MYSELF IN 1955.

LOOKING BACK

The Autobiography of a Spiritualist

BY

ARTHUR FINDLAY

Honorary Vice-President of the Spiritualists' National Union.
A Founder and past Chairman of The International Institute for Psychical Research.
Vice-President of the Marylebone Spiritualist Association.
Founder and Vice-President of the Glasgow Society for Psychical Research.
Past President of the London Spiritualist Alliance.
Honorary President of the Essex Federation of Spiritualists.
Honorary President of the Sussex Spiritualist Society.
Honorary President of the Institute of Psychic Writers and Artists.
Vice-President of the Leicester Society for Psychical Research.
Honorary Member of the American Foundation for Psychic Research.
Membro d'Onore dell' Universitaria Accademica Spiritualistica Italiana.
Honorary Member of the Edinburgh Psychic College.
Honorary Member of the Athens Metaphysical Alliance.
Founder of the Quest Club.

"Every man is a volume if you know how to read him."—*Channing*.

First Impression   1955
This Edition   1988

ISBN 0 94782 317 4

THE SPIRITUALISTS' NATIONAL UNION was left the copyright to all of Arthur Findlay's books, with the request to keep the titles in print. The SNU is the largest Spiritualist Church organisation in the UK. The SNU also owns the Arthur Findlay College at Stansted Hall.

The SNU is based at Redwoods, Stansted Hall, Stansted Mountfitchet, Essex CM24 8UD.

Two of the foremost publishers in the psychic sphere have combined their talents to produce this most important series. They are:

PSYCHIC PRESS LIMITED. Booksellers, publishers of books and the weekly "PSYCHIC NEWS."
20 Earlham Street, London WC2H 9LW.

THE HEADQUARTERS PUBLISHING COMPANY LIMITED. Booksellers, publishers of books and two Spiritualist monthly magazines "TWO WORLDS" and "HERE AND THERE."
5 Alexandria Road, West Ealing, London W13 0NP.

Printed in Great Britain by
Masterprint, Newport, Essex

CONTENTS.

ILLUSTRATIONS.

FOREWORD.

THE last thing I ever expected to do was to write my own biography. Moreover, it never occurred to me that it would be of any interest to anyone. To my surprise, an author friend said to me: "Why don't you write a book about yourself and call it the *Autobiography of a Spiritualist*, it would be very popular with many people?"

When I expressed my doubts, he remarked: "You have put over in your books, in a clear, intelligent way, the very thing humanity wants most to know about, and has been groping for in the dark up to now. You have answered Job's cry 'If a man die, shall he live again?' Your life is of great interest to many."

This set me thinking, and I asked some of my friends what they thought about the idea. They all expressed the opinion that I should start right away and tell the story of my life. So here it is. We all know many people superficially, but we do not know much about them, and I think it is because of this that biographies are popular.

To prepare this book has been a great interest to me, in fact I have re-lived my life, and the writing of it has brought back many memories of the years gone by.

Stansted Hall, ARTHUR FINDLAY.
  Essex.
16th May, 1955.

CHAPTER ONE.

CHILDHOOD.

(1883–1895.)

I was born on the 16th May 1883 at one o'clock in the morning. This happened without my being aware of the fact and, moreover, my consent was not asked beforehand. It occurred without any desire on my part, and it might have taken place, so far as I had any say in the matter, in any other country in the world. Like the rest of us, I did not choose my parents, I accepted them, and did not question the fact as to why I was born, when I was born, and where this took place.

I first saw the light in the city of Glasgow, where, in later years, I was to spend my business life and become a freeman of the city. I was baptised into the Presbyterian form of the Christian faith, but, from the first, I was a rebel against orthodoxy, because I am told that I kicked and screamed at my baptism, much to the disgust of my parents.

Then I was given two names, James and Arthur, known as Christian names, because prior to the Reformation such additions to the surname were usually the name or names of one or more saints and, moreover, they were given to the child in a church. James comes from the Latin, Jacobus, which must have come from the Hebrew, and Arthur is derived from a Sanscrit word which means noble, hence the name of

9   L.B.—A*

Aryan, the designation given to the Indo-European languages of mankind.

The name of "Findlay" is one of the oldest of Scottish names, and is to be found in the ancient poetic chronicle of the Kings of Dalriada, who figured in Scottish history in the 6th century. The name is of Gaelic derivation from Fhionnlaigh, and means "Fair Hero", our motto being *Fortis in Arduis*, or "Strong in Difficulties". What brought this into being is unknown, but perhaps it was because of the valorous deeds of the fair hero who first became known as "Fhionnlaigh" in the days of old.

Ayrshire is the county in Scotland with which my family has been closely connected, and where I spent thirty-five years of my life before I came to live in England. Our old family home was Waxford, some six miles south-west from Kilmarnock near the village of Symington, where lived my great-great-great-great-grandfather, John Findlay (1630–1697). His son William married Barbara Hodgert, and through her my ancestry can be traced directly back to the Norman Conquest. Her mother was Annabella Boyd, a direct descendant of the Fland of Monmouth, who was born about the time of the Norman Conquest and who died some forty years later. He was a scion of a Breton noble family, the Counts of Dol and Dinan. His son, Alan FitzFland, was a contemporary of Henry I (1100–1135) and was given by the King the castle of Oswestry in Shropshire, to become the sheriff of the county and a prominent courtier.

Alan FitzFland was the father of four sons, two of whom were Walter FitzAlan and Simon. Walter became the first High Steward of Scotland in 1158

and founded the royal family of Stuart, while his
other son, Simon, founded the Boyd family, the name
being derived from Boidh, meaning of fair complexion. In later years, Sir Robert Boyd so distinguished himself at the Battle of Bannockburn in 1314
that Robert I (Robert the Bruce) gave him the Barony
and lands of Kilmarnock. Kilmarnock Castle became the seat of the Boyd family, one of whom, Lord
Boyd, was Lord Chancellor of Scotland and Regent
in the time of James III (1460–1488). His son, who
was created Earl of Arran, married Princess Mary,
eldest daughter of James II (1437–1460).

William Findlay and Barbara Hodgert had three
sons, one of whom, the Reverend Robert Findlay
(1721–1814), was Doctor of Divinity and Professor of
Theology at Glasgow University, a man of considerable outstanding merit in his time. His brother
William was my great-great-grandfather.

My mother's name before her marriage was
Margaret Galloway. She was small in stature but
very dignified and good looking. She had great
charm of manner and was a delightful conversational-
ist. She was brought up as girls were in her station
of life in the Victorian age and, as there were few
girls' private schools in those days, she was educated
by governesses, to complete her education in a private
school in London. She spoke French fluently and was
a pianist of more than average merit.

My father, as a young man, became a partner in a
firm of stockbrokers and chartered accountants in
Glasgow. He was an officer in the 1st Lanark Volunteers, the army reservists of his day which preceded
the Territorials. He was a handsome man, and was

referred to by his friends as the best-dressed man in Glasgow. He had a kindly disposition and was rather retiring, but his sympathetic, genial and natural manner made everyone like him. As a father he was kind and lovable, and the only time he made me cry was when, as a baby, he once lifted me up to kiss him. I am told that I put my hand out and touched his moustache, which so frightened me that I burst into tears.

I never knew his father and mother. His mother had a gentle and sweet disposition, and her good looks were so striking that she attracted much attention. Her husband, my father's father, had a large business with the southern states of North America. Then came the Civil War in 1861, his health failed him and he died young. He could not properly look after his affairs, and he lost half his fortune. Fortunately his wife was well off, finding no difficulty in bringing up a family of six sons and two daughters, and leaving them comfortably off at her death.

My mother's parents came considerably into my early life, and to them I am ever grateful for much of the happiness I can look back upon during my young days. My grandmother was a woman of a lovable and gentle nature, a great lover of children, and her happiness came from her home life surrounded by her family of four daughters and their children. Unlike her husband, she was of a retiring disposition and was always far happier at home than travelling abroad. So she seldom accompanied him on his travels, one of his daughters usually being his companion. I never remember seeing my grandmother dressed in coloured clothes, but always in black silk with a lace cap, the

type of dress which she wore for the thirty years I
knew her and, I suppose, since she was married. She
was a woman much beloved by everyone, and I never
remember her angry or irritable, but always calm and
dignified.

Her husband, my mother's father John Galloway,
was a leading shipowner in Glasgow, being a partner
in the firm of Patrick Henderson & Co., whose sailing
ships last century, under the name of the Albion Line,
traded between the United Kingdom and Burma
and New Zealand, carrying most of the Scottish
emigrants from Scotland to New Zealand. Then
came steam and the opening of the Suez Canal. With
changing times two separate lines emerged, the
Henderson Line to Egypt and Burma, and the Shaw
Savill & Albion Line to South Africa, Australia and
New Zealand, of both of which my grandfather was
a director.

He did much public work and was for some years
President of the Glasgow Chamber of Commerce, besides being a director of various companies connected
with Burma, Australia and New Zealand. He had
many and varied interests, being an artist of great
merit, and his many beautiful landscape scenes in oil
colour now decorate the houses of members of the
family. Wherever he went for a holiday he took with
him his paint-box and canvases. Besides this, he
was deeply interested in astronomy and archaeology,
and, on returning from one of his visits to Egypt, he
brought home a mummy in its coffin, which he gave
to a Glasgow museum. When travelling he wrote to
me beautifully illustrated letters on what he thought
would interest me, and these I greatly value.

His great-grandfather, James Clark, founded the cotton thread industry of this country at the beginning of the 19th century. In those days there was no steam power, the first machine being moved by a man turning a wheel. Ingenuity, the development of the cotton thread plant (*Gossypium*), and Napoleon's embargo of 1806, when the Berlin Decree suspended trade between Britain and the Continent, thus ending the importation of Continental silk thread, combined to bring about the establishment of the cotton thread industry of this country.

Clark's cotton yarn, which produced a thread all could use, caused the business to develop rapidly, especially when the sewing-machine was invented. Consequently rivals came on the scene until they amalgamated at the end of last century under the name of J. & P. Coats Ltd., with vast mills in Paisley and elsewhere throughout this country and in many lands abroad. So when we see Coats' Thread or Clark's Thread on a bobbin or a spool, let us remember that this is how and where it first was made.

When I look back, I have happy memories of my early childhood. I have one brother, John, three years younger than myself, and no sisters, and we both spent our early days in a large nursery on the top floor of a terrace house in Glasgow. The terrace had the pleasing name of Woodlands Terrace, and our house was number eight. Woodlands Terrace was well situated on one of Glasgow's several hills, and we could see all over the city and as far as Ben Lomond. No houses obstructed our view, as a garden was on the other side of the road. Nearby was Kelvin Park, where we spent much of our time

with our nurse out of doors. Through the park ran
the River Kelvin, and there were many diverse walks
and paths bordered by flower-beds. No wheeled
traffic was permitted and we were free to play about
as we liked.

Nearby lived Principal and Mrs. Lang, whose son
Cosmo became Archbishop of Canterbury, and not
far off was the home of the boy who became Lord
Reith, in recognition of his work in building up the
British Broadcasting Corporation. Our next-door
neighbour was the sister of Sir Henry Campbell-
Bannerman, who became Prime Minister in 1905, and
here an amusing story can be told. The great man
once called to see his sister, and my mother later asked
his sister's parlourmaid what she thought of him, to
receive the reply: "Oh, Mum, I opened the door to
him, and when I had seen him into the drawing-room
I rushed back, took up his umbrella, and gave it a
good hug."

Little did we as children realise how fortunate we
all were, because not so far away conditions for both
adults and children were far different. Down below
us, about half a mile away, where the traffic was,
streets branched off where, unfortunately, many lived
in squalor, and an early remembrance is my visit to
one of these streets, to a housemaid who had left us
to be married. Her husband, a decent sober man, and
her children, were delicate, his ill-health making it
difficult to find and keep his jobs, one by one his
pieces of furniture finding their way to the pawnshop.
Such was the state of affairs I witnessed when my
mother called with me to see what help she could
give to this family in its distress. There was no

welfare state in those days, no free medical attention or cheap medicines, and the state of hopeless misery and poverty the family was in I shall never forget. Those who could not fend for themselves in those days lived on charity or poor-law relief.

Unfortunately, this was not a unique case of honest poverty, and how thankful we must be that increased wealth, education and science, have combined to enable the Government to so arrange the administration of the country, that poor health and poverty, such as existed in my childhood, have been greatly mitigated.

In those days the principal streets of Glasgow displayed extreme wealth and poverty. On the one hand, there were carriages drawn by handsome, well-harnessed horses, and driven by smartly liveried coachmen, and on the pavements walked expensively dressed people. On the other hand, children in rags, some crippled and many shivering, begged or tried to earn an honest living selling newspapers or acting as crossing-sweepers. My mother, who so loved children, had many a pang of grief whenever she saw this suffering and misery, and her father, my grandfather Galloway, finally decided that something must be done about it.

During the later years of his life he devoted his energies to collecting into two large houses, situated at Saltcoats on the Ayrshire coast, many of the waifs and strays from the Glasgow streets. Under the care of two matrons, and his own supervision, he, with the help of friends, maintained for some thirty years an average of eighty boys and girls whom he placed out into suitable work when they were old enough to fend for themselves. Many boys went to Canada and the girls into domestic service. Few were failures, and he corresponded with many of them after they had left his care.

Not only did he care for their bodily welfare, but their religious development was to him equally important. He was a deeply religious man, a strong supporter of the Presbyterian form of faith, and the orthodox outlook on life meant much to him. So every Sunday morning the children from these two homes were taken to a nearby church, to take part in a two-hour service which included a sermon of nearly three-quarters of an hour. Then back they trooped, walking two by two to a mid-day dinner, to be regaled when it was over by someone who usually took the sermon he had just heard as the subject of his talk. When this was finished, back they trudged to church for another two hours, and their Sunday ended by their being set to work to learn the Shorter Catechism or one of the Psalms.

My grandfather should have remembered his own childhood. He once told me how he hated the long morning prayers each day when he was a boy, and how on one occasion he tried to bolt from the dining-room before they finished, because, whenever they were over, his grandfather, with whom he was then staying, gave him a Bible lesson which lasted an hour. On this occasion he did not escape, as both my grandfather, and his grandfather who was praying all the time, had a race on their knees to the door. My grandfather's hand was stretched out to open it when he was stopped, his grandfather shouting out: "You will not get away from me like that," and he then continued his prayer.

Sunday morning began at home by each member
of the family repeating a biblical text at breakfast, then
came family prayers, after which I was given a Psalm
to learn, and when church time came we solemnly
walked to the Free College Church a few minutes
away. A paid singer and an organ were introduced
and this made my father and mother move to a church
further away, where only a conductor, with a tuning-
fork and no organ, led the hymns. This service tried
my patience to the utmost, as the minister prayed
extemporary for half an hour and forever talked of
"Gud" instead of God. Fortunately, I just missed
the time when the entire congregation stood during
this ordeal. The afternoon was again spent in church,
and the day ended with a Bible lesson and finally family
prayers. However, except for the misery of Sunday,
or the Sabbath as it was called, my life in those early
days was bright and happy.

Until I was six years of age we lived at Woodlands
Terrace, and for a year I went to a nearby Kinder-
garten School, which I liked, the mistresses being kind
and the childish work congenial to me. I was rather
delicate as a child and I spent much of my time at my
grandfather's home, which was at Ardrossan on the
Ayrshire coast. Glasgow did not suit me, but I was
always well at Ardrossan. Kilmeny, which was the
name of his house, overlooked a large sandy bay with
a wide and extensive view across the twelve-mile
estuary of the River Clyde to the majestic island of
Arran, with its great peaks, the highest, Goatfell,
rising to three thousand feet. The changing light and
cloud effects on these mountains were always a source
of pleasure. To the south could be seen the sugar-

loaf shaped rock Ailsa Craig, and on a clear day the outline of the coast of Ireland was visible.

Kilmeny was an ideal home for a child. It was a large handsome house with lovely gardens and lawns. In season there were peaches and grapes in the greenhouses which, as children, we could gather by lying on our backs and reaching them when the window-sashes were open. There were horses in the stable to visit, a mile of perfect sand to dig in, and the ever-changing sea to paddle and bathe in. My lessons were presided over by a governess, but my memory more easily recalls my pleasures than the knowledge I then assimilated.

My two aunts, who were then unmarried, delighted in picnics, a form of amusement which in later years I came to dislike for its discomfort and skiddle, but which, at the time I now write about, was always a joy to me. So, at times, we went over to Arran for the day by the well-known paddle steamer *Glen Sannox*, and returned in the afternoon. If we did not picnic on that delightful island there were other charming spots on the Ayrshire coast where the rocks, in which there were numerous pools filled with sea life, jutted out into the sea. At times we surprised some sleepy seals, which quickly rolled over into the water when we came close to them.

When staying at Kilmeny, on one occasion when I was about eight years of age, I had my hair cut in the nearby town of Ardrossan. My governess accompanied me, and I was not taken to the usual room where haircuts took place, but into the sitting room of the hairdresser's private house. I was set on a chair, and in front of me there was a large framed coloured picture. While my hair was being cut I stared at it, and took in every detail. It was called "The Broad and Narrow Way". It depicted two ways, one broad and the other narrow. The broad way had a large sign "Welcome", alongside of which was "Death and Damnation", and on each side of the road were different scenes.

The first one was of some people drinking beer at a table, the next a ballroom, then a gambling house and a lottery booth, other places being a loan office, a skittle alley, a theatre, a Sunday train, and so on. What startled me was a huge volcano at the top of the picture with fierce flames spurting up, and it was to this the road led, the foremost people standing on its verge or toppling into the flames.

The narrow way started from a small door marked "Way of Salvation", and then came a gruesome picture of a cross with a naked man nailed to it, next a church, a Sunday school, a mission house, and lastly a deaconesses' institute, to end in a radiant town situated on a lake, with a hill behind on which was a lamb. Only a few people were on the narrow way, but the broad way was crowded. Against each scene was the appropriate biblical text and, as the clipping of my hair went on, the barber repeated these texts to me as I went with him, first up the broad way and then the narrow way.

That picture haunted me, and every time I saw people waiting for a theatre, or going on a Sunday tram, or drinking beer, I pitied them for their wickedness. A copy of this picture, I was told, was in many homes in my young days, and, when I was older, I bought one as a curiosity and have it beside me as I write. It is, however, kept hidden away behind some furniture, a relic of the days when to be happy was considered wicked, and to be miserable was thought to be pleasing to God. Fortunately, such a state of affairs prevailed with me only on Sunday, the rest of the week being happy and joyful, but this picture shows the religious atmosphere of those days, when people would display such a caricature and believe it represented the will of God.

Sunday, to most children in my young days, was a day of gloom, and I looked forward to it each week with fearful anticipation. Fortunately, I just missed the practice of pulling down the blinds, but within our home on Sunday there was no joy or laughter. To whistle or run, or behave in a natural way for a child, was a sin. All our toys were put away, and, when I was old enough to read, I was given a religious book to keep me occupied. The children of those days had to know the answers to the Shorter Catechism, a long dreary affair full of doctrine and theology.

My memories of Kilmeny would not be completely recorded if I omitted to tell of my grandfather's coachman. His name was Robert Brackenridge, but to us children he was always "Bracky". He came to my grandfather as a young man and was with the family until his death, some forty years later. He drove my mother to her wedding, and he was a friend of the family until the end. His interest in my brother and myself, when we were boys, was more like that of a father than of a servant. He taught us to drive and to ride, he took a fatherly interest in all our pastimes, and consequently we were much about the stables, where he entertained us by his interesting stories and conversation.

He was a deeply religious man, and a firm believer in the second coming of Christ, but his talks on those subjects were to us more entertaining than dull, because he always could bring into everything he said a fund of wit and humour. The pious, self-righteous individual he never took seriously, and he looked on life through rosy spectacles. He gave up smoking because his young daughter told him that a Christian should not smoke, but he never took exception to others smoking in his harness-room, which was the place where all his friends met.

Not only was he a good coachman, but he had the gift of keeping his horses well. Seldom was a veterinary surgeon ever required, but that was not all. He was a born doctor, and my father often referred to him as "Dr. Brackenridge". His ability to cure, or relieve, bad sight was remarkable, and he had a special liquid of his own, which he dropped into the eyes to work wonders. His harness-room often resembled a doctor's consulting-room, and people came to him from all around. On one occasion, my brother was cured by him when the doctor seemed helpless. The dentist had stopped one of his teeth without removing a decayed nerve, with the result that he became very ill, an abscess forming, and his neck and face were swollen and inflamed.

In desperation, my mother consulted Brackenridge, and he advised a course of treatment by an ointment he specially prepared. This brought about a blister in my brother's neck which broke, and the pus poured out. My brother recovered, but it might have been far different if the pus had not been removed. The doctor could do no more than express his astonishment, and, needless to say, the dentist who started it all was never again employed by us.

Brackenridge was my grandfather's coachman and then, when my grandfather died, my grandmother's coachman. Then he became my father's coachman, and, when my father died, my mother's coachman and then her chauffeur. When I married he became my chauffeur. When motor-cars took the place of horses, he was as good at keeping the cars in order as he was at keeping horses well. At sixty-five years of age he became seriously ill for about the first time in his life. An operation followed but it could not save him, and he passed away to the sorrow of everybody who knew him.

To Kilmeny came many interesting people, and I have a vivid recollection of shaking hands with an old gentleman who was a guest of my grandfather and grandmother. I was then about seven years of age. My mother came to fetch me from the nursery, saying that she wanted me to meet someone in the drawing-room. He was an old soldierly man with white hair and a white moustache. He was standing on the hearthrug and he gave me a hearty handshake. He said a few words which I have forgotten. On my way back to the nursery, my mother said: "You have had an experience today that you will remember. That old gentleman is ninety years of age. He fought at the Battle of Waterloo in 1815 and is now a retired general."

I forget his name, but I have never forgotten that I shook hands with someone who fought at Waterloo, and I wonder if any other person living to-day can make such a claim. He was born in 1800 and was an ensign in the army at fifteen, one hundred and forty years ago, as I write this in 1955. I have in my possession a copy of *The Times* of 22nd June 1815, giving an account of the Battle of Waterloo bought by my great-grandmother that day in London.

The Ayrshire coast is a pleasant place for residence, and it is so sheltered that tropical plants and palms grow there out in the open. Rhododendrons and azaleas also grow in profusion. If it were not so wet, its climate, and the absence of snow and frost, would compare favourably with most parts of the British Isles, but, when it is fine, the atmosphere is so clear that the panorama of the Clyde estuary is one of majestic grandeur. Across the water from the mainland, as one travels along the coast, mountains, hills and islands delight the eye, and sailors who have been almost everywhere declare that the approach up the Clyde to Glasgow, for beauty and splendour, is difficult to match elsewhere.

This being so, it is not to be wondered that, as the railway services improved, more and more people moved from Glasgow to the Ayrshire coast, and my parents did likewise. They took a charming house at West Kilbride called Overton. It stood on high ground overlooking the sea, which was about a quarter of a mile away, and in front of the house on the lawn was a flag-pole one hundred feet high, which could be seen from a great distance. Beyond the lawn and garden only grass fields separated us from the shore, and here we lived for some years. My father could have bought Overton and all this open land around it, but he did not do so as his health made it impossible for him to travel so far each day to business, and he thus lost the chance of making a fortune. When we left, a speculative builder bought the place, built roads, and erected numerous villas, so that today Overton is surrounded by houses down to the sea.

I was about six years of age when we settled at West Kilbride. A tutor came each day to give me lessons, and we had a Norwegian governess. Looking back, I wonder why we did not have a French governess to teach us French, as it would have made it so much easier to learn the language in later years. We were only five miles from Kilmeny and so within driving distance, in fact my mother and I once walked these five miles one beautiful Summer afternoon by a road which bordered the sea all the way, only a few houses being passed. During the walk the shore was with us, covered with sand, interspersed by rocks on which the waves were breaking, and away in the distance twelve miles across the sea stood out the pile of mountains and hills known as the Isle of Arran. Pleasure steamers were crossing to and fro between it and the ports of Ayr, Ardrossan, Fairlie, Largs, and Wemyss Bay, and large liners could be seen making their way from Glasgow to lands abroad, or coming in with cargo and passengers from some distant part of the globe.

On Arran is the little town of Brodick which, about the middle of last century, had as its parish minister a well-known character. In his sermon one Sunday, when preaching on the Last Judgment, he spoke as follows: "Freends," he said, "you may think that on the last day you will be able to hang on to

my coat-tails and be saved, but you need not rely on
that, because on that day I will wear a jacket and there
will be no coat-tails for you to hang on to." That
caused a relation of mine in the congregation, a girl,
to laugh, and he pointed to her and said: "You see
that lassie in red, well, she will not be laughing when
she gets to hell." Even in my day I have heard hell-
fire preached, and on one occasion the minister stopped
his sermon and pointed to some children who were
restless. He shouted out: "You children, if you don't
keep still you will go to hell and burn and burn and
burn."

A mile from Overton is Portincross, then one of
the most delightful spots along the Ayrshire coast. It
is a small bay surrounded by rocks, and on one side
stands the ruins of a 14th-century castle, which ancestors of mine on the female side inhabited for nearly
four hundred years until 1737. The pools of water
in the rocks are a profusion of marine life, as these
are daily refilled by the tide. Lobster pots take their
toll of these crustacea, and the visitor can buy all the
lobsters he wishes. Half-a-dozen cottages are occupied by fishermen, who keep their boats in a creek
which sweeps inland up to the walls of the castle.

Across two miles of water are two islands standing like sentinels, guarding and directing the sea
approaches to the Glasgow Docks, forty miles further
upstream. On one of these islands, named the Great
Cumbrae, is the little town of Millport, and many
years ago the minister in the little parish church prayed
regularly each Sunday for blessing to rest on the
people of the adjacent islands of Great Britain and
Ireland. Portincross is, indeed, an ideal place for

picnic lovers and, needless to say, many a pleasant day was spent at this then little-known cove.

Fifteen miles further north, where the estuary of the Clyde narrows to five miles, is situated the pleasing village of Wemyss Bay, where lived my grandfather's partner, James Galbraith. His house was situated on the coast, and from a jetty in his garden he could reach his steam yacht which, during the Summer, lay at anchor some two hundred yards off-shore. This was a stately vessel, especially built to his order and named at launching by one of my aunts. It had a curved bow, was seven hundred tons in size and beautiful to look upon. It had ample accommodation on board for the owner, his friends and crew, and James Galbraith and his wife received their pleasure, and gave pleasure to others, by going from place to place in this fine yacht, which was called the *Sea Queen*. If they were not touring the Western Highlands and Islands, they were in the Mediterranean, and I heard from my mother many stories of the delightful times they had in these parts.

My mother was a favourite of Mr. and Mrs. Galbraith, and they often invited her, before her marriage, to accompany them. She was, on one occasion, very disappointed not to see Rome, but they found on arrival that fever was raging and they could not land. Rome had recently been relieved by King Victor Emmanuel and Garibaldi from the civil rule of the Pope, and after nearly fifteen centuries of priestly rule it was an insanitary foul place. Consequently, fever was prevalent. Today, with taxation as it now is, no one on his income can afford this luxurious way of seeing the world, but in those days, with income tax at sixpence in the pound and no surtax, it was possible for men of wealth to obtain their pleasure in this way.

My first experience of foreign travel was during our time at Overton, when my father and mother took me and my brother to Norway for a month. This must have been about 1892, when travelling abroad was not so popular, or as comfortable, as it is today. My father suffered from neurasthenia and his doctor thought the change would do him good. So we travelled from Leith by the steamship *St. Suneva*, and, after a stormy crossing, during which I vowed I would never cross the North Sea again, we arrived at Stavanger and then went on to Bergen. The Bergen fish market remains most vividly in my memory, so different from anything to be seen at home. The fish, mostly salmon, were alive in large tanks, and the customer made his choice. When too many people crowded round, the fishmonger lifted a fish half out of the water and its flapping tail splashed the water on the onlookers.

Bergen was so different from any town at home, the houses, the streets, the wheeled vehicles and the people's dress were such a contrast to anything I had seen before. We were all delighted with our short visit to this Norwegian port. But we had to press on, as in the afternoon our boat left for Gudvangen, near which was Stalheim, an hotel situated halfway up a mountain, so it seemed to us as our carioles took us from the pier up more than a mile of twisting road which never seemed to end. A cariole had seats for two or three in front, the driver standing or sitting behind on a small platform. When we eventually reached the top, a large spacious wooden hotel presented itself to our gaze, and the view was magnificent, mountains all around us, and down in the valley far below us we could trace the road like a ribbon winding its way to the fiord where was situated the attractive little township of Gudvangen, the place where we had landed.

We went by steamer and carioles all about this part of Norway, with its high mountains, its fiords and their steep cliffs, its long and beautiful valleys, its waterfalls and rapid rivers, but one journey especially remains a clear memory. We were one day visiting Gudvangen, my mother, the governess, and my brother being in one cariole and my father and myself in another, when on the way back to the hotel a violent thunderstorm broke upon us. The lightning was so vivid and frequent, and the thunder so loud, its echoes so eerie in that fearsome valley, that the horse of our cariole took fright and bolted. When it was stopped and quieted my father, as the driver was scared, took the reins, and our journey between black towering rocks on one side and a deep swollen river on the other was resumed. Unfortunately, a wheel of our cariole went over a large stone and we were nearly upset, the wheel hitting my head, to give me an ugly-looking wound.

There was plenty of water about, and a handkerchief was bound round the cut, which, fortunately, was not so serious as it seemed at first. At last we reached the hotel, soaked and weary, and my father was told by my mother that he should have left the driving to the driver who knew the road. In spite of the daily diet of salmon, which became monotonous, a month was pleasantly passed in these beautiful surroundings, and it was there that I was first introduced to the wranglings which are inseparable from orthodox Christianity.

A bishop was a guest in the hotel, and I remember a discussion between him and my parents about salvation. Up to now I had given no thought to the subject, my Sunday exercises being taken as part of my childish life, but here was something new, an argument on how we were to be saved, the ecclesiastic expressing the opinion that only baptised members of the Church of England could reach heaven. Presbyterians, and the rest of mankind, were consequently outcasts in the sight of God, according to this doctrine, which reserved heaven for a minute proportion of the earth's inhabitants. My childish mind remembered it all, and my mother's final remark, which ended the discussion, was: "Anyone who believes in Christ as his saviour will be saved."

To most children of nine years of age a discussion such as this would have been passed by unnoticed, but not so with me, and from time to time I wondered about it, as only a childish mind can do. To me, as the years passed, all world religions became an intellectual interest instead of, as religion is to most people, a comforting affair adopted at childhood because it is considered the correct thing to do and not from rational thought. So there was evidently something about me which made me the rationalist and heretic of after years, but one who was, nevertheless, intensely interested in natural religion, which did not conflict with my reason.

When I was about ten years of age my grandfather, who was very fond of me, took me to London, a long journey of over four hundred miles. My excitement was increased because there had been introduced from America on our main railway lines the Pullman car, in which travellers sat in comfortable armchairs, and had their luncheon, tea and dinner brought to them in baskets from the refreshment rooms of the various stations at which the train stopped on its journey. I remember the many different objects of interest he pointed out to me on the way, the source of the River Clyde and suchlike things, and so the journey, instead of being tedious, was full of interest and excitement. Little did I think that this journey was the first of over five hundred I would make in the years to come between Glasgow and London.

We arrived at the great city about seven o'clock in the evening, having been ten hours on the journey, and I received my first introduction to London when standing at my bedroom window at St. Pancras Hotel, while gazing over the vast expanse of lights and houses, which is so clearly seen from this vantage point. I was looking over the very place where lived (in the imagination of so many at that time) the amazing man called Sherlock Holmes, then being made ever more famous each month in the *Strand Magazine*. It was the London of the smoky, sooty Underground, of gaslight, of the cab, often called a four-wheeler, a growler, or a fly, the hansom cab, the horse-drawn omnibus, on top of which ladies did not go, and the crossing-sweeper. The men in the

City wore top hats and frock-coats, the ladies in the West End wearing fully flounced skirts which swept the ground, and bodices with what were called "leg of mutton" sleeves.

Such was the London to which I was introduced for the first time, and during the next few days I saw the Tower, the Houses of Parliament, Madame Tussaud's, the Bank of England, the Mansion House, and the very busy cross-roads at the Bank, this being then known as "Murder Corner". When I returned home I said that I had been to Death Street! At the Zoo a monkey relieved me of my straw hat and ate it. The memory of Madame Tussaud's lingered with me for many years, my first surprise being the dummy policeman standing at the entrance, but what awed me most of all was the Chamber of Horrors, more restricted than it is to-day, but none the less gruesome.

The Underground was a dreadful railway, its sulphur-laden atmosphere getting into one's eyes and throat, and how the engine-drivers and firemen on the engines existed, living most of their days in its smoky tunnels, is difficult to understand. Its badly gas-lit stations are such a contrast to the clean Underground stations, and the rapid well-lit trains of the present day, for all of which we have to thank electricity, which in my young days was in its infancy. The discovery of electric power has transformed our lives. Then was born the phonograph and bioscope, and I well remember the intense interest they aroused. To hear an instrument speaking and to see photographs in three dimensions was indeed the wonder of wonders.

Albert, Duke of Clarence, died on the 14th January 1892. He was the eldest son of the Prince of Wales who became Edward VII, and was engaged to Princess Mary, the daughter of the Duke of Teck. She later married George, Duke of York, to become in after years Queen Mary. Why his death is still vividly in my mind is because the day of his funeral was one of the most miserable days in my life. The bell of a church near to Overton tolled for hours, and from morning to night the rain poured down. These two factors made it difficult for me to settle down to anything, and much of the day was spent gazing out of the window at the dismal Winter scene, feeling utterly bored with life.

I was then nearly nine years of age, and shortly afterwards we left Overton and took up residence nearer to Glasgow. My father found travelling the distance of thirty-five miles from Glasgow to West Kilbride too much of a strain, and he took a house called "Hillhead" at Kilbirnie, which was about twenty miles from Glasgow. It was a nice, compact property of about four acres and with good stable accommodation. A lawn of a quarter of an acre swept down from the front of the house, and it was completely enclosed by trees. The village of Kilbirnie was unattractive, its inhabitants being principally occupied in mills for the manufacture of linen thread, but the surrounding country was beautiful. The land behind our house rose to various heights of moorland, ranging from a thousand to sixteen hundred feet, Misty Law being the highest, from the top of which could be seen the Garnock River valley stretching for miles down to the sea, across which were the mountains of Arran and the coast of Ireland. Two large lochs—Kilbirnie Loch and Lochwinnoch in the valley—added additional beauty to the scenery, which in days gone by was un-spoiled by man. To-day, it is disfigured by large iron-works at one end of Kilbirnie Loch into which is tipped the slag from its blast furnaces.

As boys, we were often up on the moor through which ran a winding river. Its pools were just made for bathing in, though very cold. About a mile up-stream stood the ruined Glengarnock Castle. This ancient edifice, its walls still standing on a site high above the river, goes back to the 13th century, and its history is well recorded. Around it is much tradition, most of it fanciful, but it is true that, as it stands to-day towering above the river, it makes a majestic picture. This stirs the imagination and conjures up in the mind the warfare between the Scots and the Norsemen, which ended in the Battle of Largs (1263) some dozen miles away, when the invaders were swept back defeated to their ships.

Grouse, wild fowl, and rabbits on the moors doubtless helped to feed the castle's inhabitants in those far-off days, as one could wander for many miles in all directions without seeing a human habitation, and wild life had this vast stretch of moorland to it-self. Other ruined castles, built in the 13th century against the Norsemen, dot the countryside, Kilbirnie Castle, known as "The Place", being wonderfully well preserved considering its age. Its Laird had a grand pew in the parish church which went back to pre-Reformation times. It was above the ground floor of the nave in the form of a gallery and took up the entire width of the church, to be known as "The Laird's Laft".

A small town a few miles from Kilbirnie is Dalry,

and through it flows the stream called the Rye, made famous by Robert Burns, the Ayrshire poet, who wrote the popular poem "Coming through the Rye" which many people think refers to a field of rye. Burns composed it after visiting Dalry, and seeing a girl wet her petticoats coming through the River Rye:

> "Coming through the Rye, poor body,
> Coming through the Rye,
> She draigled a' her petticoatie,
> Coming through the Rye."

My education was watched over at home by a tutor who lived in Kilbirnie and taught in the village school, but the time came when my schooldays were to begin. It was decided that my brother and I should go to the preparatory school for Glenalmond College, called Ardvreck, at Crieff in Perthshire, but as there was not a vacancy we had to wait for another year. To fill up this time I went each day by train to Glasgow, and there attended a private school called The Albany Academy. From the teaching aspect my parents made a wise choice, because there I was well grounded in the primary essentials of knowledge.

The headmaster, and his assistants, were first-class men and the discipline was good, aided by the fact that each master had in the pocket of his tail-coat a set of leather tawse which he did not hesitate to use on the palm of the victim's hand. Fortunately, it never came my way, but those less fortunate writhed in pain for some time after the punishment. The swimming baths nearby were something new for those days, and were much sought after by the boys.

Travelling by train in the 19th century was not so comfortable as it is to-day. At night the only light came from a smoky oil lamp in the roof of the compartment, and it was impossible to read. In Winter a warming-pan was put into the compartment in the morning and sometimes not changed until the next day, but at the best it did not give much heat. There were no corridors or lavatories in the carriages, and they did not run on bogies, so that the journey was rather rough. In such manner I got to and from school in those days, but to me at times it was rather fun, as sometimes I was allowed to drive the engine.

I do not mean that I was the engine-driver on the main line, but on a branch line. Kilbirnie was not on the main line, and at a junction we changed into a train of three carriages, hauled by a tank engine which travelled on a single track between the junction and Kilbirnie. I was on friendly terms with the engine-driver, a kindly, elderly man, who, quite against regulations, took me and my brother from time to time on the engine and let us drive it. The guard was just as hospitable to us, and we preferred his van to a more comfortable seat in a first-class carriage, because its windows made it possible to see what was coming and what was behind us.

After our Norwegian visit, my parents took me and my brother away to some place every Summer, and I have many delightful memories of what we did. It was then the early days of bicycling, and we usually took our bicycles with us, but not when we went to the Western Highlands. From Oban we visited by steamer the coast and islands of the west of

Scotland, Iona, Staffa and other places, Fingal's Cave impressing us most of all. Into it we went by a small boat, to be charmed and rather frightened by the black depth of the water and its majestic grandeur.

We visited year by year the best known holiday resorts of Northern Ireland, England and Scotland, and I remember an amusing episode when we were bicycling through the main street of Oxford. My mother's front wheel got caught in a tram line, she wobbled, and finally in desperation flung her arms round the policeman on point duty. Another amusing bicycling incident is recalled, and this time it was when we were on holiday in Normandy. We stayed at Rouen and Trouville, and, on one occasion when on the road, my brother and I were ahead of my father and mother. We had dismounted to wait for them when a French lady stopped and spoke to us. She said just a few words, smiled genially, and then rode on. Imagine our surprise, when our parents reached us, to find them terribly upset. "Why ever did you speak to that woman?" my mother asked us. "She spoke to us and did us no harm," we replied. "She is wearing bloomers, and such women are not nice." What changes in thought sixty years have brought about.

I remember when I was about twelve years of age we were sitting in Kilmeny drawing-room, when my grandfather turned to me and said: "Would you like to come to Holland with me?" "Rather," I replied. "Well, I shall take you, and your Aunt Jessie will come with us." That was an ever-to-be-remembered trip. We sailed from Leith and arrived at Rotterdam, to find men standing on the quay in baggy trousers and

wooden clogs.   They spoke a guttural language which
I was told resembled German, and now I know that
Dutch and German have many words which are
similar and that the language must have come from the
same Teutonic source.

To come from Scotland to a flat country with no
hills or mountains was strange enough, but everywhere there were canals and windmills.   Everyone
seemed to have a bicycle, and every town a church
with a high steeple.   Climbing these steeples was my
delight, my grandfather and aunt trailing behind me
in a much more leisurely fashion, urged on because of
the uninterrupted view one got from the top.

Since those far-off days, I have developed an
interest in art, but at the time about which I am writing
art galleries greatly bored me.   My memories still
remain of the wonderful pictures which fascinated my
artistic grandfather, especially Rembrandt's famous
painting called "The Anatomy Lesson".   It is a gruesome work of art, but to me now it is very wonderful,
and this I realised when I last saw it some years ago.
It depicts the dead body of a man being dissected, and
many doctors standing round the surgeon, to whom
he is explaining the operation.   This picture raised
Rembrandt to fame in 1631, and his pictures number
about six hundred.

We travelled by train all over the country, which
was easily done in two weeks, and I still remember the
attractive costumes the women wore on the island of
Marken in the Zuider Zee, but now it is an island
no more.   The canals everywhere were a continual
source of interest, as were the quaint narrow streets of
Amsterdam and the powerful dykes which stretched

for miles along the coast. It was a never-to-be-forgotten visit, and, though I have been back to Holland several times since then, one's first visit to a foreign country is always the most impressive.

Looking back, I now realise that this visit to Holland was for the purpose of producing a change of scene and thought to my grandfather, who had experienced a bereavement which also brought much sorrow to the family. My grandmother's sister, who for many years had lived at Kilmeny, died suddenly. She was a woman greatly beloved by everyone, and to this day I can clearly remember the events surrounding her death and funeral. We were first made aware of her serious illness when, at four o'clock one Sunday morning, I was awakened by my mother, who told me to get up at once as the carriage had come from Kilmeny, some twelve miles away, to fetch us. That morning journey will never be forgotten. We started just as it was getting light, the sun was rising on a world asleep, the sky was colouring, and the night was giving place to day. Yet, in spite of all our speed, we were too late and were met by sad tearful faces to hear the fateful words "She is dead".

On a beautiful Summer day her body was laid to rest in the Ardrossan cemetery. As the mourners reached the grave, a lark rose and sang joyously. Up and up it went, singing so happily, in such contrast to the black-clad mourners and their doleful proceedings. This was a phase of life which was new to me. I had never before come up against death in this personal way, and I wondered in my childish mind at the meaning of it all. I was told she had gone to be with Jesus in heaven, but nevertheless everyone was very sad. It was certainly a new experience for me, this coming to realise that life had its sorrows as well as its joys, and that to love much brought sorrow in the end.

At Hillhead we had very pleasant and friendly neighbours, and we as children did not lack companionship. We rode about the place on our ponies, had expeditions, tennis parties, and, with our dogs and other amusements, our playtime passed happily. One person to whom we were all attached was our minister, the Reverend Alexander Davidson, because he was so human and unclerical. He was an elderly man when we went to Hillhead, plain to look upon, but so kind and sympathetic to everyone. He was the first to greet us on our arrival at Hillhead, and, until his passing, I never once heard him speak outside the pulpit on theology or religious beliefs and doctrines.

His sermons were certainly long and dreary, and twice on Sunday I had to listen to him, but it was for that the congregation paid him, and in those days that kind of preaching was thought to be in keeping with the Will of God. During the rest of the week he carried on like a sane human being, giving dances to the children and other festive entertainments at the Manse, at which his charming wife officiated, all of which greatly shocked the more puritanical worthies of the parish.

Some twenty years after his death I met by chance in London, for the first time, a gentleman and his wife. We were not introduced, being complete strangers, so that they did not even know my name. Our conversation turned to Spiritualism, and the lady informed me that she was a medium. The conversation proceeded, when she exclaimed: "You once knew a clergyman, the Reverend Alexander Davidson; he is here beside us and sends you his best wishes." Names of other departed friends I knew followed correctly, and, after thanking her, we parted, never to meet again. The critic would say that she recognised me from a photograph in one of my books, but at that time I had not published any book, and—even if I had—Alexander Davidson's name occurs in none of them.

To come back to my childhood days; I can clearly remember the controversy which then raged over Home Rule for Ireland. Everyone in our family was bitterly opposed to it, principally on religious grounds. To give Home Rule to the Irish, a priest-ridden people, was to many like opening the door for the Roman Catholic Church to dominate Great Britain. I was too young to understand the subject, but events have proved these fears to be wrong. Nevertheless, my childish mind was greatly worried by the conversations I heard, especially so when I was in bed at night before going to sleep. My prayer each night consisted of the words "Please God don't let the Roman Catholics get up" and I repeated these words over and over again until I fell asleep.

As much of my Sunday reading was about the Roman Catholics torturing the Protestants and the Episcopalians torturing and persecuting the Presbyterians in the years gone by, it is not too much to say that I was scared stiff from fear of it all happening again. *Foxe's Book of Martyrs*, with its numerous lurid

pictures of people undergoing various ghastly forms
of torture, was considered suitable Sunday reading,
and these pictures haunted me at night and made me
very frightened.

The Presbyterians had suffered so much persecution
from the Episcopalians for twenty-eight years in the
17th century, that my fears were brought home to me
by the stories I heard of one of my ancestors being
hanged in 1688 at the Grass Market in Edinburgh,
because he refused to attend the Episcopalian church
as he was Presbyterian. I was shown his monument
prominently placed in Kilmarnock, and was told that
before he was executed he handed his Bible and his
scarf to someone standing by, but these have not been
passed down though every effort was made to trace
them. His brother, while this was happening, was in
the Tolbooth prison in Edinburgh, awaiting a similar
fate for the same reason, but, fortunately for him,
William of Orange landed in Tor Bay and James II
fled, an event which brought this brutal persecution
to an end.

My parents considered that any books dealing with
the martyrdom of Protestants in general, and Presbyterians in particular, were suitable for my Sunday
reading. So it is not to be wondered that I had a
horror of religious persecution. Those I most
feared were the Roman Catholics and the Episcopalians. Another Sunday book which we were
allowed to read, or was read to us, was one called
Martyrland, a record of the persecution of the Presbyterians by the Episcopalians in the reigns of
Charles II and James II. This twenty-eight years of
persecution, in the latter half of the 17th century,

made a deep impression on my mind, as it did on the minds of many other Scottish children. To read the ghastly accounts of torture, murder, banishment and imprisonment which were inflicted on twenty-eight thousand harmless people, because they wished to attend the Presbyterian Church, naturally inculcated in a child's mind the fear that it might all happen again. Consequently in Scotland there has always been an innate hostility by the Presbyterians towards the Episcopalians.

This was exemplified on one occasion when my mother was at an hotel in Bournemouth. Her personal maid, a woman of sterling character and Presbyterian upbringing, said to her one Sunday evening that she was going out to attend a church service. My mother remarked that there was a church nearby, and Barbara (this being her name) replied that she would go to it if it were not a Roman Catholic or an Episcopalian church. Another story to illustrate the feeling of many Scottish Presbyterians towards Anglicanism is worth telling here.

My father on one occasion, when at an Elders' meeting of the church we attended, proposed that the church service in the afternoon, which was held at two o'clock, be postponed until six o'clock in the evening. He said that he had just come back from a visit to England where he had found this innovation to be working well at the church to which he had been. To this the local plumber replied: "Weel, Mr. Findlay, that may be all very weel for England, but I wouldna like to copy anything frae England." My father went on to say that it had been the only church he had attended which didn't take a collection, and to this remark the local joiner replied: "Weel, Bob, you wouldna mind copying that frae England." That ended the discussion and nothing further was done about it.

In my young days the question of Home Rule was always uppermost. Gladstone became Prime Minister, in place of Lord Salisbury, after the 1886 election, when I was about three years old, and from that time onwards for eight years the question of Home Rule for Ireland was the principal topic of conversation. After being Prime Minister for the fourth time, Gladstone, at eighty-four years of age, resigned in 1894, defeated after his eight years' campaign for Irish self-government. Now we can look back and realise how right he was, and how the slanders which were flung at him were false. He was accused of being a Jesuit in disguise, and an agent of the Pope, the feeling of hatred against him being relieved somewhat by the Jubilee of Queen Victoria in 1887, which was celebrated with great enthusiasm. He ignored the strength of Protestant feeling against him in Northern Ireland, and if he had made provision for this minority to have its own Parliament, as was done too late, the separation of Southern Ireland from the Crown might never have taken place.

I can remember the excitement when, in 1896, Dr. Jameson led his famous raid into the Transvaal with a body of police troopers, an event which ended, after a few years, in the Boer War. Socially, the final years of the 19th century brought greater power to the people who, as the years passed, had become ever more enfranchised, the consequence being that free education increased and Parliament began to realise that the welfare of the people was now its duty. This has become more evident as the years have passed since then.

Many children, I am sure, ponder over the sayings of their elders, who little realise the effect their opinions have on them. Religion, which has been such a comfort to most people, has always had a sting in its tail, and I was stung by it very often. I lived my early life at a time of transition from the old order to the new, from the age of blind unreasoning faith, through the age of perplexity, to the more enlightened tolerant age in which we now live. I was born into an intolerant society, when to doubt the orthodox mode of religious thought was a fearful sin worthy only of hell-fire after death for all eternity. Those holding such a belief could not be tolerant, and woe betide anyone who showed independent thought. Fortunately, I missed the age of death, torture, banishment and imprisonment for unbelief.

In my childhood all this controversy meant nothing to me, but I remember remarks made which make me realise how bitter was the feeling of the great orthodox majority towards the enlightened, who took a more latitudinarian outlook on life. Then, the Bible was believed to be word for word true, from the first word in Genesis to the last word in Revelation, and to doubt, or interpret for oneself, a passage in Scripture was not tolerated. When the young son of a minister in the next parish to us said to me that he doubted whether everything in the Bible was true, which I repeated to my parents, a howl of horror arose, and the fear was expressed about the orthodoxy of his father.

Much discussion at this time prevailed over a heresy enquiry by the General Assembly of the Church of Scotland, the two victims being ministers who had cast doubt on the inspiration of certain passages in Holy Writ. My grandfather took a leading part in their denunciation, just as he opposed the Glasgow People's Palace, a place for relaxation, being opened to the public on Sunday. Of this innovation he spoke publicly in strong terms, because of the work it would give to the attendants, and the argument that they could have another day of rest did not satisfy him, it being their working on Sunday to which he objected.

Likewise, when the tramways began to run on Sundays in Glasgow, he, and many others, were wrathful, though it was pointed out that it would enable many elderly people to get to church who otherwise could not do so. "They should go to a nearer church" was the reply. Nevertheless, each Sunday morning his carriage and pair took my grandmother to a church a mile away, though there was one within a quarter of a mile, and if Brackenridge could take my grandmother, and members of the family, to church, why could not a tramway driver take others?

Inconsistency is common to most people, and it was inconsistent of my grandmother to drive in the carriage on Sunday and punish me for whistling on that holy day. It was inconsistent of my mother to ban all Sunday newspapers from the house, but listen to the Sunday news on the radio when that was invented, the reason being obvious. She had been brought up to consider it wrong to read a newspaper on Sunday, but did not consider it wrong to listen to the radio on Sunday, as it was unknown when she was a child. What we are taught as children influences us throughout life. However, there was one consistent man of those days, the Reverend Dr. Bonar, a Glasgow minister, who was a strong pillar of orthodoxy and a strict Sabbatarian. A ferry across the Clyde began to operate on Sunday, and, if he had gone on it, he would have arrived at his church and back home in half the time but, no, he would not take it and always walked the long way there and back on Sunday by the nearest bridge.

Religion undoubtedly comforts millions throughout the world, be they Moslems, Hindus, Buddhists or Christians. The woman who passed her ring into the mouth of a stone crocodile in Egypt some thousands of years ago, believing that the voice of the priest who spoke through it was the voice of God, or a god, lost her ring, but doubtless obtained the comfort desired. The ring has recently been found, but the priest who deceived her is not here to explain why he left the payment behind. The Moslem gets his comfort from reading and believing *The Holy Koran*, and the Hindu, Buddhist and Christian from the rites, ceremonies and beliefs of the religion to which he adheres. It is not reason that counts with the faithful, but the fact that they all think it is the truth, because they were taught it in childhood, and this gives comfort to ignorant and beset humanity in fear of its destiny after death.

This is the best side of religion, but there is also an evil side, and that is the intolerance it has produced in the past and, to a less extent, at the present time. The belief in heaven for the believers in the tenets of a cult, and the damnation in hell for unbelievers, made for intolerance and cruelty by the majority, because they had the power to be cruel and could not tolerate opinions different from their own being held. Moreover, the zealots, and those with missionary fervour, searched the Scriptures for texts to support their cruelty towards heretics, being encouraged by the words attributed to Jesus:

"But those mine enemies, which would not that I should reign over them, bring hither, and slay them before me" (Luke xix, 27).

Many other Christian texts, besides the injunction in the holy books of other religions, could be quoted to prove that intolerance and cruelty have been partners in all the religious persecutions of the past. If intolerance is less to-day than it was, this is due to mental development which has curbed the power of the fanatic to pursue his missionary zeal. It is strange but true that religion, which stands for mankind's innermost and deepest feelings, has not only been the cause of half the events of history but also of most of the persecution and cruelty which disgrace the story of the human race.

These reflections came to me as I grew from childhood to youth, and into manhood. In childhood they were in embryo, to quicken as the years passed and I too became a victim of the intolerance of the age into which I was born. It was not bodily persecution from which I suffered, but mental, the realisation, for instance, that I was considered an outcast from the Christian society into which I was born, one of the damned in the company of those who considered themselves as the saved.

However, as a child, I had nothing to complain about as everyone was kind to me and I was happy. I accepted everything because I had not the knowledge or the ability to think differently. The trouble came when, as a youth, I began to think for myself and not accept everything I was told, and that story will be unfolded as we proceed. Meantime, something must be said about my schooldays.

CHAPTER TWO.

SCHOOLDAYS.

(1895–1900.)

SHORTLY after my return from my visit to Holland in 1895 my brother and I went to our preparatory school, Ardvreck, near to Crieff in Perthshire. How well I remember the fond farewell of my parents at Glasgow, the admonitions not to lean on the railway carriage door, the journey to Crieff, some fifty miles north of Glasgow, the bus drawn by two horses which took us from the station to the school, and the arrival there to meet for the first time those of my school mates who had arrived before us. To leave a home with every comfort, where I was surrounded by love and tender care, and be ushered into a strange house inhabited by a crowd of fifty chattering boys, all of whom wanted to know my name, where I came from, and all about me, was strange enough—but that was not all.

My brother and I were taken by a kindly matron to our dormitory with six little beds, each one divided off from the other by a partition, and shown the two allotted to us. We were told to unpack and then come down to meet Mr. Frost, the headmaster. Other masters flitted about downstairs, and the conversation of the boys mostly consisted of recounting to each other their experiences during the holidays. Our

MYSELF IN 1894.

seating accommodation was made up of hard forms placed opposite our desks, and this was all that was provided for our comfort. The walls of my class-room were bare, their drabness being not even re-lieved by the usual schoolroom maps. The floor of wooden boards was inkstained and uncarpeted, but everything was clean and smelt of a recent scrub with soap and water. As I sat there and contemplated it all, I felt very homesick and unhappy.

That feeling never passed off entirely during my school life, because the thought of home was always in my mind, and the reason was because my mother wrote to us every day, and I always wrote to her every day during all the years I was at boarding school. To find something new to say each day I found to be a herculean task, but, to put my thoughts on paper, always came easily to me, and this letter-writing doubtless laid the foundation for my ability to write the books and articles I wrote in later years.

Looking back now I realise what a mistake this daily correspondence was and, though I much appre-ciated the love and news from home, my parents were never far from my thoughts. I would have been much happier if I had not received and written those daily letters. My mother's fear was that we would lose affection for our home, but the weekly letter from home received by the other boys seemed to be enough to keep the home link strong enough for all practical purposes.

Here I might add that one day a week I was re-lieved of this correspondence, as my parents asked the headmaster not to allow us to write letters on Sunday. So, when the other boys were writing their weekly letters home on Sunday afternoon, we were told to read a book. This was unfortunate, as it made us peculiar and apart from the other boys, as did the fact that, at my parents' request, we were not allowed to go for walks on Sunday, as did the other boys. Sunday was a day of gloom at home, and my parents, in their religious zeal, did their best to make it the same for us at school. Moreover, we were not permitted to read the school library books, they being secular, and instead we were provided from home with literature for Sunday which was considered suitable for that holy day.

Besides this we were made to feel even more peculiar, because the other boys went to the Episcopalian church at Crieff and my brother and I went to the Presbyterian church. At their own homes probably about half the boys went to the one and about half to the other, but nevertheless it must seem strange to many that, in a country predominantly Presbyterian, so many boys were Episcopalians, but the answer is simple. The boys at Ardvreck came largely from the land-owning families of Scotland, especially from those families living in Perthshire, Argyllshire and Stirlingshire. Their fathers were lairds, or squires as they are called in England, and most lairds in these counties are Episcopalians. The lairds in the southern counties of Scotland are about half-and-half, and the boys from business families were mostly Presbyterian.

As the days passed we all got settled down to work and play, and after a year or so of tuition I was one of eleven boys chosen for the Cricket XI. I was also chosen for the Rugby Football XV. We had a Fives

Court, a three-sided concrete structure, against the end of which the two players battled with a small hard ball, their hands protected by padded gloves. Our playing fields were situated in the valley and there we had our bathing pool in the river which flowed by them. Moreover, we had the permission of the owner of Ochtertyre to fish in his beautiful mile-long nearby lake, and the surrounding country was so wild and rugged that walks and explorations were an additional amusement to the boys in their free time. A good golf course was only a quarter of a mile away, and this was an added attraction to many of us.

In the schoolroom I was just about the average, the lessons I most disliked being Latin and Greek. I realised the use of learning the Latin and Greek roots, which are the basis of many of our English words, but I could see no sense in learning to read long passages from the Latin and Greek classics. Greatly as I admire these famous ancient authors, their works have been translated and we now have their thoughts in our own language. It is what they had to tell us that is important, and the most satisfactory way for us to absorb their teachings is through the language we know. That is how I reasoned then, and I have found no cause to change my views in the years which have elapsed. Considering how much there is to learn at school, how useful knowledge is increasing at a speed far beyond our capacity to keep up with it, it seems a waste of time for boys, who do not intend to pursue a classical scholastic career, to be burdened with dead languages which are no use in our daily life.

History was the subject at which I excelled, and

for which I received the honours. I was set an essay
to write on the reign of Queen Elizabeth I, and I
remember my keenness to succeed and how hard I
worked, with first prize as my reward. A good
memory for historical facts makes history of absorbing
interest, and those who dislike history have probably
a poor memory, which may be good in other ways.
I have always found it difficult to remember the names
of all but the common flowers we see in a garden,
whereas my wife, who has a poor memory for history,
knows the name and nature of nearly every flower
and shrub in the garden.

Ardvreck is ideally situated on the slope of a hill
known as the "Knock", which is a feature of the
landscape. Its picturesque situation, in the midst of
beautiful woodland, mountain and river scenery, could
not be surpassed for rural beauty and grandeur. The
surrounding country is rich in historic associations of
the Jacobite Rebellion of 1715 and 1745. From the
schoolroom windows we had a wonderful view which
extended along Strathearn, the valley of the "Bonnie
River Earn", for about thirty miles to the peaks of
Ben More and Ben Aan. Fifteen miles distant rose
the stately Ben Vorlich. On either side of the river
grew copses of birch, larch and spruce, and above
them towered hills, reaching up to thousands of feet
in height, intersected with valleys through which ran
rushing streams. Ochtertyre, with its lovely lake,
could be seen, and a few miles further on was the
seven-mile-long Loch Earn, from which rose heights
to over three thousand feet of rugged rocks interspersed with scrub and heather. This indeed was a
wonderful panorama of nature in her most glorious

garb, and fortunate I was to be placed in such surroundings for my education and development.

Our excursions extended far and wide, Crieff being
the centre for such famous glens and rivers as the
Almond and its long and bleak glen, the Turret and
its lonely loch and rocky valley, the Sma Glen, weird
and desolate, and Glen Artney, made famous by Sir
Walter Scott in his poem "The Lady of the Lake".
Surpassing all is the vivid colouring which enchants
the scene, and the rich life-giving air which makes the
wanderer revel in his mountain climbs and feel as if
he can go on walking for ever.

In this invigorating atmosphere of the Scottish
Highland hills and glens my mind expanded, released
as it was from the puritanism of my home life. My
boy companions were congenial, and the masters outside the classroom were our friends. In class they
were strict but always just. Some of my boy friends,
after passing through one or other of our leading
schools, rose to prominent positions in the years to
come. There was no bullying and, though the headmaster, Mr. Frost, was rather fearsome at times, he
was never unjust, and there was always a happy and
kindly atmosphere throughout the school. I have
many felicitous recollections of our work and play.
Our ramblings up the glens, our fishing expeditions,
our stopping the baker's van on our walks for "grub",
consisting of cakes and buns, our cricket and football
matches and many other agreeable episodes, will
always remain a pleasing memory of the two years I
lived at Ardvreck School.

Then there were always the holidays which came
three times a year, about three months in all, and this

meant my return to my home and my parents, who were always so glad to see us both. We invariably received such a warm welcome, and then there were the horses "Star" and "Stella" to see, and our beloved pony "Peggy", the fastest, gentlest animal imaginable. My father bought her for us in Cushindall on one of our visits to Ulster, and for twenty years, in the pony trap or riding, she gave us endless pleasure. Always gentle and always willing, she was as great a friend as an animal can ever be. When too old to work, she ended her days in comfort and peace.

During our time at Ardvreck world events were taking place which were to cause endless trouble in the years to come. Cecil Rhodes was founding the new colony of Rhodesia, fighting the Matabele, its former inhabitants, and taking their land. The year 1896 opened with the Jameson raid into the Transvaal, which was defeated, but it increased the hatred of Britain by the Dutch settlers and this ended in the Boer War. In the same year trouble commenced in the Sudan, which finished two years later at the Battle of Omdurman, when the Sudan was conquered. Then came the Fashoda crisis, when France and Britain were nearly at war, but it all ended peacefully and six years later, in 1904, came the Entente Cordiale.

The mention of the Battle of Omdurman reminds me of the return home of General Sir Archibald Hunter, who was chief of Lord Kitchener's staff during the Sudan campaign. He lived near us, and I was on the platform of the railway station with my parents to welcome him home. His red tunic, bedecked with medals, and his plumed hat much impressed me. He was unmarried and lived with his mother, who had been married three times and was again a widow. When she told her son she proposed to marry for the fourth time he strongly objected and put a stop to it, remarking that he had buried three fathers and was certainly not going to bury a fourth.

In Britain the idea of Home Rule for Ireland was shelved, but not forgotten, and here it is appropriate to go back in history and examine the causes which raised the feeling of fear amongst the Protestants, when the effort was made to grant Ireland a separate Parliament in Dublin. When doing so, we shall also find the cause of the feeling there was amongst some Presbyterians in Scotland towards the Episcopalians. Both came from the same cause, namely the Reformation and all the dynamic effects which followed.

Prior to the Renaissance in the 15th century all Europe was in religious peace, if we except the growing feeling amongst some that the Christian Church, under the Popes at Rome, was propounding unscriptured doctrine and, moreover, it was in need of reform. There were, however, no sects or divisions, and all Christendom held solidly to the accepted Catholic faith. The Renaissance in Europe came from developing mind, due to the ancient Greek learning which was brought by exiles from Constantinople just before and after the city was captured by the Turks in 1453.

Thus were the Greek classics ultimately diffused throughout Western Europe, but, before the fall of

Constantinople, the high Moslem civilisation and learning in Spain had filtered through Barcelona to the south of France. As knowledge advanced, dissatisfaction increased amongst the more intelligent of the faithful at the gross abuses by the clergy, to cause revolts in England and Bohemia. John Wycliffe in England was one of the first to condemn the abominations of the Church, and then followed John Huss of Prague who was burned at the stake in 1415 for his outspoken criticism. From this time onwards the Church of Rome put to death, massacred and imprisoned all reformers they could reach, and its torturing of heretics did not cease until the middle of the 19th century.

When the Pope, Julius II, launched his scheme for selling indulgences to obtain money for the building of the new St. Peter's Church at Rome, Martin Luther, in the year 1517, led the revolt against this means of cancelling out one's sins by a cash payment. The revolt spread throughout Germany and Switzerland, the Elector of Saxony giving this fiery coarse reformer his active support. Councils of Church leaders were called, some being for and some against the new ideas put forward by Luther. Germany was divided, some states remaining loyal to the old Church, while other states supported its reform. At the Diet of Speier in 1529, a protest was made by the reformers against those who supported the Pope worshipping in any state which had adopted the Lutheran form of worship. From that time onwards the reformers were given the name of Protestants, not because they protested against the abuses in the Church, but because they protested against those who were loyal Catholics being permitted to have churches in states which had adopted the Lutheran form of Christianity.

That, briefly, is the story of the centre of the revolt in Western Europe, but in England a quarrel between the King and the Pope occurred when Henry VIII failed to secure from his holiness a divorce from Catherine of Aragon. The Pope, Clement VII, could not grant this because he was under the control of the Emperor Charles V, who was Catherine's nephew, and he would not permit the Pope to grant this divorce to bring about his aunt's humiliation. Henry was furious and Parliament made him the head of the Church in England, which became independent of the Pope and ceased to recognise his holiness as head of the Catholic Church in England. Henry remained a good Catholic, he had no use for Luther and his reforms, but he was determined to obtain the divorce on which he was set.

Thomas Cranmer, the Archbishop of Canterbury, gave him the release he wanted from his wife, but both Henry and most of England remained faithful to the Catholic faith, all sympathisers with the reform movement abroad being persecuted. Nevertheless, the overthrow of the Pope by England, and Henry becoming the Chief Priest of the Catholic Church in England, broke the age-long control of Rome over English religious affairs. The Church of England was born, a Catholic Church but not one allied to Rome. However, in the next reign, that of Edward VI, the reformation made headway, to receive a setback during the reign of Mary Tudor who followed, and to triumph under the rule of her successor, Elizabeth I, who founded the Church of England, as we now know

it, based on the principles formulated by the reformers.

The new Church of England cut out a way of its
own, it was neither Roman Catholic nor Lutheran, and
from it many dissented. Some still remained loyal to
the old Church, the majority became members of the
new Church, but a large minority split up into groups,
to become known as Puritans and Independents. At
a later date they took the names of Baptist, Congregational, Quaker, and other names. Persecution,
prison, torture, banishment and death followed, as
the Anglican Church was just as intolerant and cruel
as the one from which she seceded. In those days
toleration was unknown, and the stronger organisation always persecuted the minority which did not
think as it did. Both organisations, the Catholic and
the Anglican, applied to itself the words attributed to
Jesus: "Compel them to come in that my house may
be filled" (Luke xiv, 23), believing that this was the
will of God.

Ireland was one of the victims of the intolerance
of the 16th century. First of all, Henry VIII tried to
force the Irish to accept his authority on religion.
He pillaged the monasteries and committed many
abominations. This was intensified when his daughter
Elizabeth I became head of the new Protestant Church
of England, she being determined to force Ireland to
adopt the Episcopalian form of worship. At this
time Spain was trying to force the orthodox Catholic
tenets on the Netherlands, by the persecution and
murder of over one hundred thousand victims.
Episcopacy, Elizabeth decreed, must take the place of
Roman Catholicism in Ireland, and both she and her

father sowed the seeds of hatred in the minds of the Irish, which grew and were watered by the intolerance and cruelty of the Anglican Church in succeeding centuries. She earned for herself in Ireland the name of "Bloody Elizabeth", just as did her predecessor the name of "Bloody Mary" in England, because of her persecution of the Protestants during her reign.

Besides Luther, there were other reformers who followed him, John Calvin and John Knox being the two who mostly influenced our country. Calvinism is the basis of Presbyterianism, and the importation from Geneva of this new form of Christianity was due to John Knox, who, after being deported, to become a galley slave on the Seine, became Calvin's most famous disciple. Escaping from his slavery, he came under the influence of Calvinism and returned to Scotland to deliver the new gospel.

At Perth, this forceful man denounced Roman Catholicism, and won to his way of thinking many of the leading men in Scotland. Doubtless many joined his reform movement in the hope of obtaining some of the loot from the monasteries that Knox advocated disbanding. Martyrdom had been rife over the past years, since the reform movement had reached Scotland in the middle of the 16th century, the Roman Catholic Church, as it came to be called, murdering and persecuting all who sympathised with the reformers. However, Knox, fearless and loquacious, escaped this fate, and gradually the Calvinistic faith grew in strength to obliterate largely the old Catholic form of belief. Only those places too inaccessible for the new ideas to reach remained loyal to the Vatican.

Presbyterianism seemed at this time to be the coming religious faith of Scotland. It differed mostly from Episcopalianism in the form of Church government, the Church being governed by Presbyteries made up of elected ministers in each district, and copied from the way the early Christian Church was organised. A General Assembly of representatives of these Presbyteries met once a year in Edinburgh. Consequently, there were no bishops or priesthood, the priests being known as ministers under the Presbyteries, and over all a Moderator took the place of an Archbishop and presided at the annual General Assembly.

The Anglican Prayer Book was bitterly resented by the Presbyterians, who objected to set prayers, believing as they did that only extemporary prayers were pleasing to God. James I, however, had no liking for the Presbyterian Church of his native land. He said "No Bishop, no King," and he and the new Church of Scotland were forever quarrelling. As King of England, as well as of Scotland, he pressed forward the Episcopalian form of Christian worship, but in the time of Cromwell Presbyterianism flourished, so much so that it seemed at one time as if it might transplant Episcopacy in England. Cromwell, however, so thoroughly defeated the Scots at Dunbar and Worcester as to put an end to that possibility.

During the following reign, Charles II supported the Episcopalians, who were again in power, in their attempt to force Scotland into their way of thinking. Then began what is called "The Killing Time", when about twenty-eight thousand loyal and harmless Presbyterians suffered the most terrible persecution between the years 1661 and 1688. These men and women, who would not abandon their religious beliefs, were hounded out of their homes to wander over the moors, chased by dragoons who tortured and shot all and sundry. Some of their moorland graves are still preserved. At Edinburgh and elsewhere, torture by the contracting boot, the thumbscrew or the rack and other hateful methods, was just as fierce as it had ever been, and then was, in Europe under the Inquisition. Protestants torturing Protestants was, however, a new feature in Britain during the 16th and 17th centuries, and nowhere was it worse than in Scotland, in spite of the fact that the Presbyterians accepted the Confession of Faith drawn up by the Westminster Divines in the year 1646.

Thousands were imprisoned, thousands were banished as slaves to the Barbados, thousands died of exposure, thousands were tortured and put to death, until twenty-eight thousand victims were put away one way or another by the Episcopalians who could not tolerate anyone holding a different idea of Church government from what they held. The Episcopalian clergy were especially fierce in their zeal to stamp out their hated rivals, and in diverse subtle ways tracked down and informed the army authorities of the whereabouts of those in hiding.

One of the most ghastly and inhuman incidents in this long-drawn-out persecution was the driving of twelve hundred victims into Greyfriars Churchyard in Edinburgh, where, without shelter of any kind, they were allowed to die from sickness and exposure. After five months those who survived were shipped to America and sold as slaves. All this savagery had the support of the King and Government in London, but it was carried out by Scotsmen in Edinburgh, by Scottish soldiers, Scottish politicians and the Scottish Episcopalian clergy. The lowlands of Scotland suffered the most, the counties of Ayr, Dumfries, Lanark and Wigtown being the most loyal to the Presbyterian faith, but all southern Scotland suffered, the highland north being spared much of their sufferings as there the Episcopalian cause was stronger because there were fewer Presbyterians.

So now it can be understood why the people of the lowlands of Scotland have had an innate feeling against the Episcopalian Church of Scotland. Now can be understood why the lairds in the Highlands support this Church and why the lairds in southern lowland Scotland are as much Presbyterian as Episcopalian.

This persecution of the Presbyterians, who were then called Covenanters, because they supported the Solemn League and Covenant which proclaimed their beliefs, had a lasting effect on human relations, and, like all persecutions, it achieved nothing except bitter hatred of the persecutors. All this, and much more, I learned as I grew older, but in my schooldays I, like other schoolboys, was much more interested in my lessons and amusements. I was then in the years when everything I was told and taught was accepted without question. This is the age when the mind of the child is moulded into its future political, social, and religious beliefs, and only the few can in after years think themselves out of the error they have been taught in childhood.

.   .   .   .   .

In this mental state, when I was fourteen years of age, I passed my entrance examination into Fettes College. Fettes is in Edinburgh, and is one of the leading boarding schools in Scotland. The college, a handsome building, is situated in its own private park. In this park are several houses where live the boys, each house being under the charge of a housemaster. My house was called Carrington, which was the most popular house at my time because its housemaster, John Yoe, was so much liked by everyone. I did not see much of the headmaster, as he taught the older boys in college.

On arrival for my first term at Fettes in the Autumn of 1897, I had not the same feeling of homesickness as I had when I first went to Ardvreck. I soon made friends, and was placed in the IVth form which I soon regretted, as it was too advanced for me. I found it very difficult to keep up with its standard of work, which was much in advance of the highest form in which I was at Ardvreck. My dormitory was comfortable, but I shall never forget my first night. Each bed was enclosed in a cubicle, across the entrance being a wooden beam about six feet up. When bedtime came I was informed by my companions that every new boy had to turn a somersault over this beam. That would not have worried me, because in those days I was supple and agile, but what troubled me was that I had no pyjamas like the other boys, and only a nightshirt!

In those days pyjamas were just coming into fashion and my mother, who thought that what was suitable for Ardvreck would do for Fettes, had not realised that what smaller boys wore at night was not now the fashion among boys of fourteen years and over. Consequently, my nightshirt caused great amusement but it was decreed that, nightshirt or no nightshirt, I had to go through the ordeal of performing the ritual every new boy had to do of carrying out the prescribed somersault. Well, I did it amidst much laughter and was rewarded by being allowed to get quietly to bed, where I was soon asleep.

Fortunately for me, my parents set no restrictions on my Sunday reading at Fettes. I could go for walks on Sunday and do what my companions did, so that I did not feel as one set apart from the rest by puritanical taboos. On Sunday, most boys went to a Presbyterian church and the others to an Episcopalian, but I remember my parents were rather shocked when they heard that the church I attended was St. Cuthbert's, because it was considered "high", it having an altar on which was set a cross. If the altar had been away from the wall and called "the Lord's table", all would have been well, but anything to them resembling an Episcopalian church was not in accordance with the will of God!

Little did I then think that thirty-five years later a minister of this church, Dr. Norman Maclean, Moderator of the General Assembly of the Church of Scotland, would deliver a sermon praising my book *On the Edge of the Etheric*. He was one of the outstanding preachers in Scotland, and his entire sermon was devoted to the contents of my book which he said "is a remarkable book which everyone should read". The sermon was given much prominence in *The Scotsman* of the following day, occupying two columns, and it created rather a sensation in Edinburgh. Needless to say, the booksellers in Edinburgh were inundated with orders from customers wishing to purchase the book, and, when I addressed several thousands in the Usher Hall some months later, Dr. Maclean was my chairman.

Edinburgh is noted for its cold east winds, and they were too much for me at Fettes. I was one day watching a football match being played between Fettes and Loretto about eight weeks after the term began. It was a cold, wet, miserable day, and in consequence I developed bronchitis, to be immediately dispatched to the School Sanatorium, where I was very comfortable but rather bored with life. The bronchitis took weeks to clear, and only when the term ended was I well enough to go home. My doctor advised my parents not to send me back to face the hard Edinburgh climate, and this meant that another school had to be found for me.

Fortunately, no permanent bad effects followed and I completely recovered, never to have a return of the illness, but the finding of another school for me was the difficulty, because a boy has to be entered years ahead for one of the leading public schools. I was now over fourteen years of age and there were no openings for me in any of these. Then it was that my parents were told of a good smaller school which was under the charge of a headmaster who had been a housemaster at Fettes. He said he could take me at once, and so it was that I went to Abbotsholme in Derbyshire in January 1898, to stay there for nearly two years.

Abbotsholme, near Uttoxeter, is a large handsome

country house adapted as a school and situated in spacious grounds. It was more comfortable than my previous schools and it was a healthy place. Every morning we had a cold bath, each boy being provided with a bath which had its place under the bed. I never got used to, and heartily hated, sponging myself with cold water after coming out of a warm bed. Our health was well looked after, and I remember that we had to sit still, and not rush about, for half an hour each day after lunch for the sake of our digestions. The headmaster, Dr. Reddie, was a Doctor of Philosophy and a Bachelor of Science, but he had made a study of health and disease, and lectured to us on hygiene from time to time.

Abbotsholme is situated on high ground, and a quarter of a mile away is the River Dove, which flows through Dovedale, not far from the school. When it reached us it was a slow and broad stream, an ideal place for boating and bathing, and moreover we had it to ourselves for over a mile. No one could go in the boats until he had swum a hundred yards downstream, but once that was done there were no restrictions, and many a happy afternoon we spent in the punts and canoes. I was chosen for both the Cricket XI and the Football XV. Between the river and the school were the football and cricket fields. The surrounding country was flat, wooded and rural, but it lacked the beauty and grandeur surrounding Ardvreck.

Abbotsholme's educational system was novel in some respects. For instance, French, German and Latin were taught orally. The master would enter the classroom and until he left, when the lesson was over, no English was spoken. If it were a French class it was French all the time, and by signs he would explain his meaning when not understood. The same with German, and I found it worked well with me, especially as the French and German masters were from the country whose language they taught, though I thought the Latin was a waste of time. To be taught everyday talk in Latin has never been the least use to me.

Another feature of the place was our outdoor work. For an hour each day we were set to work in the garden to dig or plant. I much disliked the digging, but I liked all building operations. We were the estate carpenters and kept it in repair. We were bricklayers and the doers of odd jobs. The boys came mostly from leading industrial families in the country, in fact I could mention a dozen names of boys whose fathers either founded or were at the head of great industrial concerns, or business firms, which bear their names. "What your employees have to do," said Dr. Reddie, "namely, to work with their hands, you boys must learn to do. No good being over men if you have never experienced hard bodily work." In this way we became practical workmen, but many of us expressed the opinion that the reason for this effort was to get the garden work done, and the repairs executed, at the minimum of cost.

How often in life do things work out differently from what is planned, and this is just what my parents found with regard to me. I went to Fettes instead of to an English public school so that I would not be contaminated by Episcopalianism, and here I was in England, going every Sunday with the other boys to the local parish church. As at Fettes, my parents made no restrictions about Sunday, so I was free to do as I liked that day, and read what books I wished. Sunday for me at Abbotsholme was as happy and joyful as it was gloomy in the years gone by.

Dr. Reddie, and the other masters, had no Calvinistic or puritanical views of life, and orthodox Christianity never entered into our lives, except our church-going on Sunday morning. To them, every day should be natural and happy, and Sunday afternoon after church was given over to any amusement we liked, boating, swimming, cricket, football or rambling. At last I was freed from the curse of Calvinism, but it took me some time before I entered into everything on Sunday afternoon without the feeling that it was all wicked, and my parents would be very angry if they knew about it. Of course, I never told them, and they never asked, but, looking back, I see now that Abbotsholme was far in advance of other public schools at that time, which did not permit the boys to do more than go for a walk on Sunday afternoon.

Anyone who has read the life of Daniel Defoe, an outstanding man of his time and best known as the creator of "Robinson Crusoe", though he wrote many other books, will remember how his early life was dominated by puritanical ideology. His parents were well-to-do rigid Puritans, and the Bible their only source of mental nourishment. A text therefrom was quoted on every occasion, and life was a weary round of religious exercises. His parents were determined to make him a Presbyterian minister, whereas he wanted to become rich and be a man of the world, not some-

one held in contempt by the majority in those days.
To prepare him for a ministerial career, he was sent
about the year 1674 to the Presbyterian Academy at
Newington Green three miles north of London, as
Dissenters in those days were denied the privilege of
sending their sons to Cambridge or Oxford, which
was reserved only for Episcopalians.

Fortunately for him, the headmaster was a broadminded man for that time, and advanced in his method
of education. Teaching took place in English and
not in Latin, and Italian, French, Spanish and Dutch
were taught, besides geography, history and what in
those days was known as science, including astronomy
and philosophy. Thus Defoe's mind was liberated
from the chains of Calvinism, and, when he had
finished his education there, he was determined not to
become a minister. He had freed himself from the
monotonous round of Bible reading, Bible quoting,
and from the ever-recurring prayers and sermons. My
case was not so extreme as that, as over two centuries
separated us, and, moreover, Calvinism by my time
had mellowed, but nevertheless it made my early life
miserable, as it did his.

However, we had this in common, that emancipa-
tion came to each of us through the wisdom and
advanced outlook of our headmaster. In my case
Dr. Reddie was neither puritanical nor orthodox. His
mind was not tied down to the common beliefs of his
time. His school teaching was advanced, as were his
religious opinions. The Bible to him was a book to
be read with your reason alert, and not battened down
by fear of doubt. Consequently he could not believe
in its inspiration, as it was obvious that there were

errors, contradictions and teaching which could not have come from God. In those days these were dangerous views to hold, especially for a school-master, and he was a brave and honest man to unchain the minds of his pupils from the belief in the sanctity and complete accuracy of the Holy Bible which prevailed everywhere, and largely dominated the minds of the majority of people.

On one occasion my grandfather came to see me at Abbotsholme, and he was asked by Dr. Reddie to stay the night. Another visitor that night was Prince Galitzen, a member of a well-known noble family in Russia. I was told afterwards that the talk between the three of them after dinner was concerned with the inspiration of the Bible, and how Dr. Reddie had expressed his views to my grandfather and the prince. One question he asked them was how the world could have been created some six thousand years ago in seven days, when fossils of life had been discovered which geologists claimed were millions of years old, according to the age of the stratum in which they were found. Nevertheless, his two guests were greatly shocked at this question, and also because he expressed the opinion that the Flood had not covered the entire world.

Prince Galitzen, who was a cultured and charming gentleman, visited my grandfather at Kilmeny soon after this, and his stories of Russia in those days were revealing. The vast majority of his countrymen and women were illiterate, and serfdom existed on most of the estates which were owned by the aristocracy, who did little for their mental, moral, and social upliftment. He claimed to be doing his utmost on his land to improve the conditions of his peasants but, lacking legislation, the landowner, however much he desired a change for the better, could do little.

He greatly admired the freedom of everyone in Britain, but it was the contrast between Russia and this country that appealed to him, and he did not appreciate how far short Britain fell from the aims of those who were then striving for better housing and working conditions for the labouring class. Many houses in Britain were ·miserable abodes, working hours were long, and working conditions far from what they should have been and are to-day. Trade Unions were only slowly getting strength to right the wrongs, and only by strikes could the dissatisfied workers bring their grievances before the public. This growing power of the working class, who, during the past, had had their wrongs ignored, was feared and severely criticised by many who found it difficult to change their outlook, and I remember many discussions on the subject.

It is strange how little sympathy the workers got from many of a kindly disposition in the middle and upper classes, doubtless because few knew how they really lived. Christian missions were started to save the souls of these little-considered people, and many good people subscribed to them to enable them to provide funds for charitable purposes. Few, however, realised that it was not charity that was wanted by the poor, but better education and better pay to improve their way of living, besides shorter hours and a higher standard of working conditions. My grandfather, for instance, founded the Kilmeny Mission in Glasgow, a religious and charitable organisation, and he was prominent in helping the good work done by the Glasgow Charity Organisation, but he was fearful and critical of the work done by the Trade Unions because of their agitations and organisation of strikes.

I remember what a shock came to our family by the publication of a pamphlet by Keir Hardie, which was distributed widely in the streets of Glasgow. This exposed the terrible working conditions in a well-known local industry, but the shock came to us because at the head of this prosperous concern was a friend of the family, who was one of the most prominent amongst Glasgow's evangelical workers. He was a rich man, a peer of the realm, and gave money to missions for the conversion of the heathen, but quite neglected the welfare of the men who worked for him. In the time about which I write, namely the end of the 19th century, the saving of souls from hell occupied the thoughts of Christians much more than the social conditions under which so many of the poor then lived. Only as the years passed has the pendulum swung from troubling about hell hereafter, and thinking more of making this world less of a hell and more of a heaven to its teeming masses.

The foregoing is not the only instance I can recall of Christians giving their money and energy to soul-saving, and quite neglecting the brotherhood of man. Another Glasgow man I knew well, who was a prominent evangelical leader, became very wealthy, but he neglected the welfare of his employees who blamed and despised him for his indifference to their working conditions. However, he was just typical of the mental attitude of the 19th century in Britain. The social conscience had not developed, and most of our leaders either ignored, or were ignorant, in many cases of the way in which the majority of the population worked and lived. They had lived in the past as they were then doing, the text being quoted "for ye have the poor always with you" (Matt. xxvi, 11), and it was taken to be the will of God that this should be so. Either the workers had to improve their own conditions by means of combination and strikes, or they never would be improved at all.

Most Christian people in my young days, as I said, had only one idea towards the working classes, namely to save their souls, and when the Scottish churches began, at the beginning of this century, to have a special collection on one Sunday in the year for social work, there was much criticism by some that money should be diverted from foreign and other missions to work at home of a purely secular nature. About a mile from the church we attended on Sunday was what was called "the Miners' Row", about twenty small houses in a line. Each house consisted of one small living-room and a very small one at the back, a "but and ben" as it was called, in which the coalminer and his family lived. In this house the family slept, cooked, ate and relaxed, the living-room being the only place the father could hang up to dry the wet clothes in which he came home from the pit.

My experience of these humble dwellings came when I went with my father on Sunday to deliver tracts to their occupants. These tracts, or leaflets, of four pages each contained a story which was meant to arouse interest, so that it was read to the end. The

end was usually a warning about hell and how to avoid
it by accepting Christ as the saviour. I remember
on various occasions we were asked to come inside,
and each house was a terrible place with dirty children
on the floor, the man's wet working clothes hanging
before the fire to dry, a bed in the wall where they all
slept, a few wooden chairs, and a table. No comforts,
no amenities, the lavatory and water were outside
some distance away, and there was nothing whatever
to raise these poor creatures to a higher level of
thought. This was all the miners got for doing dirty
hard work for long hours each day underground,
away from the light of the sun from year to year
throughout their lives. The memory of these hovels
will remain with me all my life.

The Trade Unions, as they grew stronger, set about
improving the workers' lives, but, because they were
purely secular organisations, they were condemned by
many for disturbing existing conditions and making
the workers unsettled. Moreover, the Unions ignored Christianity as a means for the attainment of
their policy, and consequently they were only worldly
conscious. It was not realised that the only way the
workers could have their grievances improved was by
combination and united action, which gave them
strength to make and get their demands met. Certainly the power they got brought about, at times,
impossible demands which the employers could not
meet, because of foreign competition, but time has
proved that the workers' organisations have brought
about an all-round higher standard of living for this
one-time distressed class.

Organisation has done much, but not all. Education has done wonders, and the franchise being extended to the working class brought the Labour Party into being and ultimately into power. Last, but by no means least, the inventors have done for everyone what no Trade Union or political party could do. Inventions and discoveries have improved methods of production, increased wealth, and shortened working hours. The modern house, the modern shop and workshop and our daily lives have been transformed by inventions. Electricity alone has revolutionised our lives. Compare conditions during the time about which I am writing, sixty years ago, and the present day, and think of what our ancestors lacked and what we have now. The wealthiest then had not the comforts and conveniences that the working classes have today.

Sixty years ago houses were lit with oil-lamps, or gas. Baths were not plentiful, the less favoured using tubs, and few basins were in bedrooms with running water. There were no electric fires, cookers, washing-machines, sweepers, polishers, television or radio. There were no cinemas to remove the monotony and brighten our lives. Outside, there were no electric trains or electric trams, no motor-cars, and travel by horses was slow and uncomfortable. Trains were badly lit and heated, and the streets of our towns were dimly lit by gas, while villages had no lighting whatever. There were no telephones and no electric light. So let us thank our inventors and discoverers who have transformed our way of life, and for many of us removed its drudgery.

On one occasion I was staying with an aunt, and she called me into her bedroom. Her jewel-box was open, and in her hand was a gold ring. "That ring has a great history," she said to me. "Can you believe that it was worn by a lady who produced a famous son after she was buried?" "That is impossible," I replied. "No, it is quite true," she said. "Her husband was an ancestor of your uncle, and the ring has been handed down in his family for hundreds of years." "Tell me the story," I asked, and what she told me I have had confirmed in all its details since then. So what I now have to say is true, and everyone will agree that it is one of the most extraordinary experiences that has ever happened to a woman.

More people than we care to think of were buried alive in the old days before doctors took the precautions they do to-day. Some were thought to be dead, but in reality they were in a state of catalepsy. The wife of the Rev. Henry Erskine, in the 17th century, during an illness was assumed to be dead. She was put in her coffin and duly buried. Fortunately, as it turned out, her husband could not get a gold ring off her finger, and it was allowed to remain. On the night after the funeral the family butler dug down to the coffin, opened it, and commenced to saw off the finger in order to get the ring. This started the circulation of Mrs. Erskine's blood and she sat up in her coffin, to the amazement of the butler, who fled. She scrambled out of the grave and returned home. Her husband was sitting in his library when a knock was heard at the window, and he went to the door to find his wife in her grave-clothes.

After this very unusual experience, which is just

as extraordinary as that of Lazarus coming out of his tomb, she gave birth to Ebenezer Erskine on June 22nd, 1680, at Dryburgh, Berwickshire, and this is probably the only case of a child being born after his mother had been buried. He is famous as the founder of what became the United Presbyterian Church of Scotland. That is the story my aunt told me, and I think it is certainly one worth repeating and preserving, especially as there is no doubt about it being true.

During the time I was at Abbotsholme, William Ewart Gladstone died in 1898 at the age of eighty-nine. This great and far-seeing man's passing from earthly life was felt by both his friends and foes, and I well remember Dr. Reddie calling us all together to tell us the news and something about him. He was very fond of these informal talks to us all, and one remark he once made, which impressed me, was that he was training us to be leaders of men. It was not so much the facts I learned at Abbotsholme that I remember, but he certainly taught me to think and reason, he made me feel independent and cease from troubling about what others thought of me so long as I felt I was doing what was right.

He helped to make a man of me, a thinking, reasoning individual, who thought his way through difficulties and ignored the mass acceptance of views held by the great unthinking majority. He gave me self-respect, and I ceased to think I was a damned miserable sinner, fit only for hell unless I took the Calvinistic road to heaven. For all that, I have been grateful to him all my life.

So when I returned home for my holidays I largely

ignored or doubted the wonderful forecasts which were being made about the second coming of Christ, which was then the vogue under the lead of two men who had made themselves famous for their evangelical opinions in America and in this country. Their names are well known to most people, namely Moody and Sankey, and, like others of the time, they had come from America to bring this country to Christ. I met them both, and others like them, when they came to stay with my grandfather at Kilmeny to speak to the people at a local public meeting, many of which were enthusiastically attended all over Scotland.

Moody was a plain, stocky, uneducated, kindly man with a gift of simple speech which attracted simple men and women who had feared the worst but now hoped for the best after death. He and Sankey were the forerunners of quite a number of American evangelists who came to this country towards the end of the 19th century and the beginning of this century, and their message was much the same.

They repeated what all Christians have been taught since childhood, and the audiences never heard anything different from what the clergy preached. The packed meetings, and the enthusiasm raised by the catchy hymn tunes, doubtless made their hearers minds more receptive to the gospel message. Mass psychology is now recognised, and masses of people, each influencing the other, can easily be swayed by a persuasive speaker. Some will be influenced by what they hear at such meetings all their lives, and others for only a short time. One man I knew certainly was, as each Sunday he would shout in church during the sermon "Hallelujah," much to the discomfiture of the minister, until he was asked to keep quiet, when he left the church and never came back.

Because of the conditions prevailing at their meetings, Moody, by his persuasive preaching, and Sankey, by his singing of hymns with such a fervour in them, were able to influence their hearers in a way that could not be done by the stereotyped services of the orthodox Church. Man has a soul, and he feeds it according to his mental development. Consequently, many claimed to have received light in their religious darkness, and this was revealed in different ways during the time of enthusiasm. One for instance was on the lower reaches of the River Clyde on fine Summer evenings, when the people from the coast towns, in hundreds of small boats, sang in unison many of Sankey's famous hymns. In the beautiful scenery of this stretch of the river, this unique event was one which was long remembered by those who experienced it.

When I was older, and had made a study of world religions, I found that history was just repeating itself. In the pre-Christian era, missionaries came from the east to the large cities of the Roman empire spreading the gospel of the saving power of Mithra, Osiris, and the other saviour gods of the east. Converts would stop people in the streets and ask them if they had found Mithra, and say how only he could save them from the consequences of their sins, just as converts in my young days stopped strangers to ask if they had found Christ, and tell them what they must do to be saved.

Then, as in our days, evangelists told the western Roman world of the blood shed by the slain saviour

god for the washing away of sins.   All the evangelical
expressions used by Christians to-day were then in use,
because they were taken over by Christianity from the
Pagan saviour-god religions which it superseded.
Though we find nothing new in Christianity except
the new name given to the saviour, and there is
nothing new which was not believed in long before
the Christian era, the fact remains that erring humanity
has always felt the need of something, or someone, to
lean on to help to remove the fear of death, about
which they knew nothing but feared much.

Many millions in pre-Christian days lived in the
hope of heaven hereafter, and died in peace through
the belief that their sins had been washed away by the
blood of the sacrificed saviour god.   We read in the
liturgy of Mithra that the devotee prays before receiving Holy Communion of bread and wine, at what
was called "The Lord's Table":

> "Abide with me in my soul, leave me not, that I
> may be initiated, and that the Holy Spirit may breathe
> within me.   So that I am thou, and thou art I."

God was believed to be the All in All, and the first
and the last.   Knowledge of Him increased through
grace, which brought about at-one-ment (atonement)
by belief in the Son—Mithra.   This was the message
these oriental missionaries brought to the West.   They
preached the need of a Saviour from sin, and followed
this up by telling the people of the death of their
Saviour and Redeemer.   Along with them Greeks
came to Rome, bringing with them their Mystery beliefs, and preaching that everyone must be saved by

the belief in the saving power of Dionysus. Everyone must be born again and washed from sin in the blood of the lamb. Dionysus was known as the Vine, the Saviour, the Judge of the Dead, the Deliverer, the Born Again, the Only Begotten Son of God, and his followers believed that he claimed, "I am one with my Father in Heaven." This was put into the mouth of Jesus centuries later, as were many of the utterances attributed to the Pagan Christs, the saviour gods who preceded him.

The evangelists of the Christian era, including the latest outstanding one, Billy Graham, have preached nothing exclusively belonging to the Christian faith, and all they have said was told by the Pagan evangelists, the only difference being the change in the name of the Saviour, Mediator, and Redeemer. To teach, as Christianity does, that all non-Christians, before and after Christ, are damned in hell for all eternity has always repelled me as a horrible, monstrous and wicked belief. No wonder the Pagans despised the early Christians for copying their sacred beliefs and attaching them to a new saviour god. Why this happened will be told in a later chapter.

One day I was told that a certain army colonel had called to see my parents, so I went into the drawing-room to meet him. Imagine the shock I got when I shook hands. With none of the usual preliminaries exchanged when strangers meet, he blurted out to me in a sharp military way of speaking: "Have you found Christ?" as if I had been out looking for him. I was too nonplussed to answer this pertinent and inappropriate question, so I made some excuse and left the room. It shows however how humanity, ignorant of what follows life on earth, produces for its comfort ideas which have no historical basis but, believing them, they get the comfort they require and try to pass it on to others. They are mentally unable to fathom the mysteries of existence, and, instead, they build up an extravagant ideology which, to the student of religion, is absurd, and to the deeper thinker they appear by their words to be foolish, to say the least.

Likewise the student of religion knows the simple origin of the belief in the second coming of Christ. It came from the return of the sun each morning, in all its glory and brightness, when the people gathered in their temples, and on their doorsteps, to welcome and worship the return of the god of heaven. As the different saviour-god religions developed, as I explain in my book *The Psychic Stream*, the sacrificed saviour god worshipped was expected to return once again from heaven to earth to gather his own together, and carry them off to share with him the glories of the heavenly hereafter.

The Christian belief in the return of Christ doubtless came from India, where it was believed that Krishna, the Hindu Christ, was the reincarnation of Vishnu, the second person of the Brahmin Trinity. Many think that the Greeks obtained the name "Christos" from Krishna, but, whether that was copied or not, much else was, relating to this much beloved god. In Alexandria, at the time Christianity was there being evolved, Brahmins and Buddhists mingled with the leading western theologians at the Theological College, where all world religions were freely discussed. There the theologians, who were believers in Jesus as the Christ, became convinced from their talks with those easterners that what was believed about Krishna would happen to Jesus, then coming to be called the Christ, and round whom had been draped similar legends as surrounded his Indian prototype.

Consequently, as Krishna was believed to have returned to earth as the deliverer of his people, so would Christ, to establish a kingdom of peace and justice. This idea originated in India at a time when the Hindu faith was in danger of oppression, just as was the case when it came to be attached to Jesus, who was given the heavenly name of Christ. Those Alexandrian theologians were mostly all converted Jews whose ancestors had longed for a deliverer against foreign oppression. In the person of Jesus, now accepted by them as the Messiah, they recognised the deliverer of their homeland from Roman domination, just as did the Brahmins, when in danger, in their legends about Krishna.

In the 2nd century, the belief in the return of the theological Christ became so widespread, that it found its way into the Gospels and Epistles when copies were being made by scribes who had become enthusiasts of the idea. There was no literary honesty in those days. It was quite usual for a scribe when copying out a document to put his own ideas in the margin, and these were incorporated in the next copy. Such interpolations are numerous in the Gospels, and are known to anyone who has studied the subject, because the passages do not occur in earlier manuscripts. Thus was put into the mouth of Jesus the words on which Christians from that time onwards based their belief in his second coming, all of which proves that it is foolish to accept statements from an ancient book, whose authors and compilers are unknown, and which contains many statements known to be untrue, but which can be explained when the conditions under which they were written are known.

So what was believed about these pre-Christian saviour gods was wound round Jesus, who was evolved, first by Paul and then by others, into the heavenly Christ who any day would be returning to earth to gather all believers into his heavenly kingdom. Consequently, from early Christian times, the faithful have become enthusiastic at the prospect of meeting their Lord in the air, when some would be taken and others left. History records the follies practised by these deluded people. Year after year following the 1st century the delusion took hold on Christians, they gave away their houses and gave up their means of livelihood, to regret bitterly their folly.

The first Crusade to Jerusalem was organised in the year 1096 so as to clear the land of the Infidel Turk, because of the thousand years mentioned in the *Book of Revelation*, it being thought that Christ would return any day to the spot whence he had ascended. The crusade ended only in misery, thousands being impoverished and thousands dying of disease and starvation. Each day, after departure for the Holy Land, they asked if they had reached Jerusalem and if Christ had come. A multitude of these ignorant, filthy, pious creatures was massacred when passing through Hungary because of their cruelty towards the inhabitants. Of the two hundred thousand men and women who started on this crusade none returned, they being either murdered or made slaves, or having died of disease.

So the belief has gone on to the present day, and the wave of evangelical fervour of my young days swept many off their balance and made them do foolish things. I know of people parting with their houses, giving away their property and all they had, to have to live on charity for the rest of their lives. Friends of ours, who had a large house in Stirlingshire, gathered together all their neighbours in their garden on a certain day to await the coming of Christ which was to happen on that day. How foolish they appeared to the wise, but, in spite of millions being disappointed over the centuries of the Christian era, the belief still persists.

Those who have given exact dates for the event from their study of the Bible, all of which have proved wrong, must, if still alive, bitterly regret their rashness. I know one book written by a man I met in those days who was a great Bible student, and his name was well known in the religious life of the country. It was published in 1890 and every year from that date onwards it had against it the event which was to happen and opposite it the appropriate text from the Bible. Picking it up one day fifty years later I found that not one event prophesied had occurred, and nothing was mentioned of the events which did occur during these fifty years.

Nevertheless, in spite of my lack of knowledge, which I acquired in later years, I returned to Abbotsholme from this atmosphere of make-believe, little impressed by all I had heard and witnessed, to find on one occasion I had been made a prefect of the school.

Dr. Reddie made some nice remarks about me, and I still remember with satisfaction that he stressed how my exemplary character and integrity had helped to keep up the high reputation of the school. He was anxious that when I left I should go on to Heidelberg University in Germany, but I neither wished to go to Germany to finish my education, nor to Oxford or Cambridge. I wanted to become proficient in French as well as in German, and my father consequently decided that the best place for me to go to was Geneva University, where both languages were freely spoken. So, when the year 1899 came, I went there to be comfortably settled in the home of one of the University professors.

I settled in Geneva in the late Summer that year, after I had had a delightful tour through Switzerland with my parents, my brother and three relations. I found my new home in the Boulevard Helvetique to be comfortable and my host, Professor Schoneau, to be a fat, cheery and kind man. He gave me lessons in both German and French each morning, and in the afternoon I attended classes at the University, where the students were genial and helpful. During this time the Boer War was in progress and my companions, and the other friends I met, were critical of Britain going to war with a small and poor country which, in the opinion of so many on the Continent, was fighting for its existence against a powerful imperialistic nation which had no right to be interfering in its affairs, as it had been doing for years past. However, that did not mitigate the kindness of all I met, and in every way they were friendly and tactful.

I was fortunate in having one real friend who

helped to make my stay at Geneva less lonely and more
pleasant. She was Madame Gallon, a widow who
had been the matron at Ardvreck. My parents had
been kind to her when over here, and, on one occasion,
when she was desperately anxious to see her young
son, whom she had left in Geneva, they paid her fare
there and back, which enabled her to be for two
months in Geneva during the Summer holidays. She
looked after me, and I spent some pleasant evenings
at her home where she lived with her sisters, all of
which was very good for my French.

Geneva, which I found bitterly cold in Winter, is
a place of great historical interest, being the home of
John Calvin and the centre whence Calvinism grew
and flourished. I had no reason to admire the man,
but he was to me a matter of historical interest. This
was the home of the reformer who was the friend of
the famous Scotsman John Knox, who had carried
Calvin's crazy way of thinking into my country and
into my home. So I attended each Sunday the 12th-
century cathedral, a second-rate edifice in which he
had preached, more for the good of my French than
to hear more of his doctrines.

Calvin settled in Geneva in 1536. By the force of
his intellect, and the strength of his will, he soon made
himself the leader of the Protestant party, and proceeded to work out his ideal of government and
society. This ideal certainly respected many of the
noblest elements of human nature, such as purity,
honesty and industry, but it had grievous defects.
There was no liberty of thought, and all must abide
by his ruling. Religious observances were not to be
the outcome of individual piety, but part of the

inevitable routine of daily life. The Church he produced became the state, a breach of ecclesiastical
discipline was a crime, and any innovation in the
dogmas he proclaimed was treason to the state. This
was much the same way of life as was proclaimed by
the Church of Rome and the Church of England, but
this new Church of Calvin looked to Calvin for its
lead as the Lutheran Church looked to Luther, the
Episcopalians in England to the monarch, and the
Roman Catholics to the Pope.

Calvin continued the intolerance and cruelty of the
Church he had left. It was an intolerant age, and he
was as bigoted as the rest of his contemporaries.
Nevertheless, his treatment of Servitus cannot be
excused. Servitus was a Protestant Spanish doctor
who discovered the pulmonary circulation of the
blood, but unfortunately he came up against the
theologians of his time by having views about the
Trinity which differed from those then prevailing. So
he had to leave Spain, and wherever he went he found
it necessary to leave hurriedly when his opinions
became known. He corresponded with Calvin and
took refuge in Geneva, to be recognised one Sunday
on leaving a church service. Calvin had him seized,
tried and then burned at the stake, and this was the
end on earth of this martyr to the Protestant fanatics
of Geneva.

Calvin was equally intolerant towatds Sebastian
Castellio, a venerable professor at Geneva who was
the first Christian to express the opinion that honest
error was not sinful, and other people's opinions were
worthy of consideration. This, Calvin considered a
blasphemous statement which roused his wrath, and

he had this brave man deprived of his professorship and hounded out of Geneva, to die in misery and want. Calvin denounced him as a child of the devil, a limb of Satan, a murderer of souls, a corrupter of the faith and declared that he had crucified his saviour a second time. This, then, is Calvinism, and the reason there were not numerous victims of the sect was because they did not often have the power to persecute in the wholesale way done by the Roman Catholics and the Episcopalians, who had the power to exterminate dissenters.

Another reformer, a more pleasing personality, who was born in Geneva in 1712, was Jean Jacques Rousseau, whose reforming energy was with social or political problems. He was a master novelist and also wrote many books on the political conditions of his time, the one which exerted an immense influence being *Social Contact*, to become known as the Bible of the French Revolution. This book, which set France aflame intellectually, makes clear his opinion that liberty and freedom are the heritage of mankind, that all government should come from the will of the people, and that those who govern should only do so according to the desires of those they serve. What a contrast between this mode of thought and Calvin's way, though it must be remembered that two centuries separated them. Thus Geneva produced two famous men whose ideas on liberty and tolerance, which spread widely, were exactly the opposite.

Geneva is situated on the Lake of Geneva, and, like so many other Swiss towns, has a delightful frontage on a lake, its streets converging on a large and beautiful stretch of water, the largest in Switzerland. From Geneva can be seen Mont Blanc, and along the borders of the lake are towns and villages till we reach its opposite end where tower snow-capped mountains enclosing the Rhone valley, through which runs the river on its 540 miles' journey to the sea. This river runs into and out of the lake, to be met in Geneva by another river whose water is heavy and grey with snow water. When the rivers meet they do not mingle, and for miles they run together, but separate, the clear Rhone water, which has lost its murky colouring in the lake, being clearly visible from the other.

Christmas passed and the new year came, the year 1900, and people argued and discussed whether we had entered a new century or had to wait another year until 1901. So the months rolled on. I was interested in my work and comfortable in my rooms at the Boulevard Helvetique, but this was not to last for ever, although I expected to be at Geneva for another year. However, a letter came from home one day to say that there was an opening in my grandfather's business in Glasgow, and my mother hoped I would come home at once and not lose this favourable opportunity to get a good start in my business career.

I therefore decided to leave Geneva and return home. I would have liked to have remained another year and become fluent in French and German, but the offer I had received to enter a good business was one which I thought should be accepted. If I refused it, I might have to wait a long time before it came again. Moreover, home is always home, and I had been a long time a stranger in a foreign country.

I therefore booked my passage home by a night train from Geneva, and how nice it was to land at Dover and hear my own language spoken once again. I had had an interesting and educative experience, I had met nice friends, my mind had developed and I was ready to face my new life to which I much looked forward.

CHAPTER THREE.

WOODSIDE.

(1900–1912.)

SHORTLY after my return from Geneva in 1900 I entered the office of Patrick Henderson & Co., Shipowners, Shipbrokers, and Insurance Brokers. Their office is in Glasgow and to that city I made my way each morning by train, to return home in the evening. My first duties were humble but strenuous. They consisted of going messages, as there were few telephones in those days, taking copies of all the letters before they were posted, addressing the envelopes, sticking on the stamps and taking the letters to the Post Office.

The copying of letters in those days was cumbersome and unlike to-day's methods when a carbon copy is made when it is being typed. Then a page in a book composed of thin paper was damped and the letter put into the book facing the damp page. The copy book was then put into an iron press, which squeezed it so that a copy of the letter was transferred on to the damp page. Several letters could be copied at the same time, but all this had to be skilfully done or the letters would be smudged.

My work commenced at nine o'clock in the morning when, with the help of the senior "office boy", I opened the letters, and it lasted until six in the

WOODSIDE FROM THE SOUTH.

evening. For all this exertion I was paid the miserable salary of ten pounds for the first year, fifteen pounds for the second year and twenty pounds for the third year. I was looked on as an apprentice and there was quite a demand by youths for this position. Of course, only those who had an allowance from their parents could accept it, and all the leading business men of Glasgow first started their business life in this humble way.

After six months of this kind of work I was transferred to a department, and then on to another, and so on until I had a good knowledge of the way the business was conducted. When this was going on I remember well the announcement of the death of Queen Victoria in January 1901, a cold Winter day, and I heard the news when the paper boys came rushing along the street I was in, calling it out.

There was a department for each place to which the different ships sailed from Glasgow or Liverpool or London. One department dealt with the loading and unloading of the ships going to or coming from Egypt, the Sudan, and Burma, another with the ships to and from South Africa, Australia, and New Zealand and a third with the vessels to and from the ports of Brazil and the Argentine. Other departments looked after the booking and comfort of passengers, the insuring of the ships and their cargoes, the coaling of the ships and the catering for the thousands who made up the crews. Another supervised all the boilers and machinery on the ships.

Finally, an important side of the business was the Irrawaddy Flotilla department which directed a great shipping organisation in Burma. The company owned a fleet of hundreds of paddle-steamers, barges and other craft on the Irrawaddy River, and they traded and carried passengers and cargo between Rangoon and Bhamo, a distance of some 800 miles. Besides this the company owned its own dockyard in Rangoon, which maintained the fleet and set together its ships built on the Clyde. The plan was to build the ships and then immediately dismantle them, when their parts were shipped to Rangoon and there they were reassembled. My grandfather was one of the founders of this very profitable enterprise, and remained a director of it until his death.

My father's brother, my uncle James Findlay, went out to Rangoon in 1883 and became its general manager, keeping in touch by weekly mail and daily cable with the Glasgow office. In those days Britain was in control of both India and Burma, the latter by means of a Governor, a distinguished man of high rank, but the General Manager of the Irrawaddy Flotilla Company, then the greatest business organisation in the country, was an important man and my uncle was a member of the Burma Legislative Council presided over by the Governor. Consequently, he was known as the Honourable James Findlay, but to me he was Uncle James.

He became a Companion of the Order of the Indian Empire, and attended as representative of Burma the magnificent Durbar held in Delhi early in this century. When King George and Queen Mary, then Prince and Princess of Wales, visited Burma, he was their host on the steamer which took them from Rangoon to Mandalay. At one stop on the way the royal couple left the ship alone to wander about on shore, and they were so late in returning that my uncle and the entourage became fearful that they were lost, or had come to some harm.

The foregoing gives a brief description of the organisation in which I started my business career. It will be realised that there was much for me to learn, and it was only by starting at the bottom and working one's way up that it was possible to grasp all the details, so as to fit oneself eventually to manage this great organisation. My grandfather had retired from being senior partner before I entered the office and three partners were left, one being his son-in-law who was my uncle by marriage. These three worked as hard as the rest of us, but they could not have had a proper grip over the business had they not had a capable man at the head of each department, who had started at the bottom and worked his way up to the top by his ability and hard work.

These departmental heads were the key men in the office, and from them came the future partners of the business which was one of the oldest in Glasgow, it having been started early in the 19th century by one called Patrick Henderson. He had a fleet of large fishing-boats on the east coast of Scotland which he found more profitable to employ carrying cargo than catching fish. First they made short voyages, then larger-built boats went as far as Leghorn in Italy, and finally, as their size and numbers increased, they went all over and around the world.

After I had been three years in the office and had worked my way round most of the departments, I took an opportunity which entirely changed my position in the office. "There is a tide in the affairs of

men," we are told, "which, taken at the flood, leads
on to fortune," and it was that tide I took. To this
I attribute my future successful business career. It
was a bold thing I did, but I did it and never regretted
it. It so happened that the man in charge of the
Passenger Department was the son of a late partner.
Because of this he had obtained this position, but he
was quite unfit for his responsibilities. Consequently,
the department was not being efficiently managed, and
I decided that I would speak about it to the senior
partner.

So I walked into his private room one day and told
him what I thought. Moreover, I proposed that he
put me in charge of this department, and if he did so
he would never regret it as it would be efficiently run
in future. I was only twenty then, and the other
department managers were middle-aged or elderly
men, so he must have been surprised at my boldness
and self-confidence. He took my remarks seriously
and we talked things over, to end by his saying he
would think over my proposal and let me know what
he would do. Next day he told me he had decided
to make the change, and that in future I would be the
manager of the important Passenger Department.

I may say that the man I displaced suffered in no
way. He had private means of his own, and he was
given other work to do at his old salary. He never
showed any feeling of resentment towards me, and we
always remained good friends. I think he was pleased
to be relieved of his responsibilities and much happier
with the simpler work he was given to do.

Fortunately, I was able to live up to the promise
I had made to the senior partner, and I attained a

reputation for ability which stood me in good stead four years later when another opportunity presented itself, as will be told later. If I had not made this reputation it is doubtful if this chance of a lifetime would have come my way, and that is why I look back on the bold step I took, when only twenty years of age, as the taking of the tide which ultimately swept me on to fortune.

My companions in the office were doubtless surprised at my rapid promotion, while those about my own age were amused at the keenness I showed in my work. These youths were in the office until their fathers, mostly men in good positions, could find something suitable for them elsewhere. They were not very ambitious to succeed and, with rich fathers behind them, they saw no reason to exert themselves more than was necessary. So my youthful contemporaries passed each day taking little or no thought for the morrow, and amused themselves in the present as much as an office life made possible.

I was now in receipt of a good salary and quite independent of my father. So his allowance stopped and I was on my own in life. Moreover, I was my own master to a large extent, as the partners left me to manage affairs my own way. My work took me to the Glasgow docks, to Liverpool and to London, where I met some of the leading exporters and shipowners. I was taken over different liners by them from time to time, and so got ideas for the future passenger steamers Patrick Henderson & Co. were building. I was responsible for the plans of the passenger accommodation submitted by the builders, and consequently obtained an insight to shipbuilding at the shipyard on the Clyde where there was generally always one new ship being built for the company.

Another important duty I had was to engage a doctor for each ship, and as they usually signed on for only one voyage, quite a number passed through my hands. The hospitals passed on to us doctors who had just qualified and wanted a sea voyage, but I had to check up all their credentials and make sure they were suitable and properly qualified men.

Glasgow is a first-class business city and it is well planned, the buildings being in square blocks so that the streets are parallel to each other. The various banks are convenient, and the shipping and other offices near together. It is noted for its good restaurants and tea-rooms. I joined one of the best clubs and so got to know the leading business men, being for a time the youngest member. So the years passed and to me my work was a great pleasure.

For two years after my return from Geneva we continued to live at Hillhead near Kilbirnie. My spare time was occupied with many things, such as riding or driving, tennis or golf, but I was fond of reading serious books. I became an officer in the local Boys' Brigade, with the founding of which organisation we were closely connected. It so happened that the founder of this great movement was a friend of the family. His name was William Smith, to become later Sir William Smith because of the work he did for the youth, not only of this country but of the world. The Boys' Brigade preceded the Boy Scouts by more than twenty years, and this is how it was founded.

William Smith was a brother officer of my father in the 1st Lanark Volunteers, and a business partner of my uncle, James Findlay, to whom I have just referred. Both my Uncle James and William Smith were anxious to do something to occupy the time of the many boys who had nothing useful to do in their spare time. Smith was a Sunday School teacher in the Free College Church which we attended when we lived in Glasgow. He and my uncle discussed the best way to discipline the boys and raise their thoughts to higher things. So the idea occurred to them to give the boys the feeling that they were soldiers and under discipline. In the Bible class they did not understand the meaning of discipline, but when each boy had a leather belt round his waist, a white band from his shoulder and a wooden gun he was a reformed creature.

My Uncle James gave up his business in Glasgow and went to Rangoon in Burma just as this idea began to mature, and William Smith was left to develop this wonderful creation. The 1st Glasgow Company was founded in 1883, to meet the needs of the boys who attended the Free College Church Bible class, but it was not long before other companies were formed. In fact, the idea caught on, and before long most towns in Britain were forming their Boys' Brigade companies attached to different churches. Ultimately the movement became world wide, and William Smith gave up his business to devote all his time to this new movement.

As always happens when something new comes along, it was classed by some as the work of the devil, because it was feared that it would make the boys military-minded, but this has not happened and the drills have made for discipline and good conduct. Religious teaching takes place for a short time each Sunday, but the attraction to the boys is the drilling, the marching and the band attached to each company. It smartens them up, it disciplines them, and it helps to form their characters. It helps, under the guidance of the officers, who are always picked men, to make good men of the boys and good citizens. Thus, the Boys' Brigade has always lived up to its motto, "Sure and Steadfast", and to its badge, an anchor.

My connection with the Boys' Brigade lasted for only about two years because we moved from Hillhead to Woodside, situated a mile from the little town of Beith which is three miles from Kilbirnie, and here I was to live the rest of the time I lived in Scotland —twenty-two years.

Woodside is one of the most picturesque and delightful houses in North Ayrshire. It is an old house modernised, the oldest date on the house being 1551, but another date, 1613, records the time of an addition made to the oldest part. The walls of the oldest part of the house are six feet thick, and on one window there remains the original iron bars. Timothy Pont, born about 1580, a minister of the Church and chronicler of the North Ayrshire castles of his time, refers to it in these words "Wood-syde is a proper duelling and belongs to ye Laird of Raal-stoune".

The house, as it now is, is composed of buildings of three different epochs. The proper dwelling of Pont's time, which was a square tower, still forms the south-west portion of the front of the present mansion.

To this various additions have been made, the two latest being in 1759, which date is carved on a gable near the eaves and another in 1848, when the last and largest addition was made by an ancestor of the present owner, Lady Cochran-Patrick of Ladyland. My father rented the house and grounds from her and, after his death, I did so.

Outside, the amenities surrounding Woodside are very pleasing. A flower garden was behind the house and a lawn in front, on each side of which were masses of rhododendrons. The house stood high overlooking a glen, of about a quarter of a mile in length, through which ran a stream on each side of which, intersected by paths, were trees, shrubs, rhododendrons, azaleas, and quantities of daffodils and primroses. Up to the house on the west was an avenue of about half a mile, on each side of which were stately beech trees, while another reached it from the east. Both wound through a large private park of about a hundred acres which surrounded the house, and at the entrance to both approaches were picturesque lodges.

I have already mentioned in the previous chapter the hills and moorlands behind Hillhead. Woodside was on the other side of the River Garnock valley and looked across to these hills, which rose to nearly seventeen hundred feet. They were intersected by glens, through which ran rushing streams, and the ever-changing colour of the hills made the view from Woodside one of endless delight. It was indeed a perfect residence, the old house blending in with the surrounding setting of woodlands, parks, glens, hills and moorland. About a mile away was the town of

Beith perched high on a hill, and through the valley ran the railway beside a river and two large lochs.

About the time we were taking up residence at Woodside a novel event was occuring, one such as had never happened before in the years gone by. Our means of travel on land had always been by horse or in horse-drawn vehicles. Now there was to be seen occasionally on the roads a machine which moved of itself without being drawn by a horse. It had an engine inside its metal body which made loud and fearsome noises, and emitted disagreeable fumes of gas. It was no other than the forerunner of the present-day motor-car, and how it was disliked by all road-users, especially those driving horses! These animals likewise showed their repugnance to it by shying, backing and stopping in fear whenever one approached.

During the 19th century coal was the only mineral employed to produce the power which turned the wheels of travel and industry. In the 20th century, which we have now entered, a new substance came more and more into everyday use to transform the lives of every one. Coal, formerly king, had now to compete with petroleum, a rival which in many respects is its superior, because it has made possible machines which could not conveniently be operated by coal. Last century coal enormously increased both power and speed, while this century petroleum has augmented them still more.

Millions of years ago vegetation died, and was covered over with water in the form of lakes and seas, in which floated silt brought down by the rivers. This silt sank to the bottom to form, over ages of time, a hard rock covering, which pressed ever harder on the vegetation below until it in turn became hard and brittle. This substance we call coal, which has been known to mankind for thousands of years, as it protrudes in places from the earth's surface, and its use increased as invention created machines to enable it to be raised from greater depths.

Petroleum was probably produced from the bodies of fish and animals which settled on the sea-bed millions of years ago, to become covered, as was coal, by floating sediment that sank to the bottom. Over aeons of years a deep layer of rock formed over these animal remains which, unlike the vegetation, remained liquid, to be forced out by the gas it produced in those places where the original covering of rock had been broken by earth convulsions. This released liquid was transformed by atmospheric action into bitumen and we now use it to spread on our roads to give them a smooth surface.

Petroleum has been known by civilised man from the dawn of history. Herodotus wrote about it, and, to come to more recent times, British representatives to the King of Burma referred to it in 1765 as oozing out of springs and wells near Mandalay. In 1814 it was observed in Ohio, and fifteen years later in Kentucky, when a well was sunk to obtain brine. Instead of brine it yielded sufficient oil over the next thirty years to fill 50,000 barrels, most of which was allowed to run to waste. The small quantity saved was bottled and sold as an embrocation.

That was all that was known in America in 1860 about this great power-giving substance. James Young, a Glasgow chemist, the pioneer in Britain of this new fuel, knew more about it than did the Americans, because in 1848 he commenced to refine illuminating oil from deposits discovered in Derbyshire. His success attracted the attention of the United States, where wells were sunk, deeper and deeper, with ever-growing success, and from that time to this there has been a never-ending hunt to secure land under which it was thought oil deposits lay.

Coal had for long been known as a means of producing heat, but no use was made of the gas it gave off until last century, when this was used for lighting purposes. Then it was discovered that gas in a confined space, when in contact with a light, exploded. This led Lenoir in 1860 to construct a cylinder into which air and gas were led by a pipe and exploded by an electric spark. Next, a piston was inserted which was driven out by the explosion, and then it was only a matter of cogs, wheels and timing to get the explosion to occur at the right second to drive out the piston, which, on its return journey, forced out the fumes.

Petroleum was found to become gaseous much more easily than coal, and so the next step was made by Julius Hock of Vienna (1870), who drove a gas engine by spraying petroleum mixed with air into the cylinder. Brayton, an American engineer, followed with an improved type in 1873, and then Otto, in 1876, produced his gas engine which became known all over the world. The next advance came when Daimler invented (1885) a small petroleum-gas-driven engine which he attached to a bicycle. He sold his patents to the French firm of Panhard and Levassor, and Levassor invented the motor-car.

Then in 1903 the brothers Orville and Wilbur Wright attached to a glider a petroleum engine which turned a propeller, giving sufficient forward speed for the pressure of air on the inclined wings to exert a lift which enabled the glider to fly off the ground for a distance of 852 feet. The petroleum-driven engine had made it possible to cover a distance in the air, independent of land and sea, because petroleum could be easily vaporised, whereas to obtain gas from coal requires an elaborate plant.

Petroleum, being liquid, could be carried much more easily than coal, and, in consequence, a fuel supply could be stored in the vehicle to move it a long distance. This made possible the construction of a ship to sail underneath the surface of the water, to become known as the submarine. Thus it came about that by experiment and rational thought the engineer produced the motor-car, the airplane and the submarine which, if we had been ethically developed beings, would have been used for improving our conditions without a thought of putting them to destructive purposes. Unfortunately we are not ethically developed beyond our own national boundaries, and consequently it was not long before someone thought of turning the motor-car into an armoured tank, the airplane into a bomber to carry bombs which explode as they touch the ground, and the submarine into a torpedo-carrying vessel which can carry on its deadly work without being seen.

Such then is the brief story of petroleum and the petrol engine as applied to transport by road, sea and air, and, at the time about which I am writing, the motor-car was just making its appearance in Scotland.

My cousin, who was with me in the office of Patrick Henderson & Co., and whose father was a partner, quickly became much more interested in motor-cars than in his work, and was determined to buy the first he could procure. He found one for sale and asked me to come with him on a trial run. It was a French car, a Peugeot, and our driver was the Glasgow agent whose knowledge of petrol engines was strictly limited, my cousin and I knowing nothing at all about them.

We started from Glasgow to attempt the hazardous journey to Woodside, a distance of eighteen miles. Through Glasgow we, and everyone we passed, were disturbed by loud bangs coming from the exhaust, and it was embarrassing seeing everyone turn and look at us in horror. The roads in those days were covered with stone chips rolled in to make a tolerably smooth surface, but our car had only hard rubber tyres, pneumatic tyres not then being made for cars. The journey consequently was rough, but as our speed was slow it was not too uncomfortable. A man preceding cars with a red flag was not now necessary, but we passed men breaking stones for the road, a common sight those days, but never seen to-day.

I do not remember the number of times the engine stopped on the journey, but over and over again we descended from our uncomfortable seats to lift the bonnet and tinker with the engine and the ignition. No other car was passed on the road, only horses and horse-drawn vehicles, their passengers expressing sarcastic remarks at our expense, and some asked if we wished to be towed. It took us about three hours that Summer evening to make the journey, and I made up my mind that the time had not yet come to buy a car. I had no doubt that horses were much more to be depended on, and that travelling by carriage was more certain and dignified. Not so my cousin, and he bought the car, or one like it, and had many adventures in it, some of which I shared. On one occasion we were fifteen miles from his home and the engine refused to move, no matter what we did to coax it. We left the car, had a long walk to the nearest village and went back by train.

My other relaxations were riding, tennis and golf. We had a hard tennis court at Woodside and a good golf course nearby. To drive a golf ball a long distance straight down the fairway is the delight of the golfer, it gives a sense of superiority to the one who has made a perfect drive, and this sensation must be experienced to be understood. One sport always repelled me, and that was the shooting or the hunting of animals. After much persuasion I once went shooting with friends on the nearby moors. I shot a rabbit and had such a feeling of remorse that I never shot a bird or an animal again. Hunting, I felt, was even more cruel, to kill an animal by degrees, so to speak, to enjoy oneself by making animals suffer, is to me degrading. To stop up the foxes' earths beforehand so that they would have little chance to find a refuge is to me diabolical, and all this is for the purpose of giving a dozen or two dozen men and women some excitement, which is called sport.

I therefore sincerely hope that, some day, when the people's minds develop further, all hunting of animals will cease, and we will have no more deer-hunting, otter-hunting, fox-hunting, hare-coursing, or any unnecessary cruelty to these helpless animals who doubtless suffer just as much as we would if we were hunted to death.

I knew most of the fox-hunting people in Ayrshire and Renfrewshire, and before a hunt they usually met at a private house for a drink. At times they asked permission to meet at Woodside, and it made a pretty sight, the horses, the hounds and the men in pink coats, but I never liked it, in fact I despised them all for their inflicting long-drawn-out suffering on an unfortunate animal, so as to have a day's excitement and pleasure. Otter-hunting and hare-coursing are just as bad.

I became interested in politics, and, having rather advanced opinions on improving social conditions, I became a Liberal, to be elected President of the Beith Liberal Association. Liberal principles have always appealed to me, especially the Party's attitude at that time towards the granting of Home Rule for Ireland, which I supported. I remember once addressing the Beith Literary Society on the subject of the taxation of Land Values, and I supported the arguments of Henry George in its favour, though I did not go so far as he did. This outstanding and popular American economist proposed to abolish all taxation on income as is done at present, and put a single tax on land as the simplest and most convenient way of raising revenue. He argued that as all wealth comes from the land, and as everyone one way or another lives on the land, a single tax on the assessed value of all land would be a fair and simple way to secure the necessary revenue, each taxpayer paying his share according to the value of the land he occupies.

Only a few of my audience agreed with me, and I never pursued the subject again publicly. Nevertheless, I consider that the present-day method of raising the country's revenue is expensive, cumbersome and complicated, and I am sure a simpler way could be found if we gave the matter rational thought and consideration. Remember the army of officials now employed to raise the country's revenue from taxation, and how their methods are so complicated and obscure as to require by the taxpayer in many cases the help of accountants to work through masses of figures and calculations before the tax payable is arrived at. Surely it is not beyond the wit of man to find an alternative system, simple and less distracting to taxpayers, and one which would save the country millions by employing fewer tax collectors, and putting to profitable work many of those now thus unprofitably employed.

In the year 1901 many people were interested in a newspaper report that an Italian scientist, Marconi, had been successful in transmitting signals without wires across the Atlantic between England and Newfoundland. For the previous six years the British Post Office had been attempting to transmit wireless signals, and had succeeded in doing so between the Island of Mull and the mainland, but Marconi's success was so startling that people began to talk about it, greatly wondering. That was the beginning of a new era in communication, and year by year further progress was made. The necessary instruments were manufactured and sold, and we all know what a boon the Radio has been to everyone. In those early days no one could imagine that nearly every home would

some day have a wireless receiver, and be daily receiving news, music and entertainment without the aid of
wires—hitherto the means of transmitting messages
quickly from one place to another.

In my youth there was no national service, but
many young men voluntarily joined a reserve army
called "The Volunteers", and I was one of them. The
pay was negligible, but they felt they had a duty to
their country and, like the boys of the Boys' Brigade,
they liked the drills, the marching, the uniform and
the bands. Since the time of Henry VIII volunteers
have come forward in defence of their country, and in
1779 they became an integral part of the system of
national defence. In 1859, the Indian Mutiny so
taxed our resources, at a time when France was
adopting a threatening attitude, that the formation of
a volunteer corps began in earnest, to bring about the
enlistment of 119,000 men. The following year a royal
review was held in Hyde Park, and in 1881, one
was held in Edinburgh. I remember the latter being
spoken about because the day was the worst in living
memory, the rain coming down in torrents from
morning to night. Over twenty thousand men
paraded on each occasion.

My three years of military service was not spectacular. I joined the Beith Company of the Royal
Scots Fusiliers in 1902, its headquarters being at
Kilmarnock, and I still have the document, signed by
Edward VII, addressed to "our trusty and well-
beloved James Arthur Findlay, Gentleman" to the
effect that I was a fit, proper, loyal and courageous
person to hold the rank of lieutenant. I attended
regularly the drills until I became proficient and was

always present at target practice, the shooting-range being on the moors above Beith. I was one of those who lined the streets of Glasgow when Edward VII made a state visit to the city, and that is about all I have to say, except that if I had not had an illness I would probably have been killed at Gallipoli in 1915.

I had an attack of appendicitis just before the regiment went into camp for a fortnight. I recovered without an operation, being cured by leeches, which was fortunate as the success of such an operation in those days was doubtful. The doctor said it might recur if I were exposed to bad weather in camp, and he advised me to resign my commission, which I did reluctantly. Then, in 1914, came the First World War and the regiment was sent out to Gallipoli. There, nearly every man in the Beith company, and all the officers, were killed, and if I had been one of them I do not see why I should not have shared the same fate.

I mention my doctor, and this takes me back to a conversation I had with him in 1899, when I was sixteen years of age, on which I can look back with satisfaction. His name was Dr. Milroy, a very capable and intelligent man who was our doctor during the years we lived at Hillhead, and remained our doctor when we went to Woodside. One day I confided to him how I hated the puritanical life of my home. Family worship every morning and evening, into which trooped the servants, the sprawling on our

knees over our chairs at the prayer and the dismal
Sunday, I told him, repelled me. I said how I hated
Sunday with all its prohibitions, its two church services and then Sunday School which my parents took,
and which they insisted I must attend. To all this he
was very sympathetic, as it was the way of life in which
he also had been brought up.

I expressed my doubts about the statements set out
in the Shorter Catechism. I said I could not accept
what I was told about the Bible being word for word
true, and that all this worried me because it made my
parents unhappy, they believing that all unbelievers
would end in hell. He reassured me that this would
not happen, expressing the view that such a fear on
their part was groundless, and that in his opinion their
form of religious teaching was mostly nonsense and
largely humbug. "When one knows the truth about
Christianity," he said, "one is free from fear," and he
promised to send me a book to read which would both
enlighten and satisfy me.

Never shall I forget the satisfaction and happiness
I received from reading this book, which was *Lectures
and Essays* by Robert Green Ingersoll. No man by
his writing helped me more through my early life,
especially in those days when I was groping for the
truth and did not know where to find it. What
Ingersoll had to say was just what I wanted to
know, the first chapter of his book entitled "Some
Mistakes of Moses" being headed with these
words:

"He who endeavours to control the mind by force
is a tyrant and he who submits is a slave."

Taking as his subject the many mistakes to be

found in the books attributed to Moses in the Bible, he commenced the first chapter with an opinion which strongly appealed to me and which I have never forgotten. I felt that it had been written for me, and here it is:—

> "Were we allowed to read the Bible as we do all other books, we should admire its beauties, treasure its worthy thoughts, and account for all its absurd, grotesque and cruel things, by saying that its authors lived in rude barbaric times. But we are told that it was written by inspired men, that it contains the will of God, that it is perfect, pure, true in all its parts, the source and standard of all moral and religious truth, that it is the star and anchor of all human hope, the only guide for man and the only torch in nature's night. These claims are so at variance with every known recorded fact, so palpably absurd, that every free unbiassed soul is forced to raise the standard of revolt."

When my mother first saw me reading this book she was furious, as in those days the clergy of every denomination denounced Ingersoll as a servant of the devil. She was a kind and affectionate woman and loved me dearly, but from her childhood she had been taught that to doubt the contents of *The Holy Bible* was contrary to the Will of God and consequently wicked, the punishment for which would be eternity in hell. Mentally she was not capable of throwing off this pernicious teaching, and she believed that I was heading for hel as straight as I could go.

A wiser woman than she was would have talked the question over with me, and listened to an opinion different from her own. She was not wise, in fact she was foolish in the attitude she adopted towards me, one of flat refusal to hear or discuss anything contrary to the orthodox beliefs in which she was nurtured. Hell made her intolerant of any unorthodox opinion. Hell made her intolerant with me, it made her aggressive, domineering and autocratic towards me. Hell caused a breach between us which would never have occurred if she had been willing to learn, and to read books other than the Bible and simple light novels. She could not think deeply or read deeply, she could not think for herself, and a book she set up as holy, and written by God, guided and directed her daily thoughts.

Unbelief, she held, nullified for me the salvation of my soul by Christ's death for my sins, it being written "He that believeth and is baptised shall be saved, but he that believeth not shall be damned" (Mark xvi, 16). If she had been more intelligent and had known about her Bible as much as she knew of its contents, she would have found on referring to the Revised Version that the last half of the last chapter of Mark, in which this verse occurs, is an interpolation and is not to be found in the earlier copies. Later I found that the interpolations made in the Gospels, by zealous scribes at later dates, were so numerous that when they are all withdrawn from the text, as given in the Bible, only a skeleton remains. In other words, the entire Gospel story, as given in the four Gospels, is unhistorical, unreliable, and, in their evolution, they represent only the opinions of various unknown writers over very many years about what Jesus was, did and said, not what he actually was, did say and do. In other words the Gospels are fanciful legends, and how they came into being will be explained further on.

On 21st July, 1899 I saw in the newspapers with regret the announcement of the death of Robert Ingersoll at the age of sixty-six, which occurred in the same year as I first read his *Lectures and Essays*. So I obtained a copy of the record of his life and found that he was one of the leading advocates in the United States. He became Attorney-General for the State of Illinois. He was the son of a revivalist Presbyterian preacher, and had rebelled against the religious teaching to which he had been subjected. In his spare time he made a deep study of religion, the Christian religion in particular, and, by his oratory and his writings, he stirred to its depths the thinking English-speaking world. Every calumny was hurled at him by the ignorant because of his unorthodox beliefs, and when he stood for the Governorship of the State of Illinois in 1868 he was defeated because he would not retract his unbeliefs.

His love of humanity was unbounded, his abhorrence of slavery and his kindness and generosity to all being noteworthy. His life was spent in an endeavour to raise the living conditions, and the mental level, of his fellow citizens at a time when such efforts received little sympathy from his Christian contemporaries. His home life was ideal, he was a devoted husband and father, and always a true, upright and honourable man. Yet this was the man denounced and maligned by most of the clergy in the States and in Europe, who could not find words bad enough to say of one who exposed the falsehoods they preached.

Nevertheless, he was one of the grandest and noblest characters of the 19th century, as all who read his books and learn of his life will discover.

After reading Ingersoll's essays on various aspects of the Christian religion, I went into a leading bookshop in Glasgow and asked if there were on sale any other books similar to Ingersoll's Essays. "We do not sell such books, and no decent bookshop does," was the reply, and I remember the look of horror the bookseller gave me. Today they can be bought in any large bookshop. However, I was not to be baffled and got into touch with the Glasgow Secular Society, who told me of a hairdresser in a small way in a side-street of the city who sold other such books. I called on him and left with a bundle, one being *The Age of Reason* by Thomas Paine, who lived in the latter half of the 18th century.

This revealing book contains so much that is good, and such wisdom, that it should be read by everyone. Here are some of Paine's beliefs:—

(1) I believe in the equality of man, that religious duties consist of doing justice, loving mercy and endeavouring to make my fellow creatures happy.

(2) Everyone, if he wishes happiness, must be mentally honest.

(3) Belief in a cruel God makes a cruel man.

(4) Those whose lives have been spent in doing good, and in the endeavour to make their fellow creatures happy, will be happy hereafter.

(5) One good schoolmaster is of more use than a hundred priests.

(6) I believe in One God and no more, and I
      hope for happiness beyond this life.

(7) Slavery is wrong, and one man should not
      make another his property.

(8) The key to Heaven is not in the keeping of
      only one religion or sect.

When this book was written, to criticise the Bible
and Christian orthodox beliefs, as Paine did, was considered to be as bad as treason to the State, and this
son of a Quaker, born in 1737, suffered terribly for his
boldness.   In Britain and the United States the Protestant Church was then all-powerful, and all sects in
both countries united to denounce this critic of the
prevailing orthodox beliefs.

The Age of Reason is an honest investigation of the
Bible and the Christian faith, it was written in simple
words for the average man, and Paine gave his candid
opinions.   He made the people think and put the
priests on the defensive.   He made the reader wiser
than the parson, taking the power from the pulpit and
giving it to the people who sat in the pews.   By
making the people think he struck at the power of the
Church which had kept them ignorant and superstitious throughout the Christian era.   He exposed the
folly of considering the Bible as word for word true
and written from heaven.   From this book itself he
took his arguments, and exposed its contradictions, its
stupidities, its errors, its false history and its support
for that which is evil.

How right he was came to be known in 1881 when
a new Revised Version of the Bible was produced.
Those responsible for the translation of the new

version then stated that they had discovered 36,191 mistakes in the old version, and we know that if a new version were to be published to-day the alterations that would be made would be equally striking.

For this crime of using his reason Paine became an outcast. He could not safely appear in the streets, and, until his death, every lie manufactured about him was thought to be pleasing to God. The life of a man devoted to the well-being of his fellow men was by his enemies turned into one of drunkenness, immorality and shame. Every scandal told about him was untrue. He was depicted as a drunken beast and it was said that he died a drunkard's death in destitution and want. All this and more was said to vilify his character, not one word being true, all was false and born of hatred caused by ignorance.

Paine died as he lived, an honest, good-living, kind, and upright man. He was the first to denounce American and British slavery, to champion the common man who had no vote, and no one took an interest in his welfare. He was the first to expose the injustice everywhere prevailing, and to put forward a scheme to relieve the poor in abject poverty by means of an old age pension, but this was turned down by Parliament. He lived to improve the lives of his fellow creatures and make them wiser, nobler, and better men. This was the man who, from being considered a good and honest citizen, became by this book, through the influence of an army of black-robed priests and ministers, "a filthy little atheist". He was not filthy, little, or an atheist, one of the first statements in *The Age of Reason* being "I believe in God".

Hatred, when roused to a passion, can blacken a man's character amongst those who know no better, and this continued up to my time, as such slanders as I have written above I have heard said about him in churches, and have read in the religious papers. That aggressive American evangelist, Torrey, who followed Moody in an evangelical campaign in this country in 1905, and whom I met and once listened to, repeated from time to time the above slanders against Paine. The Secular Society exposed these lies, but neither Torrey, nor the numerous clergy who had repeated them, were honest enough to dissociate themselves publicly from the slanders they spread. W. T. Stead was so furious about it all that he vowed he would use all his influence with the Press of the land to prevent Torrey ever entering this country again.

But the lies remained both here and in America, and President Theodore Roosevelt, I read in disgust, referred to Paine as "a filthy little atheist" in a speech he made which was reported at the time in this country. The British Tract Societies until recently, and they may still do so, have perpetuated these slanders about Paine, and I imagine that they are still taught to the clergy in their theological colleges, where their minds are twisted, besides the other numerous errors and historical inaccuracies for which these training colleges are famous. Lies, once they set wing, are hard to catch up with.

If it had not been for Paine we would not be living to-day in a tolerant society, as he it was who broke the hard crust of intolerance prevailing in his day. He was followed by others in this country and by Ingersoll in America. Because of them I, and others, can now write and speak our honest thoughts without molestation. Intolerance is the child of ignorance. Intolerance comes from ignorant superstition. Tolerance comes from knowledge and understanding. One lives in the night of mental darkness, the other in the sunlight of knowledge. The curse of ignorance is mankind's greatest foe, though unfortunately few there be who know it.

Paine did much more than write *The Age of Reason*. Our liberal welfare state came from his book *The Rights of Man*, for the reading and selling of which, as happened with *The Age of Reason*, many were imprisoned or banished. One Glasgow man was banished for eleven years for handing *The Rights of Man* on to a friend to read. Pitt the Younger remarked once to his niece, Lady Hester Stanhope: "Tom Paine is quite in the right, but what am I to do? As things are, if I were to encourage Paine's opinions we shall have a bloody revolution." Nevertheless, Paine was 80 years before his time in advocating general education, 120 years in advance in advocating old age pensions, 130 years ahead in his scheme for a League of Nations to prevent war, and 150 years ahead in his ideas on general social welfare. In fact, his life and work are a political and religious history of the times, and throw an illuminating light on the stupidities, cruelties and injustices prevalent in Britain, Europe and America not much more than one hundred years ago.

Under the stimulus of Paine and Ingersoll I became a student of Religion, and read all the leading books dealing with Christianity and the other world religions of the past and present. I found the study of Comparative Religion fascinating, such books as *Christianity and Mythology* and *Pagan Christs* by John McKinnon Robertson making clear to me how the old Pagan beliefs gathered round Jesus to produce Christianity. Robertson, who was Parliamentary Secretary to the Board of Trade from 1911 to 1915 and a Privy Councillor, had a powerful intellect, was a scholar of repute, and stayed with me once at Woodside to deliver a lecture to the Beith Literary Society.

I can only mention briefly a few of the outstanding books which gave me much delight and enlightenment. *The History of the Intellectual Development of Europe* by Professor J. W. Draper and his *History of the Conflict between Religion and Science* are masterpieces on the subjects they cover. Three other books which gave me great pleasure to read were *Lectures and Essays* by Professor T. Huxley, *The Riddle of the Universe* by Professor Ernest Haeckel and *The Story of Evolution* by Joseph McCabe. Another book on evolution I much enjoyed was that thoughtful work *The Evolution of the Idea of God* by Grant Allen.

After reading *The Oldest Laws in the World* by Edwards I realised how little we had progressed up to last century in our culture and way of life in Europe during the Christian era, and how many pre-Christian people, called by us the heathen, had as high an idea of righteousness as ever had Christendom. This was intensified by reading *Paganism and Christianity* by that great classical scholar J. A. Farrer in which the following, and much else he tells us, will astonish those who have accepted the orthodox history of Europe as it has come down to us, influenced as it has been so largely by the Christian Church. Farrer writes:—

"There is indeed no fact more patent in history than that, with the triumph of Christianity under Constantine, the older and finer spirit of charity died out of the world, and gave place to an intolerance and bigotry which were its extreme antithesis, and which have only in recent years come to be mitigated."

This is only too true, as my long study of history has convinced me. The good that Christianity did to the western world came from its spreading the civilisation of ancient Greece and Rome, and taking the culture of these two Pagan civilisations to those the Greeks called the European barbarians. Christianity, with its headquarters in Rome, acted as a carrier of Pagan culture, but no more, because Christianity was not the cause of the civilisation of Europe. Western civilisation and culture came from the influence of Pagan Greek and Roman thought on barbarism, brought to an ignorant and superstitious people under the cloak of religion.

By conquest or persuasion Christianity spread. Rome, when seen, so impressed the barbarian leaders, and Athens, when seen, the eastern rulers, that they returned home to force the new religion on their people. It was not the new religion that changed these people, as basically there was little between the new Christianity and the old Paganism. What did slowly change their mental outlook was the civilising influence of the laws and customs of ancient Rome and Athens, especially when their literature came to be freely read after the fall of Constantinople in 1453, to bring about the end of the Dark Ages of medieval Europe.

A few other books I might mention which greatly
enlightened me were *Christianity Before Christ* by
Charles Stone, and *The Origins of Christianity* by Whit-
taker. Canon Robertson's *History of the Christian
Church* amazed me by its frank revelations. What a
terrible history it is of an institution which claims to
represent Christ on earth! This was emphasised when
I read Robertson's *A Short History of Christianity.*
Books dealing with the study of comparative religion
revealed how Christianity is but a copy of the religions believed in at the time of its birth, its moral
teaching coming from the high Greek culture prevailing when it was being slowly manufactured over four
centuries.

Books which made this their subject were *The
Mystery Religions and Christianity* by Dr. Angus, Professor of New Testament and Historical Theology at
St. Andrew's College, Sydney, and *Myth, Magic and
Morals* by that great scholar F. C. Conybeare, a most
enlightening study of the influences which brought
the Gospels and the Epistles into being. Mention
must be made of the eleven volumes on comparative
religion, and kindred subjects, by Professor Max
Müller, which comprise his exhaustive study of world
religions, especially those of India.

The Golden Bough, that large and learned work by
Sir James Frazer of Cambridge, who was the son of a
Glasgow chemist, profoundly interested me, as it has
done all serious students of anthropology and religion, his exhaustive enquiry into the pre-Christian
beliefs about the ancient saviour gods being very revealing. A book which I found gives much valuable
information in small space is *The Churches and Modern*

Thought by Vivian Phelips, and lastly I must mention that great work entitled *Jesus* by Guignebert, Professor of the History of Christianity at the Sorbonne, Paris, which reveals Jesus as he was before Paul and others superimposed their Pagan beliefs, and changed him from a human being into another Pagan Christ.

Edward Gibbon's masterpiece, *The Decline and Fall of the Roman Empire,* I read and re-read, his 15th and 16th chapters on the early history of Christianity being most revealing. Here we have the first systematic and scholarly attempt to present in historic narrative the development of organised Christianity, and the rise to power of the Christian Church. Little wonder that he was much criticised in his day, but truth, as it always does, has won in the end.

These, and many other books, greatly swayed me in forming my opinions on the world's organised orthodox religions, Christianity in particular. They made me realise how ignorant and stupid were the religious people I was coming across, how they knew nothing about the beliefs they held and had accepted without thought. In those days ignorance was considered a virtue and knowledge a sin, and it still is amongst many of the orthodox. The thoroughness with which I have always undertaken everything serious in life I applied to my religion, as I applied it to my business. Consequently I ceased calling myself a Christian, and did not become a member of any Christian church. After fifty years I have never regretted this decision. Orthodoxy and Religion are by no means the same, and one need not be orthodox, or believe in a creed, to be religious.

I became a member of the Rationalist Press Association, and so obtained their publication called *The Literary Guide*, which gave reviews of all new books on Science and advanced thought. I became acquainted with many leaders of modern thought, one very unusual man, Stuart Ross, who wrote under the name of Saladin, being an especially interesting and forceful personality. He took the name of Saladin as his pseudonym because, as will be remembered, Saladin fought against the Christians during the Crusades.

Here I might mention a highly significant experience I once had. Calling on one occasion at the office of the Christian Evidence Society in London, to ask if they had a book to recommend which countered the statements made in books hostile to the beliefs of the Christian faith, I met the clergyman in charge of the organisation. So I put the question to him, and his candid reply amazed me. "No," he replied, "we have no such books, and there are none to be had. I would recommend you to go to the Rationalist Press Association, who publish and distribute the best books for the student of religion." This was candid enough and true, but the Christian Evidence Society was the last place on earth I expected to hear such an admission.

All this in no way interfered with my business. Every fortnight a captain of a ship would arrive home from a voyage to some distant part of the world, and come and see me to report how things had gone with the passengers. My office work gave me intense interest, but nothing out of the ordinary happened from day to day, except that one Winter in the evenings I wrote a small book on Burma for the guidance of tourists to that interesting land. This was my first literary effort. The idea of such a book was expanded, and resulted in *Burma*, a large book Talbot Kelly was commissioned to write by Patrick Henderson & Co. His great talent for painting, which was so evident in the pictures he produced in his book on Egypt, was again exemplified in this one on Burma, where he went to describe and paint scenes from that colourful land.

Otherwise, steamers sailed regularly to their destinations and returned regularly. Winter fog held them up from time to time, as was to be expected, and very occasionally mishaps and accidents occurred.

One steamer, owing to faulty navigation, ran ashore on its way down the coast of West Africa, but when high tide came it was towed off. Another in a fog went ashore on the Isle of Man on its way from Glasgow to Liverpool, but it likewise escaped destruction and returned to Glasgow to spend some weeks in dry dock. Another went ashore on a mud-bank in the Moulmein River in Burma on its way to Moulmein, and what is left of it is still there, as it never returned home, but such happenings fortunately do not often occur in the life of those who go down to the sea in ships, or manage them from land.

From the time I brought the first unorthodox book into Woodside I found I had to keep them under lock and key. Whenever I left one lying about it disappeared, and, when asked for, my mother told me she had burned it. I suppressed my annoyance and bought another copy, but on one occasion I left the cupboard, where I kept them, unlocked and she ransacked it. I shall never forget the consequences. She and my father met me in the library on my return home from the office with solemn and angry faces, one of my books being on a table and they standing behind it. When I entered the room my mother exclaimed: "What is the meaning of this?" My father, who never liked what he called "these scenes", said nothing and allowed my mother, who was always the moving spirit in this persecution, to do the talking.

This, one of many such scenes, ended by my mother saying that if I wanted to live with them I must stop reading such books, and that she was going to put them all in sacks and have them taken outside and burn them in a bonfire. I replied that, as they were quite unaware of their contents, I was sure they would do as they intended, but that I protested against the destruction of my property as I had myself paid for all these books. Moreover, I did not interfere with their beliefs, and they should not interfere with mine. My protests were all in vain, and all my greatly valued books were put on a bonfire and went up in flames. I am glad to think that during those times of severe frustration and aggravation I never lost my self-control, or said anything to hurt their feelings. Inwardly, however, I felt very bitter and longed for a home of my own.

To such lengths Christians go to please the God made in their own image, and in their efforts to save erring souls from His anger and hell, an idea which is no more than their own foolish imagination. It was, moreover, quite senseless, because I just replaced my library at my leisure, though unfortunately some of my rare books I found were out of print and impossible to get. This new library I made certain did not suffer the same fate, and I kept my books in future in a place where my mother could not find them. I never left one lying about.

That day I realised why heretics suffered throughout the Christian era. Education, over the past hundred years, has deprived Christians of their lust for bodily cruelty, so I was not thrown into prison or burned to death. Neither did I suffer from the rack, the contracting boot, the thumbscrew, or in any of those many other ways Christians had invented for enforcing their opinions on others. Nevertheless, when I stood there facing my mother, I realised what little chance of mercy those old victims ever had, and how ignorance produces fanaticism which does away with all the nobler feelings of mankind. My persecution was a mental, not a bodily, one. In one way I was a victim of the age-long tragedy of Christian persecution, but fortunately I came in for the tail-end of it, and suffered no bodily harm.

However, she now knows better and regrets her mistakes, as will be discovered from the talks I had with her after she passed on. These will be reported in a later chapter.

The history of book-burning goes away back, almost to the time books were invented following the invention of an alphabet in the 9th century B.C. The word "Bible" comes from the town of Byblus on the coast of Syria, where the first book was produced in an alphabet invented by the Egyptians. Books which were contrary to the prevailing opinions were destroyed by the authorities, and so we learn how the works of two Greek authors were burned in Athens by the Romans some nineteen hundred years ago.

The early Christian Church was not slow to follow this example of intolerance, and any books considered heretical were destroyed. The first recorded instance was the burning of all books written by Arius, whose writings against the addition of the Trinity to the Christian faith were consigned to the flames after the Council of Nicaea in 325, Constantine himself threatening with death all who had such copies. The same fate befell the books of other authors whose opinions did not accord with the findings of this council.

At Alexandria there was a famous library founded by Ptolemy I in the 3rd century B.C., and it became known as the most important library in the ancient world. Under the enlightened rule of the Ptolemys, scholars and men of science were attracted to the Egyptian capital, and made much use of the literature there available. The first Ptolemy began this collection of books, and so laid the foundation for this great library, his successors sending to every part of Greece and Asia to secure the most valuable works. No exertion or expense was spared in enriching the collection.

Books were translated by Alexandrian scholars into many languages for the benefit of the different nationalities which came to Alexandria to consult them. There were two libraries in this city, the Bruchium and the Serapeum, and both contained a large number of volumes. There were 42,800 volumes, or rolls, in the Serapeum, and 490,000 in the Bruchium. In 389 all these were pillaged and destroyed by the Christians. This act of barbarism was carried out under the direction of the Christian bishop Theophilus, and Gibbon, in his *Decline and Fall of the Roman Empire*, tells the whole disgraceful story. All the books in Alexandria, available to the public, were thus destroyed by this act of vandalism.

Then followed the destruction by the Christians of many Greek and Roman classics in 400 after the Council of Carthage, Aristotle's works being prohibited until the 14th century. All the many colleges and schools, which were established throughout the Roman Empire, were closed because Christians believed that the Holy Scriptures contained all there was to know, and that what was not therein was of the devil. Schoolmasters were banished and intellectual night fell on Christendom, to last for more than a thousand years, a period which became known as the Dark Ages.

When learning slowly returned at the Renaissance, the Church compiled an *Index* of all heretical books which, when found, were destroyed. The Inquisition forbade all books contrary to the teachings of the Church. All Europe was under this intolerant rule, and England was no exception. Among those whose books were destroyed were Gibbon, Bacon, Hallam, Milton, Locke, Stuart Mill and others. Adam Smith's *Wealth of Nations* was banned in Spain. The war against books began in the reign of Henry VIII, when the clergy gathered in every translation of the Bible into English they could get hold of, and burned them publicly before St. Paul's Church. It is better to burn books than their authors, but they did both in those days.

In Moslem lands intolerance prevailed whenever the orthodox were in power, and consequently we read of intellectual darkness coming down on the glories of Moslem culture in the 10th century. At a time when intellectual light flooded the Moslem world from the writings of Arabian scholars, when in Cairo, Baghdad, Damascus and Alexandria books were freely bought and sold, free schools were available for the poor, and culture and learning was never higher, a change came in Moslem Spain, where this learning was at its height. An orthodox Caliph, by cunning, obtained power and all books dealing with science, philosophy and astronomy were condemned to the flames.

To return to my experiences, it may be wondered why I did not live elsewhere, but that would have been a dreary form of existence. I was very comfortable at home. I paid no rent and had every luxury. My mother, when not making a scene, was loving and kind. I had a large and pleasant bedroom, in fact, I considered it the best in the house, and from it a door opened into a private sitting-room which my brother and I shared. The carriage, and, later on when we had one, the motor-car, took me to the railway station each morning and met me in the evening.

Scenes or no scenes, I was too fond of my home, too comfortable to move, and besides that I always got on well with my father, who never of his own wish would have gone to the extremes to which my mother went. We were always the best of friends, and I am glad to think that in his later years I helped to make life easier for him. He suffered from neurasthenia and was very nervous and highly strung. Consequently, he felt nervous meeting the men at the club in Glasgow, and I proposed to him that we should always have our lunch together at a nearby restaurant. This proposal he at once agreed to, and for long he and I lunched together, much to his relief and satisfaction.

In 1904 my grandfather died at the age of seventy-five. He developed pneumonia from a chill he got when on a trip on the Clyde. He was a trustee of the Clyde Navigation Trust, and each year the trustees made an inspection of the lighthouses under their authority. Doubtless they all thoroughly enjoyed themselves, and made a pleasure out of a duty, but on this occasion he returned home feeling far from well. In a few days he passed on, but just before he lost consciousness he sat up in bed and held out his arms. He looked up as if seeing someone, a bright smile came over his face and he exclaimed "Oh Mother." These were his last words, and he then fell back on his pillow, dead, as it appeared, but I think he got a glimpse of the new world he was about to enter, with the mother he loved so much waiting to meet him. It was a wonderful ending to a wonderful life on earth.

His funeral was one of the largest which ever passed through the streets of Glasgow from the railway station to Cathcart cemetery. I was in the first carriage, and after we had come down one of the long principal streets I looked back and could see the carriages still turning into it. He received, in the many obituary notices published about him, much praise for the good work he had done to so many during his time on earth. Personally, I felt his loss greatly; that such a mind should be extinguished, as I then thought, was to me inexplicable, and I pondered long and often on the mystery of death.

Never had I anything but love and kindness from him, and our affection for each other was mutual, our interest in science and kindred subjects binding us together mentally. For my twenty-first birthday he painted for me a large landscape picture in oils, a beautiful work of art which has a prominent place in my home. Never did he mention religion to me nor rebuke me for my beliefs. Never did he take up a pitying attitude towards me and say he was praying for me, as some did in the family. How I disliked hearing it said of me: "Poor Arthur, the only thing we can do is to pray for him."

Much pleasure was obtained in those days from the motor-car, its novelty and usefulness being recognised by everyone. Motor-buses in small numbers began to appear on the roads, and my cousin, who took me on my first journey by car as previously mentioned, worked out a scheme for the linking-up of all the towns in Scotland by bus. He could not get the financial backing, but some years later others did and his dream came true.

In the old days there were no maps and the roads were tracks for animals and humans. The horse-coach took a few passengers slowly, over bad roads, into new parts hitherto known only to their inhabitants, who had never moved away from the place of their birth all their lives. Then came the railways, which greatly enlarged the knowledge of our country, but not in an intimate way, as we were whirled past scenery, ugly and beautiful, without a chance to do more than get a glimpse of it. The coming of the motor-car changed that, as we could stop at will, have a meal at a country inn and ramble over land so far known only to the natives. Thus our country became intimately known to us, and, from the time of which I write, in those early days of motoring, much pleasure and instruction came from exploring our native land.

Ayrshire became known to me as it never would have been had we not made many journeys with our new car, a Spyker, into unknown parts. Twenty miles out and home was all we could risk at first, and the Spyker, which was claimed in the advertisement by the makers abroad to be noiseless and dustless, it being neither, seldom let us down. The absence of tar on the roads meant that we went along in a cloud of dust which covered the hedges. We wore goggles and thick coats, as cars were not then covered over to keep out the wind and cold, and women wore large veils to protect their hair. To go far from home was left to the enthusiastic driver, and in those days the attempt was being made to go from Glasgow to London in a day. I remember my astonishment when a man got out of a car at the Central Hotel in Glasgow, late one night, and I heard him say to the porter that he had left London early that morning.

In 1906 King Edward visited Paris, to cement the Entente Cordiale, after the General Election, when the Liberals obtained an overwhelming victory over the Conservatives. They attempted, without success, to curtail the competition in armaments then proceeding, forced on by Germany which was building three new warships. At the Hague Conference the following year Germany refused to discuss the limitation of armaments, and consequently the melancholy race continued which was to end in 1914 in the First World War.

Writing of King Edward reminds me of one of the most extraordinary church services I ever attended. As I have listened unwillingly to over two thousand sermons in my life, from which I have not been any the better, my critical faculty being fully aroused, I have had many opportunities to sample these outpourings. So, when I say that it was the most extraordinary service I ever attended, I really mean it. With some relations I went to church one Sunday at the little town of Kirkintilloch in Stirlingshire, to find to our amazement the pulpit and Communion table draped in black. The minister entered and announced that King Edward had died suddenly, and that he would now conduct a funeral service. Consequently mournful hymns were sung, funeral prayers were said and an appropriate sermon was preached, but it turned out that it was all a mistake. Someone in the town had received a telegram reading *King is dead* and the Postmaster had told the minister, who stupidly accepted it as relating to King Edward, without further confirmation. King was the name of a dog!

The year 1907 meant much to me, to my mother and my brother, as in that year my father died on 24th July. He became ill when sitting out on the lawn one afternoon at Woodside and went to bed. He developed acute appendicitis, and a surgeon from

Glasgow was called in. He said that an operation was the only hope, but that at the best there was slight prospect of his recovery. He never recovered from it, blood-poisoning set in, and he passed peacefully away at the age of fifty-one to the sorrow of everyone.

I remember making this remark to the surgeon before he returned to Glasgow. "I wonder," I said, "what death means. Does it mark the end of life or the beginning of another?" He replied: "The end, to be sure, there is no life after death. Your father only lives on in you and your brother." How wrong he was, because it was my good fortune eleven years later to speak to my father when he came back to me at a séance, where I was a complete stranger to everyone, including the medium. Here, he proved to me his identity by speaking in his own voice and telling me first his full name, and then something so confidential that it was known only to him, to me, and one other man. I was the only person on earth who knew about it, as this other man had also passed over. He came back with my father on this occasion, gave his full name and followed on with the conversation started by my father, everything said being correct. This remarkable fact will be told in greater detail in a later chapter.

My father was much respected by everyone. He was generous and kind, a good husband and father. His neurasthenia made it hard for him to take a part in public life, and he must have suffered much mentally from this illness then so little understood. A large company gathered to lay his body in Beith cemetery and we erected over his grave a beautiful monument.

His firm in Glasgow was called Findlay, Kidston & Goff, and his two partners immediately approached me to ask me to leave Patrick Henderson & Co. and join them. The business was one of the oldest firms of Chartered Accountants and Stockbrokers in Glasgow, my father being senior partner and in sole charge of the stockbroking side of the business, the other two being responsible for the accounting work. They told me that they were confident I could keep the stockbroking clients from leaving and giving their business elsewhere, the more so as my uncle, who was a partner in Patrick Henderson & Co., had called to see them to say that his firm, and everyone in it, would give me all the business they could. For my uncle's kindness and help to me in those days of change I have always been deeply grateful. He was one of the kindest men I have ever known.

A stockbroker must have rich friends who will employ him to transact their business on the Stock Exchange. Buying and selling the stocks and shares of his clients, on which he gets a commission, makes up the daily business life of a stockbroker. He must be prepared to advise them what to buy and what to sell, and, if his connection is a considerable one, he employs a large staff of clerks to carry through what is skilled and intricate work.

I was now asked to give up the business in which I was trained, and take over this new life. This meant that I had to start and learn a new business, and, when this was done, I would become a member of the Stock Exchange and be given a partnership and my father's place in the business. No one could be a partner unless he was a member of the Stock Exchange.

This was one of the standing Stock Exchange regulations, and, besides that, a sum of £3,000 had to be deposited with the Stock Exchange as security against default, and an entrance fee had to be paid. My father had left provision for this in his will and for the capital I had to put into the business, but the money was a loan and was to be repaid as I earned it.

This then was the proposition I was faced with, and the offer was one which I did not hesitate to accept. A certain partnership was offered me in a good business, my father's attractive private room was given over to me, and everyone was gathering round me and encouraging me. I felt that at twenty-four years of age I was extremely fortunate to have such an opportunity, and I set to work to learn the business, determined that it would grow and prosper in the years ahead. So I gave up my post in Patrick Henderson & Co.'s office, and entered the firm of Findlay, Kidston & Goff within a week of my father's funeral.

I became a member of the Glasgow Stock Exchange eight months later on 17th March, 1908, to become the 485th member admitted since its foundation in 1844, and I then became a partner in my father's firm. The first stockbroker in Glasgow began business in 1830. He was James Watson, who became Lord Provost of Glasgow and received a Knighthood. When he began business as a stockbroker the population of Glasgow was only 202,000, to rise to over a million at the time I write.

Glasgow, in his day, was a prosperous city, the successful citizens living over their shops and offices. Queen Street, now made up of shops and warehouses,

was then composed of private residences.   Salmon in
those days were caught at the steps of the Customs
House, and, in George Square, where now stand the
Municipal Buildings, there was a rookery.   Gas was
just coming into use, and when its inhabitants made a
journey into the country, or to Edinburgh, they went
by coach or by canal boat.

To-day, many thousands of transactions take place
daily on the Stock Exchanges of the leading cities of
this country, but in Watson's time they were few and
they took much longer to negotiate.   Then there were
sixteen Joint Stock companies in and around Glasgow,
comprising Water, Gas, and Canal companies, a few
short railway lines for carrying minerals, six Banks
and a few Insurance companies.   Investors in those
days mostly put their money in land, houses, or the
Funds, as Government securities are called.   There
were no debenture or preference stocks, and sometimes it took weeks or even months before a transaction was completed.   Then came the railways, in which
so many put their savings, a boom developed to end
in collapse and ruin to those who bought more than
they could pay for.

The Glasgow Stock Exchange Association was
formed in 1844 after a meeting held by the Glasgow
Accountants who had been acting as stockbrokers.
They decided to form an association of Stockbrokers,
and the first members numbered twenty-eight who
met in part of the Royal Exchange.   As business and
membership increased the Association moved to larger
and then larger premises, to end in their having their
own handsome building in 1898 where the accommodation was ample for all foreseeable future needs.

Present-day Scottish Chartered Accountants are the oldest body of incorporated accountants in the world and, as we have seen, their predecessors in Glasgow were the founders of the Glasgow Stock Exchange, the largest in the country outside of London.

After my father's death, my mother, my brother and I continued to live at Woodside, and, to take her mind off past events, we went on a cruise to the North Cape. She slowly recovered from the shock of my father's death, but for a year her nerves were in a very unsettled state. She and I shared the expenses of the upkeep of the house, the car and gardens, and, as her old vivacity returned, we took several long motor tours with Brackenridge, formerly my grandfather's coachman and now our chauffeur, as the days had not yet come when cars were free from breaking down. Moreover, to change a punctured tyre was a laborious business. On one occasion we went as far north as Inverness, and the wonderful highland scenery much impressed us. Our "grand tour", however, came later when we went down the east coast of England to London, across to Gloucester and home by the west coast, a distance of a thousand miles, a long journey by car for those days. This trip we much enjoyed, as everything was new to us. We visited places we never imagined we would ever see, and to us England was indeed a fair and pleasant land.

To-day, with easy access by car to distant places, it is difficult for the younger generation to realise the meaning to us in those days of such a journey. Places that had been just names became a reality, a panorama opened up, a vast vista of towns, villages, rivers, hills and dales. To see it all unfolding before us as we sped along was a never-to-be-forgotten experience, a memory that never grows dim.

When we returned home I set off on another journey, this time to Germany. Clients of ours were anxious to have a report on a new process for making cement out of blast furnace slag which had recently been invented in that country. So I spent a week in Germany, in company with an English cement manufacturer, and saw all there was to be seen. I made my report on my return home, and this new process was adopted and is still at work in this country, to the satisfaction of those concerned. What impressed me about Germany in those days prior to the First World War was the large number of army officers to be seen strutting about the streets, in fact there was a martial feeling about the country which was quite strange to me. At Cologne railway station the station-master paraded the platform in full military uniform, with a sword dangling at his side, and I wondered whatever a sword had to do with trains and travelling.

In those days I received many requests to deliver lectures on different subjects, and I have beside me three of these which were especially popular. One is headed *Capital, Labour, and Intelligence*, and it deals with their respective share in the production of wealth. Another is called *Some Interesting Archaeological Discoveries in Assyria*, a country which in those days was just beginning to reveal its ancient history to archaeologists. The famous Gilgamish tablets had recently been discovered, they, amongst other things, relating to the Flood, and some of my listeners were shocked to hear me say that the story of Noah, and others we read in Genesis, had come from Assyria and

Babylon, brought back by the Jews after their captivity.

Another lecture I gave is entitled *How our Social Conditions could be Improved*. Much of what I advocated has to-day come about, including the United Nations, and I concluded with these words:—

> "To do all the good you can is to be a saint in the highest and noblest sense. To do all the good you can, this is to be really and truly spiritual. To relieve suffering, and to put the star of hope in the midnight of despair, this is true holiness. This is the religion of science."

This, it must be remembered, was said at a time when religious beliefs, doctrines and dogmas took first place, and little was said from the pulpit about good deeds or conduct. To dwell on these was thought to detract from beliefs which alone ensured salvation.

Before closing this chapter I might mention an interesting visitor we had to stay with us at Woodside. He was Ernest Shackleton, who had become famous by approaching within ninety-seven miles of the South Pole in 1909. He was our guest for one night, as he came to deliver a lecture on his experiences to the Beith Literary Society. He was a charming man, and to hear of his exploits gave us a very interesting evening. He became Sir Ernest and conducted another expedition in the *Quest* during 1921–22, but never returned home as he died on the island of South Georgia in the South Atlantic.

How I fared as a stockbroker I shall tell in the next chapter, but, when the year 1912 came, someone else besides my mother came into my life. My bachelor days drew to a close and a new influence came upon me, which has accompanied me from that time to this. Instead of treading the stage of life alone I now had a companion to accompany me, and make life joyous, happy and peaceful. What really had happened was that I had fallen in love, and in the tale that the rest of this book unfolds I have a wife who is my loving companion. I am no longer alone.

CHAPTER FOUR.

WOODSIDE.

(1912–1925.)

To FALL in love, as the saying is, then to become engaged, and then to marry, is one of the most important events in one's life, and everyone who has gone through this experience has some story to tell as to how it came about. My story is simple. My brother, when an undergraduate at Cambridge, became friendly with a fellow student, and through this friendship I came to know his parents who asked me to stay with them at their lovely place in Argyllshire, where they spent several months in the year. The rest of the time they lived in Leicestershire, and it was when visiting them there at a later date that I met their niece, Gertrude Walker. She lived near, her home being called Glenn Hall, close to the village of Great Glenn.

I first met her when she came to dine in the evening. I sat next to her at dinner and we talked of her travels abroad, which had been extensive, she always having accompanied her father and mother who generally went abroad for the Winter. I found that, except for Australia, New Zealand and southern South America, Gertrude had been to most of the other countries in the world, including a voyage round the world when she was nineteen years of age. We got

WOODSIDE FROM THE GLEN.

on well together, and she asked me to come the next day for afternoon tea. This I did, to find other subjects in which we were both interested, and so it went on. I again visited her aunt and uncle, and Gertrude and I met again, to end in our becoming engaged within a month of our first meeting.

Her father, Theodore Walker, was a director of Wolsey Ltd., a charming cultured man with the mind of a university professor. He welcomed me as his future son-in-law in such a kind and cordial way that I knew I would like him. We always remained the best of friends, and I found him as good a father-in-law as a man could have. His wife, who could claim direct descent from the Welsh King Ludd, had died at sea a few years earlier coming back from South Africa, and he and Gertrude came home alone. Gertrude took her mother's place in looking after her father and their home, but my coming on the scene changed this arrangement and, following our marriage six months after our engagement, her place was taken by her sister.

My mother and brother decided to leave Woodside and live elsewhere, so that when we returned from our honeymoon we began our married life at Woodside. The Hon. Edward Carr Glyn, Bishop of Peterborough, and two other clergymen officiated at our marriage, to which came many of our friends, and this took place at Great Glenn church on 15th July 1913. My father-in-law kindly put his car and chauffeur at our disposal and the honeymoon was spent in Devonshire and Cornwall. When we returned home we received a great welcome from the people of Beith. The train entered the station to the sound of fog signals going off and we were pulled to Woodside by ropes attached to our car. We certainly never expected this great reception.

Thus it was we married and lived happily ever after. There were no more "scenes" and I could safely leave about any book I was reading. Morning and evening prayers were not continued. Moreover, I was free to remain away from church on Sunday and was relieved of listening to futile sermons without a fuss being made. Sunday ceased being a day of gloom, prayers and sermons, and sanity returned to my home life. When I think of the misery and inconvenience taboos have cost mankind down the ages, I am amazed at the human folly and ignorance which brought them into being.

At one time or another, at some place or another, throughout the world since the time of primitive man taboos have largely entered into his life, for some reason or other. Almost everything he would have done normally was forbidden by his religion, somewhere or sometime, as contrary to the will of God or the gods, but the taboos on the way he lived on Sunday were certainly one of the most widespread and the most obnoxious of them all. When we get down to the origin of Sunday observance, how foolish it must seem to all intelligent people.

It all started for those who were later to live in the west, when Nebuchadnezzar invaded Judaea and conquered the Jews in 586 B.C., taking many of them back with him to Babylon, where they were civilised and ceased being barbarians. There the last day of the week was known as the Sabatu, which was a holy day, given over to the worship of the saviour god

Bel, or, as the Jews called him, Baal. He was the Babylonian redeemer who died for their sins many centuries before Christ. His passion drama was copied at the beginning of the Christian era and draped round Jesus. The story of Bel's trial, death, burial and resurrection, which has been discovered in Babylonia engraved on stone, was doubtless the basis of the Christian passion drama, and its translation is given in full in a later chapter of this book.

A Babylonian king, Hamurabi by name, who lived between 1792 and 1750 B.C., decreed that the Sabatu was to be a holy day on which no work was to be done because on that day the creator finished his work of making the earth and heavens after his six days of effort. The Jews brought back to Palestine this taboo when they were released from their captivity, and incorporated it into their new *Book of the Law*, then being written by Esdras, as is told in the *Book of Esdras*.

When the Christians took over the Jewish scriptures it became part of Christian belief. This came about in the 6th century when the Hebrew *Book of the Law* was joined on to the Gospels and Epistles to form one book, *The Holy Bible*. The Christians, however, changed the day from Saturday to Sunday and called Sunday "the Lord's Day", because of the overwhelming desire of the Pagans, who became Christians, to continue Sunday as their holy day, they having been brought up to believe that their former saviour, Mithra, had risen from his rock tomb on that day. Consequently it came to be believed that their new saviour Christ had likewise risen on the Sunday. As the Mithraists called Sunday "the Lord's Day", so the Christian Sunday came to be called by this name.

All the taboos attached by the Hebrews to Saturday, the last day of the week, came to be attached to Sunday, though there is not a word in the Bible anywhere that Sunday was to be observed as a holy day, with the taboos attached to Saturday. According to the Bible, all the taboos Christians have observed on Sunday should have been carried out on Saturday, and it shews how little serious thought was given to the subject that the discrepancy of the day was passed by. Sunday, the Mithraic holy day, became the Christian holy day, and the Babylonian taboos about Saturday, which came through the Jews, were attached to Sunday. Consequently I, and millions of others down through the Christian era, have had to suffer because of the prevailing fear of offending the Christian God by not keeping the decree of an ancient Babylonian king relating to the worship of his god Bel. Such is the curse of ignorance.

Another curse due to ignorance is intolerance. It is well known that Christians, if belonging to a dissenting sect, will not be given Communion in an Anglican church, but it can work the other way about. My wife, an Anglican, attended Communion at Beith Parish Church, and its Presbyterian minister afterwards asked her not to do so in future. She asked him for the reason and he told her that once, when he attended an Anglican prayer meeting, the vicar asked him to deliver the closing prayer, which he agreed to do. Later the vicar returned to him and said: "I presume you are an Anglican clergyman?" "No," he replied, "I am a Presbyterian." "Oh," answered the vicar, "I have made a mistake so I withdraw my request." From this, and many other experiences I have had, I have formed the opinion that so long as creeds, sects and divisions remain, to talk about Christian charity and brotherly love is rather a hollow mockery.   However, the fact remains that our Beith Parish minister refused my wife Communion all the time he was at Beith.

All of us have two sides to our lives, our life of ease, and our working-day life.   The former comprises for most men an interest in their homes, their children, relations and neighbours.   Besides our interests surrounding our home life we are uplifted by beautiful music, we think about sport, politics and religion, the story we are reading, what we hear on the radio or see on the television, all of which fall outside our daily work.   For most of us our working life, on the other hand, is made up of our efforts to earn sufficient money to sustain and keep ourselves and our dependants in health and comfort.   Housewives spend much of their working day looking after the house, their children, cooking and cleaning, their relaxation coming when this work is done.   The man and woman who live a full life direct their thoughts to many things throughout the day, from keeping the wolf from the door, to their relaxations of many and different kinds.   I am giving in this book these two sides to my life.

So this my life which you are now reading has had numerous sides to it, as it comprises many and varied subjects, one following the other, as I look back and remember the incidents as they occurred to me in the years gone by.   Events that took place in my business and my home, besides my thoughts and ideas, all come back to me and I have to sort them out as they occurred. The story of my marriage, and my new home life, broke into the tale I was telling, at the close of the last chapter, of my new business life, but I shall now return to it and tell how I fared in my career as a stockbroker.

I was determined I would succeed in my new way of life, and I commenced a study of economics and finance in the evenings after my work at the office had come to an end. There, in the office, I was learning all the many and intricate ways a transaction went through, from the time a client gave instructions to buy or sell until it was settled, and he either paid us for a purchase or we paid him for a sale. I had to know all this, but once I learned how it was all done the methods of doing it were routine, and were left to the manager of each department. I was training myself for much more difficult and responsible work, and this meant great study and exhaustive reading.

A good stockbroker must be well informed. Above all he must have good judgment. He must know about all the important events that are taking place both at home and abroad, and weigh up news which might affect the course of prices on the Stock Exchange. He requires to know whether money is likely to become what is called cheap or dear, and what section of the market may become lively or dull. Besides an all-round view of politics and finance, he must have a knowledge of the leading companies in which his clients are, or are likely to be, interested.

He must know their strength, their weakness and their prospects. Briefly, he is expected to give advice to his clients as to what to buy and what to sell, and, if his advice is good, one client will tell others of his wisdom, and his business will grow. If his advice is bad his clients will go elsewhere, and his business will decline. There is no other business in which good judgment pays quicker and better dividends.

Buying and selling takes place by buyers and sellers meeting on the floor of the "house". If they agree on the price a deal takes place, and this transaction ends some weeks later when a transfer deed is signed by both buyer and seller. The actual buying and selling of stocks and shares presents nothing mysterious, what is hidden in the future is whether the buyer or seller has done the right thing, whether the buyer buys, or the seller sells, something that afterwards rises or falls in price. That brings me to the crux of the business transacted on the Stock Exchange, because that market has two distinct aspects.

It can be looked on as a place for speculation or, on the other hand, as a medium for the investment of savings. The speculator thinks a share is cheap and buys it to hold it for a short time, and, if it rises, he takes a profit. If it falls he cuts his loss. That method of trying to make money quickly is speculation and can be classed as gambling, but it has its use because it helps to ensure a free market, which means that shares can be freely dealt in.

The investment of savings is something far different, and a much more certain way to obtain capital appreciation. The investor should think of the real worth of what he buys. If he wants absolute safety he buys government stock, or a debenture, or preference shares, but, if he looks ahead, and thinks that a company will increase its dividends in the years to come, he backs his judgment and buys the ordinary shares of that company. That is the only possible way of safely increasing one's capital.

Decide on the company with prospects, get to know all about it, its history and the variation in the price of its shares over past years. If the shares are relatively cheap, and the prospects of the company are good in the years to come, buy them, and be prepared to wait years if necessary for its prospects to come to fruition. If the purchaser's judgment is right he will find that in time the value of the shares has increased since he bought them. In other words, it is wise to take a long view, as the speculator, who takes a short view, generally suffers in the end.

These, and many others, were the problems with which I was faced, but life on the Stock Exchange is not a smooth or placid one, because there comes, from time to time, booms, when fortunes are quickly made, and slumps when they are just as quickly lost. These are the events which remain in a stockbroker's memory. Several outstanding slumps and booms come to mind when thinking back, times of fear and panic, and times of confidence and rejoicing, when the moneyed class lost millions in a few days or millions were made in as short a time.

The first Stock Exchange boom was from 1844 to 1847, to be known as the Railway Boom, when new railways sprang up like mushrooms all over the country. In 1844 the public subscribed eighteen millions for the building of new railways, in 1845 the sum subscribed was sixty millions, in 1846 it was one hundred and twenty millions, and in 1847 three hundred and forty millions. This development was accompanied by much speculation on borrowed money. Then it came to be realised that some of this enormous sum would be years before it became remunerative, and, when the Bank of England refused to make any further advances on government securities, the reaction came. Prices first crumbled, then tumbled and finally crashed. Panic followed and several banks failed. The losses that were experienced were enormous, and confidence only returned slowly after the government consented to the Bank of England renewing advances on approved securities.

Twenty years later came another boom and crash. This followed the Companies Act of 1862, which limited the liability of shares to the amount paid up. Hitherto the liability of shareholders was unlimited. This new measure increased the confidence of the investing public to such an extent that between 1862 and 1865, 2,500 Joint Stock companies were formed with a capital of five hundred and sixty-seven millions. Money consequently became dear or scarce, reaction followed, to turn into panic which brought about the failure of banks and finance houses. I well remember hearing about the failure of the City of Glasgow Bank which took place in 1878. In this case the cause was the disgraceful way the Bank was managed.

Then came the Baring crisis of 1890, due to a revolution in the Argentine after many millions had been subscribed for new ventures in that country. A heavy fall in their values followed, to end in Baring Brothers, who were heavily involved, being unable to meet their liabilities. My grandfather, who had large interests in the Argentine, lost heavily. He, and others, had financed the La Platense Flotilla Company, a venture which ran vessels up and down the River Plate, but, with trade at a standstill, the company had to wind up. Fortunately, the loss did not alter his way of living, and things at Kilmeny went on as before, but there was one effect it had. His hair changed from black to white after a long visit to Buenos Aires to try and find some way to carry on until the country returned to normal.

The discovery in 1895 of the Witwatersrand Goldfields in the Transvaal led to the Kaffir boom. Speculation became rampant, to end in a slump and heavy losses following the Jameson Raid into the Transvaal. Within two years of this memorable event South African mining shares had fallen to a fifth of their pre-Raid value.

The foregoing tells of the principal booms and slumps the Stock Exchange experienced prior to the Boer War, which caused, during its early stages, much disquiet and lack of confidence. How well I remember the confidence with which Britain entered the war, and the blank despair which came over everyone when the early disasters were announced. Only when Lord Roberts and Lord Kitchener took over command did confidence gradually return, to become hilarious rejoicing when peace was signed in Vereeniging in 1902. Then came the First World War, but I have other things to tell before that terrible event befell us.

A year after I became a partner in my father's business, my partner, David Kidston, died and the business was now shared between me and my other partner, William Henry Goff, with whom I got on extremely well. He was very keen on hunting, being Master of the Lanarkshire and Renfrewshire Fox-hounds, and this meant absence from business two days a week during the Winter. Kidston was a very able chartered accountant and we both greatly felt his loss, but for some years he had been in failing health and his time in the office had become less and less. His great achievements were at the end of last century, the first being the amalgamation of all the cotton-thread manufacturers which now make up the well-known firm of J. & P. Coats. His second was the amalgamation of the linen-thread manufacturers, to become what is now the Linen Thread Company. Many other amalgamations have taken place since then by other accountants, but these two were amongst the first to be carried through, and the immense amount of new work involved taxed Kidston's great capacity to the utmost. Shortly after his death we assumed a new partner to take his place.

By this time I had obtained a grip of the business, and felt sufficiently assured of my capacity to guide my clients in making their investments that I started something new. Under the rules of the Stock Exchange members cannot approach for business purposes other than their own clients. That limits their business connection, but it occurred to me that if I wrote at the end of each month a review of what had happened during the past month, and anticipated what was going to happen in the future, it would interest our clients. Moreover, if my forecasts turned out right, our clients would speak about the review to others, or give it to them to read, and they would come of their own accord to see me.

So each month I sent out a printed review of four large pages giving names and prices of safe stocks in which to invest, besides a long article on the past month's events and the prospects ahead. This was posted to each client, many of whom, as I anticipated, handed it on to friends. I was the first Glasgow stockbroker to start this innovation, and the results were far beyond my expectations. The business steadily increased and soon I was in receipt of a large income. For fourteen years I wrote this financial article each month, after which I retired from active business.

In those days, with taxation light and not as it is to-day, one could save money, and I was soon able to pay back to my father's trust the money it had advanced to me to enable me to put capital into the business and join the Stock Exchange. Moreover, after that was done, I was able to save something substantial to invest. Then it was that the motor-car was just in its infancy, the airplane had been invented, and shipowners were thinking of using oil fuel in place of coal for their steamships. So I took the long view, that to invest in the shares of petroleum producing and refining companies would some day bring a rich reward, and this I did when a very favourable opportunity came my way.

This happened when friends of mine in London asked me if I would agree to my firm becoming the Glasgow stockbrokers to a large oil company, which was requiring more money to complete its drilling, pipe-line and refinery in Mexico. It was called the Mexican Eagle Oil Company, at the head of which was the first Viscount Cowdray, an exceptionally able business man. Before I accepted I interviewed him and others directing its affairs, men who held the highest position in the business life of this country. Being satisfied that the prospects were excellent, and, after discussing the matter with my partner, Goff, I agreed to our firm being the company's Scottish stockbrokers. This meant that we would receive all the information we desired about the company in the years to come. No oil had yet been found in any quantity, but large quantities were hoped for, and the geologists were most optimistic, so much so that a refinery and pipe-line were in course of erection in anticipation of the great day when the drills would reach the oil level.

Then came the day when large supplies of oil were discovered, and the wells were "capped", as it is called, until the pipe-line was ready, but I was to experience much worry before my ship, so to speak, came home. First of all came the Mexican revolution in 1911 when President Diaz, who was our friend and supporter, was displaced, and President Madero, whose attitude was uncertain, took his place. Imagine my anxiety, with much of my own and my clients' money now invested in the company, to hear one day that the rebels were fighting in the oilfield, and no one knew what damage they would do. Then came the first Balkan war in 1912, and the next year another revolution broke out in Mexico, when a new president took over. So far, no damage had been done to the company's property, and fortunately none was done, but these three years were the most worrying in my entire business career.

To discover oil is the first step to success, the next is to find the way to move it, first to the refinery, and then to the consumers overseas. Consequently, money was now wanted to build a great tanker fleet to move this oil to distant parts after it was refined, and this I helped to find, but, from now onwards, apart from the threatened war with Germany, I had no fear of the future, though the coming of the First Great War somewhat delayed developments. However, I was prepared to wait for years if necessary, as I was certain of great success some day if Germany did not defeat us, and here I break off the story of my business life to say something of my life at home.

My wife was delighted with Woodside, and extremely happy in her new home. Being very sociable, she soon made many friends. Her aunt and uncle, at whose home I met her in Leicestershire, were then staying at their Argyllshire home, as was their custom in Summer, and we received an invitation to visit them, which we did. Scotnish is the name of their house, and it is in the wilds of the Highlands, the nearest railway station being thirty miles away. In those days, before a good road was made, the best means of access was by pleasure-steamer, which sailed from Greenock in the morning for Ardrishaig and Inverary on Loch Fyne, to return in the evening. From Ardrishaig a horse-coach took passengers to the little hamlet of Tayvallich, near which is Scotnish.

On a fine calm day this journey, which takes six hours, is one of the most delightful in Scotland. From Greenock the first call is Rothesay in Bute on the west side of the Firth of Clyde, thence, by way of the Kyles of Bute, up Loch Fyne to Ardrishaig. No one who has ever sailed through the Kyles can forget that delightful part of Scotland, not only because of the grandeur of the scenery but because of its majestic beauty.

As the steamer sails on through the Kyles they gradually narrow until the passenger wonders if the ship will have enough water to keep it afloat. Then opens up a small deep channel through which it passes, but one can throw a stone on to either bank. Slowly the banks recede, until we find ourselves in another great stretch of water from which towering hills rise from each shore. Their grandeur is heightened by their colouring, the vividness of the scenery being enhanced by the sheen and radiance given off by the landscape everywhere, when the sun shines in that part of the world.

After calling at the little village of Tighnabruaich, where all is bustle at the pier, the steamer sails into Loch Fyne, famous for its good herrings. At the head of the loch is Inverary and its castle, the seat of the chiefs of the ancient Campbell clan, the chief being known to-day as the Duke of Argyll. When we reached Ardrishaig few cars, but many horse-drawn vehicles, were waiting to take passengers along good but narrow roads to the many hamlets for which Ardrishaig is the centre. For half of this journey we kept alongside the Crinan canal, which is cut through a broad valley from Ardrishaig to the little hamlet of Crinan. This terminus is situated on the Atlantic, and the canal is used for quick communication with the western Highlands and islands. It contains several locks, and a small steamer chugged along once a day with sightseers on board.

We, however, turned south before reaching Crinan and, over a winding hilly road cut through the hills, we arrived at the head of Loch Sween, a sea loch stretching twenty miles inland from the Sound of Jura. This is a gem of a loch, its clear crystal water reflecting its rocky shore and the golden lichen which abounded. It is called after Sweyn, King of Denmark, who conquered those parts in the 11th century. He was a bad and cruel man, the father of the good English King Canute. The ruins of Sweyn's castle remain bordering the loch, and scattered about are the remains of early dwellings and damaged Iona crosses.

Scotnish, the house which was our destination, is situated on high ground above Loch Scotnish, an off-shoot of Loch Sween, a site chosen by my wife's uncle to build his delightful home. The view from its windows embraced Loch Scotnish and Loch Sween, the first opening out of the other, and on either side were hills covered with firs, larch, and spruce. We passed few houses on this pleasant journey, and the hamlet of Tayvallich, a mile from Scotnish, contained only about a hundred people beside three churches, representing the three sects into which the Presbyterian faith was then divided. One minister resided near his church, but on Sunday the other two came some distance by rowing-boat. At each church the people stood for prayer, and sat when singing; such

an unholy thing as an organ was absent, and a conductor led the praise with the help of a tuning-fork,
all this taking place in Gaelic, except in one church
which had a morning service in English.

This out-of-the-world place had as its attraction
only its natural beauty.   The nearest town for shopping
was Oban, thirty-seven miles away, and twelve miles
separated Tayvallich from Ardrishaig where the boat
from Greenock called each day.   Nevertheless, Scotnish was delightful for its rural grandeur and, as we
approached, we saw only a motor-launch riding at
anchor on the loch.   Otherwise there was nothing to
indicate the works of man, nature in its solemn
majesty ruling over all.

When we reached the house we were welcomed by
relatives and friends.   Amongst the loneliness of the
hills and vales, here was gaiety and the days passed
pleasantly exploring by launch the various inlets and
bays which abounded.   One favourite expedition was
lunch or tea on the aptly called Fairy Isles and in this
way time passed quickly, but at the back of the minds
of everyone was the danger of Germany, which Lord
Roberts was publicly asserting was becoming ever
more menacing.

The year 1914 which followed was an uneasy one
for stockbrokers, as prices were steadily crumbling
and it was difficult to foresee the future.   To make
matters worse, Ireland was on the verge of civil war.
A change for the better, some thought, might come
in Europe, and, if it did, this was a time to buy, as

all stocks and shares were at low prices. On the other hand a European war seemed to most of us to mean ruin for everyone, in fact a large and important industrial concern announced publicly that if war came it would be unable to pay a dividend to its share-Holders. Unfortunately, a change for the better did not come; in fact, the news on the 28th June that the Archduke Francis Ferdinand, the heir to the Austrian throne, and his wife had been assassinated at Serajevo in Serbia brought matters to a crisis.

Then followed a series of events which culminated in the outbreak of the First World War. Austria sent an ultimatum to Serbia. Russia and France resented its provocative tone. Russia then declared she would not allow the invasion of Serbia by Austria. Exactly a month after the assassination Austria declared war on Serbia, and Russia called up her reserves. Germany resented Russia's action and the next day declared war on Russia. France now mobilised, and Germany invaded Luxembourg. The next day Britain warned Germany not to enter Belgium, but this had no effect and Belgium was invaded. Britain at once declared war on Germany. That was on the 4th August 1914 and, by the 12th August, open war was taking place, Russia, Serbia, France, Belgium and Britain being lined up against Germany and Austria. A fortnight later Germany and Japan were at war.

In anticipation of this calamity, between July 24th and 31st the Stock Exchanges of Paris, Brussels, St. Petersburg, Montreal, New York, London, Glasgow and elsewhere closed down, and, as there was nothing to keep me at the office, my wife and I set out by car to visit her father at Glenn Hall in Leicestershire, her old home. There we found preparations being made for a large flower show to be held in the grounds on the following Monday, which was August Bank Holiday. The day after the holiday, the 4th of August, we were at war with Germany.

The flower show was a success, and the extensive park in front of Glenn Hall was filled with people from far and near, the various side-shows beside the beautiful lake, which is such a feature of the place, giving much enjoyment to the holiday-makers. If they were aware of the gravity of the situation these pleasure-seekers showed no sign of their anxiety, and I remarked to someone, when I saw that joyous crowd, that soon they would have a severe shock. Strange as it may seem, few people had yet grasped the seriousness of the situation. Few believed a European war was possible, and some of our economists had declared that modern financial conditions would be enough to prevent war in our time. The world's delicate economic structure was thought to be such that war would bring ruin to both aggressor and victim. A book, *The Great Illusion* by Norman Angell, which dwelt on this theme, was then very popular and gave comfort to many apprehensive of the future. So the majority put this hideous nightmare at the back of their minds, and only realised the calamity when it came.

Little did we appreciate that we were at the portal of a new epoch. We were on the threshold of a new world when most things, looked upon as stable, would change for the better or for the worse. Women, because of their war work, were enfranchised, and about this time they began to paint their lips and finger-nails.

New methods, new ideas, and a new outlook were to come in the social conditions of Western Europe, in its healing of disease, in its industry, and in its financial structure. Drastic political changes and upheavals were before us, the conduct of war was about to change, and war, or the fear of conflict, was to be with us for the next forty years. Millions were to die unnatural and premature deaths, and tragedy, suffering and misery were to be the lot of many of the world's inhabitants. What a terrific event it was, as far-reaching in many ways as was the fall of the Roman Empire.

My wife and I set off for home next morning, and such a journey it was. I was warned that petrol might be scarce, so we took with us additional tins of petrol, which was a fortunate precaution as the few filling-stations of those days were very reluctant to part with their supplies. We passed Territorials on the march, or singly on the way to join their units, and at East Retford the hotel, where we stopped for lunch, was packed with officers. War was everywhere in the air, but it was not until we stopped for the night that we heard that Britain had declared war on Germany, as from 11 p.m. that night. So when we woke up next morning we knew that our country was at war, and with this thought in our minds we set out for the last lap of our journey home.

Here I must tell rather a tragic story of what happened on our journey. I was driving, and, on one side of the road, for about a hundred yards, was some high thick grass. Imagine my surprise when out of this grass rushed madly a young pig right in front of the car. I could not help hitting it, and then came another, then another, and lastly a fourth pig, one after the other a yard or so apart, and each one was hit before I was able to stop. The wonder is that I did not run over them. The car kept on the road and was not damaged, but fortunately I was not going fast. I got out and went back to find all four pigs dead. It was sudden death for them, but it might have been sudden death for us, and why we escaped unscathed I cannot tell. I saw a small farm nearby and went to the door to report what had happened.

The owner of the pigs appeared and was very angry, demanding that I pay for them and take them away. "I don't want them," I said, "and in any case I have no room for four pigs on my back seat. They are quite fit for market, and you can get the full price for them. You had no right to have them on a public road. We might have been killed, or the car seriously damaged." I gave him my name, and when I received a letter from him I passed it on to my lawyer, who wrote and told him he had no case, but that I had one against him for allowing his pigs to stray on the public highway to the danger of motorists. His lawyer evidently told him the same, as I heard nothing further from him, and doubtless he got a good price for them from his butcher, who was saved the trouble of killing them.

Without further incident we arrived home, and when I reached the office the next morning, all financial worries for the time being were set at rest by the moratorium which Parliament had just declared. Precautions were taken by the Treasury against forced realisation of securities and, but for this wise action, there would have been widespread bankruptcy and panic. Prices were fixed, under which no one could sell, and, as there were few buyers, there was little business. Members and clerks met for an hour or so on the pavement outside the Stock Exchange and discussed the news, which was bad, the German army meeting with little effective resistance on its way through Belgium.

The month of August was passed in an aimless fashion, the German march through Belgium and into France continuing, but when September came hope revived. The German advance in France was halted, and on the eventful 7th of September the British and French counter-attack was successful, the invaders having to retire some distance. From now until the end of October the Germans tried unsuccessfully to get round their opponents until they reached the sea, to be stopped each time, until eventually they were held all the way from the Channel to the south. Then static trench war began, interspersed by battles forced by both sides in an endeavour to break the line, and this continued to the end when the German defence was finally broken.

On January 4th 1915 the Stock Exchange reopened after being closed for five months, and from this time onwards it contributed to the raising of the necessary money for the conduct of the war. My staff at the office was by now greatly depleted, as a steady demand for young men for the forces made itself felt. Their places were taken by girls who had to be trained in the work, and moreover my partner Goff was a major in the Territorials, though fortunately his duties were in Glasgow. The weight of the business consequently rested on me, and for that reason my call-up was postponed, but my brother, who was in the office, became an officer in the Gunners. He was the Honorary Secretary of the Ayrshire Branch of the British Red Cross Society, and when he left I was asked by the County President to take over this work.

The County President, the Countess of Eglinton, was an able woman and nice to work with, so we got on well together. My brother had left everything in good order, so before long I had a grasp of the work, the detail of which was attended to by one of my secretaries. With my own office work and a limited staff, some untrained, I now had more work to do in the day than I could manage. Consequently much of the Red Cross work was done at home in the evening, but, so long as quiet conditions continued on the Stock Exchange, life was strenuous, but tolerable.

As the war continued and it became evident that it would last for a long time, and, as the casualties increased, the work of the Red Cross grew, the organisation being greatly enlarged. Large houses were taken over and organised as hospitals, and, when the war ended, there were nine in Ayrshire with 539 beds, some eight thousand patients passing through them. Work-parties were organised in each village for the making of comforts for the troops, making surgical dressings, and the gathering of sphagnum moss, which is found growing in bogs and peat and is normally used for packing. When cleaned and placed in bags it becomes a first-class surgical dressing.

Ayrshire had 180 men and 887 women members in the Voluntary Aid Detachments. Most of the men were called up, but the women attended daily to the wants and comforts of our soldiers in the hospitals in the county, and some went to hospitals elsewhere. These workers, who were unpaid in those days, were under the direction of the County Director. The local secretaries, hospital secretaries and local treasurers moreover relieved me of much detail work.

Besides being the Honorary Secretary of this great organisation I was also Honorary Treasurer, with sixty-two local treasurers throughout the county. From the outbreak of the war to its conclusion Ayrshire headed all the other counties in Scotland for the amount raised for the Red Cross during the war, and in the Summer of 1918 the Ayrshire Red Cross Week alone raised £100,000 by local subscriptions, by fêtes, entertainments, and other appeals, a sum worth much more then than it is now.

Before this took place I wrote a brochure of sixty-four pages entitled *Ayrshire and the Red Cross*, giving an account of the work done by the county since the war began, each district receiving a full account of all its activities. This book, of which ten thousand copies were sold, contained 134 photographs of the leading workers in the county, the working-parties, hospitals, staffs and wards, etc. I attribute to it the wonderful success of the 1918 Red Cross Week Appeal, as it must have been read or seen by nearly everyone in the county.

The Ayrshire Branch was well organised. The county was divided into twenty-two districts over each of which was a capable and active Vice-President. My wife was Vice-President for the Beith district and each lady, besides being responsible for the activities of her district, was on the County Committee which

met at Ayr, twenty-four miles from Woodside, each
month, under the chairmanship of the President.
This meeting took place in a room in the County
Buildings, one of the handsomest in the kingdom, and
Ayr, the county town, it will be remembered, is
famous for its association with Robert Burns, who
wrote of it:—

> "Auld Ayr, whom ne'er a town surpasses
> For honest men and bonny lasses."

I was present at every meeting, and recorded and
carried out the decisions of the committee. It was
always a very friendly affair and no wrangling ever
took place.

In this way my wife and I came to know many
new friends, and, besides this, places in south Ayrshire, now that motor-cars were freely used, became
known to us as they would never otherwise have been.
The coast of Ayrshire extends for seventy miles and
makes up the eastern coast of the Firth of Clyde. We
lived in the northern part of the county, and I have
already given a description of its beauty, but south
Ayrshire is just as delightful. Its coast is grand and
rugged, interspersed with bays and promontories.
Looking from north to south the beautiful moun-
tainous island of Arran, and the sugar-loaf rock of
Ailsa Craig, are to be seen across the sea and on a
clear day the coast of Ulster.

In the old days the south Ayrshire coast was
famous for its notorious characters, it was a lawless
place and smuggling was rife between it and Ireland.
Then the Kennedy family owned much of the land,

and their wild escapades gave them the name of "the wild Kennedys of Culzean", the ruins of their old castle still being in good preservation. There are numerous interesting and amusing stories told about different characters in this part of the world, one of the best being about the adventures of a south Ayrshire boy when only sailing-ships were to be seen at sea. This lad, Jock Thomson, was brought up in the village of Tarbolton, six miles from Ayr. He disappeared and was never heard of until—but here is the tale and I believe it has a true background.

The little seaport of Saltcoats on the Ayrshire coast produced many a sea-faring man, and one of these was the master of a sailing-ship which one day, many years ago, sailed into Vera Cruz Bay in Mexico. There he saw spread before him in all its glory the ships of the Spanish Navy. Much to his surprise he was invited to dine with the Spanish admiral, which he did, surrounded by all his chief officers. He returned to his ship wondering greatly why he had been so honoured, to be even more amazed to receive another invitation to dine with the admiral the next evening. He went, and this time they dined alone.

Imagine his surprise when the admiral asked him questions about Ayrshire, and showed an intimate knowledge of the people and places in the county. At last the Saltcoats captain could contain his curiosity no longer and blurted out: "How do you, a Spaniard, know so much about Ayrshire?" "Why, man," the admiral replied, in broad Scotch, "do ye no ken I am Jock Thomson frae Tarbolton? I am the wee laddie that disappeared and could never be found."

Explanations followed, and the Saltcoats captain was informed that the "wee laddie" had got on board a vessel sailing for Spain, where he joined the Spanish navy and worked himself up to the top as so many Scottish youths have done since then.

On 12th August 1916 Joan Margaret was born, a small baby with lovely brown eyes. She has brought much happiness into our lives, and, when she was six, a friend's little daughter, Jean Campbell of Arduaine in Argyllshire, came to live with us and share the governess, returning home for the holidays. They were both a great joy to us, and Jean was with us for eight years. We still look upon her almost as a daughter.

The Revolution in Russia in 1917, and her withdrawal from the war, meant that we had no ally in the east, and Germany was able to move much of her army fighting Russia to the west. A month later the United States declared war on Germany, but it took time before she was able to do much to help the hardpressed Allies. Heavy casualties continued on both sides, and men everywhere were combed out of their civilian work and forced into the army. German airplanes and airships (Zeppelins) started to attack this country and I was in London during two air raids. Every time I pass a certain place near Liverpool Street station I think of the ghastly sight I witnessed there after an air raid, and I saw a great German airship come down at Potters Bar one night in flames when attempting to raid London.

I was in an hotel in London and my bedroom window faced north. An air raid was expected, and I was looking out when a fierce blaze lit up the sky, to descend slowly until it reached the ground. Germany's pride of the sky, which it was hoped by our enemy would frighten us into a panic and bring the war to an end, thus met a timely end and, strangely enough, the British pilot who brought it down was the son of Sir Alfred Ball, from whom I bought Stansted Hall where I now live. The next day I went to Potters Bar where it fell, and brought away pieces of this great airship. For their size, they were very light in weight.

In 1917 I received a "call-up" which meant that my previous one, which was postponed because of my other duties, was no longer valid. So I was directed to Ayr to undergo my medical examination. There, the doctor, whom I had never previously met, addressed me thus, to my great astonishment: "Mr. Findlay, whatever brings you here?" "To be examined as to my fitness for the army," I replied. "You must not go into the army, you cannot be spared from your Red Cross work," he answered. "That is not for me to say," I replied. "Well, we shall see; just undress," he said. "No," he went on, "you are not fit for the army, you have varicose veins. Put on your clothes again, you must stay on here at home. Your work is too important, you are too valuable a man to be spared for the army." Consequently from that day onwards I never heard another word about my call-up, and my varicose veins have never given me the least trouble, though they might well have done on long marches. I was much relieved that no call-up came for me, because on me much of my business rested. If I had gone, there might have been no office for my clerks, now in the army, to come back to, and doubtless the recruiting authorities had this and my Red Cross work in mind when they decided not to enlist me in the army.

The following year my wife became seriously ill and had to be removed to a nursing home in Glasgow, where she had an operation, from which she recovered and was fortunately none the worse. To be near to her I stayed in Glasgow, and, when sitting with her one Sunday evening, I remarked that I would like some fresh air and would go out for a stroll. Little did I think what that walk would mean to me, but it was the beginning of an entire change in my mental outlook on life and death.

I sauntered down one street and up another rather aimlessly, to pass a church with the name "Spiritualist Church" prominently displayed in the foreground. I stopped to see what it looked like, as I did not remember having seen it before, and I was unaware that such a denomination existed. What little I knew of Spiritualism was contained in a book my wife had recently been given and which to me, by a casual glance, seemed too fantastic for serious thought. I threw it aside as not worth reading, and now that Sunday evening I was facing the entrance to a Spiritualist church. Why not enter and see what it is like inside? I thought, and this I did.

A service was going on and the speaker was telling the congregation of some wonderful things he had experienced. I sat down and listened, and when the service was over I went up to him and this is what I said: "Do you really expect me to believe what you said to-night? It may have gone down with some simple-minded people who listened to you, but do you expect a rational thinker to accept as true what you said? Can you prove it to me?"

I have from time to time challenged a parson with questions, and have received as a reply: "No, I can prove nothing, but that is where faith comes in. You must believe and not doubt." The Spiritualist, whom I now challenged, said exactly the opposite, to the effect that I could not be expected to believe without proof. "Proof is essential," he continued, "and what Spiritualists believe has come from experience. All claims made by Spiritualists can be proved, and if you want to have proof you can get it." "How?" I enquired. "By going to a medium," he answered. "Can you take me to one?" I asked. "Yes, to-morrow night, if that is convenient to you," he replied.

That reply appealed to me, and I accepted his offer. So it was arranged that the following night I would meet him at seven o'clock at the corner of North Frederick Street and George Street, and he would take me to a séance which was held every Monday evening in a house nearby. When I returned and told my wife where I was about to go, she wondered if it were a wise thing to do. To go with a strange man to a strange house seemed to her taking an unjustifiable risk, but she raised no objection and I kept the appointment next day as arranged.

Consequently on the following day, Monday, 20th September 1918, we met at the place arranged and walked along a quiet street to a house, the entrance to which was by a passage. He told me we were going to the house of John Sloan, who was a medium. We entered the passage, and my unknown guide knocked at the door on the right-hand side. It was opened, and we were ushered into a small room in which were ten people, all sitting on chairs in a circle. The light was on and talking was general. A man was playing a hymn on a harmonium. We were both given seats in the circle and no introductions were made. All that was said by my guide was a remark to the man at the harmonium that he had brought someone with him. That was all. My guide did not know my name, I did not know his, and the rest of the people were all complete strangers to me. I put them down as belonging to what is called the working class, nice, kindly, decent people who gave me a very friendly welcome.

The man at the harmonium then said it was time to start, and he switched off the light. A hymn was played and sung and then another, but before it ended the organist turned round and took his place in the circle. Shortly after this a man's loud voice spoke right in front of my right-hand neighbour. I heard everything said and the name it gave, the conversation being an intimate one between my female neighbour and this voice. She had evidently spoken to the voice before, and took it all quietly and naturally. The voice seemed to know everything of importance she had done since the last conversation, and ended with love and the promise to be back again at the next séance.

When the voice had finished speaking, she calmly

announced to everyone that she had been speaking to her husband, whom I took to be dead. This went on for three hours, dozens of voices speaking to different people, men's voices, women's voices, children's voices, all of which I was told came from people called dead. A woman's voice spoke to a man sitting on my left. It gave a name and referred to happenings at his home. It specially referred to Tom, who was giving his father trouble, and then came advice as to how he should be dealt with. Intimate family matters were discussed between my neighbour and this female voice, and finally with love it said "Good-bye". "That was my wife," he whispered to me. "I never come here but she comes back to me. She always knows everything that goes on at home."

I was now beginning to feel that I was the only one to be omitted from this strange medley of conversation which seemed to go on and on without stopping. Everything said was claimed to be correct, and I wondered how it was possible for any human being to be so intimate with all the dead friends, and the private doings of the sitters, as to be able to impersonate their deceased relations in the way that was taking place. Not only did the imagined impersonator know intimately about their dead friends and relations but every voice was different, the mannerisms were different, in fact each voice had a different personality. What a wonderful actor there must be amongst us to be able to carry on like that for hours on end, and to remember in the dark where everyone was sitting, as the right person was directly addressed every time with never a mistake.

Such were my thoughts, when suddenly right in

front of my face a strong voice spoke to me. "Yes, who are you?" I enquired, to receive the answer:

"Your father, Robert Downie Findlay."

The voice continued speaking, and referred to something that only my father and I, and one other man, ever knew about on earth, and that other man, like my father, was dead. I was therefore the only living person on earth with any knowledge of what the voice was talking about. It was a private matter that neither I, nor my father, nor the other man when on earth, ever spoke about to any other person. All this was extraordinary enough, but imagine my surprise when my father concluded by saying:

"David Kidston is standing beside me and would also like to talk to you about this matter."

Now David Kidston was the name of the other man who knew about this private affair. He was my father's partner and, as you have read, he was my partner after my father's death. Only the three of us knew about this private affair and here I was in a Glasgow artisan's house, a complete stranger to everyone, being told by two different voices about something known only to me and two dead men. Moreover, the voices which spoke claimed to be the voices of these two men, and Kidston continued the conversation quite naturally which my father had started, to conclude with these words:

"I am glad to get that off my chest at last."

When I wrote *On the Edge of the Etheric* I included in it this experience and others I had with this medium, but I gave no details as to what the voices said to me on this occasion. I thought it wiser then to give an outline of what happened and no more, as to recount what the voice, which claimed to come from my father, said, and what the voice, claiming to come from Kidston, said, would have involved too much explanation before the matter could be understood. However, now that my past life has been made public in these pages there is no reason why everything should not be told. What my father said after giving his name was this:

"I am very sorry I did not take you into my business. I would have liked to do so but Kidston opposed it. If you had been with me it would have greatly eased my life, as I found business a great strain on me. David Kidston is standing beside me and would also like to talk to you about this matter."

Then a voice claiming to be that of David Kidston spoke, saying:

"I am David Kidston. I was wrong opposing your coming into our office. I am sorry I did it but now you need have no regrets. I am glad to get that off my chest at last."

That was all true, but only my father, myself and Kidston knew about it, and the incident referred to happened when my grandfather died in 1904, fourteen years previously. When he passed on, I said to my father that I would like to enter Findlay, Kidston & Goff's office, as now my prospects of becoming a partner in Patrick Henderson & Co. were not so bright. My grandfather's influence had gone and I might have to wait years before I became a partner. My father agreed, and said he would speak to Kidston about it as I would be a great help to him. My disappointment was great when he told me that Kidston would not agree, because the business earned enough for only three partners. He evidently foresaw the day when my father would want me to become a partner, and that would mean less to go round.

Kidston was so short-sighted that he could not foresee me bringing in enough new business to the firm to justify my being made a partner, but he was a very difficult man to work with and my father had some unpleasant times with him. He was gruff, short in his manner and domineering, so much so that my father rather feared him. So I knew that what Kidston had said was final and I never raised the matter again, but, as neither he nor Goff had sons, I saw something good slipping away from me. So my request and its refusal remained known only to us three. Nevertheless, here was I listening to what had happened fourteen years previously, in a strange house, and in the company of people I had never seen before in my life.

That indeed was a problem. No spy system, however thorough it was, no fraud or impersonation by the medium or anyone else could be responsible for what I had experienced. I was up against something quite inexplicable. That, then, was my first introduction to Spiritualism, and, when the séance was over, I was introduced to the medium John Campbell Sloan, the man who was at the harmonium when I entered. I thanked him for his hospitality, and asked him if I could come back again, as I was anxious to know more about this subject.

"Certainly, any time you care to come, I shall be pleased to see you," was his reply, and I turned to someone standing near and asked how much I should pay Mr. Sloan. I have always remembered the reply.

"If you suggest such a thing as paying him he will be deeply offended. He does this as a duty, not to make money out of his mediumship." That did not impress me as the method adopted by a fraud. How could a working man earning a few pounds a week, I wondered, afford the time and the money to gather all the information I heard given to the people present that evening? I was so impressed with my strange experience that I went back to my club that night, and wrote into the small hours of the next morning a careful account of all that had occurred at this my first séance. This practice I have constantly adopted unless I had a stenographer present.

I left Sloan's house in company with the man who took me there, and he accepted my experience as a matter of course. "That is how people become Spiritualists," he said. "I told you I could prove to you what I said last night, and, you see, I have done so." He told me his name was Duncan McPherson, and I found out later that he was a much respected leader in the Glasgow Spiritualist movement, he himself being a medium. Some years later he died and returned to a séance at which my brother was present in Manchester. He, McPherson, spoke to my brother and said that it was he who had taken me to my first séance after meeting me at the Scottish Mediums' Union church one Sunday evening. My brother replied: "I think you are wrong, you met my brother at the Holland Street Spiritualist Church."

"No, I did not," was the reply, "it was at the Scottish Mediums' Union Church, 100 West Regent Street, I first met your brother and I took him the next day to Sloan's. Ask your brother and you will find out that I am right."

So my brother asked me the next time we met. He was wrong, and the voice claiming to be that of McPherson was right. It was at the Scottish Mediums' Union Church we first met, so that telepathy, if telepathy can produce a voice, which it can't do, is not the explanation of how this happened.

During the next five years I attended thirty-nine séances with Sloan, sometimes at his house and at times in places of my own choosing. Eighty-three separate voices have spoken to me or to friends I have taken with me. I have given details in *On the Edge of the Etheric* of the precautions I took to make sure it was not Sloan who was speaking. I sat with him at times alone and the voices spoke even when my ear was within an inch of his mouth, which was silent. Two and three voices sometimes spoke at the same time, but I have recorded all this already in *On the Edge of the Etheric*, and in the next chapter I shall give the subject greater consideration. Occasionally the voices were so strong that they could be heard across the street. The most convincing experiences were when I took strangers to a séance. Sloan knew nothing about them and I never mentioned their names. Here are a few instances which come under this category.

One evening I took with me the widow of a man whose body had been cremated that day and whose funeral I had attended. I introduced her to Sloan by another name. Her real name was Mrs. Louis Pearson. A voice spoke to me when the séance began:

"Why did you give the lady's wrong name? We know who she is, and her husband, Louis Pearson, is here to speak to her."

Pearson then spoke, remarking that it would take him some time to recover from seeing his earth body burned. When speaking to his wife he became very emotional, so much so that he could not continue his conversation with her, much to her disappointment.

On another occasion I took with me a professor from Glasgow University. I did not give his name, I knew little about him, but his experience interested me. A voice spoke to him in a language I did not understand. He replied in the same language, and the conversation went on for some time. After the séance was over I asked him what language he was speaking. He replied: "I was speaking Welsh, I am Welsh, and the voice which spoke to me gave the name of an old gardener I employed when I lived in Wales. He knew all about me and what he said was quite true."

These two experiences I have never recorded before, nor the fact that my father came back on other occasions and gave me good evidence of his presence and survival, but I could go on and on. Some of my experiences can be found related in my books, others I have never publicly told, in fact I have dozens of similar incidents hidden away in my memory or on record, which are as evidential as any I have published. Many departed friends and relations have returned and given their correct names, and good evidence of their survival, but nothing was more amazing than the return of Eric Saunders, as reported in *On the Edge of the Etheric*. Not only was his evidence remarkable, and everything checked later as correct, but he was seen when speaking. Many pages of this autobiography could be filled with the evidence I have received, but I must remember that this is a book recording my life and not a case-book for survival. However, I shall give just one more.

The Hon. Everard Fielding, who was such an active member of the Society for Psychical Research, once wrote to me to say that a friend of his would be coming to Glasgow, and would very much like to have a sitting with Sloan. I replied that I would arrange this, and, on the day appointed, Mr. Fielding's friend called to see me at my office. In the evening he dined with me at my club, after which we went to Sloan's house where the sitting was held. This man, during the course of our conversation prior to the séance, never gave me a hint of his occupation, and I purposely asked him no particulars. He was therefore a complete stranger to me, and neither I, nor the medium, nor anybody present at the séance, knew anything about him.

The séance was a good one, and during it a voice spoke clearly and distinctly before my new acquaintance. It addressed him correctly, and, when he asked who was speaking, the voice replied:

"When on earth I was known as King Edward VII."

A personal conversation ensued, names of people being mentioned by the voice which my acquaintance knew, and the conversation went on quite naturally just as if my friend were speaking to someone on earth. Finally, the voice said:

"I must thank you for all your kindness to my wife, Queen Alexandra. I do not know how she could have got on without you, and you have relieved her of much worry and care."

After the séance was over I asked him if he were satisfied with his strange experience, and he replied: "Most certainly." Then I said: "Will you tell me what your position is towards Queen Alexandra?" "Oh," he replied, "I am the Controller of her household." Neither I, nor any other person in the room that night, except the man himself, knew this, and it therefore follows that the voice that spoke to him was not of this world. Moreover, the person who controlled the voice knew all about him and his friends, which proves that someone, unseen to us, was present with knowledge beyond that of the medium, myself, and the other regular sitters.

Queen Alexandra, when she heard about this séance, wanted to sit with Sloan and this took place in London. I am glad to say that this gave her great satisfaction. Those also present were my friends, Sir William Barrett the eminent physicist, Sir Arthur Conan Doyle, Dr. Abraham Wallace and Sir Oliver Lodge, all believers in the reality of this phenomena after years of study and experience. Besides them were Sir Thomas Lipton and Marconi, for whose opinions I cannot vouch. Lastly, there was Mr. Byrd, the American scientist who did not believe in survival, but he came, he said, with an open mind. A friend of his came back, giving his name, and spoke to him, reminding him of the occasion when they were both together on Brooklyn Bridge and what they then talked about. The voice repeated parts of the conversation they had on the bridge and to this Byrd replied: "That is all true, but how can you speak to me when you are dead?"

When we came south to live at Stansted Hall, a friend and near neighbour of ours was the late Frances, Countess of Warwick, a charming woman and overflowing with human kindness. I told her about King Edward coming back to speak to the Controller of Queen Alexandra's household and she replied: "King Edward has often come back to speak to me. We were friends, and when he was on earth we always spoke to each other in German. After his death he has come back to me at séances, and always spoken to me by the direct voice. Just as he always spoke German to me on earth, so he spoke to me in German at these séances."

I wish I could give details of one more very evidential conversation which took place. My wife was once with me at a séance with Sloan, when a woman's voice spoke to her and said who she was. I would like to say who she was and what the voice said to my wife about a very personal matter, but I cannot do so as it is much too private. What is important is that only the one claiming to be the person she said she was could have known about it, and what she said to my wife was true and very appropriate. No one present could possibly have known about the matter to which the speaker referred.

Likewise I must pass over quickly any reference to the wonderful lights, about the size of half a crown, which moved about the room in the dark during the séances, which no one could catch however hard one tried. Lastly, it would require too much explanation to refer in detail to many other supernormal manifestations which occurred at these séances, but those who are unacquainted with what is called "direct voice" phenomena will find everything fully explained in my book *On the Edge of the Etheric*.

In the next chapter I shall give my mature opinions on what Spiritualism stands for, after nearly forty years of study and experience. Meantime, I would mention here that Sloan on acquaintance impressed me always as an upright, good, honest man, with little learning, a bad memory and just the average intelligence common to his class. He was a packer at a Glasgow warehouse, and his employer, who was a frequent sitter at his séances, told me he was a trustworthy upright man. This was the opinion of the very many other people who knew him, and I never once heard uttered a word of suspicion about the honest conduct of his séances.

Over five years I accumulated so much evidence of survival after death that I wrote and published *On the Edge of the Etheric* eight years later. I spoke on my experiences to the members of the Glasgow Philosophical Society at their headquarters, the meeting being packed, and my chairman was the senior Law Lord of the Court of Session. Then, on the suggestion of a lady, Miss Irwin, I formed the Glasgow Society for Psychical Research, a professor of the University becoming President and I the Vice-President. This new society had regular private meetings of members and arranged public ones, one being in the St. Andrew's Hall, where two thousand people heard the eminent physicist Sir William Barrett. I had the honour of being chairman, and remember Barrett in his speech recalling that forty years earlier in the same hall, at a meeting of the British Association, he had advocated the investigation of telepathy, but that no one gave him any support.

Now to return to everyday affairs. On 9th November 1918 the war came to an end, an armistice being granted to Germany. The return of peace was reflected on the Stock Exchange at a time when I had on my shoulders, not only my Red Cross work, but the office, where business during the war had been within my capacity to cope with, by working overtime. Now, increased buying started, and continued increasingly throughout the year, and more so during 1919, until a veritable boom developed, and I alone was responsible for the stockbroking side of the business which flowed in. Only months after the war had ended did all our regular staff return. During the war I had worked strenuously, and now came the 1919 boom. I could not give up the Red Cross work, and the office work had to be done. How I got through those two years I do not know, but I was so exhausted at the end that I just had to have a holiday.

Leaving our small daughter aged four years at Woodside in the charge of her nurse, my wife and I went off to Taormina in Sicily, a charming place nestling on the slopes of Mount Etna, but the noise of the motor-cars passing our hotel made it necessary for us to leave, though not before we had explored its beauties. From its ancient Greek theatre, placed on a lofty natural terrace, one gazes fascinated at the view of Etna, some miles distant, belching out white smoke, and then one looks southwards across Sicily towards North Africa. Truly this is a wonderful sight, and well named the most famous view in Sicily, a favourite resort of painters and writers.

We returned north and stopped at Santa Margherita on the Italian Riviera on our way home, and, as we arrived, the rain began to come down in torrents. The next day I stayed in bed for breakfast, and my wife suggested a day in bed. I slept all that day, waking up only for meals, and still the rain poured down. So I slept all next day and it still rained. It rained steadily for seven days, and for seven days and nights I steadily slept, to arise on the eighth day a new man. That week-long sleep restored to me my old vigour, and I left Santa Margherita thankful that during my holiday there the weather had been atrocious.

After the war it came to be realised generally what an important part petroleum was destined to play in our future, and that is just what I had anticipated seven years previously. The after-war boom, to which I have referred, was mostly in the shares of petroleum-producing companies, including the shares of the company in which I was specially interested. My ship had come home! That was a satisfaction, but it gave me great pleasure to know that the advice I had given to my clients had proved to be correct, and that our money had helped to increase the oil supplies of the world. A stockbroker's responsibility is great and, by wise advice, he can increase the comfort of his clients. On the other hand, by unwise advice, he can do the reverse.

To make a fortune one should find a good basket, put one's eggs into it and watch that basket, but, when a fortune has been made, the eggs should be distributed around many baskets, and then the chance of loss is greatly diminished. Courage and caution must be correctly balanced. Gamblers, and those who make money by chance, seldom know how to keep the money they make, and it goes as quickly as it comes.

The successful stockbroker of to-day, and the years ahead, must not only be a good man of business, but hard-working, industrious, far-seeing and highly knowledgeable about things and events everywhere which affect trade and industry. He must be well educated and skilled in his work, with more than the average quantity of wisdom, which is essential for success. Stockbroking is a very specialised profession, and a strenuous one if one is successful. The more successful the stockbroker is, the more strenuous life is, so much so that he should plan to be able to take things more easily after middle age. The Stock Exchange is not the place for old men.

My Red Cross work came to an end as time went on, and I received the grateful thanks of the Ayrshire Committee. This was in the form of a scroll signed by the President and all the Vice-Presidents. Accompanying it, I was presented with a large handsome Queen Anne inscribed silver bowl, a silver tea-pot and silver tray, gifts which I greatly value. About the same time I received a letter from the Home Secretary, on behalf of the Prime Minister, Mr. Lloyd George, informing me that in view of the service I had rendered he proposed to submit my name to King George V for my appointment as a Member of the Order of the British Empire. This afterwards took place by the King, when I was present at Buckingham Palace, and later I was presented to the King at a Levée at St. James's Palace. The Lord Lieutenant of Ayrshire, a few years later, asked me to accept the position of Justice of the Peace, which I did, and I devoted what time I could spare to the work of a magistrate on the Bench. I was then asked to become a member of the Incorporation of Hammermen, an ancient Guild, and later was given the Freedom of Glasgow.

I was now at a fork in my road of life. I had two ways I could go. I might then have stood for Parliament, or gone in for Glasgow municipal work, with the expectation of one day becoming Lord Provost with the title and honours attached to this office, but neither appealed to me. My grandfather once said, when asked why he had not stood for the City Council, that he had no desire to work his way up through the intrigues, malice and backbiting with which it is surrounded, and I felt much the same.

Party politics, which mean so much in a democracy, did not appeal to me. The misrepresentation by one party of the other repelled me. I did not mind the animosities aroused at a parliamentary election, but I never felt that I could denounce my opponent. In politics I always realised that there are two sides of every problem, and I could not contemplate making my side out to be always right and the other always wrong, as is the custom during an election. I always try to see the other person's point of view, in fact, I am not politically minded.

Once, when in Ludgate Circus, I dropped in to see

a phrenologist who flourished there. His name was O'Dell, and I was ushered by an assistant into a small cubicle and given a seat, just as if I had gone to have my hair cut, but there was no mirror. O'Dell came in and stood behind me, but he could not see my face. His hands went over my head, and he gave me an exact reading of my character which much amazed me. One of the many things he told me was that I had a well-balanced mind, never went to extremes, and always weighed up all sides before coming to a decision.

That, I think, is true, and he might have added that intrigues, or any attempt to secure an advantage over anyone for personal gain, repels me. I have never sought honours. I have never been a place-seeker, nor have I desired fame or public acclaim. I have never wished to be a prominent figure in public life, and I have always tried to tell the truth as I see it, quite regardless of prevailing opinion. I have always been interested in the deeper things of life, in the intellectual and the contemplative, ever striving after reality in a world of delusion. I am a truth-seeker, a teacher, a philosopher, rather than a politician, which to the shallow-thinking masses does not make for popularity.

So neither a parliamentary nor a municipal life attracted me, and yet I was now a free man to do as I liked, because I had all that I needed, quite apart from my business. With heavy taxation, as it then was after the First World War, and has remained since, I was just as well off out of business as in it. By taxing the taxpayers' income on a graded scale the Inland Revenue deprived me of nearly everything I made from my business. All incentive to work for gain had gone.

By such methods the war was in part paid for, and those who had the largest income had to pay the most in taxes. This method kills the rich man's desire for remunerative work, as my energy was now devoted to making money which was just handed over to the State. Why, therefore, should I not be free to live as I wished, and not be tied to the daily attendance at the office? A country life appealed to me more than life in a city, and I saw no reason why I should continue to have the responsibility of a business, which I had greatly increased, and the daily task of advising clients about their investments.

Two very wet summers decided the question for my wife and myself. She was very happy in Scotland and was quite prepared to live at Woodside for the rest of her life, but I longed for the south of England. Western Scotland is very beautiful, but the climate is bad, as sometimes it rains for days, and Woodside, situated as it is in a valley amongst high hills, got all the rain coming in from the Atlantic. So we decided to find a house in a drier part of the world. We must have gone through the catalogues of nearly a hundred houses when at last one came from my agents relating to Stansted Hall in Essex. This seemed to us just the place we wanted, convenient to, but not too near, London, in one of the driest and sunniest parts of England. There we would not have the hills, but the countryside was rural and dotted everywhere with magnificent trees. A beautiful landscape, with large and stately trees, was to me ideal.

So off I went in January 1923 to see the house,

which was situated on the Essex and Hertfordshire borders. I was so taken with it that my wife came with me on a return visit, to end in my buying the estate comprising the mansion and all the other houses and farm on about four hundred acres of land. My partnership had still two years to run, and, as the house required redecorating, we did not leave Scotland for England until February 1925.

Our remaining two years in Scotland comprised some interesting events. We were asked by the High Commissioner to the opening of the General Assembly of the Church of Scotland in Edinburgh, an important occasion in the religious life of the country. I had previously taken a leading part in the investigation this Church had made into Spiritualism. I had taken anonymously a former Moderator of the Church of Scotland, Dr. W. P. Paterson, Professor of Divinity at Edinburgh University, to Sloan's, where he experienced the amazing phenomena of a dozen or so of his previous parishioners, considered dead, coming back to him, giving their names, addresses and particulars of their lives on earth.

"Well," I said to him when the séance was over, "what did you think of that?" "It is quite beyond me," he replied. "I am an old man, this is all so new to me, so contrary to what I have preached all my life. I can't grasp it." Nevertheless, the rest of the investigating committee grasped this and much more, so much so that its report was favourable. This was all the more satisfactory considering the fact that my friend, Dr. John Lamond of Greenside church, Edinburgh, had suffered severe criticism for appearing on the platform of a Spiritualist meeting in Edinburgh, addressed by Sir Arthur Conan Doyle.

In 1910 I helped to raise the capital of a large investment company, some of the leading men in Scotland being directors. Its capital was largely invested in mortgages in Canada. It is now known as The Dominion and General Trust, having its investments in all parts of the world. I am glad to say it has been very successful. At the end of the war I was appointed a director, to become in time its chairman, which position I still hold. In 1923 I was asked by my co-directors to go to Canada to carry out an inspection of the company's activities in that country. This I did, my wife accompanying me.

We sailed in September from Liverpool to New York, and on board was Mrs. Wriedt, made famous by Admiral Usborne Moore in his book *The Voices.* She, like Sloan, was a direct voice medium, and when she visited Glasgow I had a most evidential sitting with her. So I was pleased to meet her again and get to know her better. She told me that just before she left England she had given several sittings to members of the Royal Family, and throughout her life she gave sittings to many eminent people. She was one of the world's great direct voice mediums.

We arrived in New York to experience a heat wave. There, I visited the Stock Exchange and met a number of stockbrokers and other business men, after which we went to Chicago, thence on to Winnipeg, then a town in the making, situated on a flat fertile plain. Here were the principal agents of my company and I was busy with them for several days, when we started off for Vancouver, stopping at various places on the way. Our first stop was Regina, then Moose Jaw and Medicine Hat, both queer names, and Calgary. After Calgary the monotonous days of travel through the wheat belt of the plains of Manitoba, Saskatchewan, and Alberta ended, as we approached the foothills of the Rocky Mountains. They could be seen far off as we looked at them across a sea of autumn wheat, from which they rose on the horizon. Nearer and nearer we came to the mountains, higher and higher they rose above us, and finally we were engulfed by them, our train crawling upwards through steadily enclosing heights.

We passed along the side of a long wide river, always climbing, until we reached Banff, mountains ten thousand feet and more towering above us. Here is the Banff National Park, and nearby the beautiful Lake Louise, famous for its bluish-green water, a gem of a lake surrounded by coniferous trees and so like many Scottish lochs. Next day we continued our climb out of this magnificent landscape until, after many bends and twists, the train reached the summit, surrounded by towering barren mountains. Then the descent began, past wide rushing rivers, through valleys covered with magnificent fir trees, between high mountains, to end finally at Vancouver, a fine city on the Pacific Ocean, situated on a great stretch of water on the other side of which is Vancouver Island. Across this strait is Victoria, the most English of all the towns of Canada, and I have always regretted that pressure of business prevented us from visiting it. Around Vancouver are forests of sequoia trees which grow to such a great height and girth.

After a few days' stay at this attractive spot we

returned as we came, stopping once again at Winnipeg and then continuing east to Montreal. Thence through the fruit-growing district to Toronto and Hamilton, to end in Buffalo where we stayed with a most hospitable American family. How I got to know them I shall explain.

Some time after my first experience with John Sloan, the direct voice medium, I came across a revealing book written by Edward C. Randall. He had experienced similar phenomena to what I had, and I thought that when in the United States I would make his acquaintance. So I wrote to him before I left home and received a warm invitation to stay with him when I crossed the Atlantic. That was the reason we arrived in Buffalo where he, his wife, and daughter lived. He met us at the station and gave us a hearty welcome, and we found Mrs. and Miss Randall equally hospitable and kind.

Edward Randall was a lawyer, one of the leaders in his profession, but, among other posts he held, he was President of the American Super Power Co. which supplied New York with electric light and power. We stayed a few days at his charming house, and he told me the story of how he became interested in Spiritualism. A number of his friends asked him to investigate a lady by the name of Mrs. French as, from reports, she was a magician of the highest class and the cleverest fraud in America. He himself was a complete disbeliever in the supernatural, but he undertook the task. Like myself, and others, he experienced in her presence the direct voice, to become convinced of its reality, but, after he had reported to his friends his conclusions, he continued his investigations for twenty years. He produced two impressive books, *The Dead Have Never Died* and *Frontiers of the After Life*, and the signed copies I have of these I greatly treasure.

Several times Robert Green Ingersoll came through and spoke to Randall, and this greatly impressed him. Ingersoll was one of the greatest orators the world has known, and to hear him speak when on earth was a great experience. Randall had done so, and when Ingersoll returned to him he completely convinced him that he was the one he claimed to be. No one on earth had the delightful charm in the use of his words, and, when Ingersoll returned after death, all the charm and beauty of speech for which he was famous were expressed. "No one," Randall said to me, "but Ingersoll could have used the wonderful language at those séances with Mrs. French." When Randall once asked him what his greatest surprise was on arriving in the other world, Ingersoll replied: "To find myself alive."

Edward Randall was a man who held a high place in the affairs of his country, and many leaders, known to him on earth, returned and spoke to him. He told me some of his many experiences with Mrs. French, with whom he was in close touch for twenty years until her death at the age of eighty. On seven hundred occasions he sat with her to hear the direct voice, and his experiences were the same as I had with Sloan, voices speaking from the void and claiming to come from men, women and children who had once lived on earth.

One has only to read his books to realise that his talks went far beyond the mental capacity of the medium, who was a woman of no great learning or education, and handicapped by being deaf and very delicate. Science, philosophy and physics were discussed between him and those who were men of learning on the other side, a revolutionary aspect of the universe being given which is quite beyond our present-day scientific knowledge. I could tell of several remarkable experiences he had of the survival of the individual conscience, but here I have space for only one, and I give it because there is no normal explanation possible.

At ten o'clock one morning the Brown building in Buffalo, then being repaired, collapsed. No one knew who had been killed and there was no way of ascertaining until the debris had been removed, which took some days. That evening Randall and Mrs. French had a séance, and a voice spoke saying that those who had been killed by the fall of the building were now in the other world and being looked after. They had not yet recovered from the shock of instant death, and could not speak themselves, but their names were as follows. These were given in full, both Christian and surnames, three men and one woman, and some days later this was confirmed when their bodies had been recovered. Only those four and no more were killed.

Our host and hostess drove us by car to see the Niagara Falls, a wonderful and ever-to-be-remembered sight, and the next day we went to Detroit. Little did I think, when I said "Good-bye", that the next time I would speak to him would be at a Sloan séance, when he returned to me from the other world. From Detroit we travelled to New York and on to Washingtion, where we met many interesting people. A visit to George Washington's home on the Potomac River occupied a pleasant day, and we were amused to find Mrs. Washington's small bedroom on the top floor, whereas he had a large and pleasant one on the first floor. However, I have since been told that this change took place after his death, so that she could look out and see his monument or tomb.

After a few days in this highly planned city of Washington, indeed a pleasing place of residence, we returned to New York by Baltimore and Philadelphia and took ship for home. We had good weather all the time we were in Canada and the States, we enjoyed ourselves greatly and learned much which has never been forgotten. From a business point of view it was a great success and well worth doing. We had a stormy passage back to Liverpool, but both of us were the better for the trip, and found all well when we returned to Woodside.

A year later we set to work to plan for our removal to Stansted Hall. It was a considerable undertaking, but when the time came to move all went well. When Woodside was cleared of our possessions, and the motor-vans had set off on their long journey, we left by car in February 1925, but before doing so many farewells had to be said. I had lived for forty-one years in the west of Scotland, my wife had been there for eleven years and we had many friends to bid good-bye. The people of Beith displayed their regret at our leaving them in many ways, which greatly touched us, and the following letter, which I received before our departure, is just a sample of the many kindly feelings they showed us.

L.B.—-G*

OFFICE OF PARISH COUNCIL,
BEITH.

31st January, 1925.

J. Arthur Findlay Esqr. M.B.E., J.P.,
  Woodside House,
    BEITH.

Dear Sir,

At a stated Meeting of Beith Parish Council held on the 30th inst. I was instructed to convey to you the unanimous expression of regret of the Council at the pending severance of your connection, and that of Mrs. Findlay, with this district. As the legal guardians of the poor of the parish, the Council recognise that many deserving poor people will miss Mrs. Findlay's kindly aid and sympathy.

You yourself, during a trying period, were a tower of strength to the Council as chairman, and tactfully steered them through troubled waters into sheltered seas. Your high ideals and firmness were an uplifting influence in that time of demoralising tendencies.

Permit me, as the servant of the Council, to add my personal appreciation of your kindly considera-tion and helpfulness.

Yours faithfully,
JAMES ANDERSON.
Clerk.

For quite a number of years prior to this I had been chairman of the Beith Parish Council, a body of councillors who in those days did more the work now done in England by the Rural District Councils. Our local duties were considerable, and it was gratifying to know that I had carried out my part as chairman to the satisfaction of its members.

Some who have read thus far, and to whom psychic phenomena is little known, may feel that I have left them hanging somewhat in the air by re-counting a number of strange experiences I have had, and making no explanation as to how they occurred. They are covered by the name of "Spiritualism", and Spiritualists, who have studied their subject, can account for much of what happens in the presence of a medium. For nearly forty years I have made this subject a deep study. I myself am in no way psychic, my interest being coldly scientific. So perhaps I may here break into my career and say something about this all-embracing subject, which is every year thrust-ing itself more and more on the attention of thoughtful people.

This being so, my next chapter will be devoted to this theme, but, at the best, it can only be considered as a brief and sketchy outline of a vast subject which covers human history from early times to the present day.

CHAPTER FIVE.

SPIRITUALISM.

IN THE last chapter I did not adequately describe my feelings and thoughts when the voices purporting to be those of my father and Kidston spoke to me that night at my first séance at Sloan's humble home. I was so amazed at what had happened, that without delay I wrote down word for word, before I went to bed that night, the remarks these two voices had uttered, and from that day to this I have never been able to find a normal explanation for them. However, there must be and undoubtedly there is a reason, I argued, and this I shall find out. Consequently, I set to work to discover it.

Sloan had kindly invited me to come to any séance I wished. So I returned to one the following week, and the same kind of thing happened. Numerous and varied voices spoke to the little gathering. Lights the shape of half a crown floated about the room, but I could not catch them, however hard I tried. Someone therefore must be able to see in the dark, I thought. A voice claiming to be that of my Uncle James spoke to me, and also voices which gave the names of friends who had passed on. It was all so very mysterious that when the séance was over I interviewed each person present to make sure what their reactions were.

They were all level-headed people, and two of the

men present held responsible positions in two local businesses of repute. Each person I spoke to assured me that the voice, or voices, which spoke to him or her gave the right name, the right earth address, and everything said by each voice was applicable to the dead person who claimed to be speaking. Each one was certain that the person speaking had been quite unknown to Sloan when on earth, and that the particulars given could not have been known to him. He had no time, they said, to go to graveyards to find names and dates on tombstones, and moreover he did not know where the bodies of the people who spoke were buried.

All were satisfied that fraud could not account for what happened and, in any case, this had been going on at the Sloan Circle for many years, and never a breath of suspicion had ever been aroused. The intimate private information which had come through at these séances, they all assured me, was overwhelming, and no other explanation could be given to account for it than that the individual speaker had survived death and, with his or her memory unimpaired, could return and produce his or her voice to be heard once again on earth.

Different people came to the séances, the gathering was never made up of the same people, so if fraud were the explanation this meant gathering new names and information once a week, an impossible task for a man who worked from eight in the morning until six at night, and in Summer worked on his allotment plot. The different people attending, moreover, meant that no one was a regular sitter and this excluded one or more sitters from producing the voices.

Sloan did not know who was to be present, so how could he gather his information beforehand? Anyone who had been present once could bring a friend anonymously, but that made no difference, the unknown person got just as much attention from the voices as those whose names were known.

As time went on, and séance after séance produced the same results, as more and more of my deceased friends and relatives came back and spoke to me, I decided to ask Sloan to give me sittings at private houses of my own choice, or at the séance room of the Glasgow Society for Psychical Research. This he agreed to willingly, and he would enter the room where the séance was to be held, never be introduced to the picked friends of mine who were present, and the séance would begin, he not knowing who was present.

Nevertheless, the results were the same as took place at his own house, voices of different tone and personality spoke, men's voices, women's voices and children's voices, and they always addressed the right people. For instance, a voice claiming to be that of the husband of someone present always spoke to his widow, gave the right name and correct information with never a mistake, never a fumble, always saying what would be expected from the person who gave the name.

This likewise took place when I attended, quite unknown, the séances held by Mrs. Roberts Johnson and Mrs. Etta Wriedt, both well-known direct voice mediums. At these séances exactly what took place in the presence of Sloan also happened. Voices spoke to me and others with never a mistake, and all the remarks made by the voices concerned private matters quite unknown to the mediums. On another occasion, at the house of Mr. William Jeffrey, 15, India Street, Glasgow, at a séance a light wooden table was smashed to pieces, but this happened in the presence of another medium who was controlled by those who sat on each side of him. He never moved, and the table was broken to pieces some distance from him because he supplied the necessary ectoplasm which the etherians used to show their power over matter.

I was now coming to believe that invisible people were responsible for the extraordinary experiences I had been privileged to have with Sloan, and other direct voice mediums. Consequently, after a few years of constant testing of Sloan's honesty, and becoming satisfied that the voices which spoke were something quite apart from Sloan, or any of the sitters, I decided to ask him if I could sit with him alone and bring with me my own secretary to take notes of all that happened.

He at once agreed and the next time I sat with him the three of us were alone in the parlour of his small house. No other person was in the house, as I examined all the three rooms it comprised. I next examined the walls to make sure there was no hole through which someone from another room, or the outside passage, could speak. I lifted the carpet to see if any gadget was on the floor or if a board was loose, but nothing could be found. The entire furniture was made up of chairs, a small table, and the harmonium. The window had a black cloth over it to keep out any light, as this, the voices said, interfered with the phenomena.

With only the three of us in the room we sat down after I had locked the door, and put the key in my pocket. Sloan sat opposite me, my secretary, Miss Millar, sat on my right, between me and Sloan, and so we formed a triangle, one of us at each end. The light was put out and I held Sloan's two hands, one with my right and the other with my left hand. I put my right foot on his left foot and my left foot on his right foot, and thus we sat throughout the two hours' séance. Miss Millar had a small table in front of her on which was her notebook. She had previously practised taking down shorthand in the dark, and this caused her no difficulty. Within a few minutes of the light going out she exclaimed: "My notebook has been taken from me." A few seconds later she said: "My pencil has been taken from my hand." The table then rocked to and fro, rose up and settled on her lap.

A strange voice then spoke: **"We shall do the lady no harm, there is nothing to fear."** Voices then spoke, and, when they were speaking, I bent across to Sloan but not a word was coming from his mouth, though I had my ear just touching his lips. My hands held his, my feet were on his feet, but he was as quiet as if he were asleep. Still the voices talked, sometimes two or three at the same time, and then Miss Millar exclaimed: "The table is now off my lap and is in front of me." Then she said: "My notebook is back." A second later she remarked: "My pencil is again in my hand." A bright light now floated past us and right up to the ceiling.

Here I might explain that at a direct voice séance there are two, and sometimes three, light trumpets, or megaphones, about two feet high, which are placed on the floor. These are used by the voices to magnify their power, and it has been proved by flashlight photographs that each trumpet is directed to the person spoken to. When two voices are speaking at the same time two trumpets are used, and I have thirty-eight photographs showing the people sitting around in a circle, the trumpets, or other things, being seen hanging in the air with no support except the rods of ectoplasm projecting from the orifices of the medium's body.

The basic substance needed for the production of the direct voice is Ectoplasm. It might be called the connecting link between the physical and the etheric, as it is the substance supplied by our body which, when mixed with etheric ingredients, can be handled by etherians. It is something which is half-way between physical and etheric substance, and it acts as a bridge between the two worlds. Those rare men and women, called Direct Voice mediums, have this ectoplasm in much greater abundance than the rest of us, though we all have it in a lesser degree, and, this being so, their presence is necessary before the direct voice can be produced at a séance.

So intrigued was J. Gilbert E. Wright, an American research chemist (until recently the Research Chemist to the General Electric Co. of the U.S.A.), with this elusive stuff, that he set about making a study of it. The result was his setting down ninety-six different observations on its effects and behaviour, but only the most important will here be mentioned.

When under the influence of etheric chemists, the medium's body is used as a supply basis for the ectoplasm, and they take what they can from the sitters, but under normal conditions it cannot be seen or tasted and it gives off no smell.

This stuff seems to diffuse through the tissues of the body like a gas, and emerges through the orifices because it passes more freely through the mucus membrane than through the skin, to become, by treatment from etheric chemists, an amorphous (shapeless) viscous (sticky) liquid which can be seen at times in red light. It has now some of the properties of matter, as it occupies space and can be seen. Its weight is difficult to determine, but, if the medium and sitters sit on weighing-machines during the séance, their weight will decrease, especially that of the medium, to become normal when the sitting is over. This has been proved by experiment.

This digression has been necessary so that a better understanding of the subject can be obtained, but I shall now return to our séance. Not only were lights seen moving all about the room, but the two trumpets, which were in front of us when the séance began, were lifted up and swished at great speed about the room, never hitting us, right up to the ceiling, which was used as a drum on which they beat time. Then they resumed their place in front of us and voices again spoke through them, claiming to be those of people I once knew. Sloan never knew that I knew those people, or the information they gave me, and yet no mistake was ever made, the remarks that each made being what I would expect from the person purporting to be speaking.

I was so satisfied with this private sitting, that, when it was over, I asked Sloan if I could have another sitting with him alone, and with my secretary. To this he willingly agreed, but refused any payment. He had this wonderful gift, he said, and he felt it his duty to use it for the comfort of his fellow creatures. He was a humble, simple, little-educated man, a slow, uncertain speaker, but always willing to put his gift to the service of mankind, and never asked anything in return. Besides the fact that all his adult life voices had spoken in his presence, and did so until he died in 1951 an old man of eighty-two, he also had the gifts of clairaudience and clairvoyance.

By this I mean that he could hear what normal people could not hear, and see what normal people could not see. For instance, I might be sitting and talking to him, when he would say he had just received a message for me. He would give me the name of some dead friend of mine, and then followed quite an appropriate message, each time correct, never a mistake. He said that he heard the name and the words and just passed on what he heard. At a séance his clairvoyance made it possible for him to see the speaker and describe him or her to me, and in this way many of my departed friends were correctly described just before or after they spoke to me.

At our next private sitting with only Sloan, myself, and Miss Millar present, and after we had put out the light, a voice said: "Mr. Findlay, someone near to you is very anxious to speak to you," and before I could reply I received two quick sharp taps on my right shoulder. This was evidential, as my father on earth would come up behind someone and give two taps on the person's right shoulder in rapid succession. I never knew anyone else make a practice of doing this except my father, and it was something he did all the years I knew him.

Sloan, from where he was sitting, could not have done it or I would have noticed him moving, because I always held his hands and controlled his feet, and Miss Millar could not have done it as the table was between us. Besides this it was a man's tap, not a woman's, decisive, not gentle or soft, and moreover it happened in the dark, there being no fumbling but just on the right place on my shoulder first time. After this happened my father gave me his name, and spoke to me. He described accurately Woodside, inside the house, and took me from room to room, placing each correctly. He also took me to the office, figuratively speaking, and described the rooms and its layout, mentioning that he had seen my partner Goff sitting at his desk in an attitude which was peculiar to him. Sloan had been to neither Woodside nor the office.

At this, and two further private sittings, I started asking a series of questions to which answers were given, each time by a loud clear voice. These will be found in my book *On the Edge of the Etheric*, but, for those who have not read this book, I shall give fourteen of these questions and answers out of the many related therein. These answers give an explanation of what I had experienced. The questions I asked, and the answers I received, took place at these three private sittings at which Miss Millar was present taking everything down in shorthand. Each séance lasted about two hours, and the answers were given immediately in a man's clear voice, no hesitation and in good correct English, Miss Millar recording everything said, just as it was said, no omissions or additions. Different voices answered the fifty-three questions I put during this enquiry and in each case the tone and expression were different.

Here, then, are fourteen of the questions I have picked out of the fifty-three I put to the voices speaking at those three private sittings Miss Millar and I had alone with Sloan. The first took place on the 4th December 1923, the second on the 4th January 1924 and the third on the 24th January 1924, but besides these I had a series of private sittings extending over a year. Only we three were present, the room was always searched beforehand, the door locked, and the key put in my pocket.

Question: "Here on earth we can only appreciate the physical, namely, the sun, the earth and the stars. What is contained in what we call space?"

Answer: "I can only answer you so far as my knowledge permits me. Interpenetrating your world is another world of substance in a higher state of vibration to the one you sense. The universe is one stupendous whole, but you only appreciate what you see and hear and feel. Believe me, there are other worlds of substance, finer than physical matter, in which life exists and of which you on earth can form no conception. Connected with your earth is this world to which I came after what you call death. Encircling your world are planes of different density, and these move in rotation with the rotation of the earth.''

Question: "Is your world, then, a real and tangible world?"

Answer: "Yes, it is very real to us, but the conditions in which we find ourselves depend on the condition of our mind. If we wish it we can be surrounded by beautiful country. Our mind plays a large part in our life here. Just as we live in surroundings suitable to our mental development, so we also attract to ourselves minds of the same type as our own. Like attracts like in this world. So also like attracts like so far as your world and our world are concerned. The evil-minded here are attracted by the evil-minded in your world, and the good here by the good with you. We can, at will, take on earth conditions by lowering our vibrations. Our bodies become heavier and more perceptible to the human eye, which accounts for our being seen at times by those who have the faculty on earth of sensing our vibrations.''

Question: "I cannot see you, but, if I could, what would you look like?"

Answer: "I have a body which is a duplicate of what I had on earth, the same hands, legs and feet, and they move the same as yours do. This etheric body I had on earth interpenetrated the physical body. The etheric body is the real body and an exact duplicate of our earth body. At death we just emerge from our flesh covering and continue our life in the etheric world, functioning by means of the etheric body just as we functioned on earth in the physical body. This etheric body is just as substantial to us now, as the physical body was to us when we lived on earth. We have the same sensations. When we touch an object we can feel it, when we look at something we can see it. Though our bodies are not material, as you understand the word, yet they have form and feature and expression. We move from place to place as you do, but much more quickly than you can."

Question: "What is the mind? Is it something apart from the brain?"

Answer: "Certainly it is. You bring your mind over here with you. You leave your physical brain on earth. Our mind here acts on our etheric brain and through it on our etheric body, just as your physical brain acts on your physical body."

Question: "Will you tell me something about your world?"

Answer: "All in the same plane can see and touch the same things. If we look at a field, it is a field to all who look at it. Everything is the same to those in the same condition of mental development. It is not a dream. Everything is real to us. We can sit down together and enjoy each other's company, just as you can on earth. We have books and we can read them. We have the same feelings as you have. We can have a long walk in the country, and meet a friend whom we have not seen for a long time. We all smell the same aroma of the flowers and the fields as you do. We gather the flowers as you do. All is tangible, but in a higher degree of beauty than anything on earth. Here we have no decay in flower or field as you have. Vegetable life just stops growing

and disappears. It dematerialises. There is a simi-
larity here to what you call death. We call it
transition.

"In time, as we develop sufficiently, we pass on
to another plane from which it is not so easy to come
back to earth. This we call the second death.
Those who have passed through the second death
can come back and visit us in our plane, but we cannot go to them until we have passed through it also.
This is what your Bible calls the second death. Those
who have passed through it do not often come and
speak to you on earth directly by materialising, as I
am doing now, but they can pass their messages on
to me, or someone on my plane, and we pass them
on to you."

Question: "You told me your world revolved with
this world. How does this happen, and also, do you
travel with the earth round the sun?"

Answer: "The spheres nearest the earth do so
because we belong to this planet. We cannot see
your world revolving in space, because we revolve
with you. We cannot see your world until we take
on earth conditions. In taking these on we slow
down our vibrations, and come through from one
plane to another, until we get our vibrations down
more to a level with those of which your world is
composed. We can all come down, but we cannot
go up beyond our own plane until we are prepared
for the change."

Question: "What are your houses like?"

Answer: "Our houses are just as we care to make
them. Your earth houses first were conceived in
your mind, and then physical matter was put together

to make them as your mind first saw them. Here we have the power to mould etheric matter as we think. So our houses are also the products of our minds. We think and we construct. It is a question of thought vibration, and so long as we retain these vibrations we can hold the object, which during this time is objective to our senses."

Question: "How is it that you can speak to us on earth?"

Answer: "By materialising my etheric mouth and tongue."

Question: "Can you tell me something of the method by which this is done?"

Answer: "I shall do my best to make you understand how this is done, but remember you cannot get a proper grasp of the difficulties we are faced with until you yourself come across to our side. However, I shall explain our methods as clearly as possible. From the medium, and those present, a chemist in the etheric world withdraws certain ingredients which for want of a better name is called ectoplasm. To this the chemist adds ingredients of his own making. When these are mixed together a substance is formed which enables the chemist to materialise his hands. He then, with his materialised hands, constructs a mask resembling the mouth and tongue. The spirit wishing to speak places his face into this mask and finds it clings to him, it gathers round his mouth, tongue and throat. At first, difficulty is experienced in moving this heavier material, but by practice this becomes easy. The etheric organs have once again become clothed in matter resembling physical matter, and, by the passage of air through them, your atmosphere can be vibrated and you hear his voice."

Question: "After the mask is completed, what do you do?"

Answer: "The person wishing to speak takes up his position in the centre of the circle and presses into the ectoplasmic materialisation, and then commences to speak, moving his mouth and tongue just as you do when you speak."

Question: "What about the trumpet?"

Answer: "This is used, not only to magnify the voice, but to enable it to be directed towards the person we wish to speak to. The trumpet is moved by materialised rods, and is controlled by one on this side whom we term the trumpet operator. His name is Gallacher, and he will speak to you now." (A new voice spoke, announcing himself as Gallacher, the trumpet operator.) "I am responsible for manipulating the trumpet. I have been standing beside you waiting to speak to you, and I am glad of the chance to tell you what I can."

Question: "Can you tell me anything more?"

Answer: "I would like to tell you, sir, that I was brought up in the Roman Catholic faith, but I did not come here as a Roman Catholic. Before coming here I gave up all creeds. I came here as a free thinker, but I was wrong in not believing in survival. I came here minus my physical body. When I keep in touch with the earth plane my surroundings are practically on a par with the physical world, but in the higher spheres we get away from earth conditions. Now I have for the time being taken on earth conditions, and I am part of your world. I will touch you (I felt a touch on my left arm) and I am conscious of that touch. (Sloan's hands and feet were still controlled by me. If Miss Millar had touched me she would have required to stop writing, get up and come over to me, but her pencil never ceased moving, and, when I told her immediately I was touched, she answered from her correct place in the room.) Many of us here in our normal state often touch our friends on earth, and at first are much distressed that no notice is taken of us, forgetting that, with our more refined bodies, we cannot be seen or felt. I must go now, good-bye, Greentree will speak to you again."

Question: "Can you tell me something more about the mask which you enter when you wish to speak?"

Answer: "You can call it a mask or a dummy. We gather the ectoplasm from the sitters into what I might term an urn: not a physical urn. If you wait a moment I shall try and show you it. (Sloan's hands and feet were still controlled. I waited, and gradually there appeared high above his head a luminous object which assumed the shape of a large flower-pot, and then faded away.) Did you see it? ("Yes," I replied.) Well, we gather the ectoplasm into this, and the chemist adds his ingredients. The finished product is matter slow enough in vibration to vibrate your atmosphere. The mask, until it is entered by the spirit wishing to speak, is incapable of speaking itself. The spirit has to tune down his organs of speech, and thus contact between these and the mask becomes established. When the magnetic, or psychic, power is strong enough, there is no difficulty in obtaining sufficient cohesion between the speaker's organs and the mask. When cohesion is established, the ectoplasmic material moves with the vocal organs of the spirit. It is exactly as if we coated our mouth and tongue with this material. It sticks to them and moves with them."

Question: "Has this mask weight and would it affect a balance?"

Answer: "Yes, it has. The ectoplasm taken from the sitters has weight, and the sitters' weight is reduced in proportion to the amount that is withdrawn. If you were to sit on a weighing-machine during the sitting you would find your weight decrease. The ectoplasm is returned to the sitters at the end of the séance and they become normal." (As previously stated this has been proved correct by experiment. Moreover, I have proved their statements about the materialised mask to be true, because I have various flashlight photographs showing it.)

When a voice speaks to a sitter at a direct voice séance and gives good evidence of the identity of the person claiming to control the voice, you come to think of the personality behind the voice and cease to take the voice as something impersonal. If a voice speaks to you from the other side of a wall, you think of the person speaking and not of the voice as being something impersonal. You imagine a human being speaking, and someone like yourself. You can, therefore, carry on a conversation with this unseen person even if you cannot see him. He gives his name and, if you know him, you recognise the remarks he makes as applicable to him. In other words, he can make himself known to you by what he says.

This is just what happens at a direct voice séance and, moreover, if the person behind the wall tells you what conditions are like on his side of the wall you will believe him even if you cannot see. So at a séance, once identity has been established, you come to accept what the speaker has to say about the way he is able to speak to you, what has happened to him since he died, what conditions are like in the world in which he now lives, and what this other world is like. The great difference, of course, is the fact that the man on the other side of the wall and you yourself are in the same world, and, when he describes to you his surroundings, you can understand what he is talking about.

A voice at a séance has a much more difficult task to make us believe or understand what it is talking about even if you recognise it, or if, by the evidence it gives, it makes you visualise some person you once knew, but is now dead. First of all, the person purporting to speak is dead, and all our past experience is that when someone is dead he is dead, he cannot think any more and, as his vocal organs are buried, he cannot speak. We naturally accept the obvious, what we know in favour of what we do not know.

So when we first attend a séance and one's father, for example, claims to be controlling the voice one hears, the obvious conclusion we come to is that it is produced by fraud. We continue to attend other séances and the voice returns, making statements about things and people which only one's father knew, and which the medium cannot know. If we go often enough, or if we test the medium, and are satisfied it is not his voice we have been hearing, we reach the conclusion that he is honest and is not defrauding us.

That is the conclusion I reached after putting Sloan to all the tests I could think of for a period of five years. In his presence voices spoke which did not come from him. They did not come from the other sitters as they were always changing, and the fact that voices were heard when Sloan and I, and my secretary, sat alone put that matter to rest. Consequently, I came to the conclusion that in the presence of one called a direct voice medium extraneous voices can be heard, spoken to and conversed with in an intelligent way.

That conclusion might be termed the basis on which I built up my knowledge that after death our survival follows, in a world somewhat similar to this earth, but much else was still to be learned. Spiritualism embraces far more than the direct voice. It is a name given to cover a wide range of phenomena which are beyond, or do not conform to, the physical laws of the universe. Spiritualists are those who believe from experience that these phenomena occur, and give as the cause invisible, active, intelligent beings outside our everyday world to whom is given the name of "spirits". Otherwise, these abnormal occurrences cannot be rationally explained.

The name "spirits" attached to these intelligent beings is the same as is given to whisky and suchlike liquids. Whisky, which comes from the two Gaelic words UISGE BEIDH, meaning water of life, is called a spirit because it is volatile, something that evaporates rapidly. Whisky, and the like, if left exposed to the atmosphere, disappears. A spirit is seen at times, to disappear as quickly and as silently as it came. What was obvious one moment is invisible the next. So our ancestors likened such a being to spirit, a material liquid that disappears. It is an unfortunte name, but a better one is hard to find. I have called such beings in my books "Etherians", which conveys the idea of something light, airy or heavenly, and physicists at one time applied the word "ether" to a subtle elastic fluid imagined to permeate space through which light waves travel.

These Etherians appear to us as something shadowy or cloudlike, but that is only from the physical point of view, and, as Spiritualism embraces the invisible as well as the visible universe, we realise that solidity is only a matter of degree. What is not solid to us is solid to them, because they function in what is called a different range of vibrations, and what is solid to us is not solid to them. To spirits their bodies and surroundings are solid, and we are to them what they are to us. We liken them to material spirits and they liken us to something similar. We can pass through them and they can pass through us and other material things, as if such things did not exist. It is all a question of the vibration in which the thinking being is living.

The universe is made up of countless vibrations, and only a minute portion of these are sensed by physical beings. Other beings sense vibrations of greater frequency than we do, and, living as they do affected by these, they are real to them and unreal to us. What, then, is meant by vibrations? It is the name given to the make-up or structure of the universe, but it is none other than a vast scale of agitated movement, or waves of varying frequency, which, in each range, makes conscious beings aware of their surroundings.

On earth we sense the vibrations of physical things. We live and move and have our being in a physical world which is composed of substances vibrating within certain fixed limits, to which we give the name "matter". We are born into it, and we accept it as if it comprised everything. Yet how different things are from what they seem to be! Matter, which looks so solid, is in reality not solid at all. Appearances in this world are not reality. What we see when we look at a table or a chair, for instance, are the vibrations of a certain number of electrons, which are revolving at immense speed around a centre known as the nucleus. Matter is made up of atoms, and these atoms are in turn composed of electrons, protons and neutrons. According to the number of electrons in an atom so is the substance, but the weight is conditioned by the number of protons.

Physical matter is an open network of electrons and protons, and the distance between the electrons and the protons in an individual atom, in relation to its size, is immense. If we consider the nucleus as commanding the same position in an atom as the sun does in our solar system, then the relative distance the electrons are apart from one another, and from the protons, might be taken as equivalent to the distance the planets are from each other and the sun.

If we consider an atom as something the size of a village church, then a pin-head would represent the relative size of one of the electrons of which it is composed. These protons and electrons in the atom are thus far asunder, moving at enormous speed, the electron being negative, the proton positive, and the neutron neutral. Matter is thus constructed of minute electric charges, both positive and negative within the atom, not moving haphazardly, but freely and orderly around the nucleus. It is their vibrations which cause us to see and to feel, and we would see and feel nothing without them. According to the speed of the electrons in each atom, so is the colour of the object.

The neutron, moreover, has now been found to play an important part in the mechanism of the atom. Its discovery has led the physicists to understand its properties. A uranium nucleus, after absorbing a neutron, splits into two fragments and releases the extra neutrons. Mass is lost in this fission process which is given off as energy. This is the basic fact that makes possible the atomic bomb, but, when the tremendous energy released is kept under control, as the way to do so has now been discovered, we get atomic power. Another of nature's secrets has been uncovered, and the more we know of the make-up of physical matter the more is the greatness, wonder and majesty of the universe revealed.

Only the ignorant affirm that just what we sense is real and that beyond this range of sense nothing exists. Our range of sense, our sight, our touch, our smell and hearing are limited to the last degree. We know that the spectrum of the spectroscope proves the very limited range of our ordinary vision, and that further ranges of vibrations of what would be colour, could we see them, extend on either side. It has been said that the perceived vibrations, as compared with the unperceived, are much less than is an inch to a mile. It is evident that there lies an enormous region for other life to inhabit around and within this world of ours, a region quite beyond our normal sense-perceptions.

Until we clearly understand that our senses here only respond to a very limited range of vibrations, namely those we term physical matter, that outside these there is a universe full of life, which responds to a higher range of vibrations, unreal to us, but more real to it than physical matter, we cannot grasp or understand in all its fulness the psychical phenomena which develop through mediumship.

We see things, and we feel the touch of things, by the vibrations of an object on our sense organs, and we hear by the vibrations of the atmosphere made by a noise. Our conscious life, the colour of everything we see, and the weight of all we feel, are caused by the vibrations in our surroundings within the physical range. The conscious life of those inhabiting an invisible world around us comes from it inhabiting a world of higher vibrations than those which make up the physical world.

We have two bodies, one the physical and the other the etheric duplicate, which latter passes out of the physical at death and responds to the vibrations of the etheric world. We have this etheric body on earth, but it is not visible because its vibrations have a greater frequency than those which make up our physical body. On earth the physical body is governed by mind, an image-making substance, which image-making we call thinking, and at death this mind goes with the etheric body to control it as it controls the physical body on earth.

During some of my séances I discovered that my friends on the other side could read my thoughts. I had only to think of something and they told me what it was. Thus I found from them that our thoughts are mental images, our minds picturing everything we think or do, and they can see these images. So I made a series of experiments, and everything I thought of was told me correctly and no mistake was ever made. My conclusions were, and this they confirmed, that our mind is a plastic substance always imaging what we think and see. We think of a house, and our mind images a house. I see someone, and what we might call a photograph of the person appears on the mind. I can recall the pictures at will, and that is what we call memory.

Everything we see or feel is pictured by our minds, and, if we go somewhere, we picture the place for which we are bound. Our thoughts are mental pictures of all we do or think or feel, they are in the colour of the object we see, and, when we sleep, they are not under control, these pictures being what we call dreams. This means that these coloured pictures are formed in our minds somewhat like coloured cinematograph pictures, our mind being like a screen on which pictures are always being formed. This mind-picturing makes up our life; it is something apart from the brain which is like the camera, the pictures being what the film produces.

In other words, our mind is ourselves, it is you and I, and our physical body is its abode, but it has another, which is the etheric body. At death, this picture-making substance, which we call the mind, parts from the physical body and functions through the etheric body in new surroundings, the vibrations of which produce mental pictures just as the physical vibrations produced its pictures on earth. This is a vital discovery and one which makes us realise the meaning of thought, the meaning of life, and what each human being actually is when we get down to reality. To know what man is will become the science of the future, and only through Spiritualism can this be discovered.

The foregoing is a brief and sketchy summary of how I arrived at an understanding of the way to rationalise the belief in another world, and how I was able to find a place for those who once lived on earth who now inhabit it. It came about because I was a student of physics, the science dealing with physical matter. Before I had any psychic experiences I knew something of physics and what we call matter, and I applied this knowledge to what I learned at these direct voice séances. Those who make physics their life-work are called physicists, and it is they, by their researches and experiments, who have put nuclear energy at our disposal for both good and evil purposes.

The fact that each of us has a duplicate invisible body, the etheric body, is, I discovered, the first lesson in Spiritualism. The etheric body interpenetrates the physical body during earth life, and leaves it at death. Our mind does not die, and it controls the etheric body through the etheric brain. The individual mind is the greatest factor in the universe, it is the common factor between the two worlds, and without mind the universe would cease to be. Life and consciousness would end, and without these there would be nothing.

To be able to live without a body, such as we have now, is only possible to understand by realising that we live in a world made up of vibrations visible and invisible. The physical vibrations visible to us range from 34,000 to 64,000 waves to an inch, as will be seen in the diagram of visible and invisible vibrations. Invisible vibrations of a different order make up other worlds, and it is to the world next in frequency to this world that our duplicate etheric body is in tune, though, only when death frees it from the physical, can it respond to its new environment.

To some readers this may all seem very technical, but I am trying to convey how my mind worked once I was satisfied of the genuineness of the direct voice. I had to find a place in the universe for those people who claimed to have lived on earth and gone else-where. Was it possible, with our present-day know-ledge, to have a rational understanding of how this took place? An obviously thinking individual, even if invisible, must have a mouth to speak with, and this implies a head and body. Before he can speak he must be able to think, and this implies a mind with which to think. Moreover, he must live in a world of some kind or another.

Then I went back to a book on physics which always fascinated me, *Scientific Ideas of To-day*, by my late learned friend Charles Gibson, F.R.S.E., who stayed with me from time to time at Woodside, when the subjects comprised by the word "physics" were often the subject of conversation. So I re-read all about the vibrations which make up the physical universe, and prepared the diagram on the next page of the known physical vibrations in the midst of the

VISIBLE AND INVISIBLE VIBRATIONS

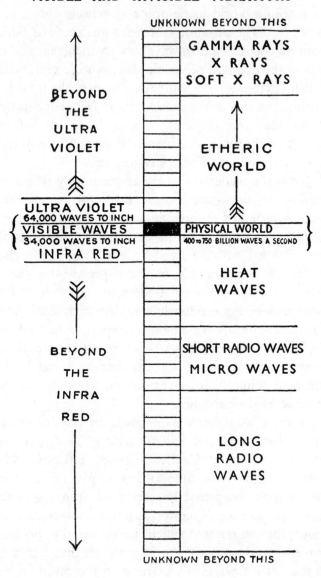

UNKNOWN BEYOND THIS

GAMMA RAYS
X RAYS
SOFT X RAYS

BEYOND
THE
ULTRA
VIOLET

ETHERIC
WORLD

ULTRA VIOLET
64,000 WAVES TO INCH
VISIBLE WAVES · PHYSICAL WORLD
34,000 WAVES TO INCH · 400 to 750 BILLION WAVES A SECOND
INFRA RED

HEAT
WAVES

BEYOND
THE
INFRA
RED

SHORT RADIO WAVES
MICRO WAVES

LONG
RADIO
WAVES

UNKNOWN BEYOND THIS

vibrations which are on either side. This diagram of physical vibrations has been carefully checked by leading physicists, and a study of it makes it possible to visualise the different ranges of vibrations, to which I have added those pertaining to etheric substance, which are assumed, because they are of a different order and cannot be proved as are physical vibrations.

When the etherians spoke to me they referred to their vibrations, and this implied that the structure of their bodies, and their world, are built up on the same principles as apply to us on earth, the difference being that they have a range of vibrations to themselves, just as physical vibrations appeal to people on earth. Our duplicate etheric body, seemingly dormant in this world, functions after death in another world of vibrations of higher frequency, and I wondered if we had on earth any visible evidence for this. That we each have a spirit body is an age-old belief, but I wanted more than that. Then I discovered that there is good evidence that ghosts, or apparitions, have been seen down the ages, and the evidence accumulated by both the British and American Societies for Psychical Research confirms this.

To put the matter on a scientific basis, the Society for Psychical Research, of London, sent out a questionnaire, for the purpose of discovering what proportion of those who replied had ever experienced the seeing of an apparition. The result, which was published in 1894, revealed the fact that, from the thirty-two thousand replies received, a sufficient number had met with this experience to establish apparitions as scientifically demonstrated. Twelve per cent. of the women, and nine per cent. of the men, who replied declared that, under good conditions, they had seen one or more apparitions on one or more occasions. Others have made the same enquiry, the American Society for Psychical Research, for instance, having obtained a similar result from its questionnaire. Various scientific men who have done likewise have had similar results.

Hallucination cannot be given as an explanation, as medical science knows nothing of hallucination amongst sane and healthy individuals such as these were. Apparitions, as seen to-day, have been seen since the time of early man, and probably also by animals, as there is good reason to believe that animals can see apparitions when they are invisible to human beings.

Anyone who doubts the fact that those we call dead can, and do, return to earth to be seen and heard should read W. H. Salter's book *Ghosts and Apparitions*. Coldly analytical, he examines the claims made by those who declare that they have had such experiences. Apparitions are seen and are heard, is the author's verdict, and no one is more competent than he is to give this decision because, as Honorary Secretary of the Society for Psychical Research, he has had exceptional opportunities to enable him to arrive at the truth.

Three very evidential cases of apparitions being seen have come to my knowledge during my lifetime. The first I shall mention refers to an apparition being seen in my own neighbourhood, the facts of which are as follows: A few miles from Stansted Hall, near the old market town of Great Dunmow, there lived a woman who shot herself one evening, Monday, 5th December 1938, after having shot her husband. They were alone in the house at the time, and the discovery was not made until 7.45 on the following morning when the daily help arrived at the house, to find the woman in the garden with part of her head shot away. She immediately informed the police, who were on the scene by 8.30 with a doctor who certified that they both must have been dead since the previous evening. The radio had not even been turned off.

There is therefore no doubt that these two people were dead at 8.30 in the morning. A husband and wife, who live near Great Dunmow, both friends of mine, who do not wish their name mentioned, gave me the following information. They were motoring to London on the morning the discovery was made, and they passed the house where the tragedy occurred about 9.20. As they came in sight of the house they saw the woman who had shot herself walking along the road towards them dressed, but without a hat. She was seen first of all by the man, who was driving the car, who said to his wife beside him: "Oh, there is Mrs. Davies. She gives me the creeps." His wife replied: "Oh, so it is," as she also saw her and, as they passed within six feet of her, they smiled in recognition and she acknowledged this with a bow and a smile.

They thought nothing more about the affair and, after spending the day in London, they bought an evening paper on their way home in which they read the story of the tragedy. This was the first time they had heard about it, and my friend went to the police on his return home, and told them that the woman could not have been dead at the time stated as he and his wife had seen her at 9.20 that morning. The police, however, assured him that they were in the house by 8.30, and that the doctor had certified that the woman they saw had been dead since the previous evening.

Such is the story that was told to me by my friends, who agree about all the facts. They have not the slightest doubt that the woman they saw was Mrs. Davies, who had killed her husband and then herself the previous evening. There was nothing about her dress which occasioned my friends any surprise, and, when I asked if she looked happy or sad, I was told "She looked just as she always did." All these details as to time of death came out at the inquest, and are to be found in the local newspaper.

This is an interesting case because, when my friends saw the apparition, they were unaware that the woman was dead and only discovered, some twelve hours later, that the woman they had seen that morning walking along the road had died the previous evening. Because they remembered the time they left home they knew the time they saw her, and the police and the doctor were able to certify that the woman was dead when they arrived at the house an hour earlier. Both my friends saw the apparition, and are quite definite that it was Mrs. Davies, the dead woman. Thus we have two witnesses who saw the apparition at the same time, which greatly strengthens the evidence.

The other interesting case occurred in Scotland. Friends of mine rented for the Summer a large old country house in Dumfriesshire. It had the reputation of being haunted, but, as they were quite uninterested in such subjects, this did not worry them. One evening their daughter, who told me this story, went out of the drawing-room to interview the cook, whom she thought she saw at the end of a passage. She spoke to her, but received no reply. Then she realised that the person she was looking at was a woman who had no resemblance to the cook. She went towards her, but the figure vanished. She returned in an agitated state to the drawing-room and told her parents, whose only remark was that she must have been dreaming.

Not long afterwards she saw the same figure and went straight forward with her arm outstretched, determined to touch her, but the apparition vanished from view. She was not the only one to see her, because some days later the apparition was seen in an upstairs passage by three young women guests, who were so overcome that they collapsed on the spot. I knew personally all the people connected with this experience and what I have related is what was told by those who experienced it. Such stories have been told down the ages, and many people are aware of one or more of a like nature.

I shall now tell one more. An aunt of my wife came home from China where she was an honorary missionary. She later became Lady Mayoress of Manchester when her father (my wife's grandfather) was Lord Mayor. She left the boat at Liverpool and it then went on to Glasgow, but unfortunately the steamer was involved in an accident in a fog on the way. It sank and the captain was drowned. Before the news reached the owners, or was known on land, his wife in Glasgow had an extraordinary experience. Her front door opened, and her husband walked in and hung up his coat near the door. She saw him do so, and heard him say, "It was the fog, Dorcas dear." She went towards him and he vanished. My wife's aunt was so upset by the death of the captain, whose name was McKinlay, as she had sat at his table on the ship and got to know him well, that she went to Glasgow to see his widow, who told her of this strange event.

It seems to me that such experiences as I have recorded point to the fact that beings usually invisible can become visible from time to time to those with clairvoyant sight, and can be heard by those with clairaudient hearing. When seen, they resemble human beings with legs, bodies, arms, and heads; in other words, they have bodies which were their duplicate etheric bodies when they lived in the flesh. Apparitions might therefore be called beings who once lived on earth and now live in vibrations, or surroundings, different from our own, functioning in the duplicate body which they had on earth and which only became real to them when they died.

Such beings go to a direct voice séance, such as Sloan's, are there seen by clairvoyants, and, from the ectoplasm the medium exudes, they materialise their vocal organs and speak to us. Therefore, by seeing apparitions, we know that these other-world beings, usually invisible to us, exist and under certain conditions can be heard to speak.

Direct voice mediums are rare, because only comparatively few human beings can supply the quantity of ectoplasm which is required by the men and women on the other side to materialise their vocal organs. Even rarer are full-form materialisation mediums, and consequently the complete materialisation of someone we call a spirit happens only from time to time as nature produces a medium well endowed with ectoplasm. This the spirit uses to bring his or her vibrations down to our level, and to appear to us in the likeness of himself or herself as he or she was when a human being on earth.

The two most common means of communication used by the men and women of the other world are trance and clairaudient mediums. Mediums, who have the gift of hearing speech not heard by normal people, are said to be clairaudient, and the comparatively large number of people who make this claim, and the correctness of the evidence they produce, establishes this phenomenon on a scientific basis. By observation and experience it can now be scientifically claimed that some, more sensitive in their hearing than others, can hear voices which are not heard by the rest of us. Thousands of investigators, over the past hundred years, have established to their own satisfaction that this is true, and I myself have had numerous opportunities to prove it to be so.

I have already mentioned how the trumpets moved about without physical contact, and how Miss Millar's notebook and pencil were taken from her and her table put on her lap. I wish to refer to another supernormal incident which I experienced at the house of John Sloan.

On one occasion I left a gold match-box, having my initials on it, in my overcoat ticket-pocket. I said nothing about this to anyone, hung up my coat in the entrance passage, entered the séance room, locked the door, put the key in my pocket, put a mat up against the bottom of the door and took my seat with the others sitting around in a circle for the séance about to begin. Two trumpets were in the middle of the circle for the voices to speak through, and it was not long after the lights were put out when a trumpet came in front of my face and a metallic object was rattled inside it. A voice said: "Please put out your hand," when something was heard to slide down the inside of the trumpet into my hand. It was the same gold match-box that I had put into the ticket-pocket of my overcoat. When the séance was over I found the window still tightly shuttered, the mat was at the door as I had placed it, and the door was still locked. That is what is called an apport.

Apports may be anything one can handle, and these objects are put, by someone unseen, into the hands of the person present or placed on his lap. On one occasion a lighted cigar was put between the fingers of a visitor when he was talking to Sloan in his house. Amazed, he looked about and finally went outside, to find the owner of the cigar looking for it everywhere on the pavement.

I only record these two marvels and do not attempt to explain them. When I asked my friends on the other side how they happened, I was told that they could, under certain circumstances, dematerialise and then re-materialise objects. Yes, strange things happen at séances which make investigators realise that what we call solid matter is only so to us here on earth, but not to those who inhabit another order of nature in which the frequency of their vibrations differ from those we experience on earth.

For a period of over twenty years I accepted invitations to address Spiritualist meetings throughout Great Britain and Ireland. I paid my own expenses and took no fee. These meetings were, as a rule, held in the Town Hall or the largest available hall in the town, and I must have spoken in over one hundred of these from the Albert Hall downwards. In every case these meetings were crowded, and I have addressed over these years more than one hundred thousand people. The attraction, of course, was the clairaudient medium who, after my address, stood up on the platform and pointed to this, that, and the other person in the audience and gave each one messages purporting to come from their relatives and friends on the other side. Let me give an example of what was said to one person spoken to.

The following is copied from *Psychic News* of 12th February 1955, and was taken down at the time in shorthand by one of its reporters. The medium was Ronald Strong, and the place was the Wigmore Hall in London.

A woman in the audience said she thought it was a message for her after Strong had asked if she knew a man who shot himself.

"Mr. Jarvis is the name of the man who shot himself through the mouth," explained the medium.

"Yes," was the reply. "He was a neighbour of mine."

"There is someone called Albert Jarvis, someone called Frank, another called Simpson, and a woman whose name is Dorothy Simpson. You knew her as Dolly Simpson," went on Strong.

"Yes," she replied.

"She was a friend of Jarvis and she lived in Park Road."

"That is correct."

"He says, 'She will remember because we had many happy times at number 28,'"

"He lived at 28," she replied.

"He says, 'We were all together, a group of us, and there was someone called Doris Sparks. They called her Dorrie.'"

Again came confirmation.

"There is someone else called Alf Patterson. He played the piano," continued Strong.

"Yes, I remember Alfy but not his second name," was the reply from the woman.

"He used to play jazz and one piece he played was 'Hold that Tiger'. Another man called Jack Stevenson and one called Bill Fowler." Here Strong corrected himself. "No, Bill Fox."

"Yes, that is right."

"There is another woman and her name was Elizabeth Westwood."

"My maiden name was Westwood," said the recipient.

"He tells me that there had been some trouble about money and that is why he shot himself."

"Yes, that is quite right."

After reference to the recipient having met the communicator and his wife, Strong enlarged:

"You met them at a whist drive and either you or his wife won a teddy bear."

"I won it."

"It became a part of your life and you called it Mickey."

"Yes, that is right."

Questioned by the medium whether she had ever been to the hall before, the woman replied:

"No, not here."

"And you have never seen me before in your life?" asked Strong.

"No," said the woman.

"What is the connection you had with Huddersfield?" went on the clairaudient.

"I always wanted to go to Huddersfield for no reason whatever," was the reply.

Diverging into details concerning the recipient, Strong said:

"When you were a little girl at school there was a boy you rather liked."

"Yes."

"The little boy you liked was Fred Peterson."

"Yes, I remember."

"Why, I can't think, but you used to call him Danny."

"That is correct."

"Your Danny you haven't seen for so many years is on this platform. Before he passed over you remember that he went to America into an hotel.

"He wants you to know there is still a great link between you although he went out of your life when he was a child. At that particular time either you or he was living at Church Street."

"We used to go hand in hand through Church Street," explained the woman.

"He tells me there was a Peter Hughes."

"Yes," she replied.

"There was Ken Roberts and a little girl called Irene whose surname was Fisher and she used to dance," said the medium, pursuing these details of years gone by.

"Yes," was the reply.

"She is not on the other side," observed the clairaudient. "She is still here. I do want you to help this man who has committed suicide because he has left his wife in a turmoil. Send out your thoughts, and do please help him.

"He says, 'Will you please tell her I am so grateful for the happy days we had together. She knows how happy I was and just tell her that I have the dog called Bobby.'

"It is a Pomeranian," explained Strong, "and there was another dog called Koko; one very white and the other black and white. You were rather worried about them because you thought they were underfed."

"Yes, that is quite right."

"He says, 'Thank you very much for helping me tonight and I am perfectly well and much happier than I was.'"

The foregoing is an example of many hundreds of messages I have heard given from the platforms of meetings I have addressed. The medium in nearly every case had arrived just before the meeting from some distant place, and often had never before been to the town in which the meeting was held. For a time I kept a record of the number of correct statements the mediums made at my meetings, but I gave it up after recording many, as they all worked out about the same. Ninety-five per cent. of all the medium said was correct and five per cent. was not acknowledged.

Sometimes people held back, and would not acknowledge the truth of what was said. For instance, after a meeting I addressed at the Town Hall in Ayr, I heard a woman say to a friend: "Oh, it was all true, every word, but I would not acknowledge it; it was no business of hers, prying into my private affairs." Sitting as I did on the platform, and seeing the faces of the people spoken to, I could tell by their expressions that what was said by the medium was true. Chance has been ruled out, as it has been worked out by an eminent mathematician that to give correctly by guessing three messages, such as the foregoing, the odds would be five million million to one against chance being the explanation. That being so, we need not consider it, especially when not three but a dozen correct messages are given at a single meeting.

The only other possible explanation is that the medium has agents in every part of the country. When going to Birmingham, for instance, his or her agents find out about people who are going to the meeting and discover all about their past lives. In a city of a million people, how is it possible to discover who intends to go to this particular meeting? How could the agent find out all the details given by the medium to the people addressed, and how could the agent arrange for the medium to speak to the right person each time and give the right name, never having seen the person before? There is no opportunity for the agent and medium to meet, as someone connected with the meeting generally meets the medium on arrival, and he or she has no opportunity to gather information before the meeting.

What an expense agents would be, how easily the medium could be blackmailed, and what does the medium's fee come to? Only two or three guineas for each meeting. So I have come to the conclusion, after very many opportunities to judge, that these clairaudient mediums hear what they tell, and the only explanation for this supernormal knowledge is that the words they hear come from people who once lived on earth, died, but still live elsewhere. They use the mediums to convey their messages to those they love or know on earth, and take the opportunity to do so at a gathering where a medium is present.

The other method etherians use to communicate is by a trance medium. Such a person seems able to detach his or her duplicate body from the physical body more easily than normal people, and thus open his or her body to the influence of these other-world beings. The medium sits down in front of you and, after a few minutes, seemingly gets drowsy and then falls asleep. If you speak the reply comes in a strange voice, but, as it gets stronger, it speaks to you as if it is passing on messages from someone present but unseen, whose name is given. It is like having speech with a foreigner through an interpreter. What is important is what is said, and, if this information applies to the person whose name is given and is correct, it is termed evidential, especially if you are a stranger to the medium who knows nothing about you or your friends.

When my mother died I had two very evidential sittings with two different trance mediums at which everything said was correct. These two sittings I give in full in their right place in Chapter VIII, but here I shall record what was told me once by the direct voice when I was having a private sitting with Sloan. Miss Millar was present and she took everything down in shorthand. I was anxious to have an explanation of trance phenomena, and these were my questions:

"When you control a medium in trance and use his or her vocal organs, what really happens?"

Answer: "When the medium is controlled, and we wish to speak through his vocal organs, we get him into a passive condition. This is the condition he is in when in trance. His spirit has left his body for the time being and is outside. When he is in this condition we are able to work on his larynx and vocal cords, his tongue and throat muscles. We do not go inside him, however, but stand behind him. We are able to get ourselves into a condition, or in tune with the medium, to such an extent that when we move our voice organs the medium's move likewise.

"There is a connecting link, etheric or psychic, whichever you like to call it, which has the same action on the medium's muscles as a tuning fork on another tuning-fork if they are both tuned to the same pitch. Thus the two sets of vocal organs work in harmony. There is no question of the messages in any way being influenced by the medium's mind, as his mind does not come into the question at all. We do not work through his mind, but directly on his vocal organs. Everything that comes through is exactly as it originates in the mind of the controlling spirit. The medium's mind and brain are switched off for the time being, and the spirit operator controls the muscles of the medium's vocal organs."

Question: "The medium is still in trance: where has his spirit been since we started?"

Answer: "When the trance state comes on it means that the medium's spirit has moved out of his body. His spirit is at present exactly on his right not far from his body."

Question: "Can you tell me more of your controlling the medium during trance?"

Answer: "I take on earth conditions, slow down my vibrations, and stand behind him. Ectoplasm is found everywhere in the human body. When I stand behind him it is similar to standing behind the mask, only in this case it is the medium's own vocal organs which I move to form the words. They move in company with my organs, whereas when we speak directly, apart from the medium, we enter the mask and form the words by our own tongues which are temporarily materialised."

What are called spirits are men, women and children who lived on earth and, after having discarded their earth bodies by death, became men, women and children in a range of vibrations of a higher frequency than we experience on earth. Their minds did not die with their physical bodies, and their duplicate etheric bodies carried their minds with them to this other world, to which their etheric bodies of greater frequency responded. In a word, this is death, an event so dreaded by mankind that it has been responsible for all the world religions, which have produced half the events of history.

The fact that ghosts exist goes a long way to help us to understand all the phenomena for which Spiritualism stands. When, moreover, some clairvoyants tell us they can see the etheric duplicate parting from the physical body at death, we conclude that their vision enables them to have a glimpse of the vibrations of higher frequency with which we are surrounded. Moreover, certain people have temporarily parted from their physical bodies and returned to them. A lady, whose honesty is unquestionable, told me that during the time she was under an anaesthetic, having an operation, she felt herself standing overlooking her physical body on the operating table. She was interested to follow everything done by the surgeon and nurses, but, what impressed the surgeon, when she told him her experience afterwards, was the fact that she saw him do something to her inside that she could not have dreamed about.

Moreover, she saw what is called in Ecclesiastes xii, 6, "The Silver Cord" connecting her physical body with the duplicate body in which she was functioning, and was fearful lest the surgeon and nurses would break it, but they passed through it, doing it no harm. It is when this invisible "umbilical" cord, connecting the etheric with the physical body, breaks or dissolves, that death takes place. We pass at birth from the womb in which we were conceived into this world. The cord connecting the foetus to the placenta is broken and we live a new life on earth. When that ends, our duplicate etheric body passes into a new world, and the cord connecting the physical with the etheric is broken, or is dissolved, to enable the etheric body to function therein.

I have heard or read of many such experiences of people parting from, and returning to, their bodies, but certain dreams are equally strange and point to the fact that when asleep we can leave the physical body and travel about in our duplicate body. Generally we forget what we have experienced, but here is a case where the narrator evidently remembered what he saw the previous night. His letter came to me and was dated 24th October 1954, and I have his permission to publish it with his name and address. The writer is a doctor in Southern Rhodesia, his name being James R. Foy, and his address is Powell Road, Parktown P.O., Salisbury. All he asks of me is not to mention the lady's name, so I have left it blank. His letter reads as follows:

"I am a doctor and about thirty years ago, while seated in my surgery, a lady knocked at the door, came in, and introduced herself as Mrs. ——, wife of our local Anglican minister, and asked me to examine a nasty bruise on the upper part of one arm.

"Suddenly I remembered a dream which I had the night previous, in which dream she was being beaten by her husband in her drawing-room, from which beating I persuaded her husband to cease. Between us we put her to bed.

"I had never met Mrs. —— before, I would not have known her from Eve, though I had met her husband at my own house. I was buying a motor-cycle and side-car from him at the time.

"To come back to my surgery and her entrance. Remembering my dream, and before she could speak another word, I said 'Mrs. ——, I can tell you how you came by that bruise. Last evening your husband was beating you while you were seated on a pink upholstered couch, and I persuaded him to stop beating you.'

"Mrs. —— said: 'How did you know all that, because it is quite true in every detail?' I told her, and some of my friends, of my dream. She and they are still marvelling.

"Can you throw any light or explanation on the matter?—remembering always that I had never met the lady before, and could not, therefore, be said to have been 'in love' with her."

I explained in reply that we are frequently told by etherians, when communicating with us, that when we are asleep our etheric bodies pass out and have experiences which are not remembered, except occasionally. I told him that it was quite possible that his etheric body passed out of his physical body and was taken by someone on the other side interested in Mrs. —— to witness what was taking place. I went on: "You saw her being beaten and tried to stop it, and then you returned to your physical body. So long as the silver cord between the physical and the etheric body is intact you can return to your physical body. I use the word 'silver cord', because it is the one used in the Bible, but you can call it the 'etheric cord' or anything else you like. It is the attachment between the etheric body and the physical body when they are apart.

Clairvoyants have seen this on many occasions, and they have even seen it dissolve when death takes place." So that was my reply.

I have had little experience of what is called materialisation, though I have read much about it. This phenomenon embraces the full materialisation of the so-called dead person who walks about the room, speaks, laughs and behaves like one of us. The most prolonged and careful investigation of this was made by Sir William Crookes, F.R.S., the famous physicist who published his experiences in *Researches in the Phenomena of Spiritualism* and elsewhere. His medium was Miss Florence Cook and his record is dated 30th March 1874. The materialised spirit gave her name as Katie King. He took numerous photographs of Katie, which I have seen, and also one of the medium and Katie together, and here I give his account of one of his many experiences with this medium:

"On March 12th 1874, during a séance here, after Katie had been walking amongst us and talking for some time, she retreated behind the curtain which separated my laboratory, where the company was sitting, from my library which did temporary duty as a cabinet. In a minute she came to the curtain and called me to her, saying: 'Come into the room and lift my medium's head up, she has slipped down.' Katie was then standing before me clothed in her usual white robes and turban head-dress. I immediately walked into the library up to Miss Cook, Katie stepping aside to allow me to pass.

"I found Miss Cook had partially slipped off the sofa, and her head was hanging in a very awkward position. I lifted her on to the sofa, and, in so doing, had satisfactory evidence, in spite of the darkness, that Miss Cook was not attired in the 'Katie' costume, but had on her ordinary black velvet dress, and was in a deep trance. Not more than three seconds elapsed between my seeing the white-robed Katie standing before me and my raising Miss Cook on to the sofa from the position into which she had fallen.

"I pass on to a séance held last night at Hackney. Katie never appeared to greater perfection, and for nearly two hours she walked about the room, conversing familiarly with those present.

"Katie now said she thought she should be able this time to show herself and Miss Cook together. I was to turn the gas out and then come with my phosphorous lamp into the room now used as a cabinet. This I did, having previously asked a friend who was skilful at shorthand to take down any statement I might make when in the cabinet, knowing the importance attaching to first impressions, and not wishing to leave more to memory than necessary. His notes are now before me.

"I went cautiously into the room, it being dark, and felt about for Miss Cook. I found her crouching on the floor. Kneeling down, I let air enter the lamp, and, by its light, I saw the young lady dressed in black velvet, as she had been in the early part of the evening, and to all appearance perfectly senseless. She did not move when I took her hand and held the light quite close to her face, but continued quietly breathing. Raising the lamp, I looked around and saw Katie standing close behind Miss Cook.

"She was robed in flowing white drapery as we

had seen her previously during the séance. Holding one of Miss Cook's hands in mine, and still kneeling, I passed the lamp up and down so as to illuminate Katie's whole figure and satisfy myself thoroughly that I was really looking at the veritable Katie whom I had clasped in my arms a few minutes before, and not at the phantasm of a disordered brain. She did not speak, but moved her head and smiled in recognition.

"Three separate times did I carefully examine Miss Cook crouching before me, to be sure that the hand I held was that of a living woman, and three separate times did I turn the lamp to Katie and examine her with steadfast scrutiny until I had no doubt whatever of her objective reality. At last Miss Cook moved slightly, and Katie instantly motioned me to go away. I went to another part of the cabinet and then ceased to see Katie, but did not leave the room till Miss Cook woke up, and two of the visitors came in with a light.

"Before concluding this article I wish to give some of the points of difference which I have observed between Miss Cook and Katie. Katie's height varies. In my house I have seen her six inches taller than Miss Cook. Last night with bare feet and no 'tip-toeing' she was four and a half inches taller than Miss Cook. Katie's neck was bare last night, the skin was perfectly smooth both to touch and sight, whilst on Miss Cook's neck is a large blister, which under similar circumstances is distinctly visible and rough to the touch. Katie's ears are unpierced, whilst Miss Cook habitually wears earrings. Katie's complexion is very fair, while that of Miss Cook is very dark. Katie's fingers are much longer than Miss Cook's, and her face is also larger.

In manners and ways of expression there are also many decided differences."

Sir William Crookes records many other séances with the medium Florence Cook when Katie King materialised. The numerous photographs he took make clear that his experiences were not due to hallucination or the medium impersonating Katie King, and until his death Sir William held firmly to all that he had recorded.

Finally I must mention just one more aspect of Spiritualism, and that is called automatic writing, when the hand of the writer is impelled to write about things of which he is not thinking. From time to time evidential information is given which is quite unknown to the automatist, but, on the other hand, much of what is written may come from the subconscious mind.

There are many phases of automatic writing, such as (1) writing in trance; (2) the more indifferent the automatist is, the more easily he will write; (3) writing something consciously with the right hand and unconsciously with the left, or *vice versa*; (4) writing in foreign languages unknown to the automatist; (5) writing in a character and style quite different from the automatist's normal; (6) writing coherently about things the automatist knows nothing of; (7) writing upside down; (8) writing backwards, each word spelt from the last letter to the first, yet readable and sensible when the paper is turned over and in this position held up to the light; and lastly (9) writing at great speed, Miss Geraldine Cummins producing parts of the *Scripts of Cleophas* at the rate of 2,000 words an hour.

Physical phenomena and psychic phenomena must be treated in different ways in our attempt to understand them. Physical knowledge is obtained by laboratory methods. We cannot dissect a living being to find the duplicate etheric body, which is invisible and must be discovered by other means. When the etheric body is in the physical body there is life, when out of the physical body and the connection broken life has gone. What psychic scientists have to rely on is the evidence we have of invisible life. A voice speaking from the void gives evidence of invisible life, and what the voice says indicates intelligence and personality. That is why Spiritualism is based on evidence, and to ignore the mountain of evidence that exists to-day, as so many do, is due to ignorance, prejudice and stupidity.

Some orthodox scientists, who have hitherto ignored the evidence, are beginning to think that they have been mistaken, and the following remark made over the radio in December 1954 by Antony Flew, the Professor of Philosophy at the University College of North Staffordshire, when giving a lecture on Psychical Research, is significant:

> "Most scientists never look at the evidence, we close our eyes, go to sleep, and hope that when we wake up the evidence will have vanished."

Orthodox Science has not yet found a place for psychic phenomena and, except for a few leading scientists over the past fifty years who have investigated it and accepted it, scientists as a body have ignored it, because it upsets their materialistic conception of the universe. Consequently, Spiritualists and their assertions have been treated with contempt by scientists and the Press, including the B.B.C., who remind me of Galileo who wanted the priests of his time to look through his newly invented telescope and see the spots on the sun and the mountains of the moon, but they would not.

An equally strong body of opinion has been against the Spiritualists, who have had to plough their lone furrow, with neither official science nor official religion to support them, and that is the Church. The Roman Catholic Church has been uncompromising in its opposition, and to it the spirits are devils, all Spiritualists being the servants of the devil. That has also been the attitude of the Protestant Church, and on many occasions Spiritualists have been termed from the pulpit the "servants of the devil", other equally rude remarks being made about them. The Anglican Church set up a committee to investigate Spiritualism, and its findings, arrived at in 1938, were favourable. Consequently, the bishops met and decided that the report was not to be published, and it was therefore suppressed.

Fortunately, for the sake of truth, a member of the committee was so angry about the suppression of this important document that he handed his copy over to the Editor of *Psychic News*, who published it, much to the annoyance of the Church authorities. Then, some years later in 1954, certain leading churchmen, doubtless impressed by this report, formed the Churches' Fellowship for Psychical Study, my two friends, the Honourable Sir Cyril Atkinson becoming President and Colonel Reginald Lester its Chairman. A number of leading clergymen joined its committee of management, and others gave it their blessing, one being Dr. W. R. Matthews, Dean of St. Paul's, and another the Bishop of Ripon. This is what Dr. Matthews had to say about Spiritualism in December 1954:

> "Anyone who is concerned to keep in touch with the development of thought must take note of the progress of psychical research, and the related subjects of faith-healing and Spiritualism. In my opinion we are on the verge of an important new insight into the nature of human personality."

Spiritualists have been saying this for the past hundred years, and the Bishop of Ripon is of the same opinion as is Dr. Matthews. This is what he had to say on the subject:

> "The recent growth of Spiritualism will at last compel the Church to look seriously upon Psychic Research, and perhaps discover, in days when it is sadly needed, a rich meaning in her own belief in the Communion of Saints."

The pioneers amongst the clergy, to whose work in the past this advance is partly due, must be gratified to find at last some progress being made, and I would particularly recall the stand taken in past years by my friends the late Reverend Dr. Lamond in the Presbyterian Church, and the Reverend Maurice Elliot in the Anglican Church, who refused to be silenced by their superiors. What an advance we are witnessing in our times. Some leading churchmen of our day are now accepting what Spiritualism stands for, whereas the clergy, up to the beginning of the 18th century, took the lead in burning or drowning witches, who, in many cases, were natural mediums.

Within our own times we have had the determined opposition of Church leaders to any enquiry into survival after death. Dr. William Temple, the late Archbishop of Canterbury, was outspoken in his opposition, his words being:

> "It is positively undesirable that there should be experimental proof of man's survival of death . . . it would make very much harder the essential business of faith, which is the transference of the centre of interest and concern from self to God."

These words will stand as a permanent monument to the Church's attitude towards Spiritualism, and I hope in the days to come all thinking people will be shocked that such was possible. Of course the explanation is that proved survival, and the knowlege that as we sow so shall we reap, is not to the liking of organised religion, as it proclaims that only through the doors of the Church can one find salvation. As I write this a leading Bishop has just announced, and was reported on the B.B.C., that "Man is a spiritual being but only through Christ can he be saved."

Nevertheless, I believe that the Christian Church, and all other world religions, will be forced by growing intelligence to absorb Spiritualism gradually, and allow their creeds and dogmas to fade into oblivion. It will come slowly, and may be little noticed, but it must come in time if the Church is to have any influence on future generations. "Semper idem",

"Always the same", cannot continue as its motto in this age of advancing thought and, if it is to survive, it must accommodate itself to the discoveries of our age.

What is called Science, the knowledge obtained by observation and experience, has so far held firmly to the belief that we live in an ordered universe, and anything supernormal must be ignored and ridiculed. It was the idea in Christendom up to within recent times that God's laws were contained in *The Holy Bible*, and had been revealed to man only through the Christian Church. So Giordano Bruno, Copernicus, Galileo and others were ignored, ridiculed, or persecuted and put to death, by the priests because they revealed to man nature's laws hitherto unknown. The laws had always been, and the work those early scientists performed was revealing them to an ignorant world. For the past hundred years Spiritualists have been asking Science to embrace within its boundaries age-old phenomena which they had sorted out in an orderly manner, only to receive the ridicule meted out to the pioneers of science some three to four hundred years ago.

Spiritualists do not claim to have discovered new phenomena, as what they accept has been taking place as far back as history goes. History and legends all tell of the interaction of a spirit world with the physical. Ancient literature refers to the direct voice, trance, materialisation, clairvoyance, clairaudience, apparitions, automatic writing, the Bible being one of the great psychic books of the world. The Pythagoreans and the Neo-Platonists were quite familiar with psychic phenomena. What present-day Spiritualists claim is, to have brought all these supernormal phenomena within our present-day knowledge. What goes under the name of Spiritualism has uncovered a world of beings who once lived on earth. It has humanised the dead, for so long regarded as vaporous creatures. This has been done in an orderly scientific way, and in marked contrast to the haphazard methods of the past which have come down to us as legends and exaggerated stories called miracles.

The Christian Church, after the 4th century, banished all psychic phenomena from its midst, and mediums, hitherto called "The Oracles of God", became known as "The Servants of the Devil". That was the work of Saint Jerome and Pope Damasus, and this unsavoury piece of Church history drove out Spiritualism, the life-spring of the early Church, and made its priests supreme. The facts will be found in *The Psychic Stream*. From that time onwards the Church claimed to be the only revealer of heaven to earth, and excommunicated, imprisoned or murdered all who ignored its commands.

As mental development proceeded, some timidly at first made the claim to believe only what was observed and experienced. Others did likewise, the numbers steadily increased and, as the power of the Church declined, what is now called Science slowly reared its head over a world steeped in ignorance. Western Europe then entered what is called the Age of Reason, when what hitherto had been called the laws of God became known as the laws of Nature. Thus we slowly accepted a universe of immutable fixed laws, every cause having its effect and every effect its cause. Unfortunately, the cause which had brought the numerous world religions into being was ignored and ridiculed, the result being that a materialistic outlook of the universe prevailed amongst the intellectuals.

Science had forgotten something, and it still ignores the fact that the visible physical world is not the only one to which we human beings are attached. There are two worlds influencing us, one the physical and the other the invisible etheric world. Science is concerned with the physical world and physical laws, but intrusions into its ideas take place which point to the fact that not only the physical exists, but something else as well. That is the point we have reached to-day, namely, the halting half-hearted admission by some scientists that there exists more than their philosophy has allowed for.

The invisible is intruding on the visible, and Science does not like it because this experience has never come within its reckoning. Nevertheless, Science must stand or fall by accepting or ignoring the basis on which it is built, to observe and to experience all things and never ignore anything. So far, except for the few, scientists have ignored psychic phenomena and, as Professor Flew, who is quoted some pages back, emphasised, most scientists never look at the evidence, they close their eyes and hope the evidence will vanish. That is a damning admission, and Science is as guilty of the suppression of facts as is religion.

If, as I believe, an invisible world, inhabited by invisible human beings who once lived on earth, is making itself realised in our age, which is capable of recording the evidence for it, there is nothing in that to scoff at, to jeer at or ignore. It does not upset the laws of nature. As in the time of Galileo, so to-day, the human mind is systematically recording something apparently new which, in the past, was loosely accepted and never accurately reported. Our ancestors mention supernormal phenomena, calling them supernatural, but they never recorded them in an orderly business-like way. Now that has been done by certain Spiritualists and psychical researchers, and we are no longer dependent on ancient writings, about which we have no evidence for their assertions.

The ignoring of some of the phenomena of nature by Science is probably due to prejudice, and has ended in ignorance. Science, because it ignored the possibility of an invisible world, pushed aside all the evidence for it and decided to reject phenomena which accounted for something it had decided did not exist. Consequently, to scientists in general all psychic phenomena were and are due to fraud, to hallucination, to bad observation and to human simplicity. Because of that, Spiritualism, in their opinion, is built up on fraud and folly, and Spiritualists, who only have been truly scientific, believing in what was experienced and observed, have been the outcasts of intellectual society.

As the Church will some day absorb the facts for which Spiritualism stands, so also will Science, slowly and gradually, only to find that the laws of the universe have not been upset by this greater knowledge. This new knowledge will add to and heighten existing knowledge. Science will be enriched by it, and a wider horizon will open before the human mind. Some day it will be generally accepted that life does not die at death, and that, instead of dying, a new world opens before it, the destiny of mankind being something far grander and nobler than human thought has so far ever dared to imagine.

At the close of the previous chapter I had reached the time when we had taken our farewell of Scotland and had set off for Stansted Hall in Essex. I shall now tell how we fared in our new home and what this change meant to us.

CHAPTER SIX.

STANSTED HALL.

(1925–1930.)

WE ARRIVED at Stansted Hall in February 1925, in the depth of winter. The trees at that time of the year have a decided charm, their leafless branches spreading upwards to form a pleasing picture against a Winter sky. In this part of Essex trees abound, and I know of no other place in Britain where finer ones are to be found. Around us are many Elms a hundred feet high, besides large and stately Oaks, Beeches, Chestnuts and Limes. South and west from the house they were planted to form vistas stretching for half a mile over undulating parkland, and rare specimen trees abound. If this so pleased us in Winter, I thought, what must it be like in Summer?

Stansted Hall is the second dwelling-house to be built on this delightful site. It stands two hundred and fifty feet above the sea, and to the north-west the land slopes down to a valley through which flows the Stansted Brook, a stream which, after passing through Stansted village, joins the River Stort on which is the old market town of Bishop's Stortford, three miles away, the birthplace of Cecil Rhodes.

Away back in 1066 the battle of Hastings was fought. It was won by the Normans, and the losers, the Saxons, became the bondsmen of their conquerors.

So William I took the lands of Stansted from their previous Saxon owners and gave them to Robert Gernon, one of his generals, in recognition of the help he had given in conquering the Saxons. William made him a baron, and he took the name of Baron Mountfitchet, the name of a village in Normandy, and that is why Stansted is called Stansted Mountfitchet.

Baron Mountfitchet built a castle on this land, and a piece of its wall is still standing, its entire outline being easily seen from the air as the foundations, though covered over, are still plainly visible. Centuries later, as fortified dwellings became unnecessary, the first Stansted Hall was built, and the old castle fell into ruins. This happened, I should think, about the end of the 16th century from the appearance of the picture I have of the first Stansted Hall, and, until the beginning of the 19th century, it was occupied by families who held a prominent position in the county.

I made a careful research into the history and previous owners of this property and, as I wish this preserved for future generations, I here give a copy of the document I prepared. Some gaps in the ownership exist, but this is the best I could do with the information available:

STANSTED HALL.

The Parish of Stansted was bestowed by William the Conqueror in 1066 on a Norman of the House of Bologne, Robert Gernon, whose name is on the Roll of Battle Abbey, and in Domesday Book is described as Robert Gernon, Baron Mountfitchet.

Robert Gernon built Stansted Castle. Since then the owners have been his son

William Gernon, founder of the Abbey of Stratford Langthorn, who took the name of Mountfitchet. His son

Gilbert de Mountfitchet. His son

Richard de Mountfitchet, created Forester of Essex in 1200, Sheriff of Essex and Hertfordshire in 1201 and Custodian of houses in the Forests belonging to King John. His son

Richard, who was one of the 25 Barons chosen in 1215 to govern the Realm in the reign of King John. In 1236 he was appointed Justice of the King's Forests of Essex and other counties. In 1242 he was appointed Sheriff of the counties of Essex and Hertford, and Governor of Hertford Castle. He died in 1258 without issue, and Stansted Castle reverted to his sister

Margery, wife of Hugh de Bolebec of Northumberland. Then succeeded her son

Walter de Bolebec. Then succeeded his son

Walter de Bolebec, who died without issue. Stansted Castle then reverted to

Roger de Lancaster, Baron of Kendal, who married Philippa, daughter of Hugh de Bolebec. He died in 1290, and his wife in 1293, leaving their son

John de Lancaster (died 1334), who sold the estate to

Thomas de Vere, son of Robert, third Earl of Oxford, in which family it remained till 1461, when the estate was confiscated because the twelfth Earl of Oxford, who was beheaded, was a Lancastrian. King Henry VII then conferred the estate in 1485 on

Queen Elizabeth, widow of King Edward IV. On her death Henry VII returned the estate to

The Earl of Oxford, in which family it remained
till the 17th Earl, when it passed in 1582 to

John Southall, and then to

Edward Hubbard, Clerk in Chancery. Then to his
son

Sir Francis Hubbard, who sold the estate in 1615 to

Sir Thomas Middleton, Kt., Alderman, Sheriff, and
in 1613 Lord Mayor of London (died 1631),
brother of Sir Hugh Middleton (friend of Sir
Walter Raleigh) who planned and constructed
the New River with the financial help of King
James I in order to supply fresh water to London.
Stansted Hall remained in the Middleton family
for several generations till Thomas Middleton (a
member of four successive parliaments in Queen
Anne's reign) died, without male issue, in 1710.
Estate then purchased by

Thomas Heath, Member of Parliament for Harwich,
and son of William Heath, an eminent Captain in
the East India Company's service. He died in
1714 and was succeeded by

Bailey Heath, Sheriff of Essex 1747, who died in
1760 and was succeeded by

William Heath, who was succeeded by

Bailey Heath, who died 1818. Family became
extinct. Stansted Hall was then bought by

E. Fuller-Maitland, who died 1858 and was succeeded
by his son

William Fuller-Maitland, who died in 1876 and was
succeeded by his son

William Fuller-Maitland, who in 1922 sold Stansted
Hall to

Sir Albert Ball, who in 1923 sold it to

James Arthur Findlay, M.B.E., J.P.

The foregoing was compiled from information
extracted from *MORANT'S HISTORY OF
ESSEX* and *RUSH'S SEATS IN ESSEX*

Early last century the first Stansted Hall was burnt
down, only one of the towers being left standing, and
that also went in time, so that its underground drain-
age system is all that now remains.　Fortunately, its
beautiful Adams fireplaces of Italian marble were
saved, and, in 1871, when the second Stansted Hall was
commenced, they were placed therein.　The new house
made its appearance near to the site of the old one,
it being a large and handsome structure built at great
cost over a period of seven years, the ceilings of the
ground-floor rooms, moulded by workmen specially
brought from Italy, being of beautiful design.

Its architect, Robert Armstrong, was a man of
great talent, as his modern Elizabethan architecture
fitted perfectly into the old surroundings.　He erected
a noble dwelling in keeping with the past history of
its situation, but modern in every respect, fireproof,
steel girders instead of wooden beams, everything
where it should be, and its large windows give ample
light to its spacious and well-designed rooms.　Armstrong would have become an outstanding member
of his profession, but he only lived long enough to
carry out one other residence of the same size.

The County of Essex, which had now become our
home, has played a prominent part in the history of
our island.　Close to Stansted runs the old Roman
Road from St. Albans to Colchester.　Its old name

for most of this distance was Stane Street, or Stone Street, just as Stansted means stone steading. To the Romans this road was a vital link in the pacification of the country, and in those days it ran through a vast forest, as most of Essex then was. When the Romans withdrew they left Essex open to the Saxon invaders. Then developed a small Saxon kingdom, to become the main battleground in the long struggle between the Saxons and the Danes. For some three hundred years it had a chequered existence, sometimes independent and at other times the vassal of either the powerful state of Mercia or of Wessex, to become later absorbed into Wessex and finally form part of a united England.

Then came the last of the invaders, the Normans, to bring internal conflicts to an end, and both Saxon and Dane became the serfs of their new overlords. England, at last, was at peace and, as the centuries passed, Essex grew rich from the wool trade with Flanders, some of its finest churches being the outcome of the wealth it produced. Thaxted, eight miles from Stansted, became the centre of the cutlery industry, its old prosperity still showing itself in the magnificent perpendicular church built from the money then made. The old borough of Saffron Walden is ten miles from Stansted on the way to Cambridge, it also having a fine perpendicular church, but, besides these centres, there are attractive villages and hamlets dotted about the countryside with their old Tudor cottages, some villages having their village greens. All is unspoilt and rural, and no one would realise, when traversing the many good side roads, that London is to most of these places not more than about thirty to forty miles away, Stansted being thirty-four.

It is said that if a man retires from his profession he should do so when he is young enough to take up something new, and, if he is too old for that, he should not retire at all. Fortunately, I was young enough to be able to interest myself in all the opportunities which had opened up before me. I was forty-one years of age, strong, healthy, and energetic. So I bent my energies to farming, and for six years gave much of my thought to building up a dairy farm, for which the land was specially suitable.

The existing farm buildings, half a mile from Stansted Hall, were old-fashioned and out of date. So everything was removed and new buildings erected, after I had made a close study of modern farming methods. Consequently, it became a Grade A farm, the first in the district. I never had any training as a farmer, but I am glad to say, after many years of experience, that if I rebuilt the farm to-day I would do so exactly as I did then. When completed, I engaged an experienced bailiff to look after a herd of eighty Shorthorn cattle and the cultivation of the land.

When all this was done a business of some size had been created, and this gave me much pleasure as the work of creation should always do. Over three hundred acres of land were thus used for agriculture, the rest of the estate being made up of woodlands, garden and the pleasure grounds surrounding the Hall. Some ten miles of fencing had to be maintained, and, besides this, private roads and many houses, large and small, on the estate required to be kept in repair. So gardeners, farm-workers and other craftsmen were employed and had to be supervised, all of which meant work, but it was all enjoyable and of great interest. Nevertheless, the fact remained that I had not really retired, when I gave up my business in Glasgow, as I had only exchanged one interest for another, but my new one was in the country and not in a town. Moreover, I could spend the day as I liked, which made all the difference.

To live in a county where the rainfall is moderate, to have the sun shining more often than it does in most parts of the country, and the sky less leaden, is a joy in itself, but to be able to ramble over one's own land each day greatly heightens it, especially if one has an object in view. I always took with me a notebook, and there was generally something to be noted that required attention. So I could spend several hours a day enjoying the walking on the springy turf of my own land with the object of improving it, or looking after the woodlands. No wonder, I sometimes thought, men will forgo an office life, with its better pay, to remain on the land and thus live a more natural life of greater freedom.

I now discovered that there was much dissatisfaction amongst dairy farmers about the way magistrates were dealing with those who occasionally sold milk which had less than three per cent of butter fat. Adulteration of the milk was presumed, and the retailer too often convicted. The truth was that the cows themselves were in many cases giving poor milk, and the retailer was not to blame. The law allowed for this, but the honest farmer found it difficult to prove his case, as cows vary in the percentage of butter fat they produce. The sample complained of one day quite possibly would have complied with the standard of three per cent. if taken the next day. Several convictions in our neighbourhood made me look into the matter, and see what could be done to secure justice for the honest farmer.

Everyone who sold milk was in danger of being in this unenviable position sooner or later, and to right a wrong I had a long correspondence with the Chief Inspector of Weights and Measures for Essex. He said he had to administer the law and could not help me. I then went to the Ministry of Agriculture and saw several leading officials, who sympathised, but could not do more than that. One stated that as the law was administered he would never be a milk-producer. Finally I decided to make out my case in pamphlet form, and send a copy to each Member of Parliament and the Chairman of every Justice of the Peace Court in the country. The pamphlet, entitled *The Law Relating to Butter Fat in Milk*, stating the case and giving copies of the correspondence which had taken place, ran into twenty-seven pages and received much publicity. I am glad to feel that, when the position was understood by the magistrates, honest farmers who were summoned obtained greater justice than they had received in the past. The pamphlet still circulates and goes on doing its good work to this day.

Gradually my outside interests grew as I came to be known by my neighbours. I became active on the Essex Committee of the League of Nations. Then I was asked to join the Executive Committee of the Saffron Walden Conservative Association, one of our duties being to select a new candidate in place of Sir William Foot Mitchell, who wished to retire after being Conservative M.P. for the Saffron Walden division for many years. In 1929 our choice fell on R. A. Butler, now the Chancellor of the Exchequer, then a young man of twenty-seven, who has been our Member ever since. I was next asked to become a member of the Board of Management of both the Bishop's Stortford Hospital and the Saffron Walden Hospital, on which I served for many years.

I was elected a member of the Stansted Rural District Council, and soon afterwards I became chairman, to remain so for several years until it was absorbed by the Saffron Walden Rural District Council when I retired. During my term as chairman the council was responsible for carrying out the first considerable building scheme in the district, and I am glad to think that I managed to bring into operation the Humane Killer for the slaughter of animals in the district. Thus these creatures came to a painless end by electrocution, instead of being butchered to death as had been the practice heretofore.

I became a Justice of the Peace for Essex and, as such, adjudicated on several shocking cases of cruelty to children, besides many major and minor offences. This office also called for my presence on the Bench at the Quarter Sessions at Chelmsford, where the more serious cases came up for trial. Lunacy, or mental cases, required the sanction of a Justice before long confinement was allowed, and I remember one case which gave me serious thought before my consent was given. However, after I visited the woman at the mental home, I had no reason to regret my decision as it was quite obvious that she was in the right place under care and supervision.

My wife, as I have previously said, is very sociable and a born hostess. If I have said little about her so far, the omission has been at her own request, as she wishes no publicity. In fact, I feel the same myself, as it is not my desire so constantly to use the personal pronoun, but, if this were not done, no autobiography would ever be written. Many people, I am told, like to read an account of the lives of those whose books they read, and it is some of these who have read my books who have urged me on to this task of writing about my experiences during an interesting but not spectacular life.

Stansted Hall was never dull, my daughter Joan, her friend Jean, the dogs, and any guests we may have making for joy and gladness. It always was, and still is, a very happy home with harmony prevailing, and our interest in those around us helps to make it more so. From time to time we have opened the grounds, or had dances and concerts in the house for charitable purposes, and this has not only been for the benefit of a good object, but has brought much pleasure to those who attended them.

The library at Stansted Hall is a spacious room, and round three of its walls rest some three thousand volumes. Let me take you into it and shew you some of them. Here are many volumes on history from early times, and then we come to the books on comparative religion. Here, the thirty-three volumes of the *Encyclopaedia Britannica* take up several yards of space, and these Hundred Best Books, all bound the same, do likewise. Now we see the books I have collected dealing with psychical research and Spiritualism. Thousands of books have been published on this subject, but I shall mention just a few of these, which I consider to be among the best published.

This one entitled *The Voices* by Admiral Usborne Moore was published in 1913, and covers many direct voice séances held with Mrs. Etta Wriedt when she came over from the United States to this country in that year. The Admiral not only records his own experiences but gives in full the reports made by the friends he took to these séances, all reporting the voices speaking to them about events quite unknown to the medium. Those two books by Dennis Bradley, called *The Wisdom of the Gods* and *Towards the Stars*, record the wonderful séances he had for the direct voice with George Valiantine, when he invited to be present in his own home some of the outstanding people in London. This two-volumed book is Frederic Myers' *Human Personality and its Survival of Bodily Death*, the first serious attempt to classify and unify supernormal occurrences. Here is Dr. Nandor Fodor's *Encyclopaedia of Psychic Science*, a great and comprehensive undertaking.

This book here, called *Psychic Adventures in New York*, is written by Dr. Neville Whymant, the world-famous authority on oriental languages. At numerous direct voice séances, from 1926 onwards, when George Valiantine was the medium, he heard fourteen foreign languages spoken, and conversed with the speakers. They included Chinese, Hindi, Persian, Basque, Sanskrit, Arabic, Portuguese, Italian, Yiddish, German and Greek. On one occasion he heard a voice speaking archaic Chinese of the Confucian period. When he asked questions in the same language concerning the correct interpretation of certain poems from the *Shih King* of Confucius, which had puzzled scholars of Chinese for generations, and had been the subject of endless controversies, the voice immediately replied, explaining and correcting the passages, which made them quite understandable. He asked question after question, and received replies which only an advanced scholar in oriental languages could understand, and no one else on earth. The voice claimed to be that of Confucius, but, whether it was or not, an intelligence was present which ruled out the possibility of the information coming from the medium. This Dr. Whymant accepted, and, from being an utter disbeliever, he came to accept the fact that those voices speaking these numerous languages came from intelligences beyond this world.

An old but good book is *Footfalls on the Boundary of Another World* by Robert Dale Owen, a man prominent in the political life of the United States, and this is Sir William Barrett's *On the Threshold of the Unseen*, a selection of carefully attested supernormal cases. Here is Professor Zöllner's book *Transcendental Physics*, an account of his many strange experiences with supernormal phenomena. The three books *Experiments in Psychical Science*, *The Reality of Psychic Phenomena* and *Psychic Structures* by W. J. Crawford, Doctor of Science and lecturer in mechanical engineering at Queen's University, Belfast, record the first attempt by a trained engineer to account for the movement of objects in the séance room without physical contact. How he did it, and the great success he attained in proving the reality of this type of supernormal phenomena, is recorded in these three books.

Another scientist's account of his successful investigation into psychic phenomena is contained in *Life after Death* by James Hyslop, Ph.D., LL.D., Secretary of the American Society for Psychical Research, and former Professor of Logic and Ethics in Columbia University. He concludes that the case for survival is abundantly proved. Here is the book of another scientist, a famous biologist, *Miracles and Modern Spiritualism* by Alfred Russell Wallace, F.R.S., who states categorically that the only explanation of psychic phenomena is that it is the work of the spirits of the dead. Another book entitled *Apparitions and Haunted Houses* by my friend Sir Ernest Bennett, a scholar and politician, records numerous cases of well-attested apparitions.

But I shall not keep you much longer. You will realise that I have referred to only a fraction of the books I have on this subject, and only two more will be mentioned. The first is *Researches in the Phenomena of Spiritualism*, in which Sir William Crookes F.R.S. gives his experiences during his investigation into the phenomena. He certainly had more extraordinary experiences than most other investigators, the account of the materialisation of Katie King, already mentioned, and the many photographs he took of her, being rare in the annals of psychical research. Lastly, here is the record and the photographs of the supernormal phenomena which occurred at direct voice séances, and admirably produced by Harry Edwards in his book *The Mediumship of Jack Webber*, which indeed is most convincing. I could go on and mention many more, but I have much more to tell.

I continued my interest in finance and remained a director of the Dominion and General Trust which I helped to form in 1910. It developed into a very successful concern, and I travelled to Glasgow once a month for directors' meetings. I also became a member of Lloyds, but that involved little work as I have agents who underwrite the risks for me. The history of this famous institution goes back to 1687, when it was a coffee house in the City of London, frequented by shipowners, seafarers and merchants who had a common interest in shipping and marine insurance. This coffee house in time evolved into a kind of club which developed into a market, to become the world centre for the insurance of ships and cargoes. Membership involves unlimited liability, but the risks are so widely spread that heavy individual losses are rare. Consequently, as the gains as a rule outweigh the losses, membership is much sought after, but strictly limited because of the large amount of capital one has to put up.

I became a member of the Society for Psychical Research in 1920, but, as I did not approve of the methods of the Council, I resigned in 1932. This is a society, founded in 1882, whose members subscribe to receive a *Journal* and *Proceedings* as they are published. As a Society it has no opinions, but its members have varied opinions and some express them publicly. Some are Spiritualists, and some prefer to say that they are interested in Psychical Research and not commit themselves as to why or how the phenomena occurs, but all agree in the importance of examining supernormal occurrences. The Society, especially in its early days, did splendid work under the direction of men notable in various walks of life, and the mass of evidence for survival it has collected in its publications is amazing. If nothing besides this existed there would be ample evidence to support the beliefs held by Spiritualists, and some of its most distinguished members acknowledged this to be so.

Richard Hodgson became its Research Officer in 1884. He may aptly be called one of the greatest investigators into trance phenomena, and, from complete scepticism, he was compelled by facts to reverse his former unbelief, to end as a convinced Spiritualist. His chief contribution to Psychical Research was his long and accurate investigation of the phenomena produced for many years through the mediumship of Mrs. Piper, of Boston, Mass., U.S.A. This was one of the most solid achievements of his life, and his years of labour can be summed up in his own words.

> "I have no doubt," he wrote, "but that the chief communicators to whom I have referred . . . are veritably the personalities they claim to be, that they have survived the change we call death, and that they have directly communicated with us whom we call living through Mrs. Piper's entranced organism."

What, of course, is greatly needed in this country is a Chair for Psychical Research at one of our universities, occupied by a professor who understands his subject and is prepared to follow where the facts lead. In America there is Dr. J. B. Rhine, the Director of the Parapsychological Laboratory at Duke University,

Durham, in North Carolina. In him it has an un-biased researcher who keeps to facts, makes no irresponsible statements, and looks on mediums as the means nature has provided to furnish us with increased knowledge of our make-up and destiny. To him we are largely indebted for the more favourable attitude now adopted by scientists towards psychic phenomena, and this is his latest pronouncement on the subject.

"Thus the scientific tests that were initiated by prophetic dreams have already led to the discovery of a new fact about the human mind, a discovery so radical as to call for an eventual revolution in basic human thought.

"Perhaps the most significant fact that has emerged is this: there is now known to be present in human personality an aspect that is unbounded by the space and time of matter—hence a non-physical or spiritual aspect. Its boundaries and its capacity for growth may well be beyond the limits of our present powers to conceive."

In his last book, called *New World of the Mind*, published in 1955, he is even more definite, and accepts certain phenomena as coming from deceased individuals who have survived death. In other words, he has become a Spiritualist.

In my spare time, when I was able to put aside the daily duties of life, I was very interested in what we to-day would call psychic phenomena in ancient litera-ture. I visited the British Museum and got to know the curators, the result being that I discovered many ancient things of interest to Spiritualists and Psychical Researchers. At one time I thought of writing a book to be entitled *Spiritualism in Ancient Literature*, and I have still beside me my notes, extracts, and references. However much I tried, I could not make a readable book out of these. I could not combine them into a coherent whole, they being so scattered in their origin. Instead of a book it would have become a kind of encyclopaedia which would not have been of general interest.

It is, of course, impossible to give more than a glimpse of the ancient literature which covers what we to-day call Spiritualism, but let me tell briefly just a few of the outstanding stories which I have collected. One of the greatest discoveries is contained in what is called the Gilgamish epic, believed to be at least four thousand years old. It was found inscribed on broken pieces of baked clay tablets in Nineveh between the years 1850 and 1872 by two famous Assyriologists, Layard and George Smith. The hero, Gilgamish, was King of South Babylonia and the story deals with his adventures and those of his friend, Enkidu.

The tablets include the famous legend of the Deluge, and from them we discover the source of many legends with which we are familiar in Greek and Hebrew literature. The epic is a long tale of the adventures of these two heroes, and of how Gilgamish set out to find the elixir of life. It contains accounts of dreams, visions, prayers and psychic occurrences, and tells how, after Enkidu died, Gilgamish, with the help of one named Nergal, a medium, saw, spoke to and embraced his dead friend. Thus he found the elixir of life which was not never-ending life on earth, but life after death in the etheric world. This must be the oldest psychic story in the world, and from it

the Greeks probably copied their legend of the
expedition of the Argonauts in their search for the
Golden Fleece.

What is called *Book of the Dead*, a title given to the
great collection of funerary texts which the Egyptian
scribes composed for the benefit of the dead, makes
clear that the ancient Egyptians not only believed in
an after-life, but pictured it as like their life on earth.
Here is a story from the days of ancient Egypt which
I have greatly shortened.   Khonsemheb, a high priest
some three thousand years ago, was at prayer in his
temple and when he looked up he saw the ghostly
figure of a man beside him.   Not only did he see him
but he heard these words: "I am the spirit of King
Rehotep's chief treasurer.   I was representative of the
army and the head of men and nigh unto the gods,"
and then the spirit went on to tell what the King had
done for him when he died, and how the King had
built a pyramid for his tomb of alabaster.   The high
priest was chided by the spirit for the neglect of his
tomb and, after many words of rebuke, the ghost
melted away.   The tomb was repaired and the ghost
returned to the priest to say "It is well."

One of the best accounts of an ancient séance is to
be found in the old book *De Anima* written by Tertullian in 202 of the Christian era.   He is accepted as
one of the most eminent advocates of the early
Christian faith, and ranks after Augustine as the
greatest of its literary exponents.   He was an advocate
by profession, and deplored how the bishops were
departing from the way intended by the apostles, because of their opposition to the use of those psychic
gifts advocated by the Apostle Paul, which, Tertullian

tells us, had been practised from the time of Jesus till his day. He was the leader of the Christian Spiritualists of his time and this is what he tells us went on in his church:

"For seeing that we acknowledge spiritual charismata, or gifts, we too have merited the attainment of the prophetic gift. We have now amongst us a sister whose lot it has been to be favoured with sundry gifts of revelation, which she experiences in the spirit by ecstatic vision amidst the sacred rites of the Lord's Day in the church. She converses with angels, and sometimes even with the Lord. She both sees and hears mysterious communications. Some men's hearts she understands, and to them who are in need she distributes remedies. Whether it be in the reading of the Scriptures, or in the chanting of psalms, or in the preaching of sermons, or in the offering up of prayers, in all these religious services, matter and opportunity are afforded her of seeing visions.

"It may possibly have happened to us, whilst this sister of ours was wrapt in the spirit, that we had discoursed in some ineffable way about the soul. After the people are dismissed at the conclusion of the sacred services, she is in the regular habit of reporting to us whatever things she may have seen in vision, for all her communications are examined with the most scrupulous care, in order that their truth may be probed. 'Amongst other things,' says she, 'there has been shown to me a soul in bodily shape, and a spirit has been in the habit of appearing to me, not, however, a void and empty illusion, but such as would offer itself to be even grasped by the hand, soft and transparent and of an ethereal colour, and in form resembling that of a human being in every respect.'

"This was her vision, and for her witness there was God, and the apostle Paul most assuredly foretold that there were to be spiritual gifts in the Church."

Anyone reading this who knows anything of Spiritualism would place this lady medium in the category of a trance, materialisation, clairvoyant and clairaudient medium, and what took place in Tertullian's church takes place in our own time all the world over in Spiritualist churches, when the medium gives a trance address, to be followed by clairvoyance and clairaudience. If it had not been for Jerome and Pope Damasus, backed up by the priests who resented the people preferring a Spiritualist service to the service taken over from Mithraism, the Spiritualist form of service, as told by Tertullian, might have continued without a break throughout the Christian era, as it had done to the 3rd century from Apostolic times. The priests proved too strong for the Spiritualists, and Jerome and Damasus, both unsavoury creatures, drove them out of the Church in the 4th century, from which time onwards mediums were called the Servants of the Devil, to be burned or drowned as witches, they having hitherto been known as Oracles of God.

On going through all the cuttings and references to Spiritualism in ancient literature I have collected, I am amazed at the mass of information I have gathered together under this subject, and realise how valuable a collection such as this would be in encyclopaedic form. From early times the people of the other world have been making their presence felt on the inhabitants of earth, and these records remain with us to-day, some crudely incorporated into the various world religions. For each religious belief held by the faithful everywhere, a psychic experience can be traced as the cause. Let me give one instance which should be known to every Christian, but is not, it being perhaps known to a few. The Holy Ghost, which became one of the three gods of the Christian Trinity, by the majority resolution carried after much quarrelling at the Council of Nicaea in 325, came from what the early Christians called the Holy or Divine Spirit, their name for what we to-day call the medium's spirit control or spirit guide.

The discovery by a Greek bishop of an ancient Christian work, written in Greek, has immensely extended the range of our knowledge of mediumship in the early Christian Church. This discovery was made in 1873 by Philotheus Bryennius, Metropolitan Bishop of Nicomedia. In that year he discovered the precious volume in the library of the Jerusalem Monastery of the Most Holy Sepulchre at Constantinople, and published it to the world in 1883. This manuscript is known as *The Teaching of the Twelve Apostles*, though it is generally spoken of as *The Didache*. Professor Harnack, and other authorities, put its date at about 130–150, and it is not likely to be much later than that, as it is quoted by Clement of Alexandria who died in 220.

Therein we have an unblemished account of primitive Christianity, to which I give the name Jesuism. There was no Christianity in those days, the Jesuians being unitarians, believing in only one God, Jehovah. Trinitarian Christianity did not develop until the 4th century, when it adopted the Pagan religious beliefs, as will be told in a later chapter. Jesuism is mostly made up of moral teachings, as the Incarnation, the Atonement, the Sacraments, and other doctrines and rites are passed by unnoticed in *The Didache*. Though we find therein nothing to support Christian doctrine and dogma, much is said with regard to psychic gifts which, during the period when this work was written, evidently continued in the early Church, just as they did in the times of the apostles. The early Church, in the 2nd century, before Christianity had been built up from Paganism in the 4th century, consisted of a community of Jesuians intent on living good and pure lives in anticipation of their Lord's return. During the interval they were consoled by communications which they believed came from the etheric world to which he had gone.

From *The Didache* we discover two things of especial interest, namely, that mediums were employed by the Jesuians in their churches in the 2nd century, and also that "Every medium that speaketh in the spirit ye shall not try nor judge, for every sin shall be forgiven but this sin shall not be forgiven." So we now know that these early Jesuians were aware of what was the sin against the holy spirit which, after mediumship was abolished, no Christian understood. Moreover, priests, in their sermons, have at one time and another made use of this undefined sin to influence their congregations in the way they wished them to think.

The words attributed to Jesus in the Revised

Version of *Matthew*, that all sins will be forgiven "but the blasphemy against the Spirit shall not be forgiven" (Matt. xii, 31), has caused as much misery as the fear of Hell. Millions of Christians in the past have lived in misery for fear of having committed this unforgivable sin, and now it turns out to be nothing worse than judging the spirit control of a medium. Everyone has the right to question and to doubt, but in those days of old, when it was considered that the spirit controlling the medium was a divine being, or a god, it was far otherwise, and all criticism was silenced by the critic being told that to criticise the holy spirit was a sin which would never be forgiven. Whether this spirit is holy or unholy matters nothing, he or she being judged, in our more enlightened age, not by his or her holiness, but by what is said through his medium.

The discovery of this old work enables us to realise the reverence the early Jesuians had for mediums and their spirit controls, but, when these discarnate beings were forgotten after the 4th century and the sin was undefined, how easy it was for the simple to imagine that they had committed this unforgivable sin. Besides the terrible misery it has caused, many have become insane thinking about some evil they may have done which, on the Judgment Day, would be termed the sin against the holy spirit.

If we go back to ancient history we find quite a number of outstanding men and women whom we to-day would describe as mediums. Many lesser known, doubtless, also lived, but their gifts have not been recorded. I recall to mind, for instance, the great Hebrew leader, Moses, whom I try to show in *The Psychic Stream* was controlled by one who was given the name of Jehovah, or Yaweh, meaning Rain Cloud, who became the god of the Hebrews. Then there was Deborah, the Hebrew Joan of Arc who, following the advice of the voices she heard, led her countrymen to victory. Samuel was a medium, in fact he was at the head of a college of mediums (1 Samuel xix, 20), and the Bible is full of psychic events. In many cases what has been translated as "the Lord said" should have been given as "a spirit said", but in those days when voices spoke out of the void, or a medium spoke in trance, everyone, both Jew and Gentile, thought the voice was the voice of God or one of the gods. All the mediumistic gifts are mentioned in the Bible in some place or other, and Paul summarises and commends them in the first Epistle to the Corinthians. Livy, the Roman historian, wrote a book on psychic healing.

Elsewhere we read of the miracles and sayings of other mediums. Krishna, the Hindu Christ, was evidently a medium, as was Pythagoras, the esoteric philosopher, and Orpheus, who was called the divine man. Socrates was a medium and greatly influenced Plato. Apollonius of Tyana was a medium, as was Jesus, and what is called the words and deeds of both these two mediums were in each case incorporated into a new religion. Plotinus, the neo-Platonist, was a medium and greatly influenced early Christian thought. Mahomet had undoubtedly mediumistic gifts, but the man who, by his mediumship, had the greatest influence on the world was undoubtedly Paul of Tarsus, who, from his writings, evidently believed that he was controlled by Jesus. His psychic experiences changed not only his life but, by his strong personality, he was the cause of the Pagan world ultimately being brought to believe in Jesus, his control, as the heavenly Christ. Lastly I have space for only one more, namely Lucius Apuleius, the author of the famous old story *The Golden Ass*, who was a medium, but these are only representative outstanding mediums and there are others to be found in ancient literature.

What then did the Pagans think of Spiritualism? Many early Christians were Spiritualists. Were their Pagan contemporaries likewise? The masses then, as now, were wedded to the religions in which they were nurtured, but then, as now, some intellectuals believed, as is the case to-day, that an invisible order of beings exists who are seen and heard at times, while others scoffed and jeered. Cicero (106–43 B.C.) championed the Spiritualists and wrote two treatises putting forward his views. Cicero was a great man in his day, an advocate, an orator, a statesman, a man of letters, and a representative of the highest culture, both moral and intellectual, of the Roman world.

In him we have one of the foremost men of an age of greatness prominently advocating what Spiritualism stands for, and remarking that it was believed in by many down the ages in all parts of the known world. His views can be encompassed in these words:

"They whose minds scorn the limitations of the body are honoured with the frequent appearance of the spirits. Their voices have been often heard, and

they have appeared in forms so visible that he who
doubts it must be partly bereft of reason."

My answer to the latter part of that remark is this:
To believe in the interaction which takes place between
the two different orders of beings one must have a
psychic experience, which means evidential proof.
Each one must learn for himself until the time comes
when everyone will believe in a general kind of way,
just as we accept other things we personally have never
proved.   Some will read about other people's psychic
experiences and be interested, but to know that it is
true each must experience for himself or herself.   That
is why Spiritualism is so little understood, as the
majority have had no personal experience and consequently take no interest in it.   To them Spiritualists
are a peculiar people, and not understood by the
majority who have had no opportunity to learn.

To me, and others like me, who have no psychic
gifts, the world was a material affair made up of what
we see, feel and touch.   If I had not had my psychic
experiences, that would have been the sum and substance of my belief to-day.   I consider that I was
fortunate, but the vast majority of the people I move
amongst have never been so favoured and why should
I chide them for their ignorance? Far better to be
tactful and never argue, or even discuss, the subject
with the ignorant, as little can come of it.   Ignorance
is the reason why so much rubbish is spoken and
written about Spiritualism, but mental development
will come in time.

It took seventy years after Copernicus proved that
the earth went round the sun, and not the sun round

the earth, before it was believed by the most intelligent. The obvious is not always the truth, just as it is not the truth that matter is solid, that we are just beings of flesh and blood, and that nothing exists that we cannot see or feel.

My interest in those ancient worthies to whom I have just referred was intensified when it became clear to me that mediumship must have been the cause of their supernormal doings and sayings. Then I turned my attention to the beliefs of primitive people, those living more closely to nature, and discovered that before organised priestly religion took possession of men's minds Ancestor worship had been practised throughout the world, in fact it was the only religion. They worshipped their ancestors, and, by means of their psychic gifts, they communicated with them. This happens to-day amongst primitive people who accept naturally psychic phenomena which the more cultured races have largely rejected or neglected.

I was fortunate one day to come across in a book-shop the two volumes of *A History of Experimental Spiritualism* written by Caesar de Vesme, a scholarly book which was laureated by the French Academy of Science. The first volume deals with the psychic deeds and beliefs of primitive people, and tells how psychic phenomena are the cause of their religious beliefs and superstitions. He takes the reader from one part of Africa to another, through North and South America and on to Asia and Australasia, giving extracts from reports made by travellers and mission-aries about the supernormal happenings amongst the natives of these lands.

The second volume is equally interesting, as herein

he deals with Spiritualism amongst civilised people of bygone days, the Egyptians, the Hebrews, the Chaldeans, the Persians, the Phoenicians, the Etruscans, the Kelts, Aztecs, Incas, the ancient Greeks and the Romans. What happens to-day happened in those far-off days, and it occurred to me how much better the deeds and beliefs of the ancients would be understood by our anthropologists if they had the knowledge possessed by Spiritualists. What a misfortune it was that Sir James Frazer was ignorant of this subject when he wrote his masterpiece *The Golden Bough*. He amassed in his twelve volumes an immense array of facts, but he could only record them and not account for them. He told us of the effects, but not the causes which produced them.

During a busy life I have managed to accumulate a great amount of knowledge which our schools, colleges and universities ignore. Fortunately, I have a good memory for anything of a scientific or historical nature, and I look back with thankfulness on the fact that I was not only able to remember what I read but to arrange it in my mind in an orderly way. After I had cleared the ground of the refuse deposited therein by my early religious teaching I was able to build anew, freed from the ignorance and superstition of the past.

My mind had been cleansed, and was now fit to receive knowledge based on observation and experience. Had this not been done before Spiritualism had entered my life I would have been befogged and bewildered in an attempt to make the new knowledge fit in with orthodox Christianity. With that first cleared away my mind was open to receive what came

my way without prejudice. Now I knew that religion, as accepted by Hindu, Moslem, Jew, Christian,
or any other form of faith, is historically, and in places
ethically, false in its outlook and teaching. So I was
able, when the truth of Spiritualism came to me, to
place all orthodox religions in their right perspective.

The origin of Religion is not what the faithful in a
particular form of faith call a divine revelation to the
people who believe. Neither is it due, as the material-
ists claim, to the imagination of the ignorant and
superstitious without a soul, who were in fear of what
follows after death. No, neither of these causes produced the effects we now call religion, but rather it is
a revelation through psychic phenomena that has
always been with all mankind of an invisible world of
beings around us.

Those supernormal happenings have revealed to
those who have experienced them that another world,
invisible but very real, is about us, and that to it we
pass at death. Death, we now know, is not a curse
on mankind for his wickedness, as was hitherto believed, but a natural event, just like birth, and the
place in which we shall find ourselves after death
depends on our character, and not on the religious
beliefs we have adopted on earth. As we sow, so
shall we reap, as our character is, so shall be our place
hereafter. Orthodox religion is a crutch and nothing
more, but it is a great help to many through life who
know no better.

Religion, moreover, as the word is understood by
the majority on earth, is the natural instinctive outcome of the fact that each of us has a destiny after

death. However, since the time of Ancestor Worship, when the etheric world was such a reality to mankind, religion has tended to become an organised, regularised, priestly affair. Supernormal phenomena was only experienced by the few, but each and all have a duplicate etheric body which has to find a place in the hereafter. Whether the instinct that this is so is strong or weak, everyone more or less feared death, which fear has had a tremendous effect on history. This fear of death made religion a universal affair, and it is equally true that if man had no soul or destiny, religion would be unknown.

The fact that religion exists everywhere throughout the world is one of the many proofs that man is an etheric being, and is made up of more than flesh and blood. He needed religion to help him through life, to comfort him, to give him something to lean upon, and to soothe his fearful mind about his destiny after death. Religion, of some kind or another, is as necessary to the mind as food is to the body and, this being so, religion, from the time of primitive man to the present day, has been as much to him as was the providing of his bodily needs. He felt cold and he invented clothes, he felt fearful of attack, and he invented weapons of defence. He lived in fear of his fate after death, and he had to invent religion.

Now the word "invent" means in this case that he had to think out something new, and, when mental development brought man from the animal stage to that of a human being, he began to wonder, not only about improving his earthly life but also about his destiny. Some around him claimed to be in touch with those thought of as dead, and thus Ancestor

Worship developed over all the world. As he settled down in towns and villages to a civilised form of life, and ceased being a wanderer in search of food, those we to-day term mediums brought the people together to see and hear supernormal deeds and sayings. As time went on those mediums became the first priests, but those who were clever and cunning amongst the people said to themselves that what was done and seen under the control of the gods they could do by pretence.

Thus the art of magic arose, and as the magicians could produce their tricks whenever they were wanted, and the mediums their phenomena only at the will of their controls, the magicians eventually won the day, to become the priests when the mediums were relegated to their charge. Based on what the mediums said and did, the priests first produced, or invented, a form of religion suitable for all the people, who thus did not depend on the manifestations of the spirit control through the medium. This was the beginning of ritual which was all a simple people could grasp.

As organised ritual came into being, Religion developed under the care of the priests, and the people received the comfort needed, by being told from childhood onwards what to do to be saved from punishment hereafter for their wicked deeds on earth. Thus was Theology born, its father being mediumship and its mother mysticism, the practical merging with the fanciful. It grew ever more mysterious, and this kept alive the spiritual side, while the ritual maintained the religious observance. Both went together, as simple man, to satisfy his spiritual desires, must worship in some material way, he must be doing something and believing something to enable him to feel his soul is safe.

So he prayed to the gods, or spirits, and he required a place wherein to pray. He required a material image of the god or spirit to whom he prayed, and he observed certain forms and practices, as that gave him religious satisfaction. He required instruction from his religious leaders, and he had to have a place wherein to listen to them. So in every community of civilised men and women there developed from small beginnings a building looked upon as sacred, and as the spiritual home of the medium protected by the priests. The medium was either kept apart for the use of the priests alone, or, on occasions, the public could hear trance utterances, clairvoyance or clairaudience coming from the séance room called the Holy of Holies, the Sacred Shrine, the Sanctuary, or some other suitable name. So developed what we now call a church, a temple, a mosque or a pagoda, originally a house built to protect the medium and watched over by the magician priest.

Now I return to my everyday life. My thoughts have been wandering over past ages, but I now come back to the present day. Stansted Hall had now become part of my life, and my wife and I were very much attached to it. We made many improvements, one of the most satisfactory being a path round the lake. Whichever way we went gave us a walk of about a mile which brought us back to the house, a

delightful walk and one we often take to get some
exercise.   We had a boathouse built with a thatched
roof which looked very picturesque, and it housed a
punt and rowing-boat.   The lake is a great attraction
to the place, and, now that we could walk round it,
we saw it in all its varying aspects, especially interesting being the number of wild birds, swans, geese, wild
ducks and moorhens which make it their home.

The farm was a constant interest, but I felt that
my life's work did not lie solely in finance and looking
after the estate.   My mind was too active for that kind
of life, and I wanted to use, for the good of my fellow
men and women, the knowledge that I had accumulated over many years.   I had so much of value to
impart, and I felt it was my duty to set to work to
make it generally known.   So why not put it in book
form?   I knew I had the gift of expressing my
thoughts in a way all could understand, as had been
proved by the way my writing on finance and Stock
Exchange matters had been appreciated when I was
in business.

I decided, therefore, I would first of all write a
book on my experiences of the direct voice, and in
such a way that all could understand.   To give an
account of what had taken place when I was present
at Sloan's séances was not enough, as I realised that
what was also needed was an explanation of how and
why they occurred.   One which would make people
realise that they were not contrary to present-day
scientific knowledge, if presented in the right way.
With this in mind, I set to work to write a book to
which I gave the title *On the Edge of the Etheric*.   If this
were well received, as I hoped, others would follow

to present to my fellow men and women a new outlook on many of the vital aspects of life.

The success my books have attained makes me feel that the need was there, and that they have met it. Otherwise, I would not now be writing this, my biography, and I would have remained known only to my friends and acquaintances. Little did I realise, at the time about which I am now writing, that for the next twenty-five years I would find a ready medium for my thoughts in ten books, some of considerable size.

One thing I had no doubt about. I would not use my knowledge and gift of writing for profitable purposes, and here I emphasise that all my books have been published exactly at cost of production. I have made nothing from them, either in the English editions or in the foreign translations, my satisfaction being the help they have given to so many who have read them. That is all I ever desired, my wish being to help mankind but to make nothing from them of a monetary nature. All my hard work and thought over the past twenty-five years has been amply repaid by the knowledge I have that my books have helped so many who have read them. That was my only wish, and it has been granted to me in full measure.

So from now onwards I am an author, having been forced out of my private life by the wish to help others. That is the story I am now about to tell in the following chapters.

CHAPTER SEVEN.

STANSTED HALL.

(1930–1936.)

WE HAD now been at Stansted Hall for five years and the year is now 1930. The world was slowly working its way out of the morass caused by the First World War, but not without labour troubles at home and widespread financial disturbance. We had experienced unsettled labour conditions which culminated in the General Strike· of 1926, but, when the Trade Union Congress realised that the country was against this form of tyranny, the 2,500,000 workers who had been called out were told to return to work.

Then followed in 1929 a terrible financial crisis which started in Austria and spread round the world, hitting particularly the United States. Prices slumped quickly on all the Stock Exchanges and continued to fall for three years, so that many were ruined, all of which showed that the world was still licking the wounds it had received during the war.

At home all men and women over twenty-one years of age were now entitled to vote at Parliamentary elections, this being the result of the Franchise Act of 1928. In consequence Britain became a democratic country. Nevertheless, so long as there are more than two parties, majority rule is in danger, and I would

STANSTED HALL FROM THE PARK.

like to see our Constitution providing for only two parties and not more. Certainly when we look abroad, and think of the numerous different parties elected and their bargaining with one another to get their measures passed, we must think that this kind of democratic government is a farce and fully justifies the Communist jeer at party politics.

The Welfare State was now making its presence felt, the school-leaving age having been increased to fourteen years, children had ceased to spend half their days at work and half at school, and the State was looking after the welfare of all children and young people from the age of two to eighteen years of age. Increased medical attention had improved the health of the people, reduced working hours had increased their leisure, and better productive methods had advanced the standard of living.

The Irish question had now gone a long way towards a settlement, by southern Ireland becoming the Irish Free State and a self-governed dominion, but it was not until 1938 that what is now known as Eire became a republic and a sovereign state quite independent of Great Britain.

The Cinema and the Radio had enlarged the life of the people who, as the years passed, were living easier and more comfortable lives due to a large extent to the greater use of electricity, the increased bus services, moreover, making travel to greater distances possible for all. Abroad, the world was at peace and the future seemed set fair by the withdrawal in 1930, five years sooner than the date allowed for in the Treaty of Versailles, of all the Allied troops placed in Germany as an army of occupation. Consequently, relations between France and Germany now commenced to improve, and great hopes were set on something really practical being done to reduce the chance of a future war at the forthcoming Disarmament Conference at Geneva, two years hence in 1932.

In this atmosphere of world peace I set to work to prepare the book which was to be called *On the Edge of the Etheric*. As a book on Spiritualism it differs from other books on this subject, because I started off by explaining what the universe really is, and from this little-realised aspect I found a place for another world to which we pass at death. In this way my book brought Spiritualism within our present-day scientific knowledge, and made survival possible to understand. Hitherto we had only the evidence to rely on, and this my book contained in full measure. This certainly pointed to the survival of the personality after death, but what I was at first puzzled about was where this survival took place. Here my knowledge of physics came to my help, and, after much pondering, the answer to my problem became clear and definite. *On the Edge of the Etheric* contains that answer.

The phenomena which go under the name of Spiritualism were undoubted. Voices did speak from the void in an intelligent way and, by what they said, made enquirers believe that they were the voices of those they claimed to be. Likewise, what a medium said in trance produced the same results. Clairaudience and clairvoyance had a like effect, and apparitions and materialisations gave us visible proof that another order of life existed around us, though invisible to most people. How was this possible?

To answer that question I made it my business to explain in *On the Edge of the Etheric*. Once a scientific rational statement, setting out a place for the so-called dead to inhabit, is laid before the enquirer and is understood, the seemingly impossible becomes quite possible.

What seems to be contrary to all nature's laws becomes quite natural, and the enquirer consequently can accept as possible what seems to be impossible. All that is necessary is a correct conception of the universe. When we know what matter really is, how it is that we see things, why things are light and heavy, and when we know the reason for colour and the effect of light, the universe becomes a new conception to us. We then realise that what appeals to our sense of sight, and sense of feeling, is the frequency of a small range of the numerous vibrations which make up the universe. This knowledge opens our minds to the possibility of another world in which the higher frequencies appeal to those looked upon as dead.

To be a conscious being, the mind must be housed somewhere, and the mind must have a body to enable it to express itself. Here again my knowledge of physics came to my aid, when I remembered that different frequencies of vibrations can occupy the same place. The physical body is made up of physical matter and, as explained in Chapter V, matter is an open network of electrons and protons moving at enormous speed within the atom in which also can function vibrations beyond the physical range. It therefore follows that within our physical bodies there is plenty of room for an etheric body, made up of higher frequencies than those which form the material body.

This being so, it is quite within the boundaries of physical knowledge for each living creature to have what is called an etheric duplicate body, which is unnoticed while we live on earth, but which passes elsewhere with the mind from the earth body at death. Consequently, we have found a place for the etheric body, and that makes it possible to believe more easily that it is a reality than if a place for it could not be discovered. Now the two problems I had before me were resolved within our present-day scientific knowledge. In the universe there is a place for a duplicate etheric body to live, and in each of us there is a place for a duplicate body to occupy.

When this is accepted the evidence we have of the survival of the personality becomes rational and understood, without our having to trespass beyond the boundaries of scientific knowledge. Moreover, we can explain the reason for much we experience which is little understood, for instance, the innate belief in a soul which survives the death of the physical body. The emotions of millions of the world's inhabitants everywhere, now and always, have been moved by hymns which had as their theme the life beyond the grave, or Heaven, as English-speaking-people call it, just as they have been moved by fear of the torments of Hell. Where reason in the past could not go our emotions have taken us, and consequently nearly everyone on earth has experienced religious emotion. The name of Religion is given to the multitude of ideas which have been formed in the human mind about a life after death, and the best way to prepare ourselves for it on earth.

Lacking reasoned knowledge, being ignorant of his make-up and the set-up of the universe, mankind has groped about for a crutch to sustain and comfort him through life and at death. The necessity of something to help and satisfy him brought religion into being everywhere, but the coming of reasoned thought, increased knowledge, better and greater observation, and more experience gave other explanations for those ideas which had become entwined with religion. Thus we entered the age of materialism, when only that which could be seen or explained was believed. Religion everywhere has always accepted survival, but in a vague and contradictory way, and this belief was one of the first to be discarded in a materialistic age, it being something for which there was no objective proof. Consequently, it was considered irrational.

There is certainly no laboratory proof for survival, and in a laboratory age that is enough to disqualify the belief. Faith only remained, and it took the place of reason, Religion being relegated to the faithful, who had to rely on ancient tradition contained in contradictory unhistorical documents which had been elevated far above their merits. Their beliefs and teachings, which were in many respects fanciful, had been handed down from one religion to another over thousands of years, and the errors they contained our scholars, in our days, made it their business to expose.

So we found during the 19th century Religion and Science in definite opposite camps, but, when knowledge increases, and the people as a whole become intelligent enough to grasp all that Spiritualism stands for, a change will follow. Increased knowledge is slowly making itself felt, and the recent discoveries of Science as to the make-up of man and the universe, together with the mountain of evidence for survival collected by Spiritualists, will some day bring Science and Religion together. Religion will then throw over its superstitions and errors, its myths and legends, and Science its materialism, and both will combine to regard the meaning of life on earth in its right perspective. Religion and Science will then be joined together, and both will contribute to the world's book of knowledge.

That is the message *On the Edge of the Etheric* gave to the world in 1931, and the reception it received revealed how much it was required. The first impression of a thousand copies was sold within a few weeks. Another thousand was printed and went just as quickly. Five thousand were then printed, and in a few months these were sold, and so it went on year by year until 1952, when the total number sold reached fifty thousand copies. I planted the seedling of a beech tree at Stansted Hall to commemorate this event, and I am pleased to say that this has grown into a strong and healthy youngster which promises some day to be a stately tree.

I was much gratified by the reception the book received from the Press, not only in Britain but also in the Dominions and the United States. Over one hundred reviews in Britain praised it for the clarity of its theme, the evidence it gave of survival being considered by many as unanswerable. It was the most reviewed book of the Winter Book Season of

1931–32.   Only orthodox Religion and Science stood aloof.   The scientific journal *Nature* disparaged the book and made several stupid observations, its attitude being coldly aloof and sceptical, as if the subject was beneath the notice of anyone claiming to be scientific.   The orthodox religious journals had nothing favourable to say about it, and even refused to publish advertisements of it.

My friends, Sir Oliver Lodge and Sir William Barrett, both physicists, were highly pleased with the book and generously expressed their gratification that it had scientifically located a place for the spirit of man after death.   Both agreed with the scientific facts put forward, and expressed their regret that they themselves had not used my method of putting them over as an argument in favour of survival.   Here, however, I must pay tribute to Sir Oliver's books on the invisible world, and say how much his advanced ideas helped me to form my own opinions.

Before long, letters began to pour in from readers of *On the Edge of the Etheric*, and I do not remember one adversely criticising it.   All welcomed it, and said what a comfort and satisfaction it was to them. Many reported having had similar experiences to those contained in my book, and I wish I had space to quote from some of them.   Many unburdened their sorrows, and a few confided in me that they had contemplated suicide through grief from the loss of someone they loved, but had thought differently after reading the book.   As it became known, I was inundated with requests to speak at every kind of gathering, from Mayfair literary drawing-room meetings to those held in our largest halls throughout the land. I accepted all I could, but it was impossible to find time to speak at them all.

I have been fortunate in having chairmen at my meetings who were well-known men in the district. For instance, at my Ulster Hall meeting in Belfast in September 1932, Colonel the Right Hon. R. G. Sharman Crawford, D.L., the Deputy Governor of Northern Ireland, took the chair, and in his opening remarks said:

> "I am a believer in survival after death, and I can say that as a result I am a better and happier man, and even more so since I read the book *On the Edge of the Etheric.*"

I could tell of many interesting events which happened at my meetings, and of the strange and unusual experiences told me by people who spoke to me when the meetings ended, but my space is limited. I can only briefly mention this period of my public life and pass on.

In this way I made many new friends in all classes of the community, and I was much gratified to discover how many thoughtful individuals this country contains. Many people, to explain the falling-off of believers in the accepted order of worship, complain that the people are becoming less religious. I have never found it so, but what became clear to me was that orthodoxy, made up of myths and legends, was not giving satisfaction to the growing number of thinkers throughout the land who, having cast off priestly guidance, were now finding in Spiritualism the comfort and satisfaction they required.

The next gratifying event was to receive many letters from all parts of the world relating the psychic experiences the writers had encountered, and, with these letters, came one by one requests to be allowed to translate the book into the native language of the writer. After being satisfied of the standing and capacity of the enquirer, I gave him or her the full rights to translate and publish the book, provided it was done word for word and nothing was added or omitted. I asked for nothing in return except two copies, and now I have a chest full of these translations, which I greatly value.

The first request came from Iceland, where Spiritualism is strongly entrenched, and then followed others from Hungary, Jugoslavia and Poland, to end in the book being translated into French, Dutch, Danish, Portuguese, Spanish, Italian, Icelandic, Swedish, Finnish, Greek, Croatian, Japanese, Singhalese, Arabic, Hebrew, and Afrikaans, besides being set up in England in Braille for the blind. It has been translated into German, but the translator has been unable to find a publisher. It was the cause of the founding of the Athens Metaphysical Alliance by my friend Commander C. Melas, one of the leading men in Greece. Then many prominent Athenians read it and, with their help, Melas started this psychic organisation, of which they asked me to be an honorary member. This was the first Spiritualist Society in Greece, and now there are four making good progress in spite of the opposition of the Greek Church. In South Africa it has been the cause of many articles in both the English and Afrikaan journals.

The Hebrew and Arabic translations have been much sought after, some appreciative articles written by well-known local men appearing about them in their newspapers. The Hebrew translator drew the attention of his countrymen to the fact that it was in the ancient Hebrew language that the Old Testament was first written, and that *On the Edge of the Etheric* is the first modern book in Hebrew also to tell of the intercourse of the inhabitants of the other world with the people of earth. The Governor of Jericho was so interested that he formed a Spiritualist Society which is well supported, and he has written to ask if he could see me the first time he is in England.

Shortly after the publication of this book in 1931 I received a letter from Maurice Barbanell, asking me to write an article for *Psychic News*, to tell how it was I came to write such a book. This newspaper had just been born, and it was only a week old, but his letter had effects much greater than the article I wrote. I met him a few days later and found that he, and the other founder of *Psychic News*, J. M. Rubens, required financial help to continue publication. This I contributed and we formed a company called Psychic Press Ltd. to finance and manage this new Spiritualist journal. Barbanell and Rubens received shares for the part they played in founding this new venture, and, in exchange for shares, I put up the necessary money and so controlled the company.

I became chairman, without salary, and Barbanell the editor, but years were to pass before the time came for the new journal to be self-supporting. Until then I had to pay out thousands to keep it going, but I never lost faith in the venture, especially as I had in

Barbanell an able, hard-working, and enthusiastic editor. Besides that we received much good advice in the early days from the well-known journalist Hannen Swaffer, and he also contributed many able articles which were much appreciated. My faith in the future was justified, and *Psychic News* now goes all over the world, it having become the best known of all the Spiritualist newspapers, with the largest circulation.

As my books increased in number, so did my friends, and I got to know many men and women who were leaders of the advanced thought of the times. To mention them all by name is impossible. Some came to Stansted Hall, where my wife and I entertained them, others I met in London, or as I went about the country speaking at meetings. Dr. Carl Wickland was one I much enjoyed meeting when he visited London on a trip from the United States. Anyone interested in obsession, or the curing of insanity by psychic means, could not have been otherwise. His famous book *Thirty Years Among the Dead* reveals his extraordinary experiences, which few others can equal. Dr. Abraham Wallace was another pioneer in psychic science whom I met from time to time, and one could not be long in his presence without being influenced by his zeal to widen the bounds of psychic knowledge.

He, like Sir Arthur Conan Doyle, was a missionary for the cause. Sir Arthur I had known for many years and had been to his home at Crowborough. We met from time to time, and he and Lady Doyle invited my wife and me to a pre-view of the film of his exciting novel *The Lost World*. He opened a psychic bookshop in London, and I remember once entering it to be met by him behind the counter beaming with pleasure to see me. He devoted the later years of his life to Spiritualism, and his famous missionary journey to Australia will always be remembered by the historians of Spiritualism.

I always derived much pleasure, and increased my knowledge, each time I met Sir Oliver Lodge. On one occasion my wife and I visited him at his home at Lake, near Stonehenge, when he took us through his laboratory. He was the least egotistical of the famous men I have known, his humbleness, considering his knowledge and experience, being remarkable. We met occasionally at luncheon at Sir William and Lady Barrett's house in Devonshire Place in London, when the conversation was always stimulating and elevating. He was a great man, and I missed these talks I had with him after he passed on, active to the last, his wish that he would never become senile being realised.

On one occasion Dean Inge, famous for his gloomy outlook on life, lunched with us at Stansted Hall, and, in the course of conversation, in which he was very pessimistic and very doubtful about everything, I asked him if he would like to meet Sir Oliver Lodge. I hoped that a talk with him would cheer him up, he being so pessimistic about the universe "running down", as he described it. He seemed quite hopeless about the future of the world in general, including his own destiny, but he agreed to my suggestion, and we three and a few others met at my club in London. I detached the Dean and Lodge from my other guests and found a quiet spot where we could talk undisturbed. Imagine my surprise when only small-talk took place, and Inge thus lost a wonderful opportunity to discover that happiness, both here and hereafter, comes from right thinking, and that as one's mind is so is one's happiness.

Sir William Barrett and his outstanding wife, one of the first lady doctors and Dean of the Royal Free Hospital for Women, we knew well. Sir William was a convinced Spiritualist, and made this clear in his book *On the Threshold of the Unseen*. He was one of the founders of the Society for Psychical Research and was at a council meeting shortly before he died. His devotion to his wife was remarkable, and she, after his death, gave in her book *Personality Survives Death* an account of the many conversations she had with him through a trance medium. My wife and I saw much of them in London, and they came from time to time to Stansted Hall. He was a delightful courteous man, and Lady Barrett made him a devoted wife amidst her life of ministering to, and operating on, women for their own particular ailments.

In the Summer of 1932 my wife and I spent an enjoyable week-end with our friends Lord and Lady Aberdeen at their home in Aberdeenshire. (I am referring to the 1st Marquis and 7th Earl.) Imagine my surprise to hear from Lord Aberdeen on my arrival that he had arranged a meeting at his house of many of his friends in the county, and that the subject of the address was "Spiritualism". "And who is the speaker?" I asked. "You are, of course," he replied. So it came about that the following evening a large gathering sat before me while I expounded to them my experiences and my philosophy. A discussion followed and a fruitful evening was spent, but not one that I had expected when we accepted their invitation.

After Lord Aberdeen died, his wife told me that just before his death he was reading *On the Edge of the Etheric*. Then Lady Aberdeen had sittings with Sloan, and my brother in his book *Reunited* tells that he was present when not only her husband regularly spoke to her, but several of the great Liberal statesmen, such as Gladstone and Rosebery, who had been her friends when she was the leading Liberal hostess of her day. Gladstone made a number of correct references to his home Hawarden which Lady Aberdeen quite understood, as she had stayed there, but no one else present could have known these facts. Bonar Law, Lord Goschen and Lord Kitchener gave their names and spoke to Lady Aberdeen. Then Lord Aberdeen said to her: "Do you remember, Ishbel, the 25th of July? That was a very happy day. Mrs. Gladstone sent you a picture." This was the day they became engaged to be married, and, on the same day, they were driving down Bond Street in London when they saw Mr. Gladstone on the pavement. They stopped and told him of their engagement, and that evening a letter of congratulation, and a small water-colour picture, were received by her from Mrs. Gladstone.

The evidence she received of their survival during these sittings with Sloan was so remarkable, and of such a private nature, that it can be termed conclusive. Later, she passed over, and the account of Lord and Lady Aberdeen's return, in company with William Ewart Gladstone, and what they said, is given in my book *Where Two Worlds Meet*.

JOAN AT TWENTY-TWO.

One day in 1933 I was lunching with Shaw Desmond, when he said to me, "I think the time has come to start an institute for psychical research." To this I agreed, suggesting that a good name for it would be "The Royal Institute for Psychical Research". He replied: "We may not get the name 'Royal' into it, but we shall get a good name for it when the time comes. Will you take the matter in hand, and I shall give you all the help I can?" I replied that I would, and so the seed was planted, to become the International Institute for Psychical Research.

I got into touch with Professor Fraser-Harris as I was anxious that this new institute should have a scientific backing. He was most helpful, and, before long, we had the names of six well-known scientists willing to act on the Consultative Committee of the Institute, besides twenty-two well-known men who agreed to join either this committee or the Executive Committee. Consequently, on 30th December 1933, the national newspapers gave the scheme prominence, and the following appeared in the *Morning Post*:

PSYCHICAL RESEARCH

SCIENTIFIC INVESTIGATION BY NEW AUTHORITY

A new body for the investigation of psychic phenomena on strictly scientific grounds has been formed under the presidency of Professor G. Elliot-Smith, the anatomist and anthropologist.

It is known as The International Institute for Psychical Research, and it has as Vice-Presidents

Professor Julian Huxley and Professor E. W. MacBride.

The Chairman of the Executive Committee is Mr. J. Arthur Findlay.

Well-known scientists on the Institute's consultative committee include Professor C. Lovatt Evans the physiologist, and Professor A. F. C. Pollard, who is an authority on the design of scientific instruments.

"It is simply a body," Professor Elliot-Smith stated to a representative of the *Morning Post* last night, "which will assume responsibility for scientific experiment."

All seemed to be set fair, though *Nature*, the scientific journal, expressed its contempt at the effort. We had set up our headquarters at a large house in Kensington, when one after another of our scientific supporters resigned. Why, I was never able to discover, but I have always had my own suspicions. However, the other well-known men remained with us, and we went on without the scientists. I was chairman of the Institute for a number of years, and then came the war which changed everything. I resigned, but so far we had obtained encouraging results, and had heard many learned lectures. Shaw Desmond gave me his support on the committee, and Dr. Nandor Fodor was its Research Officer until he went to America. Such, briefly, is the story of how I tried and failed to get some of our leading scientists interested in an organisation formed "for the furtherance of knowledge in regard to psychic phenomena". I hope, in the years to come, someone will meet with more success than Shaw Desmond and I did.

Encouraged by the success of *On the Edge of the Etheric* I now began to contemplate the production of another book. I had still much to tell which I felt should be known, and I possessed that urge which some have to impart knowledge. This meant more hard work and concentration, but nothing worth while is achieved without effort. Nevertheless, I was not prepared to accept the ordinary daily round of life just as it came, although, without the additional task involved in producing a new book, my days were fully and pleasantly occupied. My time was spent looking after the estate, doing my public work and, with the help of an efficient secretary, keeping my large correspondence up to date. When I had an hour or two to spare I found much pleasure in drawing, a great variety of pencils being used. Some of my sketches have been framed and hung up to remind us of places we have visited. Moreover, the constant ebb and flow of visitors to Stansted Hall, and the many engagements I had to fulfil, made the days pass quickly, to make me wonder how I could find time to embark on this new undertaking,

Nevertheless, I must do it, I thought, and find the time some way or another. So I set to work, and here it is opportune to answer a question I am often asked, "How do you write your books?" Briefly, this is how I do so. I have a wooden writing-board two feet long and one and a quarter feet broad, on which I first write everything in pencil on foolscap paper. I sit in an armchair with my feet on a stool, my knees drawn up to support the board resting on the arms of the chair, and make myself completely comfortable. Thus my back never tires, and in this attitude I can go on writing for hours at a time.

On my right is a little table with odds and ends on it, and on my left is a book-rest on a brass rod which can be moved about as desired. In this way a reference book, when necessary, is before me and can be referred to by moving only my left hand. Thus I am self-sufficient and need not move from the comfortable position established in my chair. Peace is highly desirable, but too often not achieved, as I am so often wanted for something or other. One thing I have to forgo, and that is my pipe, because the close concentration on my subject makes smoking just a waste of tobacco, as I have no sensation, when writing, that I am smoking.

The sheets, as they are finished, are given to my secretary to type, and her typed pages I read over carefully and check the facts, grammar and punctuation. Many have to be retyped, some several times, before I am satisfied that they can be passed on to the printer. Here the work of most authors finishes, as the author then passes his manuscript on to his publisher. The publisher arranges for his book to be printed, the proofs checked and read over, the necessary paper to be supplied, the nature of the cover and the paper jacket which protects it. This I have always done myself and in this way I get the best possible book produced. A publisher has to make his profit and I have not. A publisher saves paper where possible, and uses often too small a type so as to get more words on a page. This I never do. Consequently, I get a book produced to best fulfil my high standard of what a first-class publication should be, and I sell the book at a price to cover my expenditure and the bookseller's selling charge, no profit being taken into consideration.

Being my own publisher, and having Psychic Press as my distributor only, means much additional work, as the printer's proofs have to be read over and they are also read by at least three readers. The kind of type to be used must be settled, also the quantity and quality of the paper required, and the cardboard for the cover. So it comes about that after the writing of a book is completed some five months may elapse before it is ready for publication, and it was with all these thoughts in my mind that I decided to write another book which I named *The Rock of Truth* and published it in 1933.

It was well and widely reviewed, and its sales have come next to those of *On the Edge of the Etheric*. All the same, in some quarters it had a stormy reception because it told the truth about the origin of the Christian faith, and how very few there be who know anything about this subject. Why, it may be asked, did I write this controversial book? My answer is that before Spiritualism can be accepted, much that is false in to-day's religious teaching has to be cast aside. That is why some of the book is devoted to the true origin of the beliefs which make up Christianity, and it shows how, after what is false is discarded, a purified religion remains, under the name of Spiritualism, which all can accept without having to put their faith in place of their reason.

Those, however, who by faith alone have accepted from infancy what has been taught them as Religion, those who are fearful as to their destiny after death, and rely on a saviour to get them into heaven, naturally dislike intensely that doubt be cast on their beliefs. They are fearful that the crutch upon which they have always relied may not be so secure as they once thought it was. Thus, fear produces intolerance and this causes disharmony, which remains until mental development, due to greater knowledge, reveals to them that the new outlook is not only true but is one that is much to be preferred to the old one. It is simply put in Micah vi, 8, in these words: "O man what is good; and what doth the Lord require of thee but to do justly and to love mercy, and to walk humbly with thy God."

Spiritualism teaches that as we sow we reap, that as we think here we think hereafter, that our own minds and not a saviour determine our place hereafter, but the majority fear to rely on themselves. They have been brought up to think that God requires a fixed form of belief, besides certain ritual, such as baptism, Church membership and other forms and ceremonies, before entry into heaven is permitted. This idea has been a great help and comfort to many, and to feel that they are saved by believing something, and doing something, has eased the weight of the burden of sin, and the fear of punishment, to millions of the faithful down the ages, not only to Christians but to those of all the other world religions.

This idea of salvation by faith has been a crutch to the faithful and no more, because it is not true, and *The Rock of Truth* made its falsity crystal-clear by giving the historical origin of the Christian faith. Consequently, the book is disliked by the orthodox, but they could not reply to it by reasoned thinking and facts. Though I sent out a request to every individual Protestant clergyman in this country, 28,630 in all, to tell me where it erred, not one replied. That in itself is a testimony to the truth the book reveals, because no answer could be found to refute the facts it gave.

When the book was published I was President of the London Spiritualist Alliance, a corporate body representing no religious opinion, and open to those holding any of the world's creeds, or none at all. I received a letter from the secretary of the Alliance, asking me, in the name of the Council, to deliver a lecture on the contents of this book to a meeting of members, which I did, and this was reported in *Light*, the journal of the Alliance, the following week, the editor supporting my views in a leading article. Nothing I said differed from the contents of the book, but one member of the Council, who was a zealous Anglo-Catholic, and his wife were very angry. The reason was because I said I could not accept the Pagan belief in a trinity of gods which was incorporated into what became Christianity at the Council of Nicaea in 325. All the bitterness of a fanatic seemed to be aroused in him by this unorthodox opinion, and he set to work with the zeal of someone possessed by a fiend to achieve my downfall. So he acted in the following extraordinary way.

According to the Articles of the Society I, as President, was the one to call a special Council meeting if one were needed, but he, himself, instructed the Secretary to call one at less than twenty-four hours' notice. This was quite out of order and contrary to the Articles of Association, which stated that seven clear days' notice must be given. When the Secretary rang me up to tell me of this meeting I gathered that its purpose was to publish in *Light* a notice dissociating the Council from my religious beliefs. When I heard this I told the Secretary that I would tender my resignation, expressing the view that it was no business of the Council to question my religious opinions, that the subject of my lecture was at its request, and I had no intention of attending the meeting to be censured. I stated that this action was a direct insult to me as President, and consequently I would no longer remain in this office. Later I resigned my membership of the Alliance along with very many others, who saw no reason why my opinions should be questioned by the Council.

My resignation almost wrecked the Alliance, the outburst of condemnation in the psychic press being prolonged, forceful and unanimous, and it might well have done so had I not left it in such a strong financial position and able to weather the storm. Many members wanted me to convene a meeting so that I could be asked to reconsider my decision, but to this I would not agree. I had worked hard for nearly a year to put the Alliance on a firm financial basis, and its journal, *Light*, under my chairmanship, had made a profit for the first time in its history. I had founded the Quest Club, under the auspices of the Alliance, which had become popular with everyone, but that availed nothing to a few religious fanatics.

A small Christian clique in the Council took over the reins, and drove through all rules and regulations to impose its will on the rest of the Council. Afterwards the majority of the Council told me that they considered the calling of the meeting, and the raising of the question of my opinions at the meeting, was contrary to their way of thinking. If this were so, they were intimidated by a minority, and I felt well rid of my association with them, being glad to have the time to spare for something else of a more satisfactory nature. Throughout my life I had had more than enough of Christian orthodoxy, and I now realised that I had on the Council a clique of intolerant zealots to give me further trouble. From these I was determined to be freed, and my resignation solved the difficulty. It was more than a year before the Alliance could find someone who would accept the office of President, the revulsion of feeling against the Council being so great.

This example of Christian intolerance was so in keeping with what I have experienced from its zealots throughout my life that it worried me not a bit, and I was quite prepared for the next onslaught. One day I received a letter from Mrs. St. Clair Stobart inviting me to attend her next Sunday service in the Grotrian Hall, as she thought I should hear her criticism of *The Rock of Truth*, which she proposed to make the subject of her address. This eloquent and voluble old lady, with her fuzzy white hair which, as she once said to me, made her look more like a witch than an ordinary human being, had become an ardent Spiritualist, but retained many of the religious beliefs she had been taught in childhood. She had never studied comparative religion as I had done, and her beliefs were as simple as are those of a child. Consequently, *The Rock of Truth* came to her as rather a shock, and she rushed in to refute it with all her eloquent zeal.

I attended the service because of curiosity, but not expecting any reasoned intellectual nourishment. Eloquence and rhetoric I expected, and received, in fact she carried the large audience with her from start to finish, which shows the power of oratory over the masses. Never did she reply to the facts I gave in my book, these being passed by in her emotional eloquence, and when she had ended her audience knew no more than it did before she started. Before I published this book I gave it to Professor Burkitt, the Professor of Divinity at Cambridge University, in manuscript form, to read over to check my facts. This he kindly did, and then he and his wife came to lunch with us, when he told me that everything said was true and honestly set out. Nevertheless, this much esteemed old lady, who gloried in her eloquence, disposed of it in this reckless manner.

This experience in no way compares with the despicable affair at the London Spiritualist Alliance, as everyone is entitled to say what he or she thinks. Everyone's mind is different, and opposite opinions are inevitable. Some foolish people express their ideas volubly without knowledge of what they are talking about, but they are quite entitled to do so. I am a firm believer in tolerance, as intolerance comes from ignorance which is, and always has been, behind cruelty and persecution. All I ask is that I be given the same right to express my opinion that I grant to others, and this I do in my books but never by argument in conversation. Argument leads nowhere, and truth is bound to rise to the surface in the end when knowledge grows and mental development increases.

Consequently when the Grotrian Hall service ended that Sunday morning I congratulated Mrs. Stobart on her eloquence, though I said I could not agree with the way she had handled her subject. Moreover I thanked her for her forceful condemnation of the action of the Council of the London Spiritualist Alliance towards me, as expressed in an article she wrote which appeared in *Psychic News*. We have since remained friends, just as people of all shades of opinion stay with us at Stansted Hall. The only outstanding Communist I have met was William Gallacher, the late Communist member of Parliament for West Fife, and, when saying "good-bye" to me, he remarked: "Mr. Findlay, remember this. We Communists want no bloody revolution."

I am tolerant of every sincere belief, and whatever leads to the mental satisfaction of the individual I never argue about. So all our visitors of every shade of thought never find their ideas disturbed at Stansted Hall. Those who are upset by reading my books need not be, because they can ignore them. Unless someone speaks to me first about the various subjects they cover, I never do so, and, in consequence, harmony always prevails in my home. I am a teacher, not a missionary.

Psychic healing is a subject which has greatly interested me since the time the psychic healer F. J. Jones first came to our neighbourhood. He came by car once a week to a house in Stansted, and there gave healing to all who attended his healing circle. His power of healing was most impressive as was his gift in trance to diagnose an illness. He went into trance, and stood in the centre of the circle made up of about a dozen people who had come to be healed. I sat outside the circle and watched what took place. He went from one to another describing accurately the ailment, no questions being asked, and held his hand on the place affected. So successful was he that the local doctor came, and then sent his patients to be diagnosed and healed. The doctor became a firm believer in this form of healing, so much so that patients came to Jones for diagnosis and healing from far and wide.

Let me give an example of what took place. Jones, entranced, would stand in front of a patient, and his control would say, "You have had an operation which did you no good." "Yes," came the reply. "The surgeon cut you open from here to here," indicating the place and direction of the incision. "Yes," was the reply. "Well," the control went on, "that was not the way to cure you. What is wrong with you is this," and an explanation would follow, to end in treatment which the patient later acknowledged had cured her. The woman was fully dressed so that Jones's control must have seen through her clothes to her body to describe the previous operation, which was known to no other earth person present except herself. That is an example of what went on at this healing circle in Stansted, but he conducted others, his largest one being at Marylebone House in London.

Let me record the case of a remarkable cure which I followed at the time. Jones was the medium, and the details are accurate, being taken down from start to finish. In 1932 a girl of four years of age, named Doreen, had measles. On May 16th the doctor said that pneumonia had set in, and four days later she developed meningitis. Her parents were told she might die at any minute. The doctor called in a specialist on May 25th and he confirmed the diagnosis of meningitis. He agreed that there was no hope of the child living until the end of the week. The parents called in another doctor, who also agreed that there was no hope, and that nothing further could be done.

When all hope was abandoned, the child's grandmother, who herself had received great benefit from psychic healing, decided that at least no harm could be done by calling in the psychic healer, F. J. Jones. As Jones dealt with dozens of cases a day, he could not go to see the child, but he held in his hand for some time a handkerchief which was taken immediately and placed over Doreen's head. Whenever the handkerchief was so placed Doreen stopped screaming. The next day her temperature was down and another handkerchief, which had been held by Jones, was placed on her head.

Thinking the case was hopeless, the doctor did not call again until May 27th, and was very mystified at the child's improvement. He was not told the reason. On the next day, May 28th, he said her improvement was marvellous. The same afternoon Jones called to see her for the first time. He went into trance, and his spirit control treated her by keeping Jones's hands on her neck. The control, through the mouth of Jones, then said that he would draw the disease from the head through the back of the skull and, as there

would be much pus discharged, he asked that the hair
be shaved at the back of the head and that, when
suppuration started, the wounds be treated with a
mixture of olive oil and chalk.

That evening the discharge commenced from
eighteen places on the part of the skull which had been
treated by the spirit control. The doctor, when he
called on May 30th, was told that the grandmother
was treating the child with an African remedy. The
spirit control claimed to have been an African medicine man on earth. As the earth doctor could do
nothing himself, he did not interfere. On June 3rd
the doctor said it was a miracle that the child was still
alive. On June 8th and 9th Jones, in trance, again
treated the child. On June 17th Doreen was able to
speak for the first time since her illness, and on
June 23rd she went out for the first time for a walk
with her grandmother, soon to become strong and
well again.

How can we explain this extraordinary cure after
all hope had been abandoned? Accepting the claim
made by those who control healing mediums in trance
that they were doctors on earth, and still have the urge
to heal those who suffer on earth, we, at least, can
conclude this. That the medium's body is used by
the etheric doctor to conduct something, just as a
copper wire conducts electricity. Further that, in
some or all cases, the medium's hands transmit rays of
different frequencies to our physical rays which act on
the etheric body of the patient, and this in turn acts
on the physical body. Handkerchiefs can be impreg-
nated by them, and so carried to the patient. Especially interesting was the effect the handkerchiefs held

by the medium had on Doreen, and yet it was not new, because we read in Acts xix, 12, that Paul was a healing medium, "So that from his body were brought unto the sick handkerchiefs, or aprons, and the diseases departed from them."

By experience I myself know that rays pass from the medium, because I have felt them pass from a healing medium's hand to my spine. The medium was Mrs. Nan Mackenzie and, as her hand passed up and down my spine with my clothes on, it gave off a burning penetrating heat which was hard to bear. Up and down it went along with her hand, and there was no electric gadget about for this to be explained in a normal way. She was in trance from first to last, and her control told me how he used different rays for different ailments.

A friend, after thrombosis some years ago, lost her strength and vigour, and the doctor told her she would be in poor health for the rest of her life. She went to this medium and her spine was treated, as was mine. After four treatments she was strong and well, and had no ill-effects from her thrombosis; in fact, since this treatment she has never been in better health in her life. And now I shall turn to quite another subject.

We have had many interesting and distinguished people as our guests at Stansted Hall and, as anything relating to Royalty always interests people, I will now tell the following. In 1935 my wife received a letter from a mutual friend in Germany saying that she had heard that the ex-Crown Princess of Prussia, daughter-in-law of the ex-Kaiser, was anxious for her daughter of seventeen, Princess Cecilia, to come to England with a school-friend, Christa by name, to stay for two or three months. She wondered if the two girls could come to be our guests at Stansted Hall. My wife, anxious for my daughter to have companions about her own age, wrote to the Crown Princess inviting her daughter and friend to stay with us, and in reply she received a charming letter from her, accepting the invitation and inviting my daughter Joan to stay with them at Potsdam the following year.

She proposed bringing the two girls with her to England and suggested a date for her visit. So it came about that the Crown Princess, her daughter Cecilia, a handsome girl, and her friend Christa arrived at Stansted Hall, the Crown Princess staying with us for a short visit, and the two girls remained as our guests for two months. The Crown Princess, a daughter of the Grand Duke Friedrich Franz III of Mecklenburg-Schwerin, had a friendly and charming manner, and she seemed to enjoy her visit to us, having a delight in taking snapshots. We much enjoyed her visit, and my wife did her best to give our two guests a good time in England. We took them to a garden party at Buckingham Palace, to the Houses of Parliament, to Windsor, and some of the famous places in the land, they meeting many important people, for all of which they expressed their great appreciation. Joan was now nineteen years of age, and the three girls became firm friends, a friendship which has lasted to the present day. Our guests were very pleasant visitors, and we were sorry when the time came for them to leave us.

During 1935 I wrote and published *The Unfolding Universe*, and before the year ended it had completed its second impression, this rate of progress continuing up to the Second World War, when it went out of print because of the shortage of paper. It was re-printed in 1949, and since then its sale has been steady and large. This book completed the task I set out to accomplish, which was to make Spiritualism under-stood by all intelligent people as a science, religion and philosophy. I hope that some day its teachings will displace the errors which so far have been accepted by both orthodox science and religion. Spiritualism has nothing to fear from science, and it is in step with modern thought, in fact it is leading our present-day knowledge, a position which is slowly becoming realised by thinking people.

My two previous books had raised a new structure of thought and *The Unfolding Universe* completed the building. My attempt herein was to make clear the inherent weakness of the old-world religions, and the strength of the foundation on which the new religion and philosophy is built. Besides this, it tried to show what we sentient beings really are, and something of the geography of the real world in which we live, a world much greater than the one we sense during our temporary sojourn on earth. These three books form a trilogy, a trefoil window through which we can behold mankind's past beliefs, and a view of the beyond, a vista of greater intellectual light.

Advanced thinkers can now grasp mentally the greater world, and the chapter devoted to it enables one to comprehend its structure from the knowledge we now possess of the make-up of the physical universe. Both this world and the next seem to have the same structure at different frequencies of vibration, and from this angle of thought the two worlds are one. I was very pleased with this chapter entitled "The Greater World" and the diagrams I drew up made my meaning so clear that the theme could be followed step by step from beginning to end. A place for this other world had been found; it, of course, had always been there, but *The Unfolding Universe* completed the story of its discovery which was started in *On the Edge of the Etheric*. As our mind develops the greater world unfolds before us.

I think I can claim that my first three books, known as my trilogy, are unique, in that they are the first to explore scientifically the geography of the etheric world and place it on the map of the universe. These are not my words, but a fair summary of the many informative reviews the books received when published. These reviews were generous and appreciative. *The Unfolding Universe* is a book for the thinker, as are all my books, and it is because deep thinkers are few that Spiritualism is so little understood. The great majority seem to think that when they leave school their education is finished, and that they have been taught all that is worth knowing about religion and science.

STANSTED HALL FROM THE LAKE.

CHAPTER EIGHT.

STANSTED HALL.

(1936–1940.)

WE HAVE now come to the year 1936 and my thoughts turn to Scotland. My mother's health had been failing, and she was now eighty years of age. I saw her each month, as I stayed with her in Ayrshire when I went to Glasgow for a directors' meeting. She much looked forward to these visits, and I am glad to think that I was the means of cheering her up in her declining years. Not that she was alone or lonely, because she had a devoted companion, Mary Blair, who had been with her for thirty years and anticipated her every want. Her love and kindness to my mother were unbounded. With the other maids in the house, it was by no means a dull place, but my mother suffered from rheumatism and often stayed in bed for the day.

Her interest was in her lovely garden which each year she made more beautiful, and, as the years passed, she mellowed and was not so opinionative. I think she somehow or other came to the conclusion, in spite of her orthodox beliefs, that God would not damn me in hell, in fact my psychic experiences greatly interested her and perhaps they gave her a more rational outlook on life and death. To the end, however, she would not allow a Sunday newspaper in the house, or have her car on the road on that holy day.

With the opening of 1936 her health declined, but we received rather a shock when my brother telephoned to me on the 2nd of February that she had taken a turn for the worse, and that we should come north at once. So we took the night train from St. Pancras and arrived at her house the next morning just too late, as she passed away before we arrived. Then came the funeral and for most people there would be nothing more to tell, the Christian belief being that she would sleep in the grave until the resurrection of the dead—a dreadful idea. That, from the Christian point of view, is all there is to expect, and the comfort the mourners are given is that "time is the great healer".

I am glad to be able to tell quite a different story. My mother died on the 3rd February 1936, and I think that many will be interested to read of her return shortly after her death. This occurred at two séances, one in Glasgow and one in London.

These two séances produced what I consider to be first-class evidence that my mother returned, and it came through two mediums when in trance, and not by direct voice. Not one mistake was made, everything was correct, some statements being unknown to me and found later to be correct. In both cases the mediums could not have made any enquiries beforehand, and I am quite satisfied that neither of them knew that my mother had died. Notes were taken at the time of the sittings.

Taking the sittings with the two mediums together, 188 facts were given to me which were correct. No mistakes were made, and there was no guessing. Everything was said straight out. Nothing was vague. Everything said was correct and clearly stated. So that everyone may better understand this, I have put at the end of each paragraph the figures 1, 2 and 3, according to the number of correct statements given which could not have been known by the medium. When one correct statement was made the figure 1 is to be found at the end of the paragraph. When two correct statements were made, the figure 2, and so on.

If all these figures are added up it will be found that 188 correct statements were made at the sittings held on the 9th and 12th February 1936, and that nothing said was wrong. So the record of these two sittings can be read right through from beginning to end without question.

SITTING WITH MRS. BERTHA HARRIS IN GLASGOW, ON 9TH FEBRUARY 1936.

Mrs. Bertha Harris arrived in Glasgow from Chester on the evening of 8th February and went to the Holland Street Spiritualist Church, where she was given a bedroom and a sitting-room. My brother John and I, knowing that she was to be in Glasgow on the Sunday, 9th February, motored to Glasgow from Ayrshire and arrived at 11 o'clock in the morning. No previous appointment had been made, and we went up to Mrs. Harris's room, knocked and were asked to come in. I had met Mrs. Harris only once, some years earlier, after a meeting I addressed in Leicester, but she did not recognise me. She did remember John, my brother.

After the sitting with Mrs. Harris, I asked Mrs. Drysdale, the housekeeper who looked after her, if she had mentioned to her about my mother's death. Mrs. Drysdale said "No." When we entered Mrs. Harris's room, she came forward to greet us and said she was pleased to see us. We sat down without mentioning the fact that we had come for a séance, but just as if we had come to pay a passing visit, my brother saying that when he heard she was in Glasgow he just wanted to come and shake hands with her.

After a few words of general conversation Mrs. Harris spoke to us as follows:

"You seem to bring an atmosphere of sorrow with you to-day." Then she paused. "Someone has passed on within the past week. A lady, small, stooping, old. I should say about eighty years of age. Very closely connected with you. Nellie brings her with her." (10)

I now summarise what Mrs. Harris had still to say, but she had much more to tell us when the time had arrived for her to go downstairs and take the service in the church. So she said: "Come back after the church service, and we may be able to get more through." I mention this because, at the sitting I had with Mrs. Abbot in London, a few days later, reference was made to two separate occasions on which my mother had communicated, which was correct. Mrs. Harris had no opportunity to enquire about my mother, as she came downstairs with me and my brother and we returned to her room with her. What was said at both these sittings is now incorporated hereunder, as if it had all occurred at the same time.

Mrs. Harris passed into trance and her controlling spirit spoke as follows: "The lady had no feeling of

surprise when she passed over, only a feeling of great
joy to touch dear Robert's hand."   (1)

Mrs. Harris's control then referred to Robert (my
father) meeting her when she passed over and also "an
old gentleman who had passed on recently".   "This
old gentleman welcomed her, but he was now looking
after someone else."   (Annie, his sister, just died.)
"The lady gives her name as Margaret, and Nellie (my
brother's deceased wife) says: 'Just as I came and
brought the old gentleman to Glasgow and then to
London, so shall I bring your mother to you in
London as I have brought her this morning.' "   (6)

(This reference is to Nellie bringing my uncle to
Glasgow the day before his funeral to speak to John
and then, on a later occasion, to speak to John in
London.)

"The lady mentions Mary and Elizabeth.   She
sends them both her love and gratitude.   She has
mentioned them in her Will, giving them recognition.
It is a money recognition.   'I always like to pay my
debts,' she says.   'I have tried to repay them for all
their kindness to me.'   Her last conscious remembrance on earth was Mary and Elizabeth standing beside her.   'Elizabeth stroked my hand and face with
her hand.   She was alone with me at the time.' "   (9)

"I then asked: 'Have you seen your old school
friend?' and the reply was: 'Yes, Annie, big woman.
She would nearly fill the doorway.' "   (2)

"Your mother speaks of a red rose which was
placed on her robe in her coffin on her breast.   She
says: 'Red is my favourite colour, but why did you
not put the rose in my hand?' "   (5)

"Your mother had very small hands and feet: she

was proud of her small feet, she took size twos in shoes.' "   (4)

The medium went on: "Arthur's daughter, your mother tells me, is young and tall, but was not present at your mother's passing, as she was away from home at the time."   (5)

"Your mother mentions John's boys; one of them, who is seventeen, is tall, the other, Arthur—not this Arthur (pointing to me)—I am more concerned about. Carry out what she advises and push him forward." (5)

"Your mother mentions various small gifts she has left for people with cards attached bearing messages and names.   Arthur's daughter's gift is a necklace." (4)

"Your mother asks me to tell you she tried to retain consciousness until you Arthur, and Gertrude arrived.   You rushed up from a long distance.   She did not succeed in remaining conscious, but so long as she was conscious she kept thinking of you coming." (4)

The medium's control then spoke to John, saying that he had recently had his birthday, but that he had not yet bought his mother's present.   He had first told her he would not buy a book, and then had changed his mind and decided to buy one.   (4)

"She tells me," the control went on, "that John's books are becoming numerous, and that his library is becoming like Nellie's handkerchiefs.   Then she goes on to say that John put a piece of paper in his waistcoat pocket and that had reference to this book."   (5)

(The reference to Nellie's handkerchiefs was good, because Nellie, when she was ill, bought so many handkerchiefs at one time that there was a joke about it. As to John putting a piece of paper in his waistcoat pocket, he had done so that morning to remind him to order the book at the Church Bookstall.)

"Your mother mentions something in her bedroom with a single drawer in it containing papers which will interest you both." When we said we did not know of such a thing, she mentioned a bunch of keys and we said we did not know anything about this bunch of keys. (5)

(When we returned home we looked round her room and saw her dressing-case, which was a mahogany box about 18 inches by 18 inches. We could not open it as it was locked, and we asked for the key. This was on a bunch of keys. The dressing-case was opened, and, after examining the inside, we found a spring which released a single drawer in which we found quite a number of papers of interest. If we had not been told about this drawer it is unlikely we would ever have found these papers.)

The medium then referred to my mother having pain in her stomach and weakness of her heart, also to sickness. She referred also to her having weak knees. She then referred to one eye being very troublesome: "not blind, you know, but sore and uncomfortable. She goes like this" (the medium's right finger went up to her eye, and round it, as my mother was continually doing when her eye was troublesome). (8)

"Your mother died of something wrong here." (The medium put her hand on her stomach.) "Your father died of something here." (She put her hand on her appendix.) "Your mother has left three grown-up people and three children." (Myself, my brother, my wife, my daughter and John's two sons.) (4)

"Your mother was very fond of her Bible, and a little old village church with a bell in a small pointed steeple. She could hear the bell ringing from her home." (5)

"Your mother loved the hills, but she now sees hills like those she could see from her home." (2)

"Your mother has met Dr. Lamond. She hardly recognised him as he is looking so much younger than when she saw him last." (2)

"Your mother refers to a picture of Nellie on the piano in a room with a high ceiling with a pattern round it. It is a coloured picture." (5)

"Your mother said that during the recent church service Arthur moved up to the end of the pew, and she came and sat beside him." (1)

(This is correct about me moving up to the end of the pew, but, when I did so, the medium was in trance on the platform and could not have seen me. In any case, I was sitting far back in the church. This was said at the sitting we had after the service.)

All that was said at the sitting we had after the church service occurred with the medium in trance. Mrs. Harris, just before we left her, when saying good-bye, mentioned that before we arrived she had received a message which she had not understood. When she was dressing that morning, Nellie appeared to her and said that Arthur and John were coming to see her that morning. She did not know who Arthur and John were, but she mentioned this message to us as a matter of interest.

Everything reported above is quite applicable to my mother and the other people mentioned. Ninety-six facts were given which the medium could not have known. Not one single statement was incorrect or even doubtful.

SITTING WITH MRS. ABBOT IN LONDON, ON 12TH FEBRUARY 1936.

On the above date I had a sitting with Mrs. Abbot in a private room at the London Spiritualist Alliance. Mrs. Abbot went into trance quickly and her control stated that "an elderly lady was present, from seventy to eighty years, belonging to me. She had recently passed over." (3)

"Amongst those who were waiting for her was a clergyman who, when on earth, thought Spiritualism was the work of the devil. He was an ardent minister and used to wear a red hood, but he has now given up the foolish ideas which he preached." (4)

"Your father and mother are both in the spirit world, and they send you their love. All is well with your mother. This is not the first time she has come back to you, as she came back on two occasions before, but the first time she could not get through well. The second time, she got through what she wanted quite well." (4)

"Your mother learned a lot about the after-life from you (Arthur) before dying. She feels much younger now. She has met Nellie. Your father is very happy having her with him. Your father can never thank you enough for all you did for your mother. It will be repaid in the years to come. You have many years in front of you, and he is glad that

people look up to you.   He approves of your books."
(3)

"Nellie's mother is also here, but finds it very difficult to understand the new conditions.   She will take a long time to understand them, as she was so attached to earth and the things of earth."   (2)

"For a long time your mother was against your views and did not believe in what you believe. Though she was very proud of her two sons, yet she was so tied down to what she was taught in childhood that she could not realise that things could be different from what she had then been taught.   She feels very humble and subdued now, and is not so opinionative as she was on earth."   (5)

"Your mother saw Nellie just before she passed over.   Your father was also waiting for her.   When she got over here your father said to her: 'What do you think of all this?', to which she replied: 'I suppose I am dead, but I never felt like dying.'   Your father replied: 'You were never dead and you never will be dead.'   Your father put her to bed to rest when she got here."

"For some weeks before she died her mind was very forgetful.   She was losing a grip on earth life. She just slept away quite peacefully.   When she arrived here she was not so surprised as many other people are, because of what you had told her.   For some years before passing her legs were bad, but now she feels quite young again and her great freedom of movement is one of the things that impresses her most in her new life.   She has now a much nicer garden than she had in her own home."   (6)

Then reference was made to the two boys.   "They

are Ian's sons." (Ian is Gaelic for John, my brother, and is his home name.) "One was named Arthur, but his name has been changed, owing to the confusion with you, to a name connected with the family. Your mother objected to the change at first, but now thinks it was a good idea to change the name." (6)

Then reference was made to her furniture, and "she hoped that the big furniture would not be sold". (1) (This was her wish on earth.)

Reference was next made to old family papers, and to old family photographs. "They are not old rubbish and, though you are not interested in them, you should keep them." (3) (Correct. She knew I was not especially interested in these, and she had made this remark, in these words, when on earth, to me.)

"Her father," she said, "was like you in looks. He would push in where angels feared to tread. Very stern and at times she was in awe of him, but looked up to him, as no one could help doing so. She is very fond of him." (7)

She then referred to a visit in recent years to Bournemouth, which I had forgotten and said so, but she said this was correct. I now remember that a few years before she died, my wife and I did stay with her at an hotel in Bournemouth for a few days. (1)

"Your mother is very grateful to Nellie for her kindness to her since she arrived, and for helping her to come back and speak to you. She never could have imagined that Nellie could have been of such help. She has just been like a nurse. Your mother was not always too nice to Nellie, and used to blame Ian for spoiling her, but will not do so again, as Nellie is well worthy of it. Nellie's mother used not to be very nice to her either. Your mother is also very grateful to Gertrude (my wife) for all her kindness to her, which she much appreciated." (6)

She then referred to the pretty nurse who looked after her. She said she liked her very much indeed. She also liked drinking the powdered stuff just before her passing, as it made her mouth feel clean and relieved discomfort. (4)

I then asked my mother what G.W.G. stood for.

"The control stated that she was laughing and that, though she could not explain what the initials stood for, yet she was not that now. She was having to lie low and not say too much, as she felt somewhat subdued after all the opinions she had given on earth. She said she was not a G.W.G. any longer." (5) (Correct. G.W.G. stood for "Great Wee Girl" which we called her when she became opinionative.)

"Your mother was very autocratic, yet homely. She did not like to be pushed on one side, but liked to feel she was someone in the home. Her legs were rather bad towards the end, but now she can walk and feels bright and fresh. She so loved her country place and garden, but now she is in a place where there is no fog and dullness. Three months before her passing her sight became bad, but she can now see clearly and further than before." (6)

"She brings a stick, and says she has now no need for a stick. This is symbolic of her religious outlook. What you told her about her religion was true. When she awoke on the other side she saw a bright light which she thought was Christ, but it was your father. It will be some time before she understands all you told her, but her outlook is much brighter now than it has ever been." (2)

"She is glad Ian's two boys are getting on so well, and she wants you to look after the maid who took such care of her. Mary had to put up with so much from her and was always gentle and patient. Don't cast her aside but keep her in the family." (7)

Mrs. Abbot's control then said he would like Nellie to control the medium herself. Nellie then spoke to me, calling me Arthur throughout. She put her hand (the medium's hand) out, and shook hands with me. She started off by saying: "Your mother is all right." She then said: "I just wish my own mother had a clearer outlook on things, but unfortunately she was kept on the astral plane because of her egotism, her love of subservience, and having people always bowing down to her and loving to be the centre of everything." (5)

"Your father asked me to tell you that if you go to Sloan he will try and get your mother to speak to you by the direct voice." Nellie then said: "I would like my darling Ian to go with you to Sloan so that I can speak to him also." (2)

Nellie continued: "Your mother was conscious almost to the last and passed over without any suffering, and quite naturally. Your mother is very much more willing to learn about her new life than is my mother. It is sad for me not to be able to be with her more as she cannot rise to the plane in which we live, but this will come some day." (1)

In reply to a question, Nellie said: "Yes, we are living just above you and can come to you instantly. We have very bright diffused light which is very much more pleasant than the light from your sun, as it is not so glaring."

Then she referred to Jack who, "owing to his contrition, and the shame he felt for what he had done, had risen to be with the rest of us. He was never bad at heart, in fact he was a very warm-hearted and kind-hearted man. Until he felt shame and remorse he could not rise to where we are, but whenever that came to him, and he saw his mistakes, he was able to mix with us. He certainly did very odd things which seemed to be selfish, but not really selfishness. He was quite a good-hearted man." (7)

Then she referred to her father, who was with her. She said: "The love of money and earth's goods had not spoiled him the way it had spoilt my mother." (2)

Nellie then said: "Your mother would have to unlearn all her past religious ideas, but she would soon do that under your father's guidance."

Nellie then spoke about the conditions over there, emphasising that their world was very much like the earth. She said that when she arrived first of all she saw a beautiful little waterfall, and went and put her hand under the water. When she pulled her hand away it was quite dry, and she did not feel the water. When she bathes in their sea she gets all the pleasure and exhilaration of bathing but is never wet, and comes out of the water quite dry.

In reply to a question, she confirmed what I have already been told, that to come back to earth they come through their own surface, but it was just a question of tuning in to the vibrations of the different surface levels. Yes, they had towns and villages and everything was very beautiful, and they never had any darkness.

The sitting lasted for an hour and a half. When Mrs. Abbot came out of trance I asked her if she knew my brother, and she said: "No." She recognised me because she had seen me going about the London Spiritualist Alliance building, but that she never, to her knowledge, had met my brother, which confirms what my brother had told me that Mrs. Abbot did not know him.

This being so, the information given is all the more interesting, especially the story about Nellie putting her hand under the waterfall, because Nellie told John the same story through another medium.

Mrs. Abbot said, after coming out of trance, that she was quite unaware that my mother had recently passed on. I do not see how she could have heard of it, or known about it, as, after the sitting, I mentioned it to one or two others in the London Spiritualist Alliance, who had not heard of it. It was mentioned only once in *The Times*, but, even if Mrs. Abbot had seen it, I do not see how she could have connected her name with me, in fact I am quite certain that she never knew my mother had died.

The sitting was arranged by the Secretary of the International Institute for Psychical Research, but no name was given. That being so, Mrs. Abbot had no opportunity beforehand to make enquiries, and, when I arrived for the séance, I walked up to her room and found her waiting. She said she had an appointment with someone at two o'clock, but she did not know who it was, and I told her I was the person for whom the appointment was made.

Everything stated above is correct and applicable to my mother and the others mentioned. Ninety-two facts were given at this last séance, none of which the medium could have known. So, if we add together the facts given at the two sittings, we find ninety-six facts were given at the sitting on 9th February 1936, and ninety-two facts given at the sitting on 12th February 1936, making one hundred and eighty-eight in all.

Not one of the statements made was incorrect or even doubtful, and these two séances must be amongst the most evidential ever recorded. My mother returned again and materialised at a séance my brother John attended some years later. He is completely satisfied, as were two other sitters present, who knew her on earth, that she was his mother. As Nellie, his wife, comes into the foregoing sittings I have his permission to quote what he says in his book *Reunited* about her return as a materialised being.

"There is one form of psychic phenomena which I have not so far mentioned. That is Materialisation. I have attended a number of such séances and have seen many spirit forms fully materialised and recognised by those present. On one occasion, when visiting Aberdeen, my friend, Mr. Herbert Hill, president of the Spiritualist Church there, took me to a materialisation séance which was held in the house of one of the members of his church. I had never been in Aberdeen before, and, beyond the fact that I had spoken in the church the previous day, I was quite unknown to my host and hostess and to the other people present."

"At this séance fourteen discarnate individuals living in the Spirit World materialised, so that they could be seen by their relatives and friends living on earth. Their bodies were solid, their features exact in every detail. One man gazed into the eyes of his 'dead' brother and then said: 'There is no doubt about it. Nobody else ever had eyelashes like that.' A woman who materialised spoke to her daughter and then, after looking round the room, she enquired why her other daughter was not there. She was told that she had been prevented from coming at the last moment and was asked if she would care to write a note. On a small table lay a writing-pad and pencil. The woman picked these up and wrote. After the séance was over her daughter let me see what was written—a few words of greeting—and assured me that it was in her mother's handwriting."

"It was at that séance that my wife materialised for the first time since she had passed on. I recognised her instantly. After a few words had passed between us she said: 'I want to come right under the light so that you can be sure it really is myself.' There was a red light suspended from the ceiling in the centre of the room. The sitters moved their chairs aside and my wife walked under the light and held up her face so that I could see it distinctly. Then she did what, to other people, must have seemed a strange thing. She drew back her lips and pointed with her finger to her teeth."

"Now, my wife's teeth were one of her outstanding features. I have heard her dentist say he had never seen a more perfect set of natural teeth. She deliberately drew my attention to this feature as an item of evidential value. After the séance I took the earliest opportunity of looking carefully at the teeth of the medium. The less said about them the better! Perhaps I should add that the medium had been stripped and every article of her clothing carefully searched by two ladies before she entered the séance room."

"A few days later I had a sitting with a medium in London. (Nothing was said about Nellie materialising at Aberdeen.) The first words my wife said were: 'Tell me, did you see me quite plainly? I was rather nervous as it was the first time I had shown myself that way. It was a good idea my letting you see my teeth.' "

"On a subsequent occasion, when she had become more accustomed to materialising her spirit body, she took an electric torch from one of the sitters and for a few moments played the light over her face. It certainly was not the medium, who bore not the slightest resemblance to her either in size or features."

So my mother and Nellie are not underground asleep until the general resurrection of the dead, as the parsons say at funeral services. This erroneous teaching, which the Church has kept alive for over fifteen hundred years, while trampling Spiritualism underfoot, proves that Christianity is not a divine revelation as the Church has always claimed. About death and the hereafter it tells us little, and it has done its best to keep others from discovering what it has neglected. To tell mourners that "now we leave thy servant sleeping", or something similar, gives no comfort to anyone, and can be little distinguished from the materialistic belief that death ends all consciousness, the grave being the end of life. The Christian burial service is a dismal affair comprising a few ancient quotations of what Paul said about

Christ, besides many contradictory statements and things impossible to believe, such as the last judgment, but no more than that. However, I shall now get on with my story.

The daily correspondence I have received for a quarter of a century, from all over the world, confirmed the evidence for survival I have accumulated since my first séance with Sloan in 1918. My library of psychic books did likewise, and yet I feel sure that not one per cent of the world's inhabitants knows that anything supernormal happens in this, our material world. Is there any wonder that so many think of Spiritualism as something believed in by crazy people, and speak and write the most arrant rubbish on the subject? Very slowly the truth is dawning upon an ignorant world, and the reason is that Spiritualists, who have had these wonderful experiences, speak and write about them. The majority do so privately, and the few by means of books and lectures.

I have been privileged to have had the time to make known far and wide my own experiences, not only by my books but on the public platform. I much prefer to put my thoughts on paper than by word of mouth, but I have done the latter as well, because I felt it was my duty and that my personal feelings should not stand in the way. So I have toured Great Britain and Ireland and some of the Continental capitals. I was the first Spiritualist to speak in a Presbyterian church, which was St. Matthews Blyths-wood, in Glasgow, one of the largest churches in that city. I spoke from the pulpit on Sunday, 11th March 1934, to a crowded congregation, and told them what Spiritualism stands for. Other churches, Anglican, Congregational, and others, have welcomed me, but their ministers who take this broadminded outlook are few and far between. I could tell how others have frustrated me, refusing the use of church halls for Spiritualist meetings.

Many other places outside this country would have welcomed me if I had accepted all the invitations I have received, but, with my many other activities, I could not find the time to accept them. So I had to refuse an invitation from a professor of the University of Cairo, who translated *On the Edge of the Etheric* into Arabic, to visit the chief towns of Egypt and there give lectures, all my expenses to be paid. Likewise I refused invitations to the United States, Australia and New Zealand, to speak there at meetings to be arranged for me, all my expenses to be defrayed by the organisations which invited me.

My activities abroad have therefore been confined to Europe, Rome, Copenhagen and Stockholm, where I was at the time on holiday. At Rome, in May 1934, the large audience I addressed in English was most appreciative, my chairman being Prince Christopher of Greece. Various notables were present, and Roman aristocracy and diplomacy were well represented. Several high dignitaries of the Church were there, one, a cardinal, with whom I had a talk after the meeting, telling me that séances were held at the Vatican, but that the Pope, Pius XI, was a bad sitter, much better results being obtained when he was not present. Before I left Rome my wife and I had an audience with His Holiness, and we were both very much amused at what happened before we entered the audience room. A nun came up to my wife with a safety-pin and said: "His Holiness must not see your bare neck." So she pinned together my wife's V-shaped blouse. One would have thought that an old man of eighty, as he was, would not have been upset by a woman's bare neck! Besides that, a mantilla was placed on my wife's head in place of her hat.

I met in Denmark and Sweden many leading men and women interested in the subject, and I found that at all their Spiritualist church libraries English books on Spiritualism far outnumber those in any other language. The meetings at which I spoke were crowded and everyone seemed to understand English, many being able to speak it.

At home I have had some strange experiences when travelling up and down the country. A passenger opposite me in a railway carriage on one occasion leaned forward and said to me: "Mr. Findlay, how is Brutus?" "Quite well," I replied, "but how do you know me or about my dog?" "Oh," he replied, "your photograph, along with Brutus, is in *The Torch of Knowledge*." Many times I have been spoken to about my books in trains, buses, and other public places, by people I have never seen before. On one occasion my taxi-driver in London informed me, when I was paying him, that he had read some of my books, but, strangest of all, I received a letter from a man in Singapore to say that, while he was being driven in a taxi in that town, his Eurasian driver asked him if he had read any of my books, and, if not, he should do so. A man on one occasion came hurrying after me in Hyde Park to ask if he might shake hands with me, and so on it goes, everyone being so nice and appreciative.

At first when I went to a town to address a meeting I would accept an invitation to stay with someone, but my experiences made me in future put up at an hotel. I was paying my own expenses, so no one was out of pocket. On one occasion I was the guest of the vicar of the town, a very hospitable bachelor, but the sheets on my bed were filthy, and just as I got to sleep a loud bang came on my door. I woke up startled to hear a raucous voice shout: "Get out of here, we don't want spooks in this house." I quieted him and he went away. Next morning I told the servant of my experience, to be informed that it was the vicar's brother who suffered from shell-shock as the result of the First World War. On another visit I was starved. I think the entire family was on strict diet, as at each meal I was given only a cup of tea and two thin slices of toast. That is what the father, mother, and two daughters seemed to live upon, and it is little wonder, after having had these two experiences, that I preferred to stop at a good hotel.

In August 1936 I published my novel *The Torch of Knowledge*, a psychic story which caught on much better than I expected. Five thousand copies were sold, by which time the Second World War was on and I could not get paper to reprint it. I have done nothing further about it as, apart from the story, its teaching is contained in some of my other books, so nothing is lost. People, when enquiring into Spiritualism, should read facts, not fiction, the facts indeed being as good as any story, and, as they are true, give more

MYSELF AND BRUTUS.

wholesome nourishment than something fanciful. However, I may change my mind and republish the book some day, as it is often enquired about.

For some years I was a member of the Council of what became the University of London Council for Psychical Investigation, and was present at a fire-walking test in 1937, in the garden of a house at Carshalton in Surrey. We watched two Moslem professional fire-walkers from India run over twelve feet of glowing embers 700 degrees centigrade hot. Then followed five English volunteers. The bare feet of the professionals were uninjured, but the feet of the volunteers suffered in varying degrees from slight burning. The secret of the affair is the speed at which they run, the journey in each case taking one and a half seconds, too fast for the heat to penetrate deeply the natural dampness of the feet. So I came away feeling that there was no mystery about fire-walking, courage and speed being all that is required.

My life has not been all hard work and no play. My pleasure is certainly in my work, but to travel was also a source of enjoyment. Over the past years we always went away for a month in Summer and often abroad in March to find the sun for a few weeks. In Summer we generally took the car to Scotland or abroad, but on two occasions we cruised in Orient liners along the coasts of the Adriatic and Mediterranean, calling at the principal ports. I very much enjoyed seeing Athens and regretted that time did not allow a visit to the interior of Greece. North Africa and Morocco did not appeal to me, the smell in the native quarters of some of the ports being repulsive. Madeira, the Canary and Balearic Islands were well worth visiting but, because of bad weather, we unfortunately could not put into Lisbon, which I so much wanted to see. Vigo, in Spain, is an attractive place and at Gibraltar there is always so much to see.

Our tours abroad by car were extensive. We have covered most of France, northern Italy, Germany, Austria, Switzerland, Hungary, Czechoslovakia, Holland and Belgium in this way, and stayed with friends at old and historic castles. This came about as a result of the visit to us of the Princess Cecilia, as Joan, my daughter, was asked the following year to stay at Cecilienhof, the home of the ex-Crown Prince and Princess in Potsdam, and there she made many friends. She stayed at Cecilienhof for three months, and before she left we also received an invitation to spend a few days there. This we did, and, when Joan's visit came to an end, she received so many invitations from the friends she had made that we returned the following year to Cecilienhof, and also to visit some of her friends. In this way we spent several pleasant weeks amongst the old German aristocracy, who were unanimous in their dislike of Hitler and his regime. Only one was a Nazi, a Bavarian princess who wanted us to remain with her for a few days longer at her castle near Augsburg to meet Hitler, who was coming to visit her, but we refused as we had to get on. I was not sorry to miss him as there was no creature on earth I despised more.

Cecilienhof was built by the Crown Prince in the style of an English Tudor country house. It was a large place and regal style was maintained. In spite of the downfall of the royal house, as the result of the First World War, the Hohenzollerns had kept their private possessions, and moreover their extensive land in Silesia, snatched from Austria by Frederick the Great, brought them in a large revenue. The Crown Prince went daily to Berlin to his office where the estates were managed. I found him a perfect host, and, during our visits, he and his wife could not have been kinder or more hospitable, but I can imagine the satisfaction it gave him, a tall handsome man, parading about in uniform. He had been brought up as a soldier, and to him the army had been everything. Now he was a German citizen and lived the life of a wealthy nobleman.

On the two occasions we were at Cecilienhof we met many well-known people, including all the sons of the ex-Kaiser. The amount of beer they drank after dinner greatly surprised me. One of the guests was the ex-Queen of Spain who, with her ladies-in-waiting, maintained her regal splendour. She and I at luncheon spoke mostly about Spain, and we disagreed about the rights and wrongs of the Spanish Civil War, she upholding Franco and the methods pursued by the Roman Catholic Church towards the Liberals, who wanted the old abuses removed. I favoured the Liberals.

The brother of the Crown Princess, the Herzog (Duke) von Mecklenburg, came one evening to dine. He was an interesting man and had read some of my books which had greatly helped him. He was a liberal-minded man, and I much enjoyed the talk I had with him. My talks with the Crown Prince were mostly political. He had no use for Hitler, but he made me to understand why it was the Führer had gathered the German people round him. We were strolling in his garden at the time, and he stretched out his arm towards Russia and said: "Do you realise that between Germany and Russia is a vast plain, no barriers but rivers, not a mountain range to protect us? We are scared of Russia." After the German defeat in the First World War Germany was helpless, and it was Hitler who brought back the Germans' confidence. He used the Russian menace to obtain and keep his power, and only when Germany re-armed did the Germans feel safe against that vast multitude stretching for over three thousand miles to the east.

The German people as a whole did not want a second war, they had suffered enough in the first. Everyone I spoke to said they wanted peace, and that they could not believe Hitler would ever involve Germany in war. They believed he would make them secure against Russia, and, because of that, he took the opportunity to tie them up hand and foot. Hitler's growing power led him to think he could knock out Russia for ever, and free the Germans from their fear. A wiser man would have brought about a German-Polish-Czechoslovakian-Balkan alliance against the growing industrial and military strength of Soviet Russia, but he was not wise and chose force instead of diplomacy, all of us having to suffer the consequences.

None suffered more than the Hohenzollerns, as Silesia and their great possessions in that province went to Poland. Cecilienhof is now in Russian hands and the Crown Prince and Princess died in simple homes, the latter coming to see us at Stansted Hall in 1952 shortly before her death. Princess Cecilia married an American soldier, an architect by profession, and now lives in Texas. Her brother, Prince

Friedrich, married a daughter of the Earl of Iveagh, and farms near to us in Essex, one of his brothers being killed in the war and another died in South Africa. Some will say "How are the mighty fallen" and that their retribution came because the Kaiser brought it all about in 1914, involving millions of innocent people who likewise suffered just as much. That is true, but he was a cog in a vast military machine, and I doubt if he had the power to stop the wheels from moving in the way directed by the war-minded military leaders. General Grierson, who was military attaché at Berlin just before the outbreak of the First World War, said to my uncle that he found the Kaiser a gentleman, but his entourage abominable.

During the Hitler regime Joan went abroad to stay with our Ambassador at Prague. He is the brother of the friend who accompanied her, and they went by car. The next we heard was that Joan had become very friendly with the wife of the Commandant of the Dachau Concentration Camp, and that after her visit to Prague she was going to stay with her at Dachau. This horrified us, and, when we got word that a German Nazi officer at the camp was paying her attentions, I telephoned to her to come home at once, which she did by degrees as she had other non-Nazi friends with whom she had promised to stay on the way home. My daughter, I might here say, is a good linguist. After being at a boarding school in England she went to Paris and Florence, where she quickly learned to speak French and Italian fluently. Equally easily she learned German, but my wife and I are thankful she later married a nice Englishman and not a German.

Our fourth and last visit to Germany, since we came to live at Stansted Hall, was in 1938 at the time of the Munich conference, when Neville Chamberlain flew to Munich to meet Hitler and so postponed the war. Joan went on to stay with a friend in East Prussia, and my wife and I motored to Garmisch near Munich, at the foot of the Zug-Spitze, 9,725 feet high, the highest mountain in Germany. We stayed on the way with various friends along the German-French border. At this critical time it was interesting to see that our French and German friends along the border were on the best of terms. At a dinner-party, given at a house where we spent a night, French and Germans mixed in a friendly way, and at dinner the two languages were spoken fluently, these border people being bilingual. This house, made famous by being the headquarters of Napoleon at the time when he was striding like a Colossus over Europe, had a huge cannon in its garden. That was to help to protect Germany, and not far away was another protecting France, and yet the people on either side had no wish for war, they understood and liked each other and only wanted peace.

When we arrived at Garmisch I was beginning to wonder if we had been wise to come so far from home, as the talk of war was increasing. Fortunately, at the house where we stayed was Sir Edward Keeling, Conservative member for Twickenham, and a few days later he left for England, promising to get into touch with our Foreign Office and send me a telegram if we should return home. No telegram arrived, but I got into touch with Joan in East Prussia and told her to join us at once. I was thankful when she arrived and then my worry lessened, because at Garmisch we were close to Switzerland and could get out of Germany within an hour. The day Chamberlain arrived at Munich we left for Switzerland, and two days later we were in Geneva. We all heaved a sigh of relief when we crossed the frontier, but we were still a long way from home and to be stranded in Switzerland during a war was not a pleasant prospect.

I shall always remember the evening of our arrival at Geneva. It was the day Chamberlain had returned to London from Munich, and everyone was anxious to know what had happened. He was to broadcast at nine o'clock, and a lady we knew in the hotel asked us to join her party after dinner to get the news on her private radio. This we did, but the reception was so bad that we turned it off and talked of other things. Then my wife and I discovered that this gathering we had got amongst was made up of members of the Oxford Group, which was having a conference at Geneva. Moreover, it soon became evident that they were making a dead set at me.

This was obvious as they had all come round me in a circle, and were plying me with questions as to my religious beliefs. Then a lady started telling everyone of her past mistakes, and, when she finished, a man followed, his past sinful life being revealed in the most blatant manner. I thought this was all very disgusting, and I was moreover irritated by a man on my left who whispered to me at regular intervals: "God is your best friend. God is your best friend." Never before have I felt more moved to tell anybody to "Shut up", but I refrained.

After an hour of this kind of thing I felt I was

amongst a crazy gang of religious maniacs, and, as time passed, and they found they could make nothing of me, they faded away, all but one, who, I was told, was remaining to make a last effort to obtain from me a confession of my past sins. I had taken a dislike to this man from the first, his arrogance and dictatorial way of speech being particularly disagreeable. So I got up to go to bed, my wife having managed to get away earlier, but he insisted that I must hear him, and to a more disgusting story of a life of immorality I have never before listened.

When he ended he did his utmost to get me to tell him my past sinful life, and accept his Christian way of life. They all seemed to wallow in exposing to each other their past shameful lives, but he had to give up defeated in the end and I was glad when we parted. He was annoyed and showed it, but he could not get me to agree with the Apostle James that we should confess our faults one to another (James v, 16). I told him, if he must get relief for his sins in this way, to become a Roman Catholic and tell a priest every-thing in the privacy of the Confessional Box. Next morning I saw him, but nothing further was said, and I hope never again to have a similar experience of concentrated organised impertinence as I had on this occasion.

I am pleased to say that my experience with these enthusiasts has been pleasanter within the last year. Some of them have dropped many of their foolish ways and are now concentrating, under the name of Moral Rearmament, on the life we live and less on creeds and dogmas. Consequently, the high moral standards they advocate now appeal to many who

MY WIFE AS RED CROSS COMMANDANT.

were hitherto repelled or uninterested. By concentrating on the life one should live, and on one God, the Father of all mankind, and not on the religion one believes, the movement is making headway in the Middle East and elsewhere, where religious differences hitherto have kept Mahometans, Christians, and others apart. Anything that helps to bring about the brotherhood of man must have the sympathy of all right-thinking people, and this endeavour to raise mankind everywhere to a higher level of thought and life has my best wishes.

We left Geneva the next morning and arrived safely home. Soon afterwards I received a request from the Chief Constable of Essex asking me to become Chief Warden of North-West Essex for Civil Defence. This I accepted, and now began a series of meetings and conferences which took place once a fortnight, and this lasted for the next two years. North-West Essex had two Chief Wardens, I being allotted the west, and my friend, the Hon. Maynard Greville, the east, a police-sergeant being attached to us for help and guidance. We took turns in having our meetings at each other's houses. The Chief Constable at Chelmsford had his instructions from Civil Defence Headquarters in London, and through him all Chief Wardens were guided as to how to build up defence and organise their divisions. It meant hard work, a stiff examination to pass, and finding the proper men to be wardens in each town and village.

Constant meetings took place in Chelmsford of all the Chief Wardens of Essex, under the chairmanship of the Chief Constable, whose grasp of the innumerable details connected with Civil Defence gained my

admiration. This feeling increased the longer I
worked with the Police. A finer body of men is
not to be found, and their business methods, discipline and courtesy made my work with them a
pleasure. With their help Maynard Greville and I
worked on and, when war came, North-West Essex
was well organised and did its share in the country's
Civil Defence.

We have now reached the fateful year of 1939.
For the past two years I had devoted my spare time
to writing a large volume, a 1,200-page book which I
called *The Psychic Stream*. Herein I give a history of
religion, beginning with the first world-wide religion,
Ancestor Worship, and ending with Christianity. I
had not the space to deal with the Moslem faith, the
last great organised religion. In the first two hundred
pages I covered Magic, Sun Worship, how man discovered his spirit, Animism, Ancestor Worship, Mythology, and the beliefs surrounding sin and sacrifice.

I then made it evident that the saviour-god
religions, which followed, came from seeing the
apparition of a sacrificed victim of the priests, who
was then deified, all apparitions being looked upon
as gods. Each victim was worshipped with divine
honours, because it was believed that he had broken
the curse of death by his sacrifice and his return.
Each was given after death names such as Saviour,
Redeemer, Mediator, the Lamb of God, the Good
Shepherd, the Only Beloved Son, Our Lord, The Way
of Truth and the Life, and many other such titles,

most of which were attached to Jesus after he was seen after death as a priestly victim.

How an apparition evolved into a Christ, or Saviour god, I explained, step by step, and the process can easily be understood if the evolution is regarded as proceeding from the natural to the supernatural. An apparition changed a natural man after death in each case into a divine being, but, when the story came to be told later, his followers ignored the natural and only accepted the belief that he was born and died a god. Consequently, it was claimed for each that a virgin was his mother and a god his father. As he was believed to have been unnaturally born, he, after his suffering, had to return to heaven as only a god could, so he is reported as ascending into the sky like a balloon.

What we are told in the Gospels is not new. This we discover when we examine the close relations of Christianity, those earlier religions whose beliefs brought the Christian faith into being, namely the eastern Saviour-God religions. So I told in *The Psychic Stream* of the beliefs, from virgin birth to resurrection, surrounding the saviour-gods Bel of Babylonia, Osiris of Egypt, Prometheus of Greece, Mithra of Persia, and Krishna of India, all of which produced the Christian faith. The beliefs draped round all these gods were similar to those which became Christianity. One instance only shall I give:—

The beliefs surrounding Bel were similar to those which came, at a later date, to surround Jesus. This we know because there has been discovered, engraved on baked clay, the programme of the drama of the arrest, trial, death and resurrection of Bel which was in use at the time when Bel was worshipped in Babylon. Consequently it was in existence when the Gospels were being compiled and we find, when we consider the compilation of the Gospels, how it was used as the basis for the Christian drama.

This clay tablet is accepted by Babylonian scholars as the programme used by the priests at the drama depicting the death scenes of the life of Bel, known to the Hebrews as Baal. Its translation was made by Professor Zimmern in 1918 and published at Leipzig. When I called to discuss it with the Curator of the Babylonian Section of the British Museum, he told me that the translation is accepted as "a list of parallel instances found both in the story of Bel and of the Christ. Zimmern deduced the incidents of the story of Bel from ritual texts, which seem to describe a primitive kind of religious play."

The foregoing was written out for me by the Curator, when I was in his private room, and I have this beside me now as I write. The tablet is believed to have been produced about two thousand years before the Christian era, and it was evidently used by the priest who acted as the announcer of the drama. He would have the tablet before him, and, before each scene, would announce what was about to take place.

What follows is the translation of the tablet giving the programme of the Passion Drama enacted in memory of the sacrifice of the saviour-god Bel, the Christ of Babylonia, just as the Christian Passion Drama is enacted in our time at Oberammergau in Bavaria. A similar drama was produced in ancient Egypt, the saviour god there being Osiris. Here follows the Babylonian passion drama, and the corresponding incidents in the Christian drama:—

Babylonian Drama.	*Christian Drama.*
Bel is taken prisoner.	Jesus is taken prisoner.
Bel is tried in the Hall of Justice.	Jesus is tried in the Hall of Pilate.
Bel is smitten.	Jesus is scourged.
Bel is led away to the Mount.	Jesus is led away to Golgotha.
With Bel are taken two malefactors, one of whom is released.	With Jesus two malefactors are led away; another, Barabbas, is released.
After Bel has gone to the Mount the city breaks out into tumult.	At the death of Jesus the veil of the Temple is rent: from the graves come forth the dead, and enter the city.
Bel's clothes are carried away.	Jesus's robe is divided among the soldiers.
Bel goes down into the Mount and disappears from life.	Jesus goes down from the grave into the realm of the dead.
A weeping woman seeks him at the gate of burial.	Mary Magdalene comes weeping to the tomb to seek Jesus.
Bel is brought back to life.	Jesus rises from the grave alive.

The translation of this tablet is ignored by Christians for obvious reasons, but whoever reads what I have to say about it in *The Psychic Stream* will agree with me that the man of sorrows referred to in the fifty-third chapter of Isaiah was probably Bel, or one of the other pre-Christian saviour gods, and it was not a prophecy about Jesus as all Christians believe. Likewise it is probable that Bel was the living Redeemer, to whom Job refers and, moreover, we can now understand more about the suffering, dying victim, about whom Plato writes, when he pictured the "just man" who was crucified at the hands of his enemies.

So I compared each outstanding incident recorded in the Gospels with their counterparts in these older religions, and thus reached the conclusion that the only difference between them and Christianity is a new name for its god, which change of name was just history repeating itself. The names of the gods changed, but the legends, myths and beliefs were passed on from one religion to another.

Thus the psychic stream flowed on under different names, but it is wrong to think that the moral teaching of Christianity is higher than in those earlier religions. In Egypt, Greece and India the moralising attached to their religions was more extensive than is to be found in Christianity, and to put Christianity forward as teaching a higher morality than its predecessors is historically false. Christianity gave nothing new to the world that was not believed long before it ever existed.

My psychic knowledge made it clear to me that the origin of Christianity was the reappearance of Jesus as an apparition. Two stories are given in the Gospels about the return of Jesus after death, the oldest being about his return as an etheric being, and the other, which has been written over the first, recording his return as a man in his physical body. Scholars, who have given the text much thought, believe that the oldest psychic story gave place to the other because of a remark in the Old Testament (Hosea vi, 2) which was considered to be a prophecy foretelling the physical resurrection of Jesus on the third day after death. Obviously, it had no reference whatever to Jesus, but, when the Gospels were written, the authors and interpolators searched the Scriptures for anything that could be turned into a prophecy of the Messiah.

This scriptural authority was quoted in early Christian times, as a reply to scoffers at the belief in the appearance of Jesus as an apparition, and thus a physical resurrection came to be believed. Mithra, the rival god to Jesus when Christianity was developing, had, it was believed by his worshippers, risen from his rock tomb three days after his body had been placed in it. The early Christians felt that their god must be equal to the Mithraic god in his power over death, and so the story about the resurrection of Mithra from his rock tomb came to be attached to Jesus. Consequently it was incorporated in the Gospels along with the first one about an apparition, to make just nonsense.

Paul believed he saw Jesus after death as a spirit, and *The Psychic Stream* considers why this changed his life. In those days a spirit was believed to be a god. Paul, by his writings, was undoubtedly a medium and, from what he writes, he believed he was controlled by Jesus, now to him a god. He consequently transformed him into a heavenly Christ after the pattern of the Greek god Dionysus, the god of Tarsus. Thus he laid the basis of the Christian faith which, as my book shows, others developed as the years passed, to end in the Nicene creed, which put the new faith into words at the Council of Nicaea in 325. Thereafter, by persuasion, the sword, persecution, and the power of Constantine behind it, Christianity defeated its rivals and became a powerful organisation.

Thus a new religion was born and developed as had happened so often before. Once again a reformer, who was probably a medium, was seized by the priests and offered to the gods on the sacrificial altar. Again it was thought that his life-work had ended in failure. But no. To some of his followers he appeared after his death, and this they took to be a sign from heaven that he was the one chosen by God to break the fear of death, and end the feud between God and man.

Consequently he was termed the Saviour. He was regarded as the Chief Priest who had gone before to make intercession on behalf of the human race. His reappearance opened a new chapter in the history of man's relations with God, and round this event grew up all manner of doctrines and dogmas. A vast theology accumulated over the centuries, composed of mystical speculations relating to sin, sacrifice, and atonement. Stories were told of how the promise of a Saviour had been made to the first man, and how God had now fulfilled this promise.

A new era, it was believed, had, in consequence, opened in man's religious history, and those who accepted the saviour-god idea were comforted by the thought that their Saviour had gone before, to make intercession for them at the throne of God. Here, as heretofore, we find the psychic stream to be the cause of this western religious development, which, prior to Christianity, embraced all the countries from India to the Middle East until, as Christianity, it covered all Europe, America, and Australasia. As the result of Alexander's conquests, the east had made contact with the west, and the saviour-god idea made headway westwards, Bel, Osiris, Krishna, Mithra, Prometheus, and Dionysus supplying the theological material to drape round Jesus who likewise became another Pagan Christ.

Unfortunately, *The Psychic Stream* was published three weeks before the outbreak of the Second World War, when many newspapers ceased reviewing books. Nevertheless, those that did review it were eulogistic of its theme, two religious journals especially being so, *The Hibbert Journal* in a long review remarking:—

> "There will be many to strike at this book. But first it should be read, for it is a scholarly, well-written work, and, if its arguments are sound, it is of great importance to mankind. The book will disturb the orthodox, but they especially should read it. From a large number of the laity it will receive sympathy and approval. All must accord to Mr. Findlay admiration for his labours and his style of exposition."

The Modern Churchman, in its long review, was equally kind to the book, remarking that:—

> "In the field of psychical research Mr. Findlay may be regarded as a specialist, and this is manifest in the very careful and competent way in which he analyses and presents the evidence for the resurrection of Jesus Christ. It is a terrible danger to which Christianity is exposed in this modern world, by its failure courageously to separate truth from error."

The weekly journal *Truth*, in its extensive review, remarked:—

> "*The Psychic Stream* can be read with immense profit by followers of any persuasion for, though challenging, it is never offensive. Everyone will concede to Mr. Findlay an industry which never descends either to dullness or irrelevance. He is always the exploring individual."

Now I must tell a tale about two bishops. I shall call one Bishop A and the other Bishop B, as I cannot mention their names, they having been my guests at Stansted Hall. It would hardly be courteous to do so. They did not come together, but separately, Bishop A being the first, shortly after the time *The Psychic Stream* was published. He asked me about it in the course of conversation and I told him briefly its contents. "I shall be obliged," he said, "if you will lend me a copy. I would like to write a book in reply." "Certainly," I replied, "I shall be only too glad to read your opinion about it. Let me know when your book is published and I shall get a copy." His last words to me on leaving were: "I shall reply to it, never fear." That was in 1939, sixteen years ago, and I have never had an answer from him to my request to know when his reply will be published. He has not carried out his promise because he cannot do so, and I imagine he found he was up against something about which he was quite ignorant, Christian theological colleges ignoring the study of comparative religion.

However, Bishop B was not so bold. He came to have afternoon tea with us some weeks later, and again

I was asked about *The Psychic Stream*. I asked him if he would like to read it and he took a copy away with him. When returning it, his only comment was that the contents were quite new to him, and they greatly disturbed him. He was quite unaware of the similarities between Christianity and the pre-Christian Pagan religions, and the subject has never been discussed between us since then.

Handicapped as it was by the outbreak of war, and considering its size, it is remarkable how popular *The Psychic Stream* became, so much so that it went out of print after two thousand copies had been sold, and only after the war was over could I get enough paper to reprint it. To-day it sells at a higher rate than ever before, and I do not see why this should not continue for many years as it becomes better known and is more widely read. In America it is very popular, Dr. Marcus Bach, Professor of Psychology at the State University of Iowa, U.S.A., when speaking at a Church Congress in Chicago in September 1948, remarking:— "Then I found Arthur Findlay's *The Psychic Stream* and Findlay's other works. Very soon Spiritualism was taking on a new meaning to me and my limited horizons were being pushed back." This, and what many others have said and written in the same strain, greatly encouraged me, but I must now turn to other subjects.

When an official of the Foreign Office was staying with us at Stansted Hall in June 1939 I was shocked when he told me that the chance of war with Germany was evenly balanced—"fifty-fifty" was his expression, and, as Dr. Hubert von Dirksen, the German Ambassador to London, and his wife, were also our guests that week-end, the prevailing feeling was rather tense. Dr. Dirksen was not a Nazi, though his wife was, he being a German aristocrat doing his duty in London under difficult circumstances. He definitely stated to me that war would be a disaster for everybody, and expressed the hope that Hitler would act with caution and not cause the peace to be broken. We liked him, but his wife was a strong-minded aggressive woman, and was known to her acquaintances as "the pocket battleship".

Shortly after this we were invited to a reception at the German Embassy in London, but it was not a happy affair. The Germans living in London, who were present, were definitely fearful that the worst would happen, and the question of what their fate would be distressed them. Though there was much pomp and ceremony, the glittering gold had little effect in raising our hopes, and, when the time for parting came, I am sure no one was sorry. I have sometimes wondered what has happened to these German guests, the victims of one of the most terrible tyrannies known to humanity. Fortunately for everyone, "Heil Hitler" is heard no more, this evil-minded devil having gone hence to reap the misery he sowed so lavishly.

Joan had recently become engaged to Francis Wayne, a London Chartered Accountant, and my wife and I were greatly pleased. We could not wish her to have a better husband and we both greatly like him. Unfortunately the wedding ceremony and gathering on 9th September 1939 was a week after the outbreak of war. The marriage proceeded as arranged, but the large gathering invited dwindled to only some near relations. This was fortunate as a week previously evacuees from London poured into the country. Stansted had its share, and thirty-six mothers and children were sent to us. My wife was at her wit's end, having to arrange a wedding and find accommodation at Stansted Hall for all these London refugees. I cannot imagine a stranger setting for a wedding, but in the end accommodation and beds were found and the newcomers settled down, thankful to be out of London, which expected an immediate bomb attack.

Gradually, as the week passed, homes were found for everyone in the neighbourhood, and nothing spectacular happened as regards bombing. This war, unlike its predecessor, did not open with a flourish, and we all settled down hoping for the best, but expecting the worst. We had previously offered Stansted Hall to the Red Cross as a convalescent home, as a gift, for the duration of the war, but we heard nothing definite as to whether it would be accepted or not. Months passed and then the bombing started, and, as we were on the route between Germany and London, we had nightly air raids. For a time not many bombs fell in our neighbourhood, but, when the London defences increased, some raiders were turned back, to drop their bombs over us on their way home.

On two occasions Stansted Hall was taken over by Eastern Command, and used as headquarters for military exercises. Consequently the house, for several days during each exercise, was filled with army officers from the General commanding downwards. Officers occupied most of the rooms for their staff work, while some fifty men occupied the picture gallery and slept on the hard wooden floor. We felt sorry we could not provide them each with at least a mattress. The army itself lived outside in tents, and the house was surrounded by an encampment of thousands of officers and men. In the house sentries were posted everywhere, and we were amused to be challenged every time we walked about the house, even when going to bed at night. When it was all over the General on each occasion thanked us for our hospitality, but all we got out of this inconvenience was a large-scale military map of the district which they left behind.

Bombing went on each night, the wardens being well employed, and then came a letter to me from the Red Cross to say that it wanted our entire house at once. This quite upset our daily life, as, instead of having a small part of the house to ourselves as we intended, they asked for it all, and only reluctantly allowed us to keep to ourselves the estate office, a bedroom and a sitting-room. With our kitchen also taken from us we now decided to leave and make regular visits home, as we had to attend to our affairs. We kept the accommodation left to us, but had to cook our own meals on an oil-stove each time we returned home. No other house in the neighbourhood was available, there being such a rush out of London, and consequently we had to find one elsewhere. We were experiencing what the people living around London had to put up with when most of the population of London fled to the country at the time of the Great Plague in 1665.

We left Stansted Hall in December 1940 and how we fared away from home I shall tell in the next chapter.

NORMAN TOWERS, ENTRANCE TO COURTYARD.

Aero Pictorial L

ROCKINGHAM CASTLE.

CHAPTER NINE.

ROCKINGHAM CASTLE.

(1940–1945.)

THE Red Cross Society took over Stansted Hall in December 1940. Unfortunately we could not find another house, and a relation of my wife kindly asked us to come and stay with her for as long as we wished. This I did rather reluctantly as I knew her strong orthodox religious opinions and her hatred of Spiritualism, but we had to go somewhere within motoring distance. She lived in an attractive old historical house in the Midlands, fifty miles away, and that made it possible for us to come home for the day whenever necessary. I had to resign my post as Chief Warden and give up all my other county work. The farm and estate I left in charge of my bailiff, and the head gardener, with a reduced staff, looked after the garden and pleasure grounds. My accountant and my secretary kept things going at the estate office.

I did not anticipate the future with pleasure, the feeling that it might be years before we were again settled at home being depressing. The one bright prospect was that the house we had come to was peaceful, and we could sleep at night undisturbed by bombing. We were comfortable at our new abode, having a nice bedroom and sitting-room, and, as we paid a large rent in return for what we received, the arrangement seemed to please our hostess. She was a widow with two grown-up sons and a daughter at home.

Everything worked well for two months, when to my surprise she walked one morning into our sitting-room holding a copy of *Psychic News* between her fingers as if it was something foul. "This is a newspaper you are getting every week," she said in a solemn voice as if I were doing something terrible. "Yes," I said. "What about it?" "It is a Spiritualist newspaper, and I can have no one in my house who is a Spiritualist. You must both leave at once." I looked out of the window, the ground was white with snow, and said: "Leave! In weather like this, without a home to go to?" "Yes, as soon as you possibly can," she replied. My wife then came into the room and was naturally very upset when she heard what had happened.

I had never spoken to the family about Spiritualism or Religion, and I was pleased to feel how smoothly things had gone by being wise and tactful. Consequently, our being turned out of our temporary home in mid-winter came as rather a shock to me and my wife, but we decided to accept our fate and leave the next morning. When passing through Huntingdon we called at an estate agent's office and took the only furnished house he had vacant on his books at a little place called Hemingford Grey, a few miles away on the River Ouse, and there we stayed for five months.

Christians have done many terrible things throughout the Christian era to those they considered heretics. They have faithfully fulfilled the prophecy of their Lord: "Think not that I am come to send peace on earth. I come to send not peace but a sword" (Matthew x, 34). "I am come to send fire on earth" (Luke xii, 49). "The father shall be divided against the son and the son against the father, the mother against the daughter and the daughter against the mother, the mother-in-law against her daughter-in-law and the daughter-in-law against the mother-in-law" (Luke xii, 53).

When we remember that throughout the Christian era Christians, basing their actions on passages in the Old and New Testaments, have slaughtered 25,000,000 victims whom they called heretics, we realise how true was the forecast of Jesus. Montaigne (1533–92), the great French essayist, tells us that in the French religious wars of his time, which covered a comparatively short period of religious persecution throughout Christendom, 800,000 heretics were killed and 128,000 houses destroyed. The ferocity, treachery and inhumanity of the Christian zealots made him blench with horror, he says. Within thirty years, from 1618 to 1648, over sixteen million victims died in Germany and Bohemia during the ferocious wars between the Catholics and the Protestants. Is it to be wondered that thinking people of our day, those who know the history of the Christian Church, feel that Christianity has done more harm than good, and that mankind would have been no worse off without it, much of the Christian era, moreover, being the most debased period of civilised human history?

Before we left the house of our intolerant hostess, one of her sons came to our sitting-room to explain, as he said, the situation. "You must not think," he said, "that the decision we have made has not been come to without much prayer and thought. I have prayed earnestly to do God's will and, as Paul said: 'Be not unequally yoked together with unbelievers, and touch not the unclean thing.' We have made our decision that you must go. I made a special visit to London to consult my spiritual adviser, my friend Dr. Lang, Archbishop of Canterbury." "What did he say?" I asked with a smile, thinking this was very amusing. "He told me we must do as our conscience guides us," he replied, "and that is what we are doing."

I answered: "We have no wish to remain where we are not wanted, but in my opinion you are all intolerant fanatics. You have known for years I was a Spiritualist, and you have often accepted our hospitality at Stansted Hall. I got for you a partnership in a good firm of stockbrokers in London, and I have helped you in every way I could. In my opinion you are an ungrateful religious zealot, but your religion will not keep you from reaping what you sow. The eternal law of cause and effect supersedes all religious creeds and dogmas about being saved by belief in a sacrificed god. You may think that what you are doing is pleasing to God, but remember everyone makes God in his own image, a cruel man worships a cruel God, and a good man a good God." I then asked him to leave the room because he started quoting Bible texts about the fate of unbelievers, to justify his intolerance.

Shortly afterwards he entered the Roman Catholic Church, to entertain archbishops and bishops he got to know, but, when he became bankrupt, that ceased. The end was tragic as, lacking a high standard of ethical conduct, and, having only a crazy religious outlook, the last few years of his life were miserable. So ended a wasted life. He was a brilliant musician and had much personal charm but, unfortunately, his mind was not well balanced. So ended another experience I had with religious fanatics. When telling of my mother's intolerance, I said that I came in for the tail end of the long period of religious persecution. This age I have found out throughout my life to be possessed of a long tail, and mankind, still steeped in religious ignorance, has not yet seen its end.

My various experiences were not so disagreeable as those that befell Robert Owen (1771–1858), a Manchester cotton spinner, who was one of the greatest men of the 19th century. He was a pioneer in philanthropy, a word hardly known before his time in Christendom. He conducted his mills profitably and with great ability, but on humane lines, his employees working in clean, healthy, sanitary buildings, and for shorter hours than his competitors. He would have no child labour, and paid his workers during periods of depression. These he had educated, and, in an age of drunkenness, taught them to be sober and thrifty. He advocated an improved environment for all employees, but could find no other employer willing to support him. So, alone, he educated his workers out of their crimes, drunkenness and filth, and raised them to be respected and decent citizens.

The first Factory Act (1819), the Child's Magna Charta, was largely due to his efforts. All the abuse the Christians of his day could invent was hurled at him, to increase in intensity when he declared himself openly to be a Spiritualist and not a Christian. He conceived and carried out as far as possible all that the later Socialists worked for, and can be considered the founder of Fabian Socialism and the Co-operative movement.

He founded a non-theological school at New Lanark, and was the pioneer of all the reforms the workers now enjoy. He was a man of great liberality, and supported the unorthodox Lancaster, when he started his secular schools all over the country. Only then, in order to prevent the children of their flocks from being contaminated by heretical ideas, did the Episcopalians and Roman Catholics start their Church schools, their attitude hitherto being against the education of the ordinary people.

We did not like Hemingford Grey. It was situated in flat, uninteresting country, and the slow-moving muddy Ouse did not add to its beauty. It was now July 1941, and we looked out for something new. Fortunately, we heard from mutual friends that a wing of Rockingham Castle in Northamptonshire was soon to be vacant, and we wrote to Lady Culme-Seymour, the mother of the owner who was a Commander in the navy. She wrote back saying she would be delighted to have us for as long as we liked, and that she would so like to meet me as *On the Edge of the Etheric* had given her much pleasure to read. We motored over to see her and the accommodation we could have, and it ended by our paying her a visit.

We so liked Rockingham Castle that I took the wing offered, but, as it was not available until November, what were we to do meantime? Finally, we decided to leave Hemingford Grey at once, go up to Scotland, find a nice furnished house in the Highlands, and stay there until the Autumn. The very place we

wanted in Scotland was put before us by an estate
agent in Perth, and off we went to see it, to end in
our spending four pleasant months at Invercroskie
House, at the head of Strathardle between Blairgowrie
and Pitlochry in Perthshire. It was beautifully
situated in this lovely glen, the moors sloping upwards
to the towering hills, and the River Ardle rushing past
us, tumbling over rocks and into deep pools only about
two hundred yards away at the end of our lawn.

Our pastime was walking on the moors and fishing
in the river and a nearby loch, but we were not dull,
as we soon got to know our very friendly neighbours
in the glen, who were most hospitable to us. Our
nearest towns were Blairgowrie to the south, fourteen
miles away, and Pitlochry thirteen miles away to the
west, and a good road served the various shooting
estates on either side of the valley. If only the war
situation had been better, if only there had been no
war, our time in Perthshire would have been one of
pleasure and enjoyment, but unfortunately our
Scottish visit coincided with the German invasion of
Russia, everyone being gloomy and expecting the
imminent collapse of Russian resistance.

From the outbreak of war in September 1939, when
the German army battered its way into Poland, everything had gone well with the aggressors. By the
middle of 1940 France had fallen, and, by great good
fortune, most of our army escaped from France
through Dunkirk. ¯Britain was now in extreme peril,
as her¯outer defences on the Continent had collapsed.
Italy had by now entered the war against us, and the
Mediterranean and North Africa were in danger of
her domination. In August intense daylight air raids

began on Britain, which were taken to be the prelude to an attempted invasion, but this fortunately ended in our victory in the Battle of Britain.

Here I might say that before we left Stansted Hall, and during this strenuous and dangerous period, we were asked by the commander of the airfield, five miles from Stansted, to entertain some of the men at Stansted Hall who returned each day from their daily flights against the invading forces. Consequently, after a morning of fighting, they would come to us for the afternoon, and it was not unusual to have several airmen for lunch who had spent the morning hunting and shooting down enemy bombers. Coming to us gave them a break, by taking their minds off the terrible ordeal through which these brave men were passing, and they were all grateful for the change of surroundings we were able to give them.

In June 1941 Hitler made his most fatal blunder. With nearly all Europe, outside of Russia, now dominated by him, he felt sufficiently strong to meet and defeat the one enemy Germany most dreaded. So he attacked Russia, and the impetus of the onslaught compelled the Russian armies to fall back everywhere. A great extent of devastated country was occupied, but Russia was not conquered. Slowly her army retreated, both sides losing heavily, but the further it retreated the stronger it became.

That then was the position during our time in Scotland, and it accounted for the gloom which overhung our glen and the rest of the country, but, just as we left for Rockingham Castle, the turn came. Russia struck back, driving the enemy out of Rostov and from the gates of Moscow, thus forcing the

Germans to endure in the open one of the earliest and worst Russian winters within living memory. So the year 1941 ended with the once unconquerable German army lacking the necessary winter clothing, suffering terrible hardships, and losing by frost-bite, death in battle, wounds and illness a large proportion of the men who, six months earlier, had so confidently advanced into the unknown.

We were very sorry when the time came to leave Invercroskie House, where we had been very comfortable, but the turn in the tide of war encouraged us to hope that the time would come some day when we would be back at Stansted Hall. Meantime, we settled in at Rockingham Castle in November 1941, where we found our quarters both warm and comfortable, every modern convenience being installed. Moreover, its beautiful gardens were open to us any time for our pleasure and recreation. Lady Culme-Seymour set herself to make us comfortable in every way, and this delightful lady, whom we both came to love and admire, did everything in her power to make our stay at the castle both happy and pleasant.

Rockingham Castle is the home of Commander Sir Michael Culme-Seymour, the fifth baronet, and son of Admiral Sir Michael Culme-Seymour, who was Second Sea Lord at the time of his death. He was the fourth successive admiral of the family in the direct line. The castle was originally, in the time of William the Conqueror, a favourite hunting-box in Rockingham Forest. He converted it into a castle, and for long it was used for hunting by the Kings of England. William Rufus, in 1095, summoned to the castle a council of nobles, bishops and clergy, to settle the dispute between himself and Anselm, the Archbishop of Canterbury. For two days they debated in the Great Hall of the castle whether the King or the Pope had the authority to appoint the archbishop.

Right through the centuries there is a record of royal deeds at the castle, King John, for instance, having lived there from 1204 till 1216. Thence he went on his last journey where he lost his treasure in the Wash on his way to Newark, leaving behind him an iron-bound wooden chest which to-day is to be seen in the Great Hall. Henry V went to the castle in 1422, and likewise left behind him a decorated chest to be seen near the one belonging to King John. King James I visited the castle, and sold it to Sir Lewis Watson, whom he created Lord Rockingham. In Cromwell's time the Roundheads demolished the Keep and did much damage, which Lord Rockingham spent the remainder of his life repairing.

As the centuries passed the castle was enlarged, it now being made up of the original building erected by William I and several additions, the most modern being the part we occupied, which was built during last century. This large and stately edifice stands high overlooking the Welland valley with views extending over five counties and ranging far and wide over miles of open hilly countryside. Its massive gateway, the most impressive feature of the castle, is believed to have been repaired or rebuilt by King John, and one's imagination is stimulated by its formidable size, the two towers on either side being capable of holding a hundred soldiers ready in time of danger to let down the portcullis and shoot their arrows or bullets through their narrow slit windows.

This then was to be our home for the next four years, and here it was I wrote the greatest part of *The Curse of Ignorance*. Appalled by the folly of mankind, I had started this large work at Stansted when war broke out, but nightly air raids made concentration difficult. I tried once to write through an air raid, but, after completing a page, had to abandon the effort. I had more peace to get on with the book after leaving Stansted Hall, and at Rockingham the conditions were ideal. All my reference books I had brought from Stansted Hall, and, with little else to occupy my mind, it was my principal occupation. This work made my exile from home bearable and, in fact, pleasant.

It may be asked why I undertook such an immense task as that of writing the history of mankind. The reason was to expose the folly of humanity down the ages, and of course the theme developed the more I thought about it, but what made me decide to call it *The Curse of Ignorance* was some remarks made by a well-known man.

On the night of the 20th September 1942, while listening to the radio, a speech was relayed that was made that day by the first Earl of Halifax, who has held many important government appointments, and has received many honours. He is acknowledged as a great administrator and was Viceroy of India (1926–31), Secretary of State for War, and has held many other responsible positions, but his ignorance of the history of the Christian era made me think deeply. This report of a speech he had just made was passed

L.B.—N

on by the radio to listeners as history, and doubtless nearly everyone took what he said to be true. "The curse of ignorance!" I said to my wife, "to think that these remarks are accepted by nearly everyone as true. Ignorance abounds and orthodox Christianity flourishes. I shall call my new book *The Curse of Ignorance*."

This prominent man, doubtless typical in his religious beliefs of the great majority, stated, amongst other things to which I took exception, that Christianity had been responsible for all the hospitals, and deeds of kindness and mercy which we now enjoy, and that every one of the things we value is rooted in Christian thought. My reply to that statement is that it is not true. In my books *The Curse of Ignorance* and *The Psychic Stream* I tell what is true about the rise to power of the Christian Church, and the cause of its ultimate greatness. Here I shall mention a few outstanding facts.

At the conclusion of the Council of Nicaea in 325 the Emperor Constantine raised Christianity from being one of the despised cults in his dominions to be the State Church of the Empire. This was because of the decision of that Council to adopt the Trinity as a Christian belief. Consequently, the quarrelling and wrangling that had been going on over this question amongst the followers of Jesus for over a hundred years was brought to an end by Imperial decree. This was to the effect that all were to become Trinitarians and cease to be Unitarians, as so many of the Jesuians had been so far. By this momentous decision of the Council of Nicaea the Christian Church inherited the Roman Empire eighty-five years later, and its Pope sat on the Imperial throne.

How few there be who appreciate what this important event meant to the people of the Western World! Because of the consequences which followed I place it as the greatest event in history. Christianity, as we now know it, more or less, had come into being under the patronage of the Crown with its indisputable authority. The man Jesus had been turned into the god Christ. So the Christian priests put on the Pagan priestly vestments, officiated at all state functions, said prayers similar to what the Pagans said, and the congregations sang hymns similar to the Pagan hymns to the gods under new names. The Pagan holy days were taken over, and each local statue to Mithra, or some other saviour god, had the old god's name chiselled out and the name of the new god Christ chiselled in. The Pagan ritual and ceremonies were copied and continued, as were the marriage and baptismal services. So also were the Pagan Sunday services, morning and afternoon, as was the Pagan Eucharist, Christianity adopting from the Pagans the name of "The Lord's Table" for the place where the Pagans placed their bread and wine at their Holy Communion service.

Thus were the old Pagan saviour-god beliefs carried on under the new name of Christianity, and it was because of that the old religions faded out and the new religion spread so rapidly, to last so long. Its age-old beliefs met a need, just as it meets the needs of so many to-day. Mankind, in pre-Christian times, required a saviour, and, when Constantine made Christianity the state religion of the Empire, the people needed a saviour. From that time to the present a saviour has been a very welcome help in trouble.

Because the need was there the people got from the priests the spiritual food which gave them the comfort they required.

The Jesuians, or Unitarians, with the Hebrew Scriptures behind them, thus lost to the Trinitarian Christians. The weight of the Imperial throne, and the widespread beliefs in the Christs of the past, overcame the minority of Unitarians who were mostly the despised Jews. Later, in the 6th century, Christianity adopted the Hebrew Scriptures, because of their long tradition and the reverence attached to them, in spite of the fact that it had gone quite contrary to the dictates of Jehovah, who denounced all Trinities of Gods. Moreover Jesus is reported as saying that there is only one God in heaven. On these, and other texts, the Unitarian Jesuians based their arguments against the belief in a trinity of gods, but, by the 4th century, Christianity had adopted most of the beliefs of the other saviour-god religions, and the belief each had in a trinity of gods was too widespread to be ignored. In Rome in 493 B.C. a temple was dedicated to the Greek Trinity, Demeter, Dionysus and Persephone, and called the Temple of the Trinity.

When Rome was captured by the Christian Visigoths in 410, Constantinople had taken the place of Rome as the administrative centre of the empire. Innocent I, a strong and resolute opportunist, was Bishop of Rome between the fateful years of 402 and 417, the most momentous pontifical period in the history of the Church, as within that time Rome fell to the Christian Visigoths, when, with their consent, he stepped into the place of the Emperor. He was the first to lay claim to the status of sovereign over the entire Western Church. Though the Eastern Church rejected this bold assertion it would still be correct to look upon him as the first Pope. From this time onwards the Bishop of Rome took the title of Pontifex Maximus, and succeeded to this Pagan office. He took over all the royal palaces and became the Chief Priest, the bishops being the high priests, who ruled as provincial governors, all of whom claimed to be controlled by the Holy Spirit. He claimed moreover to be Vicar of Christ and to speak for God.

The Emperor now lived at Constantinople, but Rome had the glorious traditions of the past. The Pope, from now onwards, and surrounded by numerous slaves, received the greatest possible honour and position by becoming Pontifex Maximus, a position held in the past only by the emperors. He therefore became a theocratic monarch, and Rome the centre of his great dominion. This new theocratic empire, the Christian Church, which now ruled the old empire it inherited, thus became a temporal and a spiritual empire under the name of Christian, though in numbers it was far from Christian. Nevertheless, it was only the name that was changed, not the civilisation or culture, which continued Roman and Greek.

All the culture and civilisation of the ages, the laws and the ethics, passed down from Babylonia and Egypt to Greece, and then to Rome, were now behind the Christian Church, and to them were attached the names of Christian civilisation and Christian culture, Christian this and Christian that. The name Pagan was given by the Church to the past, and the civilisation and culture which Paganism had produced was now claimed to have come from Christianity, and was their possession alone.   Pagan is a word which means country people, because they were the last to adopt Christianity.   Christianity now became elevated and sanctified, and Paganism derided and scorned.   Pagan thought and religion were related to the Devil, its gods were termed devils and everything for the good and glory of the Church was attributed to the Christian gods.

Thus, a state-organised religion, with a supreme and all-powerful pontiff, was successful in changing history and imposing what was false on what was true, besides giving its name to the civilisation and culture of Greece and Rome with which it had nothing whatever to do.   Christianity, moreover, is also indebted to Paganism for its belief in heaven and hell, Satan being none other than Pan, the god of the mountains, with horns, hoofs and tail.   There are two beliefs prevalent in Christianity, one in the resurrection of the dead at the Last Judgment which was taken from Egypt, and the other, that of reaching heaven immediately at death, which was taken from the Greeks.

From the time of Pythagoras (580–500 B.C.) the belief in the survival of the soul was widely held and expressed by outstanding Romans and Greeks, Plutarch for example, when writing to his wife after the death of their daughter, expressing the belief that she was now in the presence of her saviour Dionysus. This is what he wrote:—

"The death and resurrection of Dionysus teaches us that the soul is immortal, so why trouble unduly about our daughter, as her soul is with Our Lord, and, when our turn comes, we shall be with her again."

Cicero, the famous Roman statesman, was a fervent believer in survival after death and wrote freely about it, remarking on one occasion: "Is not almost the whole of heaven filled with the human race?" Many other quotations could be given from Pagan literature to show that the Greeks and Romans, called "the heathen" by Christians, had a lively hope of survival and of being reunited after death in a better and happier world.

The Christian Church took the sole credit for the wonderful past it had so fortunately inherited. Though Christianity had produced no civilisation or culture, and had in no way raised the standard of life, the Church attributed to Christianity the prevailing culture and civilisation. It denounced the true origin of its new-found greatness, and derided as Pagan what had come from the wisdom and glory of Greece and Rome. Its leaders deliberately befouled the nest from which its new-found status and prestige had come. Instead, they claimed that Christian teaching, which was taken from Paganism, had come from heaven, was in accordance with the will of God, and for that reason the Church had been elevated to its now high position. All that was Pagan was denounced, its histories and its literature burned or banned, and it was proclaimed that Christianity was responsible for all that was good in the Western World.

Thus the Christian Church turned history upside down, and from that time onwards Christianity has thrived on falsehood. It has flourished on the immense prestige it secured, and, in consequence of the false claims it made, it obtained the obedience and subjection of the ignorant multitude. History was thus twisted, and in time most people accepted as true that which was false. Those who doubted, and those who thought for themselves, were murdered or excommunicated, the people being told that excommunication meant everlasting Hell after death, and that it was right and proper to kill an excommunicated person. Hell was the potent weapon of the Church and with it it ruled Europe. To keep the people in mind of their possible fate, pictures of a fiery hell were prominently exhibited in most churches. Christendom was, until last century, what Germany was under Hitler, the clergy being the Inquisitors of the Faith as laid down by the Theodosian Code enacted in the later part of the 4th century.

By persuasion, slaughter, and force the Church increased its adherents, but it was not until the year 507, at the momentous battle of Vouillé, near Poitiers, in France, between the forces of the Trinitarians and the Unitarians, that it was finally decided that Christianity accepted Jesus as God. Up to this time, in spite of the decision of the Council of Nicaea, the Popes had been either Unitarians, and denied this, or Trinitarians, and accepted this belief that Jesus was one of three gods. However, from now onwards, the Trinitarians only were supreme and allowed to live. Clovis, the Trinitarian, at this battle defeated Alaric II, the Unitarian, and this conflict finally decided the momentous question as to the nature of God for the Western World.

For the Middle East it was not so. There the Christian Trinity was not accepted, and, when Mahomet arose, he took from the Christian faith about half its followers. In disgust, at the dividing of God into three parts, his supporters turned from the polytheism and image-worshipping of Christianity and vowed that Allah, the god of Abraham, is the one true and only God. Mahomet's followers also took from Christendom its most precious possessions —Palestine, with all its sacred associations, Asia Minor, where its first churches were established, Egypt, whence originated the doctrine of the Christian Trinity, Carthage, famous for its Church councils, and finally Constantinople, the first Christian city. Before this time the chief seats of Christendom were Rome, Constantinople, Antioch and Alexandria. Only Rome remained.

The history of Christianity from the 4th century onwards for fifteen hundred years is revolting in the extreme. Its popes, bishops, patriarchs and primates were mixed up in all the evil doings of the time, and devoted their energies to excommunicating and cursing their enemies. Assassinations, poisonings, immoralities, torture, murder, riots, treason and the lust for domination and power are associated with the lives of the leaders of Christianity. Sixteen thousand square miles of Central Italy came into the possession of the Church by means of a blatant forgery. It was amidst these atrocities that Mahomet appeared in the 7th century, denouncing it all as evil and repellent.

Then, five hundred years later, followed the Crusades, when Christendom fought to recapture the Holy Land. For two hundred years this fruitless effort kept Europe in a turmoil, wretched and poor. The people were in misery, yet everything was diverted towards this one aim, the recovery of the Church's lost possessions. The history of the Crusades is one of the blackest spots in Christian history. Treachery, cruelty and lust were rampant everywhere as a result of this inter-religious war. Millions of lives and vast wealth were sacrificed. On both sides the fiercest passions were roused and kept aflame, to such a degree that the worst barbarities and atrocities ever recorded in history took place under the flags of Christ and Islam.

Christianity has undoubtedly comforted its followers in the past and does so to-day, but, on the other hand, there is no crime known which its followers have not committed in its name and under the authority of *The Holy Bible*, where appropriate texts were found for every villainy. This religion has supported every wickedness, every cruelty, every lust and every crime that ever entered the mind of man, and a Bible text was readily found in support of each. Yet the word Christian is used to-day as if it stood for all that is good. People talk of "Christian charity", "Christian ethics" and "Christian ideals". No word in the English language is so misapplied, but the last few pages have told how it came about.

Under priestly rule, social and cultural conditions quickly deteriorated throughout the old Roman Empire. Education was encouraged by the Pagans throughout the Empire, and banned in Christendom. Ignorance became a virtue and knowledge a vice. Serfdom and slavery flourished in Christendom up to last century. Surgery was practised in ancient Egypt, whereas the first Christian surgeon was banished from Europe in the 16th century. Hospitals and curative centres, in considerable numbers, existed in ancient

Greece and elsewhere twelve hundred years before there was a hospital in Christendom.

Throughout the Roman Empire the virtues were expounded by its great Pagan philosophers and their numerous followers from the time of Pythagoras onwards. Plutarch, a Pagan, taught that we should love our enemies. Galen, the first outstanding doctor, was a Pagan, and there were many others who healed the sick long before the Christian era. In both Greece and Rome there were widespread organisations for charity and mercy, the ancient Greeks especially being renowned for their kindness and sympathy towards those in distress.

Moreover, the Greeks seldom descended to gladiatorial sport and amusement, and they termed the Romans barbarians for doing so. Undoubtedly it was through Greek, and not through Christian, influence that these contests came to an end, though they continued for one hundred years after the Romans had adopted the Christian faith. Salvian, the Presbyter of Marseilles, wrote of the delight the Christians took in seeing their fellow men torn and devoured by wild beasts in the amphitheatres, "numberless thousands of Christians," he tells us, "being daily spectators."

Under Christianity, Christendom entered what is known as the Dark Ages, which lasted for more than a thousand years, to be enlightened by the Pagan classics reaching Europe just before and after the fall of Constantinople in 1453, where they had been hidden away from the priestly inquisitors. Paganism, denounced by the Church, was therefore responsible for raising Europe intellectually at the time which became known as the Renaissance after a thousand years of squalor, ignorance, persecution, and one of the worst periods in the history of mankind. This state of affairs the Church wished to remain, and, for more than two hundred years, after learning and culture first reached Europe from Constantinople in the 15th century, many millions were persecuted and slaughtered to prevent its effects from spreading throughout Christendom.

Christians speak and write as if charity were something which was the outcome of the Christian religion, and, as most Christians know little about the origin of their religion, this is the prevailing belief in the Western hemisphere. "Christian charity", which is nothing more than humanitarianism, first made its appearance in Christendom in the 19th century of the Christian era eighteen hundred years after the birth of Jesus, which is a long time between the alleged cause and the effect. It was in no way a novelty, because, as just mentioned, the charity claimed by Christians took place in ancient Greece and the Roman Empire long before Christianity was born.

The Oxford Dictionary's definition of Charity is "Christian love of fellow men", but this is quite wrong, as the word comes from the Latin *caritatem* meaning high regard, and, if Christians would elevate their minds by reading the writings of Seneca, and other Pagan Greek and Latin writers on Charity, they would realise how ignorant they are of the charitable ideas and deeds of the Pagans towards the poor and needy. Love of our fellow men is in no way confined to Christians and Christendom, as it is just the practice of kindness, and kind deeds are confined to no one religion, race or place. "Only Christians know how to die because only Christians know how to live" is the latest clerical howler I have noticed in the newspapers.

This dishonest Christian propaganda has now been going on since the 4th century, and Christians should be ashamed of the mis-statements and fabrications which seem inseparable from their faith. The clergy are notorious for the false claims they make for their religion, but, when a leading statesman such as Lord Halifax associates himself with priestly lies, and the B.B.C. gives his mis-statements world-wide publicity, the time has certainly come for the people to study history for themselves. They most assuredly cannot rely on either politicians or the clergy to tell them the truth, and the foregoing is only one example of many to which the B.B.C. permits no reply from those who put truth before falsehood.

Most people acquire the religious history they know from the Old and New Testaments, and from what they are told at Sunday School or from the pulpit by priests trained and paid to enhance the Christian Church. The clergy are taught at their theological colleges that only one religion is true, and that God only favours Christianity, all other religions being false. The priests of all the other world religions teach the same about the religion they are paid to propagate. This ignorance produces intolerance, and from intolerance comes disharmony, whereas, if natural, and not supernatural, religion were accepted by mankind, the same religion would be world-wide, and all the social troubles which to-day come from religious differences could be avoided.

.   .   .   .   .

Having now explained how the book I worked on at Rockingham Castle received its name, let me briefly record its object and contents. The object is educational, to inform the reader of the follies and achievements of mankind. The latter are better realised than the former, they are more spectacular and more evident to everyone, so much so that the mistakes our ancestors have made are glossed over by historians. My book emphasises these mistakes so that future generations do not repeat them. Likewise, historians have minimised the influence Religion has played in history. Religions wax and wane throughout history and historians record the fact, but never explain it.

History tells us that kingdoms rose and fell. It dwells on the eternal problem of government and on man's search for a livelihood, only to be directed into poverty and misery by his appointed rulers making use of him for their own ends. What indeed has the common man gained for himself in the past by attaching himself to a leader, a chief or a king, who used him only for the furtherance of his own power and wealth, to throw him aside when this had been gained? Power by the few over the many meets us on most pages of history. On the other hand man's aggressive propensities make firm rule necessary, and government of some kind or another has been essential to civilisation.

Nevertheless the masses, before education became general, were always overpowered by the few, because of their ignorance and disunity. They have been made to obey the law by fear, and, except for those of a thieving disposition, to make war by compulsion. In other words, the human being has been dictated to by those who claimed the right to rule over him. Consequently, the story of mankind is one of folly as well as achievement, the pulling down of what his sweat and labour have achieved. History records that man generally is no better than a child, in fact he has never grown up. When Hitler's war started, these thoughts flooded my mind, and *The Curse of Ignorance* contains the facts to support them as well as much else.

Moreover, I stress the fact that history tells us nothing about the origin of the many world religions in general, or even Christianity in particular. Religious origins are passed by, their effects only being recorded. True, we know nothing historically about Jesus, and all we know is what was thought about him many years after he lived. The Gospels are not history, but after-thoughts. Nevertheless, something occurred to produce these ideas, and there was a cause to produce the effect. That cause, in the case of Christianity or any other religion, is ignored by historians because it pertains to the etheric and not the material world. Psychic phenomena produced every religion, and every religion is the effect of this cause, but apparitions cannot be classed as history, and something which is not of this world must be ignored by historians.

Historians consequently pass by supernormal phenomena, the cause, and so it happens that supernormal phenomena, which produced history, are ignored. Nevertheless, what Spiritualism stands for has brought every religion into being. The interaction of this world and the next produced supernormal phenomena. This made man conscious of his destiny, and those with theological and mystical minds built from their imagination on this structure, which was based on the supernormal. The supernormal was the cause, it alone was the revelation, but the creeds and dogmas were the work of man. The dogmas, creeds and doctrines of every religion are the products of man's mystical nature, but they are not history, they being the stuff that dreams are made of. Nevertheless, they have greatly helped and comforted man during his earthly pilgrimage, and made the problems of life and death tolerable.

Lacking direct knowledge of his destiny, man's great achievement has been Religion. Its basis is true, and, if he could only have kept within the bounds of psychic knowledge, nothing more would have been necessary. If he had been content to know that life persists hereafter, that as we sow here we reap mentally there to the uttermost, that death itself is nothing to fear, and that for every parting here there will be a reunion hereafter, if it is desired, nothing more in the way of religion would have been produced. This, however, was not so, as he required something much more solid to help him through life, and only by doing something, or believing a creed which he could repeat from time to time, did he get the satisfaction he required. Psychic phenomena to the masses are too sporadic, too abstract, to help them, even though the religion they believe developed out of them.

I estimate that half of the events of history have come in one way or another from Religion. I believe that every religion has come from the effects of psychic phenomena. Consequently the interaction of the two worlds has had a profound effect on humanity in one way and another. Though the cause is unrealised, or ignored by the vast majority, the effects are apparent. If there had been no supernormal phenomena in the past there would to-day be no temples, churches, pagodas, mosques or synagogues. There would be no priests, ministers of the gospel, rabbis, mullahs, pongis or any other organised body of men to direct the many, who are fearful of their destiny, into a path of thought that gives them satisfaction and comfort.

If man was made up of only a physical body there would have been no apparitions. If there had been no apparitions, or ghosts, there would have been no saviours. If there had been no saviours there would have been no organised saviour-god religions. If there had been no organised religions, then ritual, which plays such a part, would never have developed. On the other hand, if there had been no psychic phenomena there would have been no abuses which produced witchcraft, superstition and much else that is evil, such as intolerance which led to wars, cruelty and murder. Man's misuse of nature's revelation has so often been his undoing, and only mental development, leading to greater knowledge, will lead him from folly to wisdom. Religion was, and still is, a necessity, but it has had, and still has, its bad as well as its good side.

So in *The Curse of Ignorance* I led the reader onwards from primitive man down the ages, telling the history of each important country from both the secular and religious point of view. Consequently, the reader travels with me from primitive times through the oldest civilisations of China, India, Sumer, Babylonia and Egypt on to that of the Hebrews, Greeks, Romans and Arabians. This occupies more than half of the first volume, the remainder being devoted to Christian and other civilisations up to the Reformation. The second volume deals with world history from that time onwards to the end of the Second World War.

I have just said that if there had been no apparitions there would have been no saviour gods. Consequently, the Egyptians would not have believed that Osiris broke the curse of death and suffered for their sins. There would have been no Krishna for the teeming millions of India to look to for salvation, no Bel for the Babylonians to regard as their mediator, no Mithra to save the Persians and the Roman world, no Dionysus, or Prometheus, to act as the Redeemers of the Greeks and Middle East, no Devatat to save the Siamese, and no Quexalcote to be looked upon by the Aztecs of Mexico as the divine sacrifice for their sins. There would have been no heavenly Christ, the creation of Paul, and no Christians to consider their future hereafter assured through the suffering, death and resurrection of Jesus.

Moreover, there would be no Mahometan religion if Mahomet had not been considered a medium, *The Koran*, so his followers thought, having been dictated to him by the angel Gabriel. No Koran meant no revelation from Allah, and no revelation meant no Moslem religion. If Moses had not been a medium there would have been no Hebrew scriptures or religion. Jehovah, meaning Rain Cloud, was evidently the spirit-control of Moses, and he guided the Hebrews through his medium. This is made clear in *The Psychic Stream*. Mediumship has had an immense influence on religion and history, but here I have only space to mention it and pass on.

If there had been no psychic phenomena there would be no belief in God in the image of man. The evolution in the belief of God started from seeing apparitions, because, from early times, an apparition, or ghost, was considered a god, a supernatural being. This phenomenon was seen to be in the likeness of man, which accounts for God being thought of as an anthropomorphic being, or one like unto man. From early times many gods and goddesses were believed to exist in another world in contact with this one, but, as the unity of the laws governing this one were realised, each religion had its own Father God, who was surrounded by minor gods, to be called by different names, such as angels, or messengers, by the Greeks, and saints by the Christians.

So it came about that the spirit control of a trance medium was regarded as the Divine Spirit, a voice out of the void as the voice of a god, and the movement of objects without physical contact as the deeds of one or more gods to manifest their power. When writing was invented, one who wrote automatically, allowing his hand to write without willing it, was considered to be inspired by a god. Clairaudience was listening to speech by a god, and Clairvoyance was seeing a god. Out of this vast throng of heavenly divinities grew the belief in the Christian God, the Moslem Allah, and all the other Father Gods who it was believed created the earth and its creatures. Out of this grew a heavenly hierarchy, all races and each religion having its own divinity or divinities who watched over their worshippers and led them to victory in war.

The hierarchy which mostly influenced Christianity

was the one this religion took over from Greece. When Christianity triumphed Christians called the Greek gods devils, little realising that all that had happened was a change of name. Zeus to the Greeks, and Jupiter to the Romans, became the Father God of the Christians, Jupiter, or Deus Pater, meaning God the Father. The Holy Spirit took the place of Mercury, the messenger of Zeus, and the gods surrounding Zeus came to be known as saints and angels. Briefly, I would put it that psychic phenomena produced the belief in the gods and goddesses, each of which had his or her allotted task in the management of this world. Out of this has grown the belief in one supreme God and many minor gods or angels. To-day the Spiritualist calls the minor gods spirits, or etherians, who once lived on earth, and I, and others who think like me, look upon God as Mind.

Mind we look upon as the directing force of the universe. This to us constitutes God. We are all part of this directing mind and, through mind, we are related to the guiding intelligence of the universe. Each one of us is part of God, or, as some put it, we are the sons or daughters of God. In consequence, we believe in the brotherhood of man. By mind we live and move and have our being, and by mind we are conscious of our existence. Without mind the universe would cease to exist. Consequently God, or mind, makes conscious life possible to each of us. Nevertheless each one of us is finite, and God or Mind is infinite. The finite cannot explain or comprehend the infinite, and so it is well to dwell carefully on our words when we speak of God, as far too many talk foolishly and loosely about something of which they know next to nothing.

If there had been no psychic phenomena there would have been no such thing as prayer and worship. Prayer started by someone asking the spirit controlling the medium what was desired. Worship arose out of respect for the controlling spirit. So it became the custom to ask the spirits, even when not manifesting through a medium. Etherians tell us now, and doubtless told those they spoke to on earth in times past, that to think intently of an individual etherian can bring him or her to you. This was the beginning of prayer, and to-day people pray to saints and angels just as they have done under different names down the ages. As the idea of the Father God developed, prayer was offered to him as the supreme deity, his will being considered more powerful than that of the saints and angels.

It will be remembered that before I became interested in Spiritualism I had made a deep study of Comparative Religion. If my knowledge of religion had been confined to this only I could not have written the books I have done. What made them possible was the combination of my knowledge of the sciences of Comparative Religion and psychic phenomena. With my knowledge of these two subjects I feel that I have been able to throw a new light on religion. Now we know how religion began, now we know the origin of the saviour-god religions, all resembling each other, and why our many religious beliefs came into being. We now know the origin of the belief in God in the likeness of man, in angels and demons (the good and bad spirits who controlled mediums) and in prayer and worship. We now know how the belief in Heaven and Hell originated, because when both good and bad spirits returned each were given by us on earth their own abode.

Lacking this knowledge, historians and theologians can give us no reason for the rise of religious beliefs. They can only refer to myths and legends, but they know nothing of their cause and origin. Now we know that a real cause produced religion, which has had such a powerful influence on history. Consequently, I assert that religion can only be understood by those who accept and understand psychic phenomena. Those who deride psychic phenomena as something too fantastic to accept, are blind to the cause of half the events of history. By prejudice, wilful ignorance, or the misfortune never to have had psychic experiences, they are mentally blind, though they know it not. Enlightenment must come some day, and meantime I have done my utmost to make use of my knowledge of comparative religion and psychic phenomena for the purpose of clearing away the dark cloud of ignorance surrounding religion everywhere.

The Psychic Stream was my first systematic effort to enlighten my contemporaries as to the right way to regard religion as a whole, and Christianity in particular. Then came *The Curse of Ignorance*, which took a world-wide sweep of religious and secular history. These two books should be read in this order, first *The Psychic Stream* and then *The Curse of Ignorance*. By so doing the reader first discovers the origin of each leading world religion, and secondly learns the history of the human race and the effect religion has had in the making of the story of mankind.

Now I shall turn to a matter of more topical interest. Most people in this country know the strange story of John Brown, the gillie of Queen Victoria, and nearly everyone wonders why she employed such an uncouth highlander to be her servant. Only two people in this country knew the answer to this question, so I made it my business to interview them myself and produce in writing the true story which has their approval as correct and accurate. This I did, and what I now tell has their hall-mark of accuracy.

When we were at Rockingham Castle, which is about thirty miles from Leicester, my wife and I motored there by invitation to pay a short visit to this lady and gentleman, Miss Eva Lees and her brother, Mr. Lees. The latter is a well-known photographer in that city. They welcomed us and kindly gave us tea, while Miss Lees told us their story. Her father was Robert James Lees, a man well known and respected in Leicester. I took notes of all Miss Lees told me, wrote out a report, and sent it to her for her and her brother to check and return to me. What follows is my record of what she told me, and I think that most people will agree with me that such an interesting story is well worth preserving.

A fact worthy of mention, and one which is quite unknown to historians, is the interest Queen Victoria took in Spiritualism, even before the death of her husband. The following facts are recorded because she was a prominent woman, and not for any other reason, her experience being typical of what hundreds of thousands of people have also discovered. Her deep interest began shortly after the death of her husband, the Prince Consort, and this is how it happened.

Robert James Lees (1849–1931), then a boy of about thirteen years of age, was so mediumistic from early childhood that his family and friends were converted to the belief that discarnate men and women spoke through him when in a state of trance. Soon after the death of the Prince in 1861, while the Lees family was having a private sitting in their own home, Robert Lees was controlled by a man from the other world who gave the name of Albert, the Prince Consort. He then made the request that Queen Victoria be told that he could communicate with her through this boy medium.

The editor of a newspaper, a friend of the Lees family, was present at this séance, and published this request purporting to come from the late Prince Albert through Lees while in trance. This came to the notice of Queen Victoria who, prior to her husband's death, had been convinced by her experiences with other mediums that such communication was possible. So she sent anonymously two members of her Court to the home of Lees, who requested that they might have a sitting with him. They did not mention who they were, or from whom they came, and gave assumed names, but the boy was not long in trance before the Prince Consort purported to speak, and he greeted these two courtiers as his friends, calling them by their correct names.

Then the boy in trance shook hands with them, and gave them correctly the highest Masonic handshake, which normally he did not know. The Prince, through the boy who was in trance, then told the visitors that he knew they had come from Queen Victoria, and, though at first they denied it, he forced them by the evidence he gave of his identity to admit that this was so. Before the séance ended he had given them such accurate information, which only the Prince Consort could have known (some of it being of a very private nature, known only to the Queen), that when her envoys returned to Windsor she was quite satisfied that these communications could have come only from her husband. She was especially impressed by a letter the boy wrote when controlled by the Prince. This was of a particularly personal nature, and he then signed it by a unique name used only by the Prince in letters to the Queen when he was on earth.

She then sent for Lees, and asked him if he would give her a sitting, which he did, and the Prince again spoke through the medium. The Queen then said to her husband that she wanted Lees to remain permanently at Court so that he would be available at all times, but the Prince objected, saying that he did not wish this boy to be his medium. He, however, told the Queen that he could speak to her equally well, and just as easily, by using the vocal organs of the son of a gillie on the Balmoral estate whose name was John Brown. The Queen immediately sent for Brown, and thus began the long and strange friendship of Queen Victoria with John Brown who, up to his death, was used as the medium of the Prince Consort to communicate with his wife, whom he advised on many questions until her death.

Robert James Lees, when he grew up, became a highly respected journalist and author. He wrote several books, of which the best known is *Through the Mists*, it being a record of the communications he believed he had received from the etheric world. Queen Victoria ordered six specially bound copies, which she presented to members of her family. The acquaintance of the Queen with Lees did not end with their first meeting, in fact it continued throughout her lifetime, and on five different occasions the Prince Consort spoke through him in the presence of the Queen. Shortly before she died she sent for Lees and thanked him for all he had done for her. From time to time she offered him honours, a comfortable annuity for his lifetime and gifts, all of which he refused. He would take nothing, he said, in return for his services.

The Queen, knowing the prejudice there was at Court, and by the Church, towards everything relating to Spiritualism, never wrote to Lees and always sent her messages by a special courier, but she kept a record of all that transpired at her sittings with both John Brown and Lees. Dr. Davidson, the Dean of Windsor, who afterwards became Archbishop of Canterbury, was always hostile towards the lady who carried the title of "Defender of the Faith" being so unorthodox, but she entirely ignored his advice to discontinue her communications with her husband, and brought up the members of her family to believe in the principles of Spiritualism. That is why the Royal Family have had sittings from time to time with the world's leading mediums.

After John Brown's death the Queen wrote a monograph about him and wished to publish it. Dr. Davidson and Sir Henry Ponsonby, her Private

Secretary, firmly objected to this proposal, the former threatening to resign his position as Court Chaplain. Moreover, Ponsonby destroyed Brown's private diaries, so that what was written therein would never become known. Thus it was that the influence of two Court officials prevented the Queen from publicly testifying to the comfort she had received from the communications she believed she had had with her husband, through the mediumship of her highland gillie.

Lees never spoke to anyone outside of his own family about his close contact with Queen Victoria, or of her communications with her husband, and consequently only the members of his family knew what was happening, and this they only spoke about to a few of their friends. I am grateful to Miss Lees for the trouble she took to give me the information I desired, and also for her and her brother's kindness in allowing me to make public what they had up till then considered a private matter.

Life with us at Rockingham went on smoothly day by day. We were quite independent of our friends in the rest of the castle, as only a passage connected us. We had our own kitchen and servants, one of whom was Mary Jakeman, who for many years served Sir Arthur and Lady Doyle, and went with them on their missionary visit to Australia to look after their children. From time to time we were invited to meet the friends of our hostess, and to lunch or dine in the famous 11th-century Great Hall. Her guests came to see us, and so the time passed in a very pleasant fashion. The garden was a great joy to my wife, and she made so many new friends that her severance from her home interests was somewhat counter-balanced.

In one room where I wrote part of *The Curse of Ignorance*, Charles Dickens, a great friend of a former owner of the castle, wrote *David Copperfield*, and about the castle he weaved the setting of another of his stories. Pictures of men and women by famous old masters, such as Morland, Van Dyck, Reynolds, Lely, Botticelli, Zoffany, Stubbs, Ben Marshall, Kaufman, Zucchero and Holbein adorned the principal rooms of the castle, one being of Queen Elizabeth I and another of King Francis I of France by Clouet.

Each month we motored the sixty-five miles to Stansted Hall, stayed for one or two nights, and then returned. In the black-out at night we had a few uncomfortable experiences, especially during fog, through lack of sufficient headlights, but nothing of a serious nature happened. At Stansted Hall everything was active, the noise made by the convalescent soldiers being very disturbing, so much so that we were glad we were not living there under these conditions. From first to last 5,500 soldiers, recovering from accidents, wounds and illness, recuperated within its walls and enjoyed the beauties and pleasures of its surroundings. Generally there were about a hundred patients at a time, and over and above that some thirty nurses and staff.

Fortunately, the house was never hit by a bomb, but at midnight, on the 21st March 1945, one of the last rocket bombs fell within four hundred yards. It was flying directly towards the house and fell just before reaching it. About fifty plate-glass windows were smashed, besides the roof and glass in the conservatory attached to the house. Fortunately, no one was hurt. The soldiers very naturally did not want to return to army life after their time at Stansted. They could go anywhere they liked in the pleasure grounds, but were not allowed in the three-hundred-year-old walled kitchen garden. In Summer they had games on the lawn, and spent much of their time sitting there.

Lady Culme-Seymour, after the death of her husband in 1925, became a firm believer in Spiritualism, because of the evidence he gave her through mediums of his survival. During the war he kept her informed about her son in the navy, and what he told her was always accurate. She kept written records of her conversations with her husband, and other friends who have passed on, and these now comprise a formidable pile. A rector of Rockingham was a good direct voice medium. I was sorry we went there after he had gone elsewhere, but the descriptions Lady Culme-Seymour gave me of the séances she had with him place him as a first-class medium.

Strangely enough he was quite uninterested in his gift, and only to oblige her did he give her private sittings. He took no intelligent interest in mediumship, and Spiritualism was to him a subject about which he knew little or nothing. That, however, in no way affected his psychic power, which came from a superfluity of ectoplasm in his body. Out of this the etheric speakers materialised their vocal organs, and spoke so that they could be heard on earth, his mental outlook having nothing to do with the phenomena.

Shortly after my mother's death my brother wrote to me to say he had had a sitting with a trance medium through whom my mother spoke to him. Amongst other things said, which were correct, was a request that he would write to me and say she was very pleased that I had her wedding-ring, and that it was now attached to my watch-chain in my right-hand waistcoat pocket. He asked me to tell him if this was so, and I replied that it was. When my mother died her nurse brought me her wedding-ring, which I put in my pocket, and, on the first opportunity, got a jeweller to fix it on to the end of my watch-chain, the end which rests in my right-hand waistcoat pocket. Consequently it is unseen, and moreover, I never told anyone what I had done, forgetting even to mention it to my wife.

Now for what followed. Lady Culme-Seymour had a lady friend who came to visit her at Rockingham Castle, and this lady was a trance medium. She gave me a sitting, and, amongst others who spoke to me, and gave me good evidence, was my mother. She referred to her wedding-ring and said she was so pleased I had it attached to my watch-chain in my right-hand waistcoat pocket. This she repeated on a later occasion when I had a sitting with another medium in London.

At the sitting I had with this lady at Rockingham another evidential statement was made. One of the staff of Patrick Henderson & Co. of Glasgow, when I was in that office in my youth, purported to speak to me. He had died many years previously, and remarked that he had with him others who had been with me in my early business days in that office. "Now," I thought, "this is the opportunity for a test," as the lady medium knew nothing whatever about me. So I asked my etheric friend this question: "Tell me, please, the telegraphic address of Patrick Henderson & Co." In reply he said: "Carthage, Glasgow," which is correct, and could not have come from the mind of the medium. Most people, if they hear such stories, say "How extraordinary!" and think no more about it, being oblivious of the fact that there is a natural explanation, the one given by Spiritualism.

As the years passed, so the war drew slowly to a close. We had experienced a general closing in on Germany on all sides, the Russians now being in Poland, the allies were half-way up Italy in Rome, and the British and Americans had landed in Normandy. Thus 1944 witnessed the enemy being gradually overwhelmed. When 1945 opened, his complete defeat was assured. On 2nd May of that year the flaming ruins of Berlin were surrendered, after both Hitler and Goebbels had committed suicide in a deep shelter in the Chancellory, their last refuge in the doomed city.

One by one the other leading Nazi mass murderers did likewise, or were rounded up, to be tried at Nuremberg for their crimes against humanity and put to death, leaving their miserable dupes to drink to the dregs the cup of misery and hatred they had been responsible for brewing. On the other side of the world the same fate was quickly approaching Japan, and, on the 14th August, the Japanese surrendered unconditionally, when followed the landing of

American troops, who took over complete control of the country.

These events brought nearly to an end our exile from home, as the Red Cross now made arrangements to evacuate Stansted Hall. When this was done we returned home, on 3rd October 1945, after an absence of four years and ten months.

MYSELF IN 1943.

CHAPTER TEN.

STANSTED HALL.

(1945–1955.)

ON ARRIVAL home we found Stansted Hall in rather an uninhabitable condition, as most of the good furniture was in store. Only the two rooms we had kept for ourselves, a bedroom and a sitting-room, were fit to live in, and the house needed repair and paint everywhere. For thirteen months, after coming home, three decorators were busy at work, and for six months a carpenter was employed repairing the damage done, several weeks being spent in scraping out ink stains from the parquet floors. The Red Cross faithfully kept to their agreement with me that, in return for having the house rent free, they would put it back into the condition they had found it in when they took possession.

Ladders were left about outside night and day by the workmen, and there is, consequently, little wonder that three weeks after our return we were burgled. A few days previously I said to my wife that all these ladders about were just asking for trouble, with so many burglaries then taking place, but she thought I was unnecessarily fearful. Then a day later a weedy sort of creature arrived to ask if he could mend any old mats. "Yes," I said, "there is plenty to do. Will you start at once?" "No," he replied, "I shall come back to-morrow," but he never came back. He, I am sure, was a scout sent forth to spy out the land by the thieves who employed him. He saw the ladders, and so the stage was set for a very smart piece of criminal work.

A few nights later we were listening to the radio, to *Escape* by Galsworthy, a very appropriate story as it turned out, and at eleven I went to a side door to let out the dogs. To my amazement I saw a ladder up to our bedroom, but it was too long and heavy to move. I called to my wife, and ran upstairs to find our bedroom door locked. So I telephoned the police, and the long and short of the story is that we did not get to bed until two o'clock in the morning, in a room littered everywhere with clothes the thief had thrown about in his search for jewellery. The police wanted everything to be left as it was, as they were coming next day to take finger-prints.

Fortunately, not much jewellery was in the room, and our loss, covered by insurance, came to £250, but, as happens to most people, the things that were stolen had sentimental value. The thief was not caught, but the police suspected one or more of the convalescent soldiers to be the guilty party. They discovered that amongst the thousands who had benefited from their stay at our home were five expert burglars. They followed up three of these unsuccessfully but could find no trace of the other two.

Gradually we got our house put in order, a staff engaged, and I was able to complete *The Curse of Ignorance*. Then came one difficulty after another. Paper was very difficult to get, but I could wait for that, as I knew the setting up of such a large book would take a long time. No printer I approached could undertake the task, they had huge arrears to work off, and many of their men had not been de-mobilised. It was months before I found one, and I am sorry now I did. He was in a fairly large way in London, but, after he had set up some two hundred pages, he informed me he would take many months before he could complete it as, now that the war was over, he was overwhelmed with work.

By now the company that had done all my printing in the past was ready to set up the book, and I took the work away from the London firm and gave it to my pre-war printers. It was annoying to have to pay the London printers for the work they had already put into the book, now useless, but, as they had not refused to complete the book, there was no way out.

From the time I started to write this work until the writing was completed five years had elapsed, an average of six hours a day being devoted to it. As with all my books, I wrote it with my own hand, and brought the manuscript back to Stansted Hall each time we returned home, to be typed out by my secretary. Two years, however, elapsed after the writing was finished before the book was published, delays in the delivery of the paper, delays by the printers, and delays by the binders being the cause. The consequence was that from first to last seven years elapsed from the time I started until the book was in the hands of the public.

The Curse of Ignorance is in size my largest book, and I feel that if I had written that alone, my life would have been of some value to mankind. Its two volumes have 2,366 pages which contain about 780,782 words. If to this is added the number of words, comprising my other books, I have written within the space of twenty-five years, the total comes to well over two million words, covering 6,693 pages. This is an output which any professional author of books of an educative nature would be pleased to accomplish, in fact this is the number of pages in thirty average-sized books. Books of a serious and informative nature are not produced as is a novel. Much research is needed for books such as I have written, besides great care and thought. Often a page was retyped three or four times before I was satisfied with it, and every important statement was checked and verified from the very best sources. Sometimes a day was spent on a single page. Consequently to write books made up of facts is a slow and tedious business, and only the urge I always had to impart knowledge kept me going.

I planted the seedling of an oak to commemorate the publication of *The Curse of Ignorance*, it now being a tree three feet high, and it should some day become a great majestic oak. The book has justified the many flattering words written in the Press reviews, which are too long and too many for me to do more than just mention. So far it has flourished, in spite of the fact that one newspaper editor informed me that he had burned the two volumes I sent him to review because of its unorthodox treatment of Christianity. This book is now to be found in most of our public libraries, though I have been told that it is hard to get as it is so much in demand. It is now in its fourth impression.

I soon got back into doing some public work, as shortly after we arrived home I was asked to become a General Commissioner for Income-Tax for the Saffron Walden district. About a dozen qualified men in this area meet about every two months in a room of the Saffron Walden Town Hall, an ancient and picturesque building, to hear appeals by those dissatisfied with their Income-Tax assessments, or to determine the facts about those who are not giving the Inspector the information he requires to make their assessments. The Inspector of Income-Tax is present and the appellants, or their accountants, come before us to state their case. Thus we hear both sides and then give judgment, about thirty cases being dealt with at each session.

Each Commissioner gives his time voluntarily and receives no payment for his services, as is done by so many in other ways in our country, so different from the method adopted abroad, where voluntary unpaid work is not the custom. After a few years I became Chairman of the Commissioners, and this position I still hold. The work is interesting, though sometimes rather tedious, but some who have been trained in accountancy, and with knowledge of Income-Tax law, must do it. To know that all the Commissioners are quite impartial, and only intent on justice being done, gives all who come before us a sense of fair play, our verdict always being accepted with good grace.

When the war ended Maurice Barbanell, the editor of *Psychic News* since this newspaper commenced, told me he wished to resign. I much regretted this as we had been associated for fourteen years, and I greatly appreciated the way he had carried the newspaper

through the difficult years of the war.   However, he
would not yield to my persuasion that he should remain, and consequently I had to find a new editor.
That was very difficult, as so many journalists were
still in the army.   The one I eventually appointed was
Stuart Martin, but he had little opportunity to express
himself as he died suddenly shortly afterwards.

When A. W. Austen, the assistant editor, had been
demobilised from the navy, he took Martin's place as
editor, and conducted the editorial side with skill and
resource.   During the printers' strike in London in
1950 he flew backwards and forwards to Brussels,
where *Psychic News* was being printed, and this enabled its publication to be maintained throughout this
very difficult time.   I was very sorry when, in 1953,
he gave up his position as editor to go with his wife
to Perth in Australia, her health being unable to stand
our climate.   He was a great loss to us, but his successor, Fred Archer, is ably maintaining the good
traditions established by his predecessors.

Austen's greatest journalistic achievement was in
obtaining from a member of the Committee, which
Dr. Lang, the Archbishop of Canterbury, set up to
enquire into Spiritualism, the report of its findings.
Otherwise it never would have been published, because the majority were in favour and the minority
advocated further enquiry.   The member in question
was annoyed at the decision of the bishops to suppress
the report, and his action brought to light this under-
hand way of doing things.   The action of *Psychic
News* in publishing the report greatly perturbed the
bishops, and I saw the letter written to the editor by
the Archbishop which was anything but agreeable.

To be responsible, as I am, as chairman, for the weekly publication of a newspaper is an exacting duty. Not that the actual work I have to do is heavy, because that is lightened for me by a loyal staff, ably supervised by Percy Wilson, M.A., the Managing Director, but there is always some problem or other cropping up to which I must attend. So long as I am able I shall direct its activities and, to make sure that it always expresses the best of Spiritualism, I am leaving my controlling interest to the Spiritualists' National Union after my days. Likewise, I am leaving to the S.N.U. the copyright of my books on the understanding that they are always kept in print.

In 1947 the directors of Psychic Press Ltd., the proprietors and publishers of *Psychic News*, decided to hold a Spiritualist rally in the Royal Albert Hall. I found the supervision of the arrangements very interesting. There was so much to think of beforehand to ensure that the meeting would be a success. The vast hall was crowded, the audience being drawn there by George Daisley and Ronald Strong, who were the clairaudients. For an hour they kept the meeting enthralled as one name after another was given and recognised by the people to whom they pointed. This was supplemented by a wealth of detail from the etheric communicators, to prove that those who claimed to be there were really so, and that they were just using the mediums to pass on the evidence that they were giving to prove their survival.

The two addresses delivered were well up to standard, and the meeting lasted exactly two hours, as it was timed to do. I acted as Chairman at this meeting, and, just before it ended, I asked everyone in the audience to stand up who had obtained evidence which had convinced him or her of survival. With few exceptions everyone stood up, which was a wonderful advertisement for Spiritualism, and it much impressed the newspaper reporters present.

The experience I have gained, when speaking from time to time in the Albert Hall through the microphone, is that the audience hears the speaker much better if he reads slowly what he has to say. On one occasion I remember being told, after reading my remarks, that every word was heard distinctly in every part of the hall, whereas the speaker who followed me was not well heard, as he spoke extempore. To be heard through the microphone one must keep the right distance from the instrument, and this is not always done when speaking extempore. In the old Queen's Hall, which was shattered by a bomb, it was quite different as the speaker there could be heard clearly in all parts without the use of a microphone. An extempore speech there was consequently appreciated by the audience.

Here it is appropriate to mention the opening of the Psychic News Bookshop in May 1946. This venture, which belongs to Psychic Press Ltd., has been most successful, and has fully justified all that was anticipated. Many thousands of psychic books have been sold by post and in the shop during the nine years it has been open. Many enquiries are received from all over the world, books are despatched far and wide and assistance in what to read is freely given to the many who enquire. I think it is the only bookshop in the world entirely devoted to psychic books, and its annual catalogue, containing titles of about six hundred books, is in great demand.

Some of my time has been given to writing articles for the newspapers, especially the Spiritualist Press. I did this without payment, and I cannot count the number I have written on many varied subjects. Moreover, the letters I receive daily sometimes constitute a formidable problem, the questions I am asked at times being quite beyond my knowledge. I wish I had kept count of the number of letters I have received since I first published *On the Edge of the Etheric*. I regret I did not keep them all in special files so that I could give some samples of those I have received and answered. Letters come from all over the world and can be divided into the following four categories: (1) thanking me for this or that book or for all my books; (2) reporting similar phenomena experienced by the writer; (3) asking the name of a good medium in the district where the writer lives; (4) reporting some relation or friend just passed on, and asking assurance that some day they will meet again.

I have, however, found a letter from someone who is quite a stranger to me, and it may be of some interest. I have the writer's permission to publish it:—

> 117, Kelverlow Street,
> Clarksfield,
> OLDHAM.
> 1st October, 1951.

Dear Friend Findlay,

I call you friend for you have been a real one to me. My dear wife has just "passed on" (Sunday, September 30th), and I am left alone in my old age

L.B.—O*

to finish my earthly journey. But what a blessing your books have been to me! Your trilogy is my great favourite. Just now I have been reading *The Rock of Truth*, page 305, philosophy, poetry, science and true religion, all in harmony. How the words comfort me at this moment!

What a grand work you have done in the world, are doing, and will do for your fellow men in the future. Your books will live for long, long years, and radiate light across the bridge which spans the two worlds. God bless you, dear friend— which is a certainty, for he who rescues his fellow-men from the pit of ignorance and opens their eyes to eternal truth, is blessed a thousandfold.

I can say no more at the moment, for my heart is full and the tears are near to my eyes.

With my love and good wishes. I am in my 75th year—a lame old man.

One of your disciples who understands his wise master.

FREDERICK TAYLOR.

On occasions people ring me up on the telephone to thank me for my books, or to ask advice. I was much touched when a blind man telephoned to me from Chester, to tell me what a difference life was to him now that he had read *On the Edge of the Etheric*, which is transcribed into Braille. From all over the world letters come to me reporting the same psychic phenomena as I have experienced, and it is surprising the number of private circles which exist, of which the public knows nothing, the medium being a member of the family or a friend. Finally, those whose grief is so hard to bear get great comfort from the knowledge they receive through mediumship, that their loved ones still live and await them.

Several bereaved people have written to tell me how they have been on the point of committing suicide when the new outlook came to them from reading one of my books, to give them strength to decide to be brave and not give way to despair. I must have given to many hundreds of enquirers the names and addresses of good mediums, and their experiences with them gave them great joy and satisfaction. Many grateful letters have I received from these enquirers, telling me of the evidence they had obtained which had satisfied them that their friends still lived. Out of these many successful results I remember only one who wrote to say that nothing had happened to convince her.

In September 1948 the International Spiritualist Federation met in London. This International Congress, comprising Spiritualist organisations throughout the world, meets in different European capitals each year, and this year London was chosen. I was asked to welcome the guests in the Conway Hall, and this I did, first in English and then in French, the two official languages of the Congress. From my notes I see that I said that "truth always wins through in the end and some day natural religion, which is what Spiritualism stands for, will be accepted in place of the orthodox faiths which are slowly passing away in every country in which education exists". I remember that this was heartily applauded. The hall was crowded, and the professional singer was much appreciated.

After this, my wife and I received the delegates at

Stansted Hall. They numbered 160, and with them came their friends. The delegates came from all over the world, and twenty-two countries were represented. They spent a very pleasant afternoon, and the opportunity was taken by them to get to know each other better. The previous week had been strenuous and, at the Conway Hall, they had heard addresses given on many subjects of interest to Spiritualists. I thought when I perused the subjects to be discussed how ignorant are our opponents of the many and varied aspects embraced by Spiritualism. Each paper read was of a high educational order, and might well have been delivered to any scientific gathering, if only the scientists could have understood it.

At the request of the Cambridge Historical Society I delivered an address to its members in 1948, and the subject I chose was the effect of Religion on history. Here I had an opportunity to tell these young undergraduates something which I hoped would make them think in a way they had never thought before. I was aware that much of what I intended to say would be new to them, and that the minds of most of them would be prejudiced against my bringing psychic phenomena into history. However, I have always told the truth as I see it, and I consequently prepared a lecture, parts of which I quite expected would receive the disapproval of the majority.

I took much trouble in preparing this address, and, as it may interest some of the readers of this my autobiography, I incorporate it as an appendix at the end of this book, just as I delivered it. I have given it elsewhere since then to audiences as far apart as Glasgow and London, and some years ago it was pub-

lished in pamphlet form. This method is not sufficiently permanent to please me, and moreover its
incorporation in this book makes it likely that it will
be much more widely read.

To my surprise I received little criticism from my
Cambridge audience, but a number of questions were
put to me, mostly relating to the psychic phenomena
of which I spoke. After it was over I was hospitably
treated in a private sitting-room, when the opportunity
was taken to question me further on the subject of
my address. It was all a very friendly affair, and I
much enjoyed meeting new friends.

In December 1950 Spiritualism won its long-
drawn-out battle to overcome the effect of the old
Witchcraft Act, under which Spiritualism was considered illegal. Any honest medium could be arrested
as a fraud and fined or imprisoned, because under this
old Act he or she was pretending to bring back the
dead. To do so was considered impossible as the
dead did not, or could not, return, and consequently
every medium was a fraud and justly deserved punishment. Such was the law, and honest mediums were
fined and imprisoned, until one outstanding case of
injustice, that of Mrs. Duncan, brought matters to a
head. No evidence of fraud was produced, the witnesses in her favour were overwhelming, and yet she
had to serve many months in prison. A Private
Members Bill was passed through Parliament in
1950 to bring this scandal to an end, and, from
that time onwards, all genuine mediums have been
safe.

It was called the Fraudulent Mediums Bill, because
no one could think of a better name, and all the other

names suggested were too long. The important thing about it was its provisions and these legalised mediumship, the Bill passing with no opposition. To celebrate the event my wife and I were present at a dinner in the House of Commons, when thanks were tendered to those who had worked so hard, and so successfully, for justice to be done. Especially was this due to Lord Dowding in the House of Lords, and T. J. Brooks in the House of Commons, they having behind them the support of the Home Secretary, Mr. Chuter Ede, who gave the Bill the Government's blessing, and Mr. Clement Davies, who gave it the support of the Liberal Party. They and three other members spoke at this private dinner, the speeches going on well into the night.

At the close of 1950 I received from a lady in Glasgow a letter asking me if I would care to see the records of some sittings she had taken down in shorthand at séances she had with John Sloan between 1942 and 1945. Her name is Jean Dearie, and she offered to send them to me. I accepted her offer with pleasure, and, when they arrived and I had time to read them over with care, I realised what a valuable collection she had produced. Every word said at twenty-four séances had been recorded, and for this great task she asked nothing in return when I proposed to her that they be published.

I told her that when I had made a book out of them I would, as is always my custom, sell it at the exact cost of production, and I myself would make nothing from it.   As she likewise was of the same mind, she received no payment for her work, but as a memento accepted from me a watch bracelet.   Sloan, moreover, had given his services as the medium free, as was his custom, so here was a book produced without any monetary gain to those who were responsible for its contents.

The name I gave to the book was *Where Two Worlds Meet*, a very appropriate title, and it contains nineteen of the séances Miss Dearie recorded.   I could not give more, as these nineteen made up a book of 624 pages, which was quite big enough.   At these séances no attempt was made to control the medium, and Sloan sat like the others in the circle.   He remained normal throughout, and, when he was talking to someone in the circle, one or more voices would break in and take part in the conversation.   At times, when he was speaking, these supernormal voices were heard.   No one can produce two voices at the same time.   Often he carried on a conversation with a voice, in fact he behaved just as did the other sitters.

When *Where Two Worlds Meet* is read it will be realised that no one person alone, or with accomplices, could produce what took place at these séances.   No actor or impersonator could do so, and Sloan was far from either, a slow-witted, slow-speaking man, with the intelligence of the average artisan.   Moreover, he had a bad memory.   Let us, however, suppose that what took place is the work of a clever swindler, who deluded for two to three hours each night the many hundreds of people who attended the Sloan Circle for over fifty years.

What would a deceiver need to do to produce

effects similar to what occurred at the Sloan Circle when Miss Dearie was recording all that took place? First of all he would have to engage a script-writer. Between them they would have to think out each week a new performance, showing an intimate knowledge of the lives and ancestors of forty or so different individuals who attended the Circle at irregular intervals, but who provided an audience of eight to ten people each week.

These people changed week by week, and those who are coming are known only when they arrive at the meeting. Consequently the producer and script-writer must continually be finding out fresh information about their possible audience, past incidents in their lives, their dead friends and relations, the pet names they used, and all the intricate family relationships of the living and the dead. Not until eight or ten out of the forty are actually seated in the Circle will the producer know who is to be present, and the script must have been written for these sitters only. Many hundreds of different people have attended the Sloan Circle over the past fifty years for weekly sittings, large numbers coming anonymously with regular sitters, and few have ever been disappointed.

When the script is finished, and everything is ready for rehearsal, the actors and actresses would assemble in considerable numbers, as on an average forty separate voices speak at each séance. Moreover, the private house where the séance is being held is decided on at short notice. No strangers would be able to visit it prior to the performance, and they can bring nothing with them. The performers would be given their parts to learn which they must memorise, and then would come the final rehearsal, but their parts would vary according to the sitters who are to be present.

Everything on the night of the séance would take place in the dark, and there must be no fumbling or hesitation. The pretence must always be kept up that the speakers live in another world. Bright lights must appear and noises be produced without any appliances. For fifty years this must have gone on without the performers being seen, or anyone being surprised or suspicious, or discovering that secret enquiries were proceeding all the time about different people. Moreover, the cost of this imaginary production would come to at least a hundred pounds a week, but no member of the audience who attends is ever asked to pay anything.

Can anyone imagine that all this is possible?

But in the Sloan Circle much more happens than merely the conversations between the living and the dead. So our producer must also arrange for two trumpets to fly around the room in the dark without knocking into each other, but frequently touching the ceiling and beating on it, the movement being at a great speed, without wires, attachments or any visible contrivances. Never must they touch anyone to hurt, but they must gently touch, stroke or caress the sitters, and at other times hit Sloan on the head without hurting him, or beat in time on the floor. Fingers are to be passed through the hair of the sitters and over their faces. Lights, which cannot be felt or caught, are to dance about the room, and any part of the body must be touched on request. Moreover, a sitter has only to ask the time to have it correctly told. All this is accompanied by a regular flow of intimate conversation between the voices and the sitters, and takes place in the dark where nobody can even see the person sitting next to him.

Finally, the actors and actresses must be present in the room whenever the light is put out, and disappear from the room just before the light is put on again. How they would manage to do this it is impossible to imagine, as in a small room with the sitters present movement is difficult. However, all this shows the absurdity of attempting to explain the phenomena as if it were produced by material beings. This can be definitely ruled out, and every time we come back to the fact that what happened was not produced by any individual living on this earth.

There can be only one explanation of all these various supernormal phenomena, namely that unseen intelligent individuals are at work at the Sloan Circle. Only someone who has not been present at these séances can think that these occurrences can be produced by ventriloquism, conjuring, faking, or any such fraudulent means. That is why this book *Where Two Worlds Meet* must be judged as a whole, and, as its contents rule out a normal explanation, a supernormal one is all that is left.

Moreover, it was emphasised by those who spoke to us from the other world, that belief in one or other religious doctrine is quite unnecessary. Neither is it necessary to perform any ceremonies or ritual, to be baptised, confirmed, partake of the eucharist, or attend religious services. All these are man-made ideas, but what is important is what each one of us is. The good, unselfish, kind, just and merciful will be happier hereafter than the bad, selfish, unkind and those lacking pity. It is what we are that counts there, just as it matters here on earth. What we sow we reap, what we give we get, but if each one of us does his or her best no more can be achieved.

Those who attended the séances reported by Miss Dearie were all sincere, good people who took the opportunity Sloan gave them to converse with their friends in the other world who came back to speak to them. Consequently, they learned much that is of value, such as how best to live here to enable us to take our places as good and worthy inhabitants of the etheric world when our time comes for us to go there. After each séance Miss Dearie sent copies to each of the sitters of what she had typed out from her short-hand notes, and they were always passed as correct. To take down shorthand in the dark is not so difficult with practice, and Miss Dearie developed the art to perfection.

Where Two Worlds Meet met with a good reception from the Press, and the fifth impression has now been printed. The question the reader should ask is this. Is it possible for the contents of the book to have come about in a normal way? To my mind it is easier to conclude that a supernormal explanation is the answer rather than a normal one, in fact it seems to me to be the only one. I can think of no other explanation than that the reported conversations were carried on between those living in the flesh, and invisible but real men and women and children. They have bodies such as we have, and have found a way to adjust their hearing and speech so that they can hear what is said on earth, and speak so that we can hear what they have to tell us.

The idea then came to me to collect together everything of an educational, but not evidential, nature which had come through Sloan's mediumship and which had already appeared in all my books. My intention was, when this was done, to group everything in chapters each devoted to a specific subject. This was a slow and arduous task, but I accomplished it in the end.

The result was *The Way of Life*, which was published in 1953, and the reception this book has received fully justified my hard work. After the introductory chapters come the chapters devoted to the questions asked, and the answers given by the etherians who spoke. (1) There is a chapter about the etheric body, (2) a chapter on the passing over, (3) one on the arrival, (4) on the other world, (5) on the conditions in the other world, (6) on their way of life there, (7) on their contact with us, (8) on their religion, and lastly on the views they expressed as to how we should live, progress and develop. Its 240 pages contain 419 extracts from the verbatim records of fifty-eight sittings with Sloan, every one of value to us on earth.

I was very pleased at the way this book was received, and I am sure it will provide a useful reference book for those who wish to have a guide as to how best to live in this world. It comes from those who once lived on earth, and who now can speak with their accumulated wisdom and knowledge about both worlds. They tell us how we should live here on earth, and they give us all the information we can understand about their new abode which will some day be ours also.

The month of July 1951 was very gay at Stansted Hall, as this was the year of the Festival of Britain. Consequently, there was staged a wonderful pageant on the lawn of Stansted Hall, four acres in extent and surrounded by large and stately trees. At one side the lawn rises slightly to make an ideal stage. Mr. Muir, an author who lives at Stansted, wrote the script and Mrs. Muir, his wife, directed the pageantry. Mrs. Muir is a most talented producer, she has a natural gift for this, and, because of her genius, the pageant was an overwhelming success. It was called "Stansted Through the Centuries", and each of its seven episodes depicted some important event connected with the district from early days.

Over one hundred actors and actresses took part, and the costumes, many of which were hired, were of the best and faithfully represented the different periods. Fortunately, the weather was perfect and the horses did no great damage to the turf. A large appreciative audience witnessed the performance, which lasted over two hours, and in my opinion it was one of the best pageants of this year of pageants throughout the country. I attended the one at Hampton Court, and I think that ours at Stansted was just as effective in its theme and splendour.

Then came 1953, the Coronation Year, and we offered to entertain some of the Commonwealth visitors. Those invited were decided on by the Victoria League, in consultation with the Committee in London responsible for the entertainment of our overseas guests. Amongst our visitors were some important and interesting people, one a Nigerian chief robed in splendour. Mrs. Muir, and those who took part in the previous pageant of 1951, agreed to repeat some of its outstanding episodes, and once again we were favoured by brilliant weather. The history of the Homeland, passing as it did before our guests, much impressed them, especially as it all took place in surroundings so different from those to which they are accustomed in their own country. "Dear old England, how I love everything about it," was said to us so often, to be followed generally by the remark: "There is no place like it, I shall be sorry when the times comes for me to leave. How I would love to live here for the rest of my life."

For some years past we have welcomed to our home as guests various members of the Victoria League (for the help and guidance of Dominion and Colonial visitors) who had expressed the desire to stay in an English country home. In this way they experienced something of English life, and everyone who came to stay with us was overflowing with affection and appreciation of the land of their ancestors. Consequently, we came to know many pleasant and interesting people, some at the head of their country's affairs and others ordinary citizens, loyal to their own land but full of affection for the country which all called "home".

Since then we have had fêtes and other entertainments, the one following the two pageants being for the benefit of the British Legion. I calculated recently the approximate number of visitors we have entertained at Stansted Hall, one way and another, since we came to it thirty years ago and, excluding the soldiers who were here during the war, I reached the rather astonishing total of about thirty thousand.

In our neighbourhood are stationed quite a number of men of the American Air Force, and from time to time we ask the officers and their wives for afternoon tea, but on one occasion we gave them a special entertainment. Most ladies would have enjoyed it, as it was a parade of dresses since the Middle Ages. Mrs. Muir arranged it all, and both borrowed and hired twenty costumes. Ladies in the neighbourhood kindly acted as mannequins. Our American guests sat in the picture gallery of Stansted Hall, and watched each mannequin coming down the main staircase, while, at the same time, we were given a short history of the United States and Britain at the time the costumes were worn. It was very effective, and so much enjoyed, that we were asked by our guests to repeat it so that each lady could be photographed by their photographers. This was done, and I understand that some of the photographs appeared in illustrated journals in the United States.

We are blessed by having four attractive grandchildren, three boys and a girl, and my daughter Joan and her husband live only some twenty-five miles away. Consequently, in the holidays we see much of our grandchildren, who always spend part of their holidays with us. Last year we took the two eldest, Peter, aged thirteen, and Margaret, eleven, on a motor tour in France. We went along the north coast, staying at different seaside resorts until we came to the Atlantic coast. Thence we returned by the valley of the Loire to see its numerous châteaux, visiting Versailles on the way back to Boulogne. As we neared the end of our tour, and the car was approaching Boulogne, Margaret, who had been chattering unceasingly, turned to me and said: "Granpie, when we get home you must not expect too much from me, because it will take me some time to get back my English!"—This, from a child who knew only a few words of French, amused us very much.

I said earlier in this book that everyone lives two lives, one the practical everyday life, comprising our work and daily duties, and the other what I might term the contemplative life, when we allow our thoughts to reach out to other things. By reading, and day-dreaming, we live for a time each day in another plane of thought apart from the things about us. Consequently, this book is a mixture of both phases of my life, the one practical, and the other contemplative. Both aspects have been told to make up my life-story, and they come one after the other in these pages in rather an irregular fashion. The practical is followed by the contemplative, which in turn runs into an account of something practical. In such a way we live our daily lives, and when the tale is told the personal pronoun is bound to become prominent.

I feel that this may make the reader, who does not know me, think I must be rather egotistical, but there was no way to avoid it as this is a book about myself. I am in reality far from being an egotist, a person I much dislike, and in my daily life I try to be humble and modest. I have therefore, when relating facts, done my best to maintain this attitude throughout my book, which now nears its end. This story must come to a finish, but I do not propose, as Moses is reported in the book *Deuteronomy*, which is attributed to him, to write my own obituary and tell of my death and funeral.

That is for some scribe to do at some future time. Meantime, this, my tenth book, now draws to a close, the last chapter being given over to what I call AFTER-THOUGHTS on looking back from my seventy-second milestone.   All my life I have enjoyed good health and, endowed as I am with a cheerful disposition, I see no reason to end on a funereal note.   In any case, one must end one's earth journey sooner or later, a few years more or less, if one takes the wider outlook, being of no importance, as I look on death as a bend in the road of life.   If not alive on earth I shall be in a better world.

CHAPTER ELEVEN.

AFTERTHOUGHTS.

WHEN one can look back over seventy-two years, memory's storehouse is well filled. To be able to survey the past helps us in the present, and is a guide to the future. I have warmed my hands at the fire of life, and am thankful for the experiences that have come from a full active existence.

Our memory is something very wonderful. It is accepted, but its marvels are seldom considered. To be able to recall the past, and record it in the present, is the great achievement of mind over matter. It confounds materialism, and proves that we are beings with powers far beyond those possessed by physical substance.

This record of the important events of my life has been recalled by memory, helped by several well-filled scrapbooks containing newspaper cuttings which I have collected over the years. No diary has come to my aid, and yet, from start to finish, each event has come back to me clearly, one leading on to another, until the entire story has been built up in a form which all can read. Our memory is an aspect of our mind. What constitutes the mind we do not know, but it is not physical substance. Probably it is substance at an extremely rapid frequency of vibration. When we see something our mind images what we see. What we experience, the mind records. These mental

MY WIFE, MY GRANDCHILDREN AND MYSELF IN 1953.

images can be recalled, right back to childhood, and we now know that death does not destroy them, those who have passed on being able to recall their experiences on earth just as we do.

To unravel the mystery of being has been to me an endeavour well worth the effort, however far short I have come of my goal. The finite cannot comprehend the infinite, but still the urge remains to penetrate further a problem that by effort will unfold before one. As the mind develops, so unfolds the mysteries of our existence, which become less mysterious as we come to realise the meaning of death. As the mind is, so we are, and prehistory and history tell us the result of developing mind. Without mind there would be no conscious existence, and our selves and our surroundings would cease to be. Mind acting on substance makes what we call conscious life. Without mind we would be unaware of substance, and without substance the mind would have nothing on which to act. Both are consequently required to produce consciousness.

The discovery that our mind is permanent, and that it is the substance it acts upon that changes, is a vital addition to our knowledge. Our mind, and its memory, are carried over from earth substance to etheric substance, from a lower to a higher range of vibrations, without the loss of our individuality. In other words, we have found that life is not confined to earth substance only, but also functions unseen in a finer substance. Life, or mind, survives death, and death only means that the effect of life ceases to be experienced on earth by physical beings. Instead, life or mind, which has made us conscious beings on earth, makes us conscious beings in another, but finer, environment.

The universe unfolds as our knowledge increases, and then the wonder of man becomes more apparent. The individual is MIND, which is something not of this world. Mind can operate outside of space and time as these are understood on earth. It is the common factor between the two worlds, and each of us is part of the universal mind governing the universe. We each are mind housed in a physical body, to enable mind to express itself in the physical world. When mind discards the physical body it uses the etheric duplicate body in which to perform the same functions in the etheric world. Mind always persists, its surroundings change but its memories remain. Nothing of value is lost by death, as the individual mind retains the memories of the past which form our character, our individuality and our experiences. It is these which determine the place we shall occupy hereafter.

What are called rewards and punishments are consequences, each cause has an effect, each effect produces a cause, and as we sow so we reap. The eternal unbreakable law of cause and effect is ever with us. We cannot shake it off, as we are for ever coming face to face with it. Each deed produces its consequence, good or bad, just as is the deed. A good action produces that which is good, and an evil action that which is bad. A foolish deed produces regrets caused by the consequences which follow. A child tries to handle fire and is burned. It remembers, and does not repeat it.

Likewise, the human race has learned from past experiences that consequences follow deeds, and, from this memory, it has built up a code of ethics which, if followed, produces good and happy consequences, whereas those who do not follow it reap evil and misery. To have learned the right way to live comes from experiencing the consequences which come from living the wrong way of life. When man learned the law of consequence, or that effect follows cause, he produced from his imagination the saviour-god religions to ease his fears of the consequence hereafter of his mistakes on earth. He imagined that death was a curse laid upon him by the gods for his wickedness. The consequence of sin is death, so he thought.

A subject already mentioned, but worthy of some amplification because of its importance, is that all the saviour gods were produced by the apparition of a slain victim, whose etheric body, in the days of cannibalism, the priests declared the gods liked to eat. It was a peace offering to the gods, and in that age of cannibalism the people imagined the gods were likewise cannibals. When the victim's ghost was seen after death it was believed he had conquered death, and that the gods had removed the curse of death which they had pronounced over mankind for his wickedness. It was believed that the victim had mediated for the release of his people from their curse. Consequently, he was worshipped as their Mediator, and called by that name. Likewise his death was taken to be for the salvation hereafter of mankind, and in consequence he was called the Saviour. He was, moreover, called the Redeemer, because he had bought back by his death the human family. His death, it was thought, had paid the price the gods demanded.

Many other titles were given to him, as were given to the Christian Christ after Paul had raised Jesus, after seeing his apparition, to the level of a deified sacrificed victim who had returned after appeasing the wrath of God. Years later the gospels were written, incorporating this old idea then so prevalent in the Middle East. The consequence of man's sins and wickedness was thus placed on the back of the saviour gods, as they were fashioned one by one over the two thousand years before the Christian era. In this simple way mankind eased his conscience and his fears, to receive comfort from the thought that the consequences of his wickedness had been carried by another. Humanity had found a "whipping boy" to take the punishment of its misdeeds. "Safe in the arms of Jesus" is a very comforting thought to many.

This passing on of sins to a sacrificed lamb, sacrificed animal, or sacrificed human victim was the common practice of those who have lived before us. It was, and still is, the feature of supernatural religion, and those who believe that they can rid themselves of the consequences of wickedness in this easy way get much comfort and satisfaction, but history does not reveal that it has made them better men and women. To feel that all is now well for one hereafter, by accepting this form of belief, certainly gives great satisfaction, but it does not make for righteousness. To have passed the consequences of sin on to another does not relieve one from the effect of natural law. The history of Christendom, in the Christian era, reveals that this side-tracking of natural law is unethical and has made for wickedness and abominations such as were never exceeded before or elsewhere.

The virtues have a small part in supernatural religions, though they are attached to most of them, but religion and ethics are not the same. Supernatural Religion comprises performing some ceremony or ritual, or believing some creed for the purpose of obtaining a place in heaven, and from this the believer gains comfort and satisfaction. Mankind has required this crutch, the mystery of existence was too obscure for him to penetrate, and he produced what he required.

To-day, however, Spiritualism reveals that it is not what we believe that makes for happiness hereafter, but what we are and how we live. Our mental outlook secures for us the place for which we are fitted, and we go there and nowhere else. Our mental outlook, the cause, produces the plane of thought on which we live hereafter, which is the effect. Our mental development determines our future abode, which is the consequence of what we are. When man realises the truth, that he himself must save himself, when he faces facts and does not obtain comfort from his false imaginings, the human race will receive ethically an immense move forward. Natural Religion will by then have replaced Supernatural Religion. Natural Religion can briefly be described as meaning that as we sow here we reap hereafter, and Ethics teaches that as we sow on earth we reap here on earth.

These thoughts, unpopular as they are to-day with Christians, will nevertheless in time mellow their outlook. As it is, I am at least allowed to express them, whereas not so long ago I would have been put in prison and, further back, tortured and burned to death. So Christians have become kinder and more tolerant, and this I realise when looking back over my span of life. Likewise, a few admit that so-called miracles did not cease two thousand years ago, and that under the name of psychic phenomena they happen to-day. Moreover, under the influence of Spiritualism, they imagine a more natural heaven which one reaches at the time of death, and not at some future far off Resurrection when the sheep are separated from the goats.

The mention of torture reminds me of two experiences I have had which greatly impressed me. Some years ago at an Exhibition held in Glasgow there was a place set apart for the display of instruments of torture used during the Christian era. There I saw the way Christians reasoned with heretics, those who dared to think for themselves and not as orthodox Christians thought. I saw the thumb-screw which was tightened up until the thumb became a mass of pulp, then a contracting boot which had the same effect on the foot and leg. The rack was there on which, when in use, lay the victim whose arms and legs were torn asunder. Many other fiendish devices were displayed for all to see how intolerance could make men worse than beasts, which never premeditate cruelty.

Again I saw some years later the same dispay at Ghent in Belgium where, in the old castle, an even greater array of instruments of torture was displayed. There must have been at least a hundred different inventions for the purpose of producing pain and suffering on the victims, who only asked to be allowed to hold their own thoughts. This is what comes from ignorance, as this breeds intolerance from which springs cruelty, and I thought to myself that, as one knows more, one becomes less a zealot and more humane. Only within the last two centuries, as the power of supernatural religion has decreased, has religious cruelty declined. This should continue as education increases, and as knowledge takes the place of ignorance in the years to come. All this cruelty came about by men and women holding false religious ideas, which it was thought had the approval of a God made in the image of man.

Education has stimulated mental evolution. I remember the ban placed on the word "Evolution", and to mention the name of Charles Darwin caused a pious silence in the conversation. This illustrious man, after many years of thought and research, published in 1859 his famous book *Origin of Species*, in which he traced man's ancestry from the animal kingdom. Since the time when Copernicus declared that the sun did not travel round the earth, no greater shock has been administered to complacent mankind, because it upsets the age-old belief, held by nearly every race and every religion, that man was a special and spontaneous creation of God, or the gods, to crown the creation of the earth.

The consternation, anger and antagonism caused by the opinions of Darwin in the average upper- and middle-class families of Christendom can hardly in our time be realised. Anyone showing the slightest sympathy with this famous biologist's theories was immediately regarded as one who was swiftly travelling on the broad road that leads to destruction. All books, which in any way cast doubt on the orthodox outlook, were regarded with fear and distrust, and to read such a book was considered to be a grievous sin. Moreover, the clergy vied with each other in their ridicule and abuse of one who had uncovered another of nature's secrets.

The Christians of the 19th century were quick to see that if Darwin's theory was true, that man and the apes had a common ancestor, their entire theological edifice was shattered and, for the next fifty years, they ridiculed and vilified this noble man. If there were no Adam then there was no fall or original sin, and, if this be so, a saviour was irrelevant and all the Christian beliefs and ceremonies meaningless. Man, argued Darwin, instead of having fallen, was a developing, progressive creature, he having reached his present position after countless years of slow evolution from primitive protoplasm. Consequently, he threw over his belief in Christianity, but it took seventy years before his main conclusions were finally accepted, and he was acknowledged as the pioneer of a new age of thought.

Besides this, his theories gave the idea of ordered progress, one quite new to Christendom, which, so far, had always looked back for guidance to the past, and given little thought to the possibilities ahead of the human race. Darwin's discoveries set a new outlook before human thought, and it became realised that another of nature's secrets had been revealed by means of improved scientific methods of observation and research. So it came about that the 19th century became brilliant with new discoveries and the advance in knowledge.

Mental development made all this possible, because Darwin, and his contemporary scientists, were allowed to live peacefully and pursue their investigations without fear of persecution, as was the lot of so many of their forerunners. The Church, however, was not so tolerant to those over whom it had the power, because not only did the clergy debase themselves by their condemnation of this brilliant naturalist, but theological professors, who accepted his conclusions, were deprived of their Chairs and cast out as heretics.

In politics I can look back and see improvement. Intolerance here has likewise lessened. I remember the time when Liberals and Conservatives were bitter towards each other, when a Liberal newspaper would not be tolerated in a Conservative home and *vice versa*. To-day, the Conservatives have become the Liberals, and the Liberals likewise more advanced in their outlook. It is all a question of mental development, as an intolerant person is one who has such a narrow outlook on life that he fails to realise that every mind is different, that each one's environment is different, and consequently each individual thinks differently. We think as our minds direct, and honest sincere thought and expression, instead of being denounced, should be encouraged so long as it is not subversive. Each one is open to disagree, but not to prohibit expression as was done not so long ago, and still is in some countries to-day. This is a retrograde attitude to adopt.

Now, much more is done for the poor and needy than in my young days. The extremes of wealth and poverty are much less evident. In the 19th century the kind and charitable took pity on those in distress, but to-day relief is better organised and the State does much of what was then done by individuals in an irregular way.

In one way my parents and grandparents lived more enviable lives than we do to-day. The fear of war did not trouble them as it does us. To imagine a world war never occurred to them, at most an Indian frontier war, a war with naked savages or a suchlike localised affair was the worst that could happen. To be told that, in the future, weapons would be devised to fly in the air and drop bombs on our towns would never have been believed. Atom bombs shot from Europe, or dropped from the air, to spread widespread destruction in our country would have been dismissed as fantastic. Nevertheless, the utter ruthlessness of war has come about, and Britain is no longer the island it was last century.

The Franco-Prussian war of 1870 was the last one they remembered until the Boer war of 1899, but neither of these caused the terror we experienced by the two world wars, especially the last. Bombing has brought everyone into war, and both professional soldiers and peaceful civilians run the risk of wounds and death. Modern war makes most people soldiers of one kind or another, and conscription embraces the youth, both men and women, of every land. Certainly the majority live in greater comfort and luxury than did our grandparents, but this greater power we now possess over matter has brought with it the haunting fear of wholesale destruction to life and property.

Can it be wondered that some say "Give us back

the good old days"? Then, the countryside was peaceful and no airplane disturbed the harmony of nature. Then, roads were safe and accidents few; now, speed dominates the mind and a place for quiet contemplation in tune with nature is more hard to find. No telephone disturbed their quiet days, as our ancestors lived in an age of quietude and we live in one of noise and rush.

Are we any happier now than were our easy-going forebears? Certainly we have much that they had not. Think of the houses the workers now occupy, and all they contain to make life easier and more complete. Think of the improved and varied food they eat. Think of the health services, and how disease, pain and suffering have lessened. Think of the reduced hours of work and the pleasures the people now enjoy, the cinema, television, radio and increased travel. Contrast this, and much more, with the drab misery of the poor, and their lives of squalor, one hundred years ago, with wages low, working hours long, and in constant fear of illness and old age. Up to the beginning of the 19th century the way of life had changed little down the ages, but science and discovery have now raised enormously the standard of living for the great majority, though, because of two world wars, the once wealthy minority are unable to maintain the luxury their ancestors enjoyed.

I look back to the opening of this century, and see how to-day we are reaping the benefit of its rich discoveries. Then, we first heard of X-rays, radioactivity, the electron and the nuclear atom. Matter ceased to be looked on by physicists as solid, and I remember mentioning this in a lecture I then gave, to be greeted by cries of derision. These discoveries set the stage for our enormous advance in knowledge over the past fifty years. Research spread from the universities to industry, and great factories now combine research with production such as our grandfathers never imagined. Man is winning more and more wealth from nature, the chemist, for instance, by experiment and research, producing greater quantities of useful things to make life fuller and more comfortable.

Synthetic materials, new clothing, new medicines and new articles come in increasing quantities from the laboratory. Petroleum has changed our lives, the modern oil refinery being so efficient that a product, which was first used as an embrocation, is to-day turned into all sorts of useful things, and the same with many other raw materials. The development in the use of electricity is enormous, great rivers once running to waste now being used for its production. Electric computers are now saving countless hours of mental work hitherto used for mathematical calculations, and what is called electronics will save labour in many different ways. Finally, we have discovered the force hidden away in seemingly inert matter, and nuclear energy will amplify the energy so far obtained from coal and oil. On the other hand, our power of destruction has increased to such an extent that everyone is terrified, and this world-wide fear may keep the world at peace. Knowledge without wisdom is dangerous.

Meantime, while peace reigns, wealth is increasing and, taking it overall, some of the world's inhabitants, but by no means enough, do get more out of life than their predecessors, but are they any happier for all they have gained? Increased wealth brings increased nourishment, security, comfort and enjoyment, but happiness is a mental condition and many a poor person lives a happier life than some who are rich. Nevertheless, I am sure that the average of happiness to-day is greater in Britain than it was in my young days. Better health, greater security from want, less toil, less drunkenness, brighter, better homes, and a wider field for enjoyment, all make for happiness. Our surroundings affect our minds, and as these improve the harmony of life increases.

As the mind evolves, so do our surroundings improve, and my time on earth has witnessed a surge forward of thought which has been translated into action. The placid Victorian era has passed, and education has brought about a new age in which most of the people enjoy better living conditions than did their grandparents. Instead of the few having all the good things of life, they are now much more fairly spread among the many. That is all to the good, and it makes me hopeful with regard to the future.

Fifty years ago, only amongst the working classes was a Socialist to be found. When a friend of mine, a wealthy shipowner of Glasgow, publicly declared himself a believer in Socialist principles, he was denounced and ridiculed. Because of his wealth he was considered a traitor to his class. Now, we are more democratic and, whatever our financial position is, sympathy for the less fortunate today permeates every class of the community. John Burns' idea that no one should have more than £500 a year is not now the aim of the Socialists, any more than the living conditions of the poor, which existed last century, would be approved by the Conservatives.

Just as education has enabled the franchise to be extended to most adults, so the masses have made Parliament, which hitherto had quite neglected them, bring about legislation for their good. In the years prior to my birth the upper and middle classes, through their members of Parliament, legislated for themselves, whereas to-day all the adult people legislate for all the people. Seventy years ago education for the people was just beginning, and to-day we see the result. That is a great achievement to have witnessed throughout a lifetime.

Mind can make a new and better world for everyone, if thought is directed aright. If the reverse, so much the worse for everyone. People in democratic countries, therefore, get the government the majority desire and consequently the living conditions for which they are mentally fitted. Mind is King. It produces the thought which creates the action, and what remarkable changes the last seventy years have brought about! If thought can produce such discoveries, inventions and ideas as it has done within this time, what will happen in the years to come? What, indeed, will our children and grandchildren experience?

Developing mind has likewise altered our outlook on the universe. In science, materialism, in the 19th century, was rampant, and matter was looked upon as something solid and made up of atoms, just as a rice pudding is composed of grains of rice. To-day, matter is accepted as something etherial, and the physicist thinks of it in terms of electrons and protons, in perpetual orderly movement and never at rest. Physical science has enabled Spiritualists to locate another world in terms of vibrations, and it has confounded the materialist, who accepts only what he sees and feels.

Science has uncovered something of the universe, but it has not explained it. It has given us a wonderful array of facts, but the eternal question, which Science has not so far answered, is ever before us. How did it all come about? To answer that God made and maintains the immense universe is no answer to the question, because the intelligent person then wants to know who made God. To this there is no answer and we are just where we were. Nevertheless there is one answer which satisfies me, and that is this. The universe, embracing both the physical and the etheric, has been from all eternity and will exist for all eternity. What is has always been and will always be, and what we call creation and destruction is change of form and aspect. Eternity has always been and always will be, and that to which we give the name of time relates to our finite consciousness, but not to infinity.

We are conscious of so little that appertains to the universe. We are not conscious of the etheric world, but we are conscious from evidence that it exists. When our consciousness can embrace the greater world our outlook will change. Relatively when we reach Etheria we shall be in another world, but in the same universe. An intelligent inhabitant of the other world has different answers to our eternal questions than we have here on earth, but he is still facing the same problem. So let us sum it up in these words.

The universe unfolds itself before us as our minds develop or unfold. The problem is a mental one, and, only as the mind develops, and we advance from plane to plane in the etheric world, will the perplexing question of the universe come to be better understood.

By ignoring psychic phenomena official Science has passed by its means of informing us of that phenomenon which we call life, and its destiny after death. To-day, some of its exponents are waking up to the fact that something very vital has so far been ignored, and, now that it cannot be denied, they are at a loss to make it fit in with their other discoveries. What Science has cast aside Spiritualists have recovered, and to-day many scientists are timidly making themselves conversant with the claims made by Spiritualists over the past hundred years. Triumphant as Science was in the 19th century, it is still seeking reality, and to-day some of its leaders realise that there are more things in heaven and earth than its past materialistic philosophy encompassed.

Likewise, I have seen in my lifetime the once triumphant Protestant Church becoming more tolerant, less aggressive or assertive, and humbled by the advance of knowledge. When it opened the door of Westminster Abbey for the body of Charles Darwin to rest within its precincts, it admitted to the world that its leaders had cast aside the first and second chapters of *Genesis*, as the basis on which its creed rested. "For as in Adam all die, even so in Christ shall all be made alive" (1 Cor. xv, 22). Up to last century nearly everyone was a professing Christian, but to-day it is not so, and, though the Church still controls the radio and prevents the free expression of thought, very many thinking people pass Christianity by and think out for themselves their own salvation.

This is the natural result of developing mind. When the people were ignorant they placidly accepted leadership in religion, as in political affairs. To-day the intelligent think for themselves, and do not rely on a priest to guide them. Last century the Church was the centre of the lives of the people, the minister in Scotland made his regular visits to his congregation, prayed with each family and asked the children questions from the Shorter Catechism. I knew it almost word for word, and what an exposition it was to set before a child! I was expected to learn it, but not to understand it. A copy of this document would now be difficult to purchase.

Many people think to-day that orthodox religion is too much a matter of creeds and dogmas, formulated by men many centuries ago when knowledge was slight. These doctrines do not embrace the wider wisdom of our times. They have divided nations and set one against another. Natural religion, on the other hand, embraces all mankind, as each one of us has the same destiny and most have the same aspirations, hopes and fears. The time, I think, is coming when people generally will accept the seven principles of Spiritualism as sufficient for their guidance and comfort through life.

Spiritualism and natural religion stand for the same thing, and mean the same thing. Spiritualism is contained within the following seven principles, and these summarise all that I have already written on the subject:—

(1) The Universe is governed by Mind, commonly called God. All we have sensed, do sense, or will sense is Mind expressing itself in some form or another.

(2) The existence and identity of the individual continues after the change called death.

(3) Communication, under suitable conditions, takes place between us here on earth and the inhabitants of Etheria, into which we shall pass at death.

(4) Our conduct must be guided by the golden rule first proclaimed by Confucius, of doing to others what we would wish to be done to ourselves.

(5) Each individual is his own saviour, and he cannot look to someone else to bear his sins and suffer for his mistakes.

(6) Each individual reaps as he sows, and he makes his happiness or unhappiness just as he harmonises with his surroundings. Each one gravitates naturally to the place in Etheria in harmony with his desires, as there desires are gratified more easily than here on earth.

(7) The path of progress is never closed, and there is no known end to the advancement of the individual.

These principles dispel despair, give a feeling of hope and satisfaction, and emphasise how right was Confucius to compress ethics into doing to others as we would be done by. They make clear each one's responsibilities for deeds done, and that consequences follow our thoughts and actions. What counts is what we really are, and not what we think we are. Finally, no one need despair, as progress is open to all, even the worst being able by effort to outgrow past wrong-doing by mental development.

Religious doctrine and creeds have helped mankind in the years gone by, but, with greater knowledge, increased intelligence and a better understanding of life, many people have now outgrown the beliefs of the past. They realise that how we live is what is important. Let us therefore think back to the pre-Christian days when flourished the great moralists, and realise how right they were in emphasising the importance of good conduct. The Pagan philosopher, Epicurus (341–270 B.C.), emphasised the need for improved ethical conduct and taught that only through right living could happiness be attained. Zeno (340–264 B.C.), the founder of Stoic philosophy, placed virtue and right conduct before all else. No closer approach has since been made to a higher system of human conduct than was reached by these two noble Pagans. Righteousness, they taught, was the remedy for most of the world's troubles, and to do what is right on every occasion produced character which is more precious than wealth.

Epictetus, the Greek, who in early life was a slave, had to leave Rome in A.D. 90 because of his opposition to the tyrannical emperor Domitian. He represents the highest in Greek culture and thought of this period, the practical ethical philosophy which he advocated being so high, noble, pure and logical, that his influence for good has been felt from his time to the present day. Another Pagan, Plotinus (A.D. 205–270), was the leading exponent of Neo-Platonic philosophy, a mode of thought which aimed at uniting the wisdom of all the ages into one great comprehensive system of thought, embracing the belief in one supreme God, and that this life is a preparation for the one to come.

Such then was the teaching of these four representatives of Paganism, but very many more could be mentioned, all of whom had numerous followers who did their best to live up to what their masters taught. One more I must mention, namely Hypatia (A.D. 350–415), the most outstanding woman of her time. She was a philosopher and a distinguished lecturer in Alexandria. This gifted woman continued to conduct her lectures to advance knowledge and righteousness, at the time the Christians in Alexandria were torturing and slaughtering the Jews (30,000 being butchered), Pagans and heretics. So it does not surprise us that she met a tragic end. Urged on by Cyril, the Archbishop, the congregation of his church invaded her classroom, cut her to pieces with oyster-shells and finally burned her body piece by piece. With her death died philosophy and learning in Alexandria, and ignorance became supreme because Christianity banned all education. Consequently the seed of ignorance was sown, and Europe entered that long and tragic period known as the Dark Ages.

I have received from many thoughtful people encouragement for my efforts to bring light into dark places. Compared with the masses still lacking knowledge, and indifferent to the deeper problems of life, the number of enlightened people is unfortunately very small, and many years will pass before a higher level of thinking prevails. We must remember, however, that education came to the majority of our people only eighty-five years ago (1870), and that there was a blank of some fifteen hundred years of mostly theological teaching to the favoured few.

If only education had been allowed to develop during the Christian era, a solution would surely have been found by now for many pressing problems, including that of war, and it is one of the greatest of human tragedies that this did not happen. Just as Christianity extinguished the lamp of learning in the Roman Empire from the 5th century onwards, so did it repeat the process in the 13th century when it smothered, with its superstitions, the advanced knowledge accumulated by the Arabs. Thus, for the second time, it denied to the Western World the benefits which come from knowledge.

Only during the last eighty-five years has education occupied the attention of the British administration. Fifteen hundred years earlier flourished the great academies of the Roman Empire which lit Europe, the Middle East and North Africa with intellectual light, and they attained their highest development and efficiency in Gaul. With the coming of Christian "civilisation" went all learning, one by one the schools were closed, and the teachers murdered or banished. Christianity and knowledge could not live together, and so the Greek and Roman attempt to enlighten mankind was extinguished. Need we wonder that the great majority to-day are still children, and give little profound thought to the deeper things of life?

Need we be surprised that everywhere these grown-up children produce guns, airplanes and explosives to destroy what has been constructed, in just the same irresponsible way as a child destroys the sand castle he has spent hours in erecting?

Education of the young first commenced in Greece, and spread all over the Roman Empire, Quintilian (A.D. 35–96), a Roman citizen, born in Spain, continuing to lead the Roman world in education on the lines laid down by Plato. His high conception of conduct could hardly be surpassed, his wonderful work, devoted to the training and instruction of the young, being rewarded by the Emperor Vespasian appointing him to a professorship, and liberally endowing his schemes with public money, to enable him to extend education all over the Empire. To-day we would call him the Minister of Education, a government office which was not created in Britain until 1870, some eighteen hundred years later, and only then after much religious opposition. His life-long work for education was so · much appreciated that the Emperor Domitian raised him to the rank of consul, and also entrusted his two grand-nephews to his care.

This refined, unassuming, kindly Roman, this noble representative of intellectual Paganism, with his clear vision and wide sympathies, one of the most attractive figures of the time, laid the foundation for the extensive system of Roman education. This most outstanding of all the Roman schoolmasters loved liberty, justice, truth and mercy, besides abhorring all forms of cruelty and oppression. He lived a noble life, instructing the young in all the knowledge of the time, his aim being to cultivate the young mind in the pursuit of wisdom and the development of righteous living, while injustice and oppression in every form always received his severe condemnation.

These observations let us realise how much we have lost throughout the Christian era, in fact, progress was stopped for at least a thousand years. However much this is to be regretted, we can all be thankful to have lived in a land where education and freedom eventually prevailed, as they have done in our time.

I have always found that my fellow men and women are, as a rule, kind, honest, tolerant and decent people to live with, it being the fanatics who make for disharmony and intolerance. If everyone would be unselfish and think of others, and less of himself or herself, the happiness of the human race would greatly advance. When analysed, it will be found that unrighteousness can be attributed to one failing only, namely selfishness. The unselfish person is the good and righteous man or woman, the bad and unrighteous being the selfish, those who think of themselves always first and others last. How the world would be transformed if the golden rule were practised by everyone!

In every land and clime there are good and righteous people, just as there are bad. It is not the tenets of the religion they profess that makes them good, but their natures. Some are naturally unselfish and some selfish, some are kind and others are cruel. To divide the world into Christians and non-Christians, and speak, as many do, as if the Christians stand for righteousness and the others do not, is wrong and stupid. Good and kind people abound everywhere quite irrespective of their religious beliefs, the ethical code being world-wide.

I am thankful to have had the supernormal experiences which have come my way. I have been greatly privileged. Moreover, I have been able to help so many, and this thought gives me great satisfaction. My mind has unfolded, and I have been able to take a wider and more satisfactory outlook on life. Neither materialism nor supernatural religion give, in my opinion, the true solution to existence, but I appreciate the reason why one or the other has its adherents. The enigma of life is so profound that either the negative or the positive outlook appeals to different minds. My aim has been to purify and rationalise religion, not to destroy it.

So very few are privileged to have had the opportunity to obtain proof of survival after death, and discover the answer to the riddle of existence. Without this direct knowledge, acceptance of Spiritualism is difficult, as to hear or read the psychic experiences of others is not the same as to experience them oneself. For those not so fortunate, faith is a very present help in trouble, and agnosticism gives mental satisfaction to the logically minded. Spiritualism, however, gave to me the answer to the deeper problems of life, and for this knowledge my life has been happier and I have obtained the mental contentment which satisfies me.

Spiritualism explains and clarifies so many problems. To the Spiritualist this life is such a brief span in our journey onwards that its seeming injustices can be appreciated in a wider perspective. The poverty, misery, suffering and deformities from which so many suffer take on a different aspect when we realise that after death our perfect etheric body replaces our imperfect physical body. In the other world, our surroundings will be determined much more by our thoughts than they are on earth. Disease, deformities, the want of sight, the lack of hearing, and our various bodily ailments, will then be no more as the etheric body is not subject to any of these handicaps. When we reach the after-life the sufferings here on earth will be found to fade away and be forgotten in the joy and fullness of the life to come.

So far as our destiny is concerned, if everyone does his best no more can be expected, and the place he or she will reach in the hereafter, a world in many respects like this one, will be in accordance with the character of the individual. The religious beliefs held are a comfort for this world only, and mean nothing in the world to come. Everyone, therefore, should do the utmost possible to diffuse kindness, love, sympathy, justice, tolerance and all that makes for increased happiness. If that is done, no one need fear death, because the consequence of righteousness is happiness. That indeed will be the state of every good man, woman and child, who will experience it in full measure when the time comes for them to pass on to the life beyond.

Looking back, I can see progress to a higher level of thought and action during my lifetime. Discarding the fanatics and zealots who are amongst us, the general level of conduct throughout the world is rising, and for this we can thank the increase there has been in education everywhere. The more people there are who think aright, the more error is replaced by truth, the happier will be the human family and the greater will be the chance of peace. So let us hold high the torch of knowledge, which will give light to the path the human race is forever climbing onwards and upwards, to higher thoughts and grander deeds.

My life has been happy, my health has been good, and to my devoted wife I pay tribute for much of the happiness I have enjoyed. For forty-two years we have lived together in loving harmony, and for all she has been to me I am deeply grateful.

To John Deans Blair, my private accountant, who has served me faithfully and loyally for forty years, and still does, I give my thanks, and here acknowledge how much his good work has meant to me.

I now finish this record of my career, but my life on earth is not yet ended. This is the end of my autobiography, but of my life here it is

NOT THE END.

APPENDIX

THE EFFECT OF RELIGION ON HISTORY

A lecture given to the Cambridge Historical Society

I have chosen this title because I feel that historians in the past have not given sufficient attention to this aspect of history. Half the events of history have been brought about by religion, and, this being so, it seems eminently desirable that we should know more about religion, its various origins and its effect on history. Historians in the past have accepted the claims of different religious organisations as to their origin, but increased knowledge now discloses that religious beliefs have a much deeper significance and can be traced back into the mists of the past.

The study of Comparative Religion reveals all too clearly how wrong it is for any one religion to make claims of a special revelation. To claim that it only is unique and has the sanction of the powers that rule in Heaven is historically wrong. Every religion makes this claim, and yet all religions have a common origin. We can trace the links in the chain of beliefs back and back until we arrive at the earliest and most prevalent of all religions, Ancestor Worship. Modern psychic knowledge, moreover, now enables us to understand how Ancestor Worship originated, and this I shall briefly explain.

The word religion means to bind back, re-ligare. In other words it means to become in touch with another order of life and existence which has been believed in from earliest times. This belief came about by the observance of what is to-day called Psychic Phenomena. In the presence of certain psychically endowed people, to-day called mediums, supernormal phenomena occurred. They went into trance and spoke in voices other than their own, the claim being made by the new intelligence that it was not the medium who was speaking, but someone else was who had lived previously on earth.

Moreover these psychically endowed people, these mediums, claimed to see people who were not seen by normal sight, and this faculty is now called clairvoyance. They were also clairaudient, in that they heard voices that were not heard by normal people. Besides this, other psychic phenomena developed in their presence, so much so that extraneous voices, which were quite apart from the human vocal organs, were heard by everyone, they being not the voices of people on earth. Beings suddenly materialised and as quickly disappeared. Bright moving lights were seen, objects were moved without physical touch, and other supernormal events took place.

We may well ask how it is that we know that all this happened, and to this question I reply that ancient literature is full of these abnormal events, which were called visions, wonders, miracles, the conversation of the gods, and other names to differentiate them from ordinary everyday events. We find them written in what is probably the oldest record in the world, *The Epic of Gilgamish*, believed to be at least four thousand years old. This has been translated from the old Sumerian language, written in cuneiform characters, on baked clay. We find these marvels recorded in the Egyptian *Book of the Dead*, Egypt supplying us with one of the oldest stories of ghostly visitors and their conversations. In the Hindu *Bag-av-ad Gita*, the Hindus named an apparition Devata, which in Sanskrit literally means "The Shining One", just as mediums to-day likewise describe another world being.

The Hebrews believed in Jehovah as an invisible super-man, seen at times by their clairvoyants, who went about their tribes and controlled the tribes' medium in the Holy of Holies. The word "Lord" which occurs so often in the Bible should have been translated "a spirit", and, if this is remembered, the Bible will come to be appreciated as the most psychic of all ancient books.

In Greece we find the same marvels told about Aga-memnon and Orpheus, also in the "Odyssey" of Homer, and in Plato's dialogues of Socrates. Socrates claimed to hear supernormal voices. In Roman literature the writings of Cicero, Livy and Apuleius contain accounts of super-normal happenings. Tertullian, in the 2nd century A.D., gives us a vivid account of a séance, and elsewhere we read of Roman séances where occurred exactly what happens in our own days. Apollonius, of the first Christian century, was probably one of the greatest of ancient mediums. However, the burning and destruction of mediums, called wizards and witches, by the Christian Church during the Christian era, largely stamped out all psychic phenomena in the West during that period, and only as this terror ceased do we find mediums arise, such as Swedenborg of the 18th century.

Later also came modern Spiritualism into being in the 19th century, in consequence of the extraordinary occur-rences which took place at Hydesville in the United States. From this time, 1848, onwards mediumship became the object of scientific investigation, and the old belief in witch-craft died out. Spiritualism claims to have scientifically proved that when we die, we live on in another world of higher frequency vibrations surrounding and interpene-trating this world. This is possible because each one of us has a duplicate etheric body which separates from the physical body at death, carrying mind and its memory with it to the new order of existence.

Under suitable conditions the so-called dead can lower their vibrations by means of a lace-like substance called ectoplasm, which is found in mediums in greater supply than in ordinary human beings. Thus these other-world men and women can regain contact with physical conditions, vibrate the atmosphere and be both seen and heard. This, I believe, not only happens to-day but has happened from early times. Only now, with our greater scientific knowledge, have we come to record with care and accuracy these extraordinary events and investigate them in a scientific manner. The ancients experienced them right enough, and attributed them to gods and devils under the all-embracing name of miracles, but to them there was no order in the universe and everything happened in a haphazard way according to the whims of these benign or evil invisible beings whom they believed ordered the universe.

With the foregoing in mind we now re-read our history, and find that every religion in the world has come into being by mankind misunderstanding psychic phenomena. Our ancestors saw and heard supernormal beings, both gods and devils. They were as children wandering in the wilderness of ignorance, unable to account for the phenomena of nature, and they attributed to a god or devil everything that happened, this being the simplest way to account for natural phenomena. Nevertheless the gods and goddesses of Europe and America, of India, China, Babylon, Egypt, Greece and Rome, the gods and goddesses of our Pagan ancestors, were none other than the men and women who had lived and died on earth. Thus can be understood the ancient saying that we are all children of the gods.

The chief of the tribe died, and returned to control the tribe's medium and govern the tribe, "He being dead yet speaketh." The ruling chief took his instructions from the dead chief, who became magnified and glorified, to become a superman and then a divine being. So religion came into being, the dead chief becoming the tribal God to the people, while those who held lower ranks on earth were, when dead, given similar positions in heaven. Thus began, in a primitive way, the building up of a heavenly hierarchy.

Consequently, in time, a god was made responsible for every phenomenon of nature. Lightning became the axe of the god of thunder who was regarded as an omnipotent superman who had the power to fell trees in a way no ordinary man could do. In this way the Pagan pantheon was constructed over the ages, and Zeus in Greece, Amen-rā in Egypt, Brahma in India and all the other Pagan father gods came to be regarded as the Kings of heaven and the fathers of mankind. Jupiter, meaning Deus Pater, was worshipped and revered just as Christians worship and revere Jehovah, the father god of the Hebrews.

This very brief and sketchy introduction to my theme gives an idea of how religion came into being with its accompanying ceremonial, ritual and dogmas. Truly it was a revelation, but not one confined to the Hebrews or the Christians, but to all mankind. Consequently everywhere we go to-day, and all we read about the past, reveals the vital fact that man has believed in an after-life, and his religion has consisted of his numerous attempts to please and placate those beings he elevated to the rank of the gods. He prayed to them, cajoled them and even threatened them to obtain his desires.

So he came to believe that only through being on good terms with the powers in heaven could his wives be fruitful and the fields yield their increase. Consequently he sacrificed to them, because early man, being a cannibal, believed that the gods were likewise cannibals, and enjoyed eating the etheric duplicates of the offered-up victim. So we read in Genesis that the gods, which is the correct translation, preferred the sacrifice of Abel, the shepherd, to that of Cain, the gardener, the latter offering only the herbal fruit of the earth whereas the former offered up animals which, it was believed, the gods preferred. This is still the belief amongst primitive people.

Sacrifice led to the belief in what is known as the Saviour-God religions. A victim was offered to the gods after being anointed with oil, so as to enable him to burn better, and make the eating of his body a more succulent meal. Consequently he was called the Christ, or the anointed one, a word first found in Sanskrit and copied by the Greeks. So we have Krishna, the Hindu Christ, who was believed to have died for the sins of humanity about one thousand B.C. Sixteen other Saviour gods, or Christs, are known to history, and surrounding them all were the beliefs and ceremonials attached to Jesus when he, likewise, because he was a victim of the priests, became the Christ.

Why was it that an offered-up sacrificed victim became, in the eyes of his worshippers, a saviour god, a Christ? The reason was because on each occasion he was seen after death as an apparition and it was consequently believed that he had broken the curse of death. The gods had been appeased and death was now regarded as the entrance to another life. The curse of death had been removed by the gods, and the victim came to be regarded as Saviour, Mediator and Judge of mankind.

Thus this apparition subdued the people's fear of death, but, when the priests theologised and organised religion, the idea of salvation became a matter of belief in the tenets of the particular religion. Only believers could be saved, and the comfort natural religion gave to the ancestor worshippers was lost in the labyrinths of dogma and doctrine. When the priests took over the organisation of religion they kept the people obedient by the fear that unbelief would mean punishment hereafter instead of bliss.

Primitive man, before the days of priestcraft and theology, believed that he passed on to be with the ancestors he worshipped. So food was laid in his tomb, besides other things that might be useful to him. The chief's horse was killed, so that he could ride on his duplicate etheric horse. Everything then was much more natural and simple than it became under priestly rule, as, over the ages, the priests reared the elaborate mental speculations which came to be known as theology, or the knowledge of the gods.

The priesthood originated amongst the men who took charge of the tribe's mediums, but, by mimicry and deceit, they were often able to impress the people more readily than did the tribes' medium, who could speak only under the influence of a controlling spirit. Likewise psychic phenomena was of sporadic occurrence, whereas the priest could delude the people at will. Thus came into being the priest-magician who sat within his magic circle, and gave to the people an imitation of the wonders and signs which had originally come from the genuine medium endowed by nature with psychic gifts.

Consequently we read in the Bible of the constant quarrelling between the priest and the prophet, which latter is the Greek name for a medium. With priesthood came sacrifice, and the belief that by releasing the etheric body at death the gods were pleased with the food and would reward the givers. With priesthood came the belief in sin, which is something quite apart from ethics, as sin relates to theology and the numerous beliefs contained therein.

With priesthood came churches or temples where eucharists, ceremonials and worship took place. Originally these places of worship were the séance rooms of the medium, but the Sanctuary, or Holy of Holies, is all that remains from the time when the medium was the centre of the service. When these sacred buildings were used by a saviour-god religion they became the eating-house where the body of the sacrificed victim was eaten, because it was believed that by so doing the "manna", or the vital part of the victim, could be absorbed by the communicant. Out of this developed the Pagan eucharist to be later re-named the Christian eucharist. Theology, or the knowledge of the gods, inaptly called the Queen of Science, is the accumulation of beliefs mankind has gathered together regarding these invisible beings called the gods, who are none other than the men and women who have lived on earth and died.

The first man to emphasise this was Euhemerus, a Greek of the 4th century B.C., who declared in his book *Sacred History* that the gods were none other than the men and women who had lived on earth. For this blasphemy he was termed an atheist. We must, however, remember that theology to our ancestors was what science is to us to-day, and that the gods were very real factors in the lives of the people, who had no idea of the unification of nature. When the belief in unity came about one divine being became the creator, and the numerous individual gods played more minor parts in the directing of the universe.

By means of theology our ancestors gave the best explanation they could of the universe, and its speculations comforted them in death while satisfying their wonderings in life. To attribute everything to a god satisfied their childish wish for an explanation of something not understood. They were but enquiring children who, without instruments, had just to take nature as they found it. So they worshipped the gods, sacrificed to them and received the comfort needed for their undying souls.

The Greeks first began the scientific method of forming opinions by direct observation and experiment, but only within the last 300 years, when instruments have been developed, have we entered the scientific age, and the gods have been put in their proper place. However, amongst some religiously minded people the old belief still prevails, and a Roman Catholic will appeal to St. Patrick or the Virgin Mary with the same confidence as his ancestors prayed to the mother goddess Demeter or the father god Zeus.

This all being so, what effect has it had on history? At the beginning of my address I said that fifty per cent. of the events of history were caused by religion, but historians have ignored and misinterpreted much that went under the name of religion because of their ignorance of the origin and meaning of religion and the phenomena which has brought it about. Religion has entered into every phase of the life of our ancestors, and caused them to do things and think thoughts that we now consider foolish and repugnant.

Religion was very useful in the regulation of society, fear kept the people obedient, but, on the other hand, we must remember the millions of lives sacrificed to the gods and the wars supernatural Religion has brought about, its greatest failing being the intolerance it caused. Too often we find that the majority thought that only those who believed in the prevailing creed had the right to live and obtain salvation hereafter. This intolerance has been particularly evident amongst the followers of the Christian and Moslem faiths, because by then religion had become fixed in definite creeds which all must believe or perish. So, if we keep in mind all I have so far said, we can now go back to early times and observe the effect of religion on history.

We all know the story of Abraham, a native of the city of Ur, in the land called Sumer, at the mouth of the rivers Tigris and Euphrates. When the Euphrates changed its course, and the wonderful canal system became useless, Abraham left Ur to eventually find himself in the land of Canaan. This, and subsequent events, had a great effect on history, because some of his descendants, the Hebrews, when captives in Babylon, copied many of the stories current in Sumer, and the adjoining country of Babylon, which have come down to us in the Old Testament. The Bible is one of the thirteen great books which have had a very marked effect on history. Up to within our own time it dominated the mental life of Christendom, and gave Christians the idea that they had received a special revelation from God. On its teaching the Christians patterned their lives and justified their actions.

One of the many great events in history, which came from this Bible worship, was the scattering of the Jews throughout the world. In A.D. 70 Jerusalem and the Temple were destroyed by Titus in the reign of Vespasian. Three hundred years later the Emperor Julian, a Pagan, decided that the Jews could again return to their native land.

He was tolerant to the Jews, and gave them permission to rebuild the Temple at Jerusalem. By this act he annulled the edict of Hadrian, and consequently the Jews had access once more to the Holy City. They were enthusiastic and vigorous in making their plans for the new Temple; the foundations were laid, and building was about to commence, when they were destroyed by an earthquake. Julian died about the time of this catastrophe, and the attempt to rebuild the Temple was abandoned because of the hostility of the Christians, who looked upon the disaster as an act of God.

Looking back, we now see how unfortunate it was that religious hatred thwarted the Jews in this their last opportunity to recover their old sacred city, and again build up a home for their nation. What a difference it would have made to them if they had had a home, and been no longer strangers in foreign lands! Christianity prevented this materialising, as Christians argued that it was contrary to the Scriptures that the Temple should be rebuilt, it having been foretold that it was to remain desolate (Matthew xxiii, 38). Instead the Christians built churches in Jerusalem, and it became a place of religious pilgrimages.

Another sacred book which has had an enormous effect on the way the people lived and thought is the Hindu Bagav-ad Gita which, together with the Indian Vedas and the Buddhist Suttantas, determined the lives of many millions of Indians and Asiatics. Neither must we forget the effect of the Koran on the lives of millions who became Mahometans, its division of India into two hostile camps lasting to the present time. Its moral effect curtailed drunkenness and theft, but it permitted slavery and war. Mahomet, in the 6th century of our era, declared that he had received this book clairaudiently from the angel Gabriel, and, during the three centuries following his death, the zeal of the Moslems to spread their religion brought the Arabian Empire into being, so much so that it spread from the Persian Gulf to Spain.

The same religious zeal for the conversion of unbelievers, and for expansion, produced the Ottoman Empire and brought the Turks up to the gates of Vienna. The Turkish victory at the battle of Mohacs (1526), which brought about this invasion of Austria, so altered the political structure of Europe that Charles V, the Holy Roman emperor, dared not crush the Reformation in Germany for fear of civil war. Thus the superior forces at the disposal of the Roman Catholic Church could not be deployed as they otherwise would have been, and this great event in history, known as the Reformation, led to the increased enlightenment of Europe, because the forces for reform during this time of Turkish invasion became too strong to be defeated.

Thus Moslem Turkey made possible the Reformation and all that followed this outstanding event, which would probably have died an early death if it had been possible to use the substantial potential Papal forces available against it.

Truly, religious fanaticism has been the cause of many wars. One of the few exceptions to this is to be found in King Asoka, whose kingdom in the 3rd century B.C. extended from Afghanistan to Madras. When he adopted the Buddhist faith he gave up his contemplated conquest of the Indian Peninsula. Instead of continuing to conquer by force he set out to do so by kindness, sending missionaries everywhere to spread the teachings of Buddha, a word which means the Enlightened One. Buddhism, of all the world's leading faiths, has spread more by persuasion than by force, and Buddhists can look back with satisfaction on the fact that their religion has not been guilty of persecution or war. It spread from India eastwards through China to Japan, but, as a religion, it did not penetrate further west than Alexandria where it greatly influenced the Middle East.

The conquests of Alexander the Great in the 4th century B.C. opened the door for oriental religious speculations to enter Europe, and they quickly took advantage of the opportunity. Buddhism introduced the Monastic system into Europe, and the oriental belief in a divine monarch was taken up by Alexander the Great to spread throughout Europe. This idea, for some two thousand years, kept the people in awe of divine majesty, but, with mental development, came the desire for greater freedom. Divine kingship fought hard against the growing demand for greater liberty and against an increased say of the people in the management of their own affairs. In England it brought about the wars and conflicts between Parliament and the King in the 17th century, while in France the King would not forgo his divine prerogative until forced to do so as the result of the French Revolution.

The same belief in divine kingship started the European Revolution of 1848 in Germany. Whereas, in England, Parliament slowly and laboriously took the place of the divine king, in Germany this was not so, and the 1848 Revolution for democratic government, and the education of the people, was stillborn, just as it was in France, Italy and Austria. The belief in divine kingship lasted in Russia until the 1917 Revolution. One lasting effect religion had on the British political system was the constitution of its two leading political parties, which grew out of the religious beliefs of the time. In the 17th century the Tories were mostly Anglicans and the Whigs mostly dissenters. These religious beliefs divided the Parliament of the time, and produced the two great political parties which ruled Britain up to our own lifetime. On the Continent most countries have a strong Catholic party, the other religious persuasions joining other parties who as a rule were more radical and progressive, to become the Socialists and Communists of our time.

The greatest event in history, in my opinion, was the calling together by Constantine of the Council of Nicaea in 325. Prior to this, Christian belief was very fluid, in fact we can hardly determine exactly what Christian beliefs really were. But to make things clearer let us go back to the beginning of the Christian era and see what actually happened. We have no history to guide us, as the gospels are not looked upon by historians as historical documents. Everything is surmise, and all that the gospels and epistles tell the historian is what the followers of Jesus believed about him. Not what actually happened.

A study of earlier Saviour-God religions always reveals the fact that the first cause to bring a new religion into being was the seeing after death of the priestly victim, either as a ghost or an apparition. This led to the belief that the victim's death had reconciled the gods and removed the curse of death. Consequently the victim was worshipped as the Christ, the Redeemer, Saviour and Judge of mankind. All the phrases of love and devotion his worshippers could think of were wound round each priestly victim who was seen after death. A story was generally spun about him being born of a virgin mother, having lived the life of a god-man, having performed miracles, to be finally arrested by the priests. Then he was tried and put to death, only to leave his tomb and return to be with the father-god in heaven, his work being to judge the dead on their arrival before his throne.

More or less this is the story told of sixteen saviour-gods who lived before the Christian era in different parts of the world. The most outstanding were Krishna the Christ of India, Osiris the Christ of Egypt, Mithra the Christ of Persia and Dionysus the Christ of Greece. Some of these myths were originally told of the sun-god, each phase of the sun having a different tale told about it from virgin birth, it seemingly arising from mother earth in the morning, to death at night and resurrection the next morning.

When the priestly victims were sacrificed they were just ordinary men, but, when they were seen again after death, they came to be regarded as gods. So much so that divine honours were paid them, and the story was told about their miraculous births on earth, their godlike lives, and how they were sacrificed as victims for sinful man, to receive adulation from their worshippers on earth and eternal praise from the inhabitants of heaven. The episode, namely the apparition, which gave rise to all these wonderful stories came last in the actual earth experience of the victim; he a natural man was sacrificed and reappeared, which reappearance turned him into a supernatural man, and then the story was spun making him out to be a supernatural man from his birth onwards. His earth life was written down to portray him as a divine being from birth to death.

So the true story, which should have depicted him as an ordinary being, was gradually elaborated until he became a divine being both on earth and in heaven. This deifying process, which took place with all the saviour gods, is quite noticeable in the gospels where the oldest records depict Jesus as a man born in a natural way. Gradually they were elaborated, and doctrine and dogma took the place of simple moralising.

In the case of Jesus how did all this take place? It is evident from Paul's epistles that he believed he saw Jesus after his death and in consequence thought that he had seen a god, a common belief in these days. Brought up in Tarsus, where the Saviour god Dionysus was worshipped, he came to believe that Jesus was none other than Dionysus returned to earth. So he wound round Jesus all the beliefs, and many of the sayings, that were draped round Dionysus, and most of the expressions he used he copied from the ritual and liturgy relating to this beloved Greek god.

Paul, figuratively speaking, lifted Jesus from his Jewish cradle over to Greece, and consequently we find the new religion which developed closely associated with Greek life and thought. However, the original disciples of Jesus, plain simple Jews, had no such extravagant ideas about their lord and master. To them he was a reformer and a medium, "a man of God", which was the expression in those days for one who had psychic powers, and this Jesus evidently displayed, especially in his gift of psychic healing.

So there was an early split amongst the followers of Jesus, some following Paul and others Peter. The Paulines became known later as Christians, the influence of Greece giving their beliefs a recognisable name. Those who followed after Peter I would call Jesuians, for want of a better name. When the converted Pagan priests entered the

Christian Church they brought with them many of their own Pagan beliefs, and so we find Jesus becoming the second member of a trinity of gods and the other Pagan beliefs likewise becoming part of the new religion. Infant baptism, a Pagan ceremony, was introduced instead of adult baptism and the Pagan holy days were reverenced instead of the Jewish. Sunday, the first day of the week, took the place of Saturday the Sabbath, but the Christian Sunday became the principal Holy day because the Pagans reverenced that day as the one when the Pagan God Mithra rose from his tomb. This day the Mithraists called "The Lord's Day", a name to be used by the Christians from that time onwards.

On the other hand, the Jesuians continued to worship in the Temple and remained a sect of the Hebrew faith. The destruction of the Temple by the Romans in A.D. 70, and the scattering of the Jews, altered everything for them. It gave the Paulines, who later became known as Christians, the lead, and the Jesuians developed into followers of Jesus who believed that he had ordained he would keep in touch with them through the Holy Spirit, until his early return. In those days the name Holy Spirit was given to the medium's spirit control, and we read in early Jesuian literature that the unforgivable sin was to disbelieve in mediumship. Consequently, their church services were more like Spiritualist services of to-day, and the medium, who gave a trance address, took the leading place in the service.

The Minister, who carried on his ordinary occupation during the week, was responsible only for guiding the service and reading the scriptures. This is the description Tertullian, the early Christian Father, gives us of an early Jesuian church before the domination of the converted Pagan priests and Pagan worshippers. By the 4th century these two main bodies of opinion, the Jesuians and the

Christians, were resolutely divided, the Christians believing that Jesus was equal to God and the second person in the Trinity, whereas the Jesuians did not accept the Trinity and did not believe that Jesus was one with the Father.

When Constantine decided to make Christianity the State religion of Rome, he found an acute division of opinion in the Christian ranks. The Unitarians, or Jesuians, who did not consider Jesus equal to God, were led by a presbyter called Arius, a pious and good-living man, and the Trinitarians by Alexander, the Bishop of Alexandria. Constantine made attempt after attempt to bring these two opposing parties together without success, and finally he was compelled to call all the Bishops of the Church together to decide on a creed which all must believe. He chose Nicaea as the place of meeting and there in 325, 318 Bishops, accompanied by minor clergy, assembled to decide on the definition of God. After much wrangling and disputing, after blows were struck and books were thrown about, the Unitarian amendment was lost and the Nicene Creed, somewhat as we know it to-day, was produced and passed. The Arians or Unitarians were thrown out as heretics, murdered, persecuted and banished, only to do the same to the Trinitarians when the Emperor was a Unitarian.

Thus began the Christian Church, and Constantine kept his promise that when the priests produced a creed they could agree on, he would recognise their religion as the State religion of the Empire. So also began Christian civilisation in the year 381 when Theodosius the Great issued his edicts which defined all unbelievers in the Nicene Creed as traitors and subject to death. Only briefly can I refer to the great events which followed from Christianity taking the place of Paganism, but you will now realise why in my history, *The Curse of Ignorance*, I refer to the Council of Nicaea as the greatest event in history, as no other single organisation has had more effect on the lives of the people of the West than the Christian Church, which dominated and moulded the outlook of the most virile part of the human race, that part of it which made the most important contribution to the history of mankind.

Its triumvirate were Augustine, Jerome and Ambrose who started the Christian Church off on its career of World domination. They were paralleled in our time by the Nazi triumvirate Hitler, Goebbels and Himmler, and I shall tell you why. Hitler wrote an aggressive imperialistic book called *Mein Kampf*. Augustine, likewise, wrote a book, which he called *The City of God*, in which he envisaged a world empire for the Church with the Pope as supreme head. All who would not accept the Nicene Creed were to be put to death by the sword, and this form of conversion he adopted towards all heretics, his principal activities being against the unorthodox sects called the Donatists and the Pelagians.

Jerome was the Goebbels of the Christian Church, and its most fiery propagandist. He translated the Old and New Testaments into Latin, and altered the text as he thought fit, to bring the gospels and epistles into line with the Paganism which had now become known as Christianity. Jerome was the most uncompromising and bitter writer and speaker against all who were accused by the Church as being unorthodox or heretics. He it was who influenced Pope Damasus, whose secretary he was, to abolish mediumship in the churches. Jerome had been to séances when he was criticised by people on the Other Side for his inaccurate translation of the gospels, he having added much that was Pagan to the original simple Jewish story. If that got about the unity of the Church was threatened, and consequently mediums, from being called Oracles of God, were from now onwards termed Servants of the Devil.

The third member of this contemporary trio is Ambrose,

who can be compared to Himmler because their methods were the same.   He was responsible for Article 9 of the Theodosian Code making torture, death or banishment the penalty for unbelief in the Nicene Creed.   This Code also established a body of priests as Inquisitors of the Faith and set the Inquisition in being.   Ambrose was the founder of the Inquisition which for 1,400 years was to turn Christendom into a vast slave camp, wherein no one could question or doubt for fear of the reprisals which would come upon him.

When Rome fell in 410 the Christian Visigoths poured over Italy.   There was no Emperor then in Rome, the seat of government being in Constantinople.   Consequently Innocent I, Bishop of Rome, a strong and resolute opportunist, took the place of the Emperor, and was recognised as such by the Invaders.   He became the Pontifex Maximus, and thus held the sacred office hitherto honoured only by the Emperor.   From this time onwards the power and majesty of the Papacy began.   The Pope, as the Bishop of Rome came to be called, had his own army, and Gregory the Great was attended by one thousand slaves.   From now onwards Christian Emperors ruled in Constantinople, and the Holy War began against Paganism, the troops being accompanied by the Inquisitors of the Faith.   In the Middle East alone upwards of 200,000 were massacred or sold into slavery, but this was only a beginning, as, throughout the Christian era, the number of victims who suffered death by massacre or torture, because they were considered heretics, reached the appalling figure of 25,000,000.

Persecution spread throughout Europe, and, as each King or Chief was converted to Christianity, by persuasion or force, archbishops and bishops were placed over large districts to supervise and collect the tithe which passed into the treasury of the Holy See. Already patriarchs had been appointed in Greece and the Middle East for the same purpose. Europe was thus converted to Christianity by persuasion or force, the people accepting wholesale the new religion adopted by their King. This process was almost complete by the year 1000, and then came the first disruption in 1054. But I must go back five centuries.

In the 5th and 6th centuries the dissension between the Unitarians and the Trinitarians had increased to such a degree that there were often two popes at the same time, one a Unitarian and the other a Trinitarian. In the 6th century Europe was so divided that the Trinitarian pope decided that unity could only be achieved by war. So, by marrying the niece of the Duke of Burgundy, who was a Trinitarian, to Clovis, the Pagan king of the Franks, the stage was set for the triumph of Catholic or Trinitarian Christianity.

This girl's duty was to convert Clovis to the Catholic belief, and this she did to such effect that he became a fanatical Trinitarian, and waged war against Alaric II the Visigoth, who was the leader of the Unitarians. On the bloody field of Vouillé, near Poitiers, in the year 507, the definition of the god-head was decided, because Clovis was triumphant and Alaric was defeated, he being personally killed by this ardent Trinitarian. From now onwards there was no place in Christendom where Unitarians could live, they everywhere being massacred, and it was not until after the Reformation that this once important section of the early Apostolic Church again made its very halting appearance.

From 507 onwards Christendom was united until we come to the disruption in the year 1054. This came about because it had been decided at a council of priests at Toledo to insert the word "Filioque", meaning "and from the son", into the Creed, to make it read that the Holy Ghost proceeded from the Father and the Son. Christian Europe, by

that one word, was split in two. The Eastern Church protested against this tampering with the Creed, an action which
it declared was blasphemous, unwarranted, unjustifiable and
a sin against God. So the Greek Orthodox Church came
into being, with its Patriarch at Constantinople, to later set
up his throne in Moscow. From this time onwards Popes
and Patriarchs have abused and cursed each other without
restraint, and an iron curtain came down to divide the people
of Europe in two, so much so that Constantinople was
captured in 1453 by the Turks because of the lack of unity
on the part of the Christian defenders. What repercussions
this caused and how it influenced history both in Europe
and the Middle East all historians know too well.

Had there been concord within this ancient bastion of
the Christian faith, it could have successfully withstood the
Moslem onslaught, but, because there was not, it fell.
Constantine XI (1448—53), the Emperor, and the last of
the Caesars, was a statesman and a hero in the hour of peril.
To secure unity amongst his Christian subjects he tried in
vain to persuade the Catholic Church authorities in Rome
to send him help, on the understanding that he and his
people would in future believe that the Holy Ghost proceeded from the Father and the Son and not from the Father
only. On this one word "Filioque", which the Catholics
added to the Creed in 1054, hung the fate of the first and
greatest Christian city. The Emperor, to save his city, was
now prepared to accept a belief which he had been brought
up to consider to be untrue, and against which the Greeks
had protested vehemently since its quite unjustified insertion
into the Creed of the Christian Church.

While Mahomet the Second's artillery was battering at
the city's walls, the Greeks turned in fury against the
Emperor for making such an outrageous offer, as to them
such a belief was nothing less than blasphemy. Moreover,
he had permitted a Catholic celebration of the Eucharist to

be held within St. Sophia, at which the hateful word "Filioque" had been heard by the congregation for the first time. Such shocking heresy made the beleaguered citizens forget their peril, and many hoped for a Turkish victory rather than experience such unbelief within their walls. The correct interpretation of Christianity meant more to the orthodox Greeks than the salvation of their city, and so the theological conflict continued between the Greeks, on the one hand, and the Catholic Spaniards, Germans and Italians who helped to make up the garrison. Meantime, as this dispute continued, the Turks, profiting by it, worked their way into the city, subduing one defence after another, intent on its capture, and the subjection to their will of the Christians within who could not agree upon the definition of their faith.

The Crusades started in 1097, over three centuries earlier than the fall of Constantinople, just after the Eastern Christians had split away from the Western Church. The primary object of the nine different crusades was to free the Holy Land from the Turks, and this could easily have been accomplished if the entire Church had been united. A great stimulus to this undertaking was the belief that the Lord Jesus was about to return to Jerusalem, the thousand years absence mentioned in *The Revelation* having now expired. However, the want of unity, and the hatred displayed between the East and the West, made this great attempt to recapture and retain the Holy Land a dismal failure. Thousands perished, and the misery these Crusades caused to all Europe and the Middle East can never be appreciated. Cruelty, breaking of faith and folly were triumphant in these days of stupidity and ignorance, and after it was all over Europe took a century to recover.

Many landowners had appointed the Church as their trustee during their absence in the East, and, as large numbers never returned, the Church continued as the administrator of their lands, to become the owner when it was not reclaimed. By this, and other methods, it became the owner of one third of Europe and the wealthiest organisation in the world.

After the heretical Albigenses in the South of France had been liquidated by Pope Innocent III in the 12th century, and after the Portuguese, Prussians and Poles had been Christianised by force by the Knights Templars, a religious but not a political peace reigned in Europe for 200 years. Then came the Hussite War and later the disruption of the Catholic Church at the time called the Reformation, because the vice and corruption, which had been so long pronounced in the holy places, could no longer be tolerated. Council after council had met in a vain attempt to reform the Church, and finally Luther carried half of Germany with him in the revolt which brought about the Reformation.

This outstanding period in history was caused by ancient Greek learning penetrating Italy by way of Venice, when the Greeks fled from Constantinople prior to its capture by the Turks. Then it was that the writings of Aristotle came to be read and pondered over, and the Greek classics, which had been banned by the Church, were read by Europeans for the first time for a thousand years. This period is called the Renaissance, or new birth. Then came the Reformation. After wars and bitter persecution Germany settled down to be half Lutheran and half Roman Catholic, but, with the coming of Calvinism, religious bitterness again became inflamed, to bring about the Thirty Years War in the 17th century.

Then the Pope, in collaboration with the fanatical Holy Roman Emperor Ferdinand II, the man next to Hitler responsible for more deaths, misery and suffering than any other, decided that the time had come when all Protestants must be destroyed. So one of the bloodiest wars in history commenced, and, when it was ended, Bohemia's population was reduced from three million to less than a million, only 6,000 out of 30,000 villages remained, and Germany had become a land of utter desolation, her population being reduced from 20 million to 6 million. Berlin's inhabitants declined from 24,000 to 6,000. Germany for one hundred years ceased to be a force in Europe.

Religious persecution continued in Europe up till the 19th century, and the Church dominated politics right up to our own times. Already it had secured complete power in both North and South America, but to pursue this subject in any detail is impossible because my time is coming to a close.

Religion has comforted millions, and helped them on their way through life. During the darkness of ignorance it gave many millions something to live for, and it helped them to die in peace. All religions have helped and comforted believers, but, on the other hand, religion has brought about an intolerance which is difficult for us to realise in our more enlightened age. Even as recently as the middle of last century it was the cause of the Crimean war, because the Greek Orthodox Church and the Catholic Church quarrelled over the holy places in Jerusalem, to set Russia, the protector of the Greek Orthodox Church, moving her armies towards Constantinople which Britain and France did not wish her to occupy.

I have not the time to touch on the wars and persecutions of the 17th century in Britain between the Anglicans, Puritans and Presbyterians, or the terrible persecutions and massacres in France, or the rebellions and massacres in Ireland because of the aggressiveness of the Anglican Church from the time of Elizabeth onwards. Religion split Ireland in two. The same Church caused equal bitterness in Canada, while Scotland will never forget the persecutions and slaughter of the Presbyterians by the Episcopalians. On the other hand, the Treaty of Edinburgh

(1560) between Scotland and England was made possible because both countries feared the return of Roman Catholicism. Thus Scotland's long alliance with France was broken, the Border Wars came to an end, and the foundation was laid for the union of the two countries, which, in the centuries to come, helped in the building up of the British Empire.

Religion brought about the populating of North America. Archbishop Laud's determination to force everyone to attend the Anglican Church caused many dissenters to cross the Atlantic and found New England. Those who remained at home eventually rebelled and overthrew the King, to bring Oliver Cromwell's Commonwealth into being.

We cannot realise to-day how much religion entered into the lives of our ancestors. It dominated their politics, it was their science and explanation for everything. The church was the only place for instruction, and this was only of a theological nature. It was the only meeting-place, and round it centred everything in the parish. The theological age was the time when ignorance was elevated to a virtue, and knowledge treated with contempt. Even to-day we are suffering from the effects of the theological age.

Prior to the rise to power of the Christian Church, the Roman and Greek educational system was conquering ignorance and spreading education far and wide under the influence of the noble Quintilian, the Minister of Education under Vespasian. Schools were established throughout Gaul, Italy, North Africa and Greece, but, when the Christian Church came into power, it was decreed by Pope Gregory that all learning, apart from the Scriptures, was sinful. By the time of Justinian in the 6th century, all school-masters had been either massacred or exiled, and night settled down on Christendom.

This was one of the greatest tragedies in history, and,

if it had never happened, we would probably have been more than a thousand years in advance of what we are to-day. The Council of Nicaea, which brought Christianity into being as a powerful political force, was not only the greatest event in history but one of the greatest tragedies of history, because the power of the Church, unfitted for its role as dictator of Europe, came from what happened in the fateful year of 325 at the town of Nicaea in Asia Minor.

So religion has been the cause of many wars. It has been a powerful force in both home and foreign politics. From fear of offending the gods it has kept back progress and encouraged ignorance in place of knowledge. Some day I hope that when people accept natural religion, instead of supernatural religion, many of the follies of mankind will pass away. Supernatural religion is based on a misinterpretation of the next world and its inhabitants. When we come to realise that the saints and gods, who were believed to reign over mankind, were just men and women, who had passed through death to another life in a world similar to this world, of finer substance surrounding and interpenetrating this world, we shall appreciate how mistaken theology has been in its speculations and mysteries. Half of history has been determined by the theories and dogmatic assertions of theology, or, in other words, by the speculations of mankind about those who once lived here on earth and died to enter the etheric world.

This does not mean the end of religion, as each one of us is an etheric being and this world is but the nursery stage of our career. In future, religion must rely on facts, on observation and experience. Those who wish for these can have them, or accept what others have discovered. Natural religion, I believe, will some day take the place of supernatural religion, to give as much and even more comfort and consolation than has hitherto been supplied by the speculations of theologians.

Let us therefore hope that with the passing of the theological age, the scientific age, which has taken its place, will bring about healthier, better and happier conditions for all mankind. This, however, will only be possible if we put the practice of the virtues before all else. If justice, truth, toleration, kindness and fair dealing between the nations do not reign to a greater extent in future than in the past, civilisation will be engulfed in a war of atom bombs and other deadly weapons, to produce misery, famine, disease and destruction beyond our imagination.

We all hope that this and future generations will never experience that dreadful calamity.